AUSTRALIA & NEW ZEALAND

NEW
GUINEA
CORAL
SEA
PACIFIC
OCEAN
GREAT BARRIER REEF
Cooktown
Cairns
Great Dividing Range
A
NSLAND
Brisbane
NEW
SOUTH
WALES
Sydney
CANBERRA
Australian Capital
Territory
VICTORIA
Melbourne
TASMAN
SEA
SMANIA
Hobart
SYDNEY
Manly
Bondi
Beach
BOTANY
BAY
Auckland
NEW
ZEALAND
WELLINGTON
Christchurch

Green **Line**

5

von
Marion Horner
Elizabeth Daymond
Jennifer Baer-Engel
Peter Lampater

herausgegeben von
Harald Weisshaar

Ernst Klett Verlag
Stuttgart · Leipzig

Green Line 5 für Klasse 9 an Gymnasien
und für den Bildungsstandard Klasse 10 in Baden-Württemberg

Herausgeber: Harald Weisshaar, Bisingen
unter besonderer Mitwirkung von Frank Haß, Kirchberg

Autorinnen und Autoren: Marion Horner M. A., Cambridge; Jennifer Baer-Engel, Göppingen; Elizabeth Daymond M. A., Kiel; Peter Lampater, Ehingen
unter Mitwirkung von Michael Mattison, Stuttgart sowie Rosemary Hellyer-Jones M.A., Ehingen

Beratung: Paul Dennis M. A., Lahnstein; Hartmut Klose, Seevetal; Antje Körber, Merseburg; Axel Plitsch, Wülfrath; Elisabeth Renner, Freiburg

Zusatzmaterial für Schülerinnen und Schüler zu diesem Band:

Workbook + Audio-CD + Lernsoftware	3-12-547168-9
Workbook + Audio-CD	3-12-547165-8
Lernsoftware CDR (Einzelversion)	3-12-547355-3
Fit für Tests und Klassenarbeiten	3-12-547205-1
Fit für Tests und Klassenarbeiten Niedersachsen	3-12-547305-8

1. Auflage 1 8 7 6 | 14 13 12

Redaktion: Andrew Hutchins M. A., Dr. Gregory Fuller, Anette Dangelmaier M. A.
Herstellung: Anita Bauch

Gestaltung: Anita Bauch
Umschlaggestaltung: Koma Amok, Stuttgart
Illustrationen: David Norman, Meerbusch; Christian Dekelver, Weinstadt; Lorna Egan, Köln *(Grammar)*
Satz: Satzkiste GmbH, Stuttgart; Wiebke Hengst, Ostfildern
Reproduktion: Meyle + Müller, Medien-Management, Pforzheim
Druck: Stürtz GmbH, Würzburg

Printed in Germany
ISBN 978-3-12-547160-3 (fester Einband)
ISBN 978-3-12-547161-0 (flexibler Einband)

Hallo und herzlich willkommen bei Green Line 5!

Den Unit- und Buchaufbau von **Green Line** kennst du jetzt gut. Die beiden **Revisions**, drei **Projects** und die **Free section** sind wie bisher nicht verpflichtend. **Mediation** und der gesamte Anhang mit **Grammar**, **Vocabulary**, **Dictionary**, **In the classroom** und **Irregular verbs** sind auch in Band 5 zu finden.

Aber in diesem Band hat sich etwas verändert:

- Erinnerst du dich noch an die Zoom-in zu den USA in *Green Line* 4? Als Bucheinführung gibt es in diesem Band eine neue, verpflichtende ***Zoom-in: The world speaks English***. Dieser Band behandelt unter anderem das Thema Englisch als internationale Sprache, und die Zoom-in leitet in dieses Thema ein. Die letzte Seite der Zoom-in führt über in das aufregende Thema der Unit 1: Australien.
- Im gesamten Buch wird in britischen Originaltexten nur **britisches Englisch (BE) und die britische Schreibweise** verwendet, in amerikanischen Originaltexten nur **amerikanisches Englisch (AE) und die amerikanische Schreibweise.**
- Von den insgesamt vier Units sind **Unit 1 und Unit 3 Kurzunits**, deren Aufbau du schon aus Band 4 kennst. Units 1 und 3 haben zwar etwas neue Grammatik, aber das Schwergewicht liegt auf der Textarbeit. Deswegen beginnen Unit 1 und Unit 3 je mit zwei Texten **zur Auswahl**. Du kannst mit deiner Klasse **entweder Text A oder Text B** lesen und bearbeiten. Natürlich **darfst** du auch beide lesen! Nach den Units 1 und 3 findet sich auf drei Seiten ein interessanter **Text** zum Unitthema, der nicht verpflichtend ist.
- In **jeder der vier Units** gibt es eine zusätzliche Seite ***Writing texts***, auf der du lernst, Texte zu strukturieren und überzeugend zu schreiben.
- In der **Grammar** gibt es nach jedem Pensum eine englische Zusammenfassung (*English summary*), jetzt mit Beispielsätzen und Erweiterungen. Die Uniteinführung der Grammar *In this Unit you will learn* und die mit Ausrufezeichen versehenen Kästchen sind in Band 5 auch auf Englisch.
- **WICHTIG!** In der **Free section** findest du das spannende ***Battle of the books***, mit dem du schon im Herbst beginnen kannst.
- **WICHTIG!** Auf vielen Seiten gibt es **Online-Links** (z.B. S.8 oben) mit Aufgaben zum jeweiligen Thema.
- Am Buchende steht eine ***Time line of Australian history*** mit interessanten Fakten aus der australischen Geschichte. Du kannst jederzeit dort nachschlagen, wenn du mehr zu den historischen Zusammenhängen wissen willst. Außerdem gibt es **Übersichten über die politischen Systeme des UK und der USA.**

- Diese Texte und Übungen sind nur auf den Lehrer-CDs zum Schülerbuch enthalten.
- Diese Texte und Übungen sind auf der Schüler-CD im Workbook *und* auf den Lehrer-CDs.
- Partnerarbeit
- Gruppenarbeit
- Schreibübungen
- Übungen/Übungsteile für den *English folder*
- ⟨ ⟩ Wahlfreie (fakultative) Übungen/Übungsteile oder Kapitel
- Besonders knifflige oder anspruchsvolle Übungen/Übungsteile
- Empfohlen, um die Kompetenzerwartung des Kernlehrplans in Nordrhein-Westfalen zu erfüllen

Die Angebote in *Green Line* 5 sind nicht obligatorisch abzuarbeiten. Die Auswahl der Texte und Übungen richtet sich nach den Schwerpunkten des schulinternen Curriculums.

Zoom-in The world speaks English

DID YOU KNOW?

- The English language has the world's largest vocabulary (ca. 700,000 words). German (ca. 175,000 words) and French (ca. 100,000) are in 2nd and 3rd place.
- The English language grows by about 25,000 new words a year – a world record.
- In France, the *Académie Française* makes official rules for the French language. 'Computer' and 'e-mail' are just two examples of foreign words which are not allowed. In countries like the UK or the US, there is no official regulation.

Just another pizza order in Manhattan

a) *Listen to this strange dialogue a New York City radio station recorded for its 'Believe it or not' show. Manhattan banker Dale Dupont called in with his story. But first look at the three photos above. Guess what the story is about.*

b) *Say what happened to Dale.*

c) *How does this story show that 'The world speaks English'?*

The world speaks English

When Queen Elizabeth I died in 1603, the English-speaking world had a population of just 8 million. Today there are over 400 million people who speak English as their mother tongue, and for another 600 million it is an official language.

The British founded many colonies, from America to Australia, Asia to Africa. In the year 1900, the British Empire controlled a quarter of the planet. By the 1940s, when the Empire started to break up, English had become important in the world. But it still wasn't quite *the* world language.

That changed after World War II with the growing influence of the United States. America had become a superpower and more people were dealing with English-speakers than ever before. Hollywood, jazz and rock 'n' roll helped to make English the world language of pop culture – a status the language still has today. The leading American role in science and technology has also given the world the PC, the Internet and e-mail, all of which have taken English to every last corner of the world. Now whole fields of business (e. g. IT and marketing) are dominated by English terms.

Now take a tour of four big English-speaking countries.

INDIA

Population:
1.1 billion
(2nd in the world after China)
Area: 3.1 million sq. km (7th)
Independent from Britain since: 1947

"Namáste! I'm from India, the world's largest democracy. My country is rich in culture and tradition. English is not the mother tongue of most Indians – there are over 20 other languages as well as many dialects of the main language, Hindi. But English is used a lot in government and business. Especially in the IT industry, India has become a huge success story. Foreign businesses see the great possibilities of the millions of English-speaking workers. But so far, only a small number of people in just a few regions of the country have felt our new success. Most Indians have not seen a change in their standard of living. India is still a very poor country.

Many people who love our Indian culture never actually go to India and see the poverty in the streets and in the country. But they needn't travel so far to enjoy what they like most about the country – food, music and films. In Britain, Indian food has become so popular over the years that in a survey, Britons said that *chicken tikka masala* was their favourite dish, not fish-and-chips! And our Bollywood films with their love stories have millions of fans everywhere in the world."

CANADA

Population: 33 million
(36th in the world)
Area: 9.9 million sq. km (2nd)
Independent from Britain since:
Legal independence in 1982

"Hi! For me, Canada is forests, tundra, the Rocky Mountains, and big cities with big skyscrapers. But there is a strong European feeling, too: Canada has a large French-speaking population (Québec was a French colony first) and the British monarch's portrait on Canadian money is just one reminder that Canada and the UK still share the same head of state. For tourists it is often surprising how some places in British Columbia and Québec can look, sound and feel almost more British than Britain or more French than France."

SOUTH AFRICA

Population: 47 million (26th)
Area: 1.2 million sq. km (25th)
Independent from Britain since: 1910

"Howzit! In 1994, in my country's first free elections, our civil rights leader Nelson Mandela became South Africa's first black president – after 27 years in prison. Mandela had been the great figure in South Africa's fight against white South Africa's racist *apartheid* ('separateness') system. Apartheid kept control of the country in the hands of the small 10 % white minority. Going from a police state to a free society has gone surprisingly well, although poverty and crime are huge problems for us. The white minority still controls much of my country's wealth, and many of us blacks still live in poverty in the crowded townships. But a new black middle class is slowly growing."

AUSTRALIA

Population: 21 million
(53rd in world)
Area: 7.7 million sq. km (6th)
Independent from Britain since:
1901 (British monarch still head of state)

"G'day! Let me tell you something about my country, Australia. Lots of visitors to Australia love the endlessness of the dry outback, where you can drive for days without seeing another car. The same visitors are sometimes surprised to see just how much of the country is covered by rainforests, too. But deserts and rainforests aren't the best places for settlement. That's why most people live on or near the coasts, and that's where the big cities have grown. Now 85 % of us Aussies live in cities.

The outback is the home of Australia's indigenous population, the Aboriginals. These Australians had already been living on the continent and developing their unique culture for over 40,000 years before the British began settling here in 1788. There was systematic killing of Aboriginals, and forced relocation tore families apart. During the 19th century, Aboriginal culture was almost destroyed. Relations have improved a lot over the past years, and in 2008 the Australian government apologized to the Aboriginals for past crimes.

For beach fans like me, Australia's the perfect place with its warm climate and beautiful coasts! But huge holes in the ozone layer mean a much higher risk of getting skin cancer. So at the beach, people wear more clothes than you would ever see on European beaches.

Australia has been a continent for 50 million years, completely separated from the rest of the world, so it's no wonder that Australia's animal world has become unique. Platypuses, koalas and kangaroos (we call them *roos*) are just a few of the animals you can only find 'down under'."

Unit 1 Australia

Walkabout (Choice A)

Read the introductions to the texts on this page and on page 14. Then decide with your teacher which text your class will read: Choice A or Choice B?

It is the 1950s. Mary and her young brother Peter – two Americans – are the only survivors of a plane crash in the Australian outback. They will die in the desert if they don't get help quickly.
In this scene Mary and Peter finally meet another human being: suddenly an Aboriginal boy appears. Few Americans had ever seen Aboriginals then. Brother and sister are terrified – especially Mary.

1 Reason to be afraid?

Have you ever been afraid at the sight of something/someone new – and then realized that you had overreacted?

The girl's first impulse was to grab Peter and run. But as her eyes examined the stranger, her fear died away. The boy was young – surely not older than she was. He did not carry a weapon, and he looked more inquisitive than threatening.

The desert sun burned down on them. The three children stood looking at each other in the middle of the Australian desert. Motionless as rocks they stared, and stared, and stared. Between them the distance was less than the length of an arm, but more than 100,000 years. Brother and sister had been fed pre-digested foods, provided with continuous push-button entertainment. The basic realities of life were something they'd never had to worry about.

It was very different with the Aboriginal. He knew what reality was. Among the secret water holes of the Australian desert his people had lived and died, unchanging.

They walked from one water hole to the next. Their lives were simple because they were devoted to one purpose, dedicated to fighting one battle – the battle with death.

Mary had decided not to move. To move would be a sign of weakness. She remembered a story about a man who had come face to face with a lion and had stared it down until it had quietly slunk away. That was what she'd do to the black boy; she'd stare at him until he felt the shame of his nakedness and slunk off.

Peter had decided to follow his sister's strategy. He held her hand and stood waiting – waiting for something to happen.

The Aboriginal was in no hurry. Time meant nothing to him. His next meal – the rock wallaby he had killed – was a sure thing. Tomorrow was also a day. For the moment, he was happy simply to examine these strange creatures. Their strange movements intrigued him; their lack of weapons told him how harmless they were. His eyes moved slowly, from one to another, examining them from head to foot. They were the first white people a member of his tribe had ever seen.

Mary began to dislike this examination more and more. She intensified her stare. But the bush boy did not care; the examination continued.

After a while Peter started to fidget. The delay was making him nervous. He wished someone would do something, wished something would happen. Then, he himself started a new train of events. His head began to waggle, as he raised his nose to the sky; he tried to hold his breath, but he could not. It had to come. He sneezed.

It was a big sneeze for such a little boy, all the more violent for having been held back for so long.

To his sister, the sneeze was a disaster. She had just intensified her stare to the point of winning when suddenly the spell was broken. The bush boy's attention went from Mary to Peter.

There was no time to show her brother how angry she was with him. Because before she could react, a second sneeze, even stronger than the first, broke the silence of the bush.

Mary raised her eyes to the heavens, wondering how the gods could have allowed this to happen. But the force of the second sneeze could still be felt when a *new* sound made her whirl around – a gust of laughter, melodious laughter: low at first, then becoming louder, uncontrolled.

She looked at the bush boy in amazement. His laughter was out of control, and infectious. It woke in Peter an instant reaction: an appreciation of the ludicrous. The guilt that the little boy had started to feel died away. At first shyly, then with no holding back, he too started to laugh.

The distance of 100,000 years disappeared in the twinkling of an eye.

(from: *Walkabout* by James Vance Marshall; adapted and abridged)

2 From different worlds

a) 1. *How does each person in the story react to the new situation?*
   2. *Why do they react like this?*

b) *How would you have reacted in the same situation?*

c) 1. *Explain this:* "Between them the distance was less than the length of an arm, but more than 100,000 years." (line 11)
   2. *Why does this distance disappear?*

d) *Have you ever had a wrong preconception about someone? How did he/she turn out differently?*

WB p. 4/1; 2

3 Characterization

1. *Find sentences in the text that show how the characters feel and behave.*
2. *How well do these adjectives describe the three characters?*

(over)protective | confident | brave | careful | direct | strong

3. *What other adjectives can you think of to describe them?*

4 Listening: *Walkabout*

Listen to what two Australian teens say about "Walkabout" on the phone. What do they mean by "symbolic"? Find an example of this from something you have read or seen.

5 Writing texts

Go back to line 56 in the story. What could have happened if Peter had not sneezed? Continue the story.

WB p. 4/3

Angela (Choice B)

Until recently, Angela and Gracey were best friends. Gracey is part-Aboriginal and from a poor background; Angela is from a rich white family in Brisbane. Since Gracey has found politically active Aboriginal friends at university, she has started to see Angela as one of the whites who treat Aboriginals badly.

Now the two girls are waiting for Gracey's new friends at a mall before they all attend a rally for the Aboriginal cause. Angela wants to attend, too. The scene is told from her point of view.

1 Why did I have to say that?!

Have you ever said something to someone – and just seconds later wished you hadn't? If so, what made you regret saying it?

It felt great to be in the mall with Gracey again as we made our way through the buskers and the shoppers. There was always a buzz about the place, so many people, from slobs in thongs and footy shorts to girls who thought they were strutting the catwalk.

I was enjoying the sensation and didn't notice her mood. I was going to pay for my negligence, but didn't know that yet …

"Hey, remember that coffee shop I fell in love with?" I called to Gracey.

She didn't answer and I thought maybe she was trying to remember its name. "We always went in there just for the smell. Listen: After the rally is over, I'll buy you a short black to celebrate."

"Yeah, if you want to," she said quietly, and still I didn't see what was happening, didn't realise how on edge she was. We arrived at the Information Booth on time but there was no sign of Shirley or Wendy. I didn't notice how nervous Gracey was.

"Look, Mum wants me to pick up her watch from a place just a few doors down. Come on. We'll do that while we're waiting." She slouched off after me, hands in the overalls she had worn to the public meeting the other day. It was only a few steps to the jewellery store. When she hesitated at the entrance and looked back towards the Information Booth, I said, "You wait here. I won't be long."

And I wasn't. It only took three minutes to get the watch and sign for it before I turned around to leave. But as I got close to the door, I heard Gracey's angry voice. "No, I'm *not* going to move!" she said hotly.

A girl in a black skirt and white blouse was standing in front of her now. As I came closer, I could see that this was no girl. The swept-back hair and confident stance spelt manager.

I guessed what was happening right away. This was an exclusive jewellery store and Gracey didn't exactly look the part.

I hurried to Gracey. "It's all right," I said. "She's with me." A handful of words, but I regret them now as much as anything I have ever said.

Suddenly, Gracey forgot the manager and turned to me instead. "What did you say?" she began incredulously. Her surprise quickly turned to rage. "I don't need *you* here so I can stand at the door of a fucking jewellery shop! Who do you think you are?! 'She's with me.' And that makes it all right, does it? Doesn't matter if I'm black as long as there's a friendly white girl nearby to speak for me. Is that the way you see it, Angela? You don't want me to get lumped in with the other blacks around the place, the ones that don't count for anything, the ones that have no right to stand around in the mall by themselves."

There were people stopping to look now. Gracey's angry voice had drawn a crowd, and the people formed a semicircle around us as if we were buskers.

"That's not what I meant," I managed to say when Gracey paused for breath. But she was just getting started.

"Yes, it was. You don't even realise it yourself. Just like Tom and Cheryl, like mother like daughter. Generous as can be on your own terms. 'Come for dinner.' 'Have a coffee, I'm buying.' It's all part of your power over me, isn't it?"

I was angry. And how could she just talk so badly about my parents? It wasn't right. "That's not fair, Gracey, and you know it! Mum and Dad have always been good to you. So have I," I added, suddenly in tears.

"Oh Angela, you poor thing. Your head's so full of boys and clothes, there's no room to see what you were doing to me. You colonised me, Angela. From the day we met, you moved in and started changing me. New hair style, a dress you stole off your mother. But they were just things. What you did *inside* my head changed me a lot more."

There was no holding back now. I shouted at her, as I let go all the frustration and fear I'd bottled up over the weeks. "I don't understand how you can just throw it back in our faces now. Anything we've ever done was because we cared about you!"

"Cared about me as long as I was the good little black girl, yes. But when I step out of line, start telling you things you don't want to know, you turn on me quick enough."

And with that, she stormed away through the crowd which parted quickly to let her pass.

(from: *Angela* by James Moloney; adapted and abridged)

2 Feelings

a) *What exactly makes Gracey so angry?*

b) *Whose feelings can you understand better – Gracey's or Angela's? Why?*

WB p. 5/1; 2

3 Characterization

a) 1. *Find sentences in the text that show how the characters feel and behave.*
   2. *How well do these adjectives describe Angela and Gracey?*

   aggressive | (not) fair | direct | ungrateful | hypocritical | racist

   3. *What other adjectives can you think of to describe them?*

b) 1. *Angela makes three mistakes. What are they?*
   2. *Do her mistakes fit in with the adjectives you found for her in a)? How?*

4 Listening: Understanding *Angela*

a) *Listen. What examples of discrimination do the teenagers mention?*

b) *Do you agree with what they say about Gracey and Angela's characters?*

5 Writing texts

Go back to line 46/47 in the story. What else could Angela have said? How would the scene have developed differently?

WB p. 5/3

LISTENING SKILLS

Listening: Taking notes

On this page you can practise taking notes in English. You will hear a talk where the message – the *gist* – is important. You will also hear a situation where the *details* are more important. But remember, what is important depends on your point of view.

1 At the Reef in a glass-bottom boat

Listen to Derrick Reese – a young Australian park ranger at the Great Barrier Reef – greet his guests. What sounds different from the way people in the UK or the US speak?

2 Listening for gist

a) *Work with a partner. Each of you takes the role of one of two passengers on board:*

1. someone who works for Greenpeace
2. someone who is interested in Aboriginal culture

b) *Think about what could interest you in your role.*

c) *Listen to what Derrick tells his guests about the Reef. Take notes for your role.*

d) *Compare your notes with your partner's.*

TIP
To help you write faster, develop your own shorthand (e.g.: b/c = because, sth = something, w/o = without, etc.)

3 Listening for details

After the tour, the guests have a choice of two activities.

a) *Listen to what Derrick says about each activity. Then choose the activity that interests you most.*

b) *Now listen closely to the details of your activity and note them down.*

c) *Tell a partner what he/she needs to know about your activity if he/she wants to take part.*

TIP
If you don't know how to write a new name, write it any way – at least you'll know how it ***sounds*** when you reread your notes.

4 Team activity – an Internet project: The Great Barrier Reef

The Great Barrier Reef is one of the great natural wonders of the world and a UNESCO World Heritage Site. Find out more about what makes it so special and what its future could look like. You will find project ideas under Green Line-Online.

WB p. 6/4; 5; 6

First time in 'Oz'

Blake Serafino, a 19-year-old from Sydney, regularly posts bits of information on his popular website for young first-time visitors to 'Oz'.

"Wow, Oz was one big jail!" (posted 30 July)

A lot of young visitors get excited by the idea that Australia used to be a penal colony. And yes, it's true. In 1788 the British started sending shiploads of prisoners to Oz. They made thousands of convicts spend the rest of their lives here. And they made them do a lot of the heavy work in the new colony, like building roads. OK, some were dangerous criminals, but judges also had people sent to the other side of the world for stealing apples! Anyway, you'll find it easier to make friends on your travels if you don't start conversations with "So what awful things did your ancestors do?".

Oz and Britain (posted 12 Aug.)

Don't let anyone tell you that Oz is just a sunnier version of Britain. Oz will always have its British background, but while most immigrants used to come from Europe, now they almost all come from Asia. Today our role in the Asian-Pacific world is very important to us. Aussies also spend their holidays in nearby Singapore or Bali much more often than in far-away Europe.

Yummy! (posted 17 Sept.)

You've seen the animals on Australia's coat of arms, right? Well, how would you like to have them served to you on a plate?! Weird, huh? Some of our food is odd, but you shouldn't let preconceptions stand in your way. Learn from my example! For my 16th birthday, my parents let me have a huge party. But they also had all kinds of exotic dishes delivered by a local restaurant: green ants, witchetty grubs, and emu, kangaroo and crocodile meat! I didn't use to like that stuff at all. Just the idea of it made me feel sick! But not any more. Emu, roo and crocodile are OK, but …

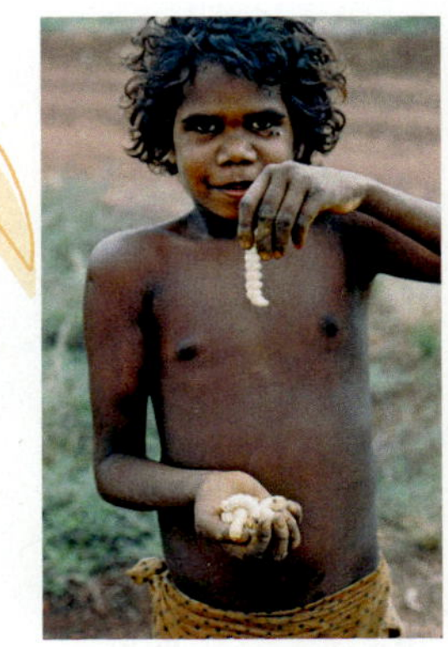

1 Understanding Oz

1. *What does Blake **not** recommend for small talk, and why?*
2. *Why is Australia becoming less European? Give two reasons.*
3. *Which aspects of 'Oz' that Blake mentions are the most interesting to you? Why?*

WB p. 7/7

2 Find the rule: *Used to*

a) *Find the examples of **used to** in the text. Explain what it means and how you use it.*

b) *How is the negative form made?*

3 Your turn: Then and now

Talk about things you used to do / like, but don't any more, and what you do / like now.

Examples:

I **used to** listen to music on my CD player, but now I only listen to my mp3 player.
I **didn't use to** like healthy food, but now I think it's OK.

WB p. 7/8

4 Find the rule: *let, make* and *have*

a) *Explain the difference between* ***let, make*** *and* ***have (sth done)***.

She **let** the boy kiss her.

He **made** his son clean the swimming pool.

They **had** the pizzas delivered.

b) *Find all the examples of* ***let, make*** *and* ***have*** *in the text on page 17.*
Translate each example into German. Can you find one German verb with which you can translate every example? What ***other*** *German verbs can you use to translate them?*

WB p. 7/9

5 Blake's barbie

Blake is talking to his best friend about a Barbie he wants to have. Put in ***let, make*** *and/or* ***have***.

"Yeah, good news, mate: My mum and dad are going to [1] me have the barbie at their place. I said, 'Please don't [2] me invite my friends to *my* little place at university. *You've* got the rooftop terrace and the fantastic view, not me!' (…) Of *course* I mentioned the pool, mate, I'm not stupid! Anyway, they'll [3] me use their flat. (…) Huh? Yeah, really! But I can't [4] anyone sleep in their flat. And Mum and Dad are going to [5] me do all kinds of stuff for the barbie. They've been wanting to [6] the pool cleaned for weeks, so guess who's going to do it now? (…) Yeah, they're [7] *me* do it. And then Mum said with a smile, 'Oh, and I'd *love* to [8] the windows cleaned, too. Hm, I wonder who could do that for me…?' Yeah, guess who."

WB p. 8/10

6 How to: Explain a problem to the police

You are visiting Australia for the first time, but your passport and some of your money were stolen. So you go to the police station.

Make a dialogue between yourself and a police officer. The phrases on the right can help you.

You: Give your name, address, tell the officer what happened, ask where you can get help …

Police officer: Be nice, ask questions, make notes, inform your partner where she/he can get help …

WB p. 8/11

USEFUL PHRASES

- Hello there, may I help you?
- My passport and some money were stolen.
- Would you let me use/May I use your telephone?
- Please fill out these forms so that I can help you.
- Could you describe exactly what happened?
- The German consulate can give you a passport for your flight home.

REVISION

〈Using relative clauses〉

GRAMMAR

- A **defining relative clause** gives necessary information. Without it you don't know who or what is being talked about.
- A **non-defining relative clause** gives extra information about someone or something.
- When a relative pronoun is followed by a subject and verb, you can leave it out and make a contact clause: *Koalas are the animals ~~which/that~~ I like best.*

For more details see → G 3.

1 Australia's animal world

*Match the correct parts and use the relative pronouns **who / that** and **which / that** to make defining relative clauses.*

1. Australia is a continent
2. So it has many animals
3. The animals are an attraction for tourists
4. They love to see marsupials like kangaroos
5. Koalas are also popular, with sweet faces
6. But watch out! Those koalas bite people

... make them look like teddy bears.
... carry their young in pouches.
... has been an island for 50 million years.
... try to hold them!
... travel down under to visit Oz.
... are not found anywhere else in the world.

WB p. 9/12

2 The Tasmanian devil

*Link the sentences with non-defining relative clauses. Use **who** or **which**.*

1. The Tasmanian devil is the symbol of the island of Tasmania. It could die out soon. → The Tasmanian devil, which could die out soon, is the symbol of the island of Tasmania.
2. Australians are proud of their special animals. They are worried about the situation.
3. The devils have a loud scream. They are being killed by a form of cancer.
4. The cancer attacks their faces. It is contagious.
5. Australian scientists have little hope. They have been doing research into the problem.
6. The animals love to fight and bite. They are giving the cancer to each other.

WB p. 9/13

3 *Which/that, whose* or contact clause?

1. A law ▢ was introduced in 1997 gives protection to sharks. It is the great white shark ▢ swimmers worry about most. 2. The platypus is a strange animal ▢ long nose helps it to feel its way in the water. Its young develop in eggs ▢ it lays near lakes and rivers. 3. Dingoes are wild dogs ▢ live in the outback. They are hated by farmers ▢ sheep they kill. 4. Exotic birds ▢ you only see in zoos in Europe fly around wild in Australia. The laughing kookaburra gets its name from the sound ▢ it makes. 5. Australia has large crocodiles ▢ teeth are strong and dangerous. But there are also small spiders like the 'red-back' ▢ can easily kill you, too.

WB p. 9/14

WRITING TEXTS

Elements of a story

Last year you learned how to use *plot*, *setting* and *atmosphere* in story writing. Now see how story elements are introduced at the beginning of a story and how they are developed later.

1 Story elements

Read the beginning of a story and look at the examples of some important story elements.

Plot (gives a story its main idea or ideas)

Characterization (gives you a first idea about someone's qualities – but much more can be written later!)

It was the first weekend of summer and the Christmas holidays, and we were excited. Four good friends on their first road trip into the outback! No parents for a week! It was just my best friend Donovan (the star rugby player), Dani (his nice but princess-like girlfriend), Ruby (my girlfriend and the school's cleverest girl) and me, Angelo. I've always been quite the worry wart, and I wasn't sure this road trip was the best idea. Two guys and two girls – was this going to work in the *outback*? But it was summer, school was over, so I didn't care. I should have. Four friends left together on that Sunday, and four friends returned to Sydney a week later. But not the *same* four people …

Setting (gives you a first idea about time and place)

Perspective (tells the reader who is telling the story)

Foreshadowing (gives the reader hints – also false hints: 'red herrings' – of what will/might happen)

2 Develop the storyline

Continue the story from exercise 1. Before you write it, make notes for the storyline. Go through each element point by point and write down how your story could continue.

- **Setting:** Is there an interesting part of Australia near Sydney to set your story in?
- **Plot development:** Things need to happen in your story. What? What could happen on a road trip? And on a road trip in the *outback*?
- **Characterization:** Give your characters *real* character, e.g.: What kind of a person do you think a 'star rugby player' is?
- **Perspective:** Your story needn't be told by the same person the whole time; a change of perspective can keep things interesting.
- **More foreshadowing:** Don't forget more hints about where your story is going – or *not*!
- **Turning point and climax:** Every story needs a *turning point* (a big change). Look at Choice A or B and find it in each text! The *climax* is the story highlight.

3 Write your story

Now continue the story from exercise 1. Don't forget to give it a good title!

4 Peer editing

Exchange texts with a classmate. How well has she/he developed her/his story? Check with ex. 2.

WB p. 10/15; 16; 17; 18

1 Australia in words

a) *Complete the grid. Write in as many words as you can think of for each topic.*

Aboriginal culture	European settlement	animal world	geography / climate
indigenous …	penal colony …	kangaroo …	outback …

b) *Think about what you have learned about Australia. What is the one aspect you like most about the country? And the least? Write a short paragraph about each.* WB p. 11/19

2 ⟨Real Australian⟩

A surfie is phoning his best mate. Can you guess what the marked words mean?

Bastard, you missed a lot of rippers today at the beach. It was ace! (…) Yeah, chocka with sheilas. (…) Sure, met a hottie. (…) Er, good question. Can't remember. Alexia? Alena? (…) Hey, don't rubbish me, I just met this sheila without a bloke! She's from – uh – Latvia? Lithuania? Hot chick, anyway. I invited 'em over for a party tonight. She's bringin' a friend. (…) Hey, that's *your* problem, mate: If you weren't with your oldies this weekend, you could be here, too. (…) Yeah, that was the doorbell, they're here! I can see 'em through the window. With *empty* plates! (…) No, bloody oath! I wanted 'em to bring plates; but where's the *food*?!

3 That's what people say

a) *Compare the English and German sentences on the right. Which English phrase is used for more formal situations, and which for less formal?*

USEFUL PHRASES

Australians **are said to** be very friendly.
= *Australier gelten als sehr freundlich.*
Australians **are supposed to** be very friendly.
= *Australier sollen sehr freundlich sein.*

b) *Write sentences with **said to** or **supposed to** for more formal and less formal situations.*

1. *(in a magazine)* The Great Barrier Reef/in great danger.
2. *(speaking to a friend)* Bondi Beach/best beach in the Sydney area.
3. *(on an Internet website)* 'Muriel's Wedding'/BEST film about Australia.
4. *(at a barbie)* I've never tried green ants/really sweet.
5. *(in a guide to Australia)* Some Australians/quiet about their family's convict history.
6. *(in a newspaper)* The new Prime Minister/very environment-friendly.

4 ⟨A song: *Beds are burning* by Midnight Oil⟩

… The time has come, a fact's a fact –
It belongs to them, let's give it back.

Chorus:
How can we dance when our earth is turning?
How do we sleep while our beds are burning?
How can we dance when our earth is turning?
How do we sleep while our beds are burning?

NOW YOU CAN

- ✔ Talk about Australia (Aboriginals; settlers; nature/animals).
- ✔ Take better notes while you listen for gist and details.
- ✔ Use 'used to' correctly.
- ✔ Recognize when to use 'let', 'make' and 'have' (for *lassen*).
- ✔ Write a story with different elements.

1 Before and after (→ G 1)

Talk about Australia. Say how things used to be and then how things are now.

WB p. 12/22

2 Use *let, make,* or *have* (→ G 2)

1. A: I hate my hair right now. It looks worse than ever! B: Stop worrying and ___ it cut!
2. A: My kids never clean up around the house, they're so lazy. B: Then ___ them do it – you're their father, remember?
3. A: Oh no, look. It's snowing, and I lost my hat last week! B: Oh, I'll ___ you borrow mine, no problem.
4. A: We're never going to have the food ready before the guests arrive! B: Don't worry. It's not too late to ___ something delivered.
5. A: Carol, that outfit is *so* ugly! B: Dad, ___ him shut up, now! He's a stupid little twelve-year-old who knows *nothing* about fashion!
6. A: What are *you* so happy about? B: Mum and Dad are ___ me fly to Bali next summer!

WB p. 12/23

3 Your turn: A talk about Australia

Give a three-minute talk about what interests you most about Australia. Make notes first.
Or: *You were in Australia and had an adventure. Give a three-minute talk about it.* WB p. 12/24

⟨Down under⟩

"Down under" was written by the American travel writer Bill Bryson who lives in the UK. "Let me say right here that I love Australia," he writes. "The people are immensely[1] likeable[2] … But Australia has more things that will kill you than anywhere else. Of the world's ten most poisonous snakes, all are Australian. Five of its creatures – the funnel-web spider, box jellyfish, blue-ringed octopus, paralysis tick and stonefish – are the most lethal[3] of their type in the world. … You may be chomped[4] by sharks or crocodiles, or carried out to sea by irresistible currents[5], or left to stagger[6] to an unhappy death in the baking outback. It's a tough place."
In this episode, two Australian friends of Bryson's, Deirdre and Glenn from Sydney, are trying to teach him "boogie boarding".

"Excuse me for interrupting," I interrupted, "but what is boogie boarding exactly?"

"Oh, it's fun. You'll love it," Deirdre said quickly.

"Yes, but what is it?"

"It's an aquatic sport. It's heaps of[7] fun. Isn't it heaps of fun, Glenn?"

"Heaps," agreed Glenn.

"You take a kind of miniature surfboard and paddle out into the sea, where you catch a big wave and ride it back to shore. It's easy. You'll love it."

"What about sharks?" I asked uneasily.

"Oh, there's hardly any sharks here. Glenn, how long has it been since someone was killed by a shark?"

"Oh, ages," Glenn said. "Couple of months at least."

"Couple of months?" I squeaked.

"At least. Sharks are way overrated[8] as a danger," Glenn added. "Way overrated. It's the rips that'll most likely get yer."

"Rips?"

"Underwater currents that run at an angle[9] to the shore and sometimes carry people out to sea," Deirdre explained. "But don't worry. That won't happen to you."

"Why?"

"Because we're here to look after you," she smiled.

Three hours later, we stood at a place called Freshwater Beach, near Manly. It was a big U-shaped bay, with what seemed to me awfully big waves pounding in from a vast[10] and moody sea. In the middle distance several people in wetsuits were surfing; nearer in, paddlers were being continually and, it seemed, happily engulfed by explosive waves.

Urged on[11] by Deirdre, we began to strip down – slowly in my case, eagerly in hers – to the swimsuits she had told us to wear beneath our clothes.

"If you're caught in a rip," Deirdre was saying, "the trick is not to panic."

I looked at her. "You're telling me to drown calmly?"

"No, no. Just keep your wits[12]. Don't try to swim against the current. Swim *across* it.

[1] **immensely** [ɪ'mensli] = extremely • [2] **likeable** ['laɪkəbl] = easy to like • [3] **lethal** ['li:θl] = If sth is *lethal* it can kill you. • [4] **to chomp** [tʃɒmp] = *here:* to bite until dead • [5] **current** ['kʌrnt] = Rivers and oceans have underwater *currents* that can be much faster than the water at the top. • [6] **to stagger** ['stægə] = to walk with no control (e.g. because you have no more energy) • [7] **heaps of** ['hi:ps‿əv] = lots of • [8] **overrated** [ˌəʊvə'reɪtɪd] = not as good/true as what people say • [9] **angle** ['æŋgl] = The two lines run at an *angle* to each other. = The two lines do not run parallel to each other. • [10] **vast** [vɑ:st] = endless • [11] **to urge sb on** [ɜ:dʒ] = to tell sb (who isn't sure he/she should) to do sth • [12] **to keep one's wits** [ˌki:p wʌnz 'wɪts] = to make sure you know what is happening around you (e.g. in a dangerous situation)

And if you're still in trouble, just wave your arm like this" – she gave the kind of big, languorous[13] wave that only an Australian could possibly consider an appropriate[14] response to a death-at-sea situation – "and wait for the lifeguard to come."

"What if the lifeguard doesn't see me?"

"He'll see you."

"But what if he doesn't?"

But Deirdre was already wading into the surf, a boogie board under her arm.

I dropped my shirt onto the sand and stood naked but for my sagging trunks[15]. Glenn, never having seen anything quite this grotesque on an Australian beach, certainly nothing still alive, snatched up his camera and began excitedly taking close-up shots of my stomach. *Bizeet, bizeet, bizeet, bizeet,* his camera sang happily as he followed me into the surf.

Let me just pause here for a moment to tell two small stories. In 1935, not far from where we stood now, some fishermen caught a fourteen-foot shark and took it to a public aquarium at Coogee, where it was put on display[16]. The shark swam around for a day or two in its new home, then to the surprise of the viewing public, regurgitated[17] a human arm. When last seen the arm had been attached to a young man named Jimmy Smith, who had, I've no doubt, signalled his predicament[18] with a big, languorous wave.

Now my second story. Three years later, on a clear, bright, calm Sunday afternoon at Bondi Beach, also not far from where we stood, from out of nowhere there came four freak[19] waves, each up to twenty-five feet high. More than 200 people were carried out to sea in the undertow. Fortunately, fifty lifeguards were in attendance that day, and they managed to save all but six people. I am aware that we are talking about incidents that happened many years ago. I don't care. My point remains: the ocean is a dangerous place.

Then Deirdre showed me how the boogie board works. It was simple in principle. As a wave passed, she would leap aboard and skim along on its crest[20] for many yards[21]. Then Glenn had a turn and went even further. There is no question that it looked like fun. It didn't look too hard either. I was eager to have a try.

I positioned myself for the first wave, then jumped aboard and sank like an anvil[22].

"How'd you do that?" asked Glenn in wonder.

"No idea."

[13] **languorous** ['læŋgərəs] = A *languorous* hand movement is relaxed, slow and gentle. • [14] **appropriate** [ə'prəʊprɪət] = The *appropriate* thing to say when you first meet sb is "Nice to meet you". • [15] **trunks** [trʌŋks] = swim shorts • [16] **to put on display** [ˌpʊt‿ɒn dɪ'spleɪ] = to show to the public • [17] **to regurgitate** [rɪ'gɜ:dʒɪteɪt] = to spit out • [18] **predicament** [prɪ'dɪkəmənt] = a situation in which one has a serious problem • [19] **freak** [fri:k] = *here:* totally different from what is normal • [20] **crest** [krest] = the top of a wave • [21] **yard** [jɑ:d] = 1 *yard* = 0.91 metres • [22] **anvil** ['ænvɪl] = a heavy metal block

I repeated the exercise with the same result.

"Amazing," he said.

There followed a half hour in which the two of them watched first with amusement, then a kind of astonishment[23], and finally something not unlike pity, as I vanished[24] beneath the waves again and again and was scraped over an area of ocean floor about the size of Polk County, Iowa. After a lengthy period, I would surface, gasping and confused, at a point anywhere from four feet to a mile and a quarter away, and be immediately carried under again by the next wave. Soon people on the beach were on their feet and placing bets. It was agreed that it was not possible to do what I was doing.

From my point of view, each underwater experience was essentially the same. I would diligently[25] attempt to replicate[26] the dainty[27] kicking motions Deirdre had shown me and try to ignore the fact that I was going nowhere and mostly drowning. Not having anything to judge this against, I supposed I was doing rather well. I can't pretend I was having a good time, but then it is a mystery to me how anyone could wade into such a merciless[28] environment and expect to have fun. But I was resigned to my fate[29] and knew that eventually it would be over.

Deirdre grabbed my arm just before I was about to go under again and said: "Look out! There's a bluey."

Glenn took on an immediate expression of alarm. "Where?"

"What's a bluey?" I asked, appalled to discover that[30] there was some additional danger I hadn't been told about.

"A bluebottle," she explained and pointed to a small jellyfish of the type (as I later learned from reading a fat book called *Things That Will Kill You Horridly in Australia: Volume 19*) known elsewhere[31] as a Portuguese man-of-war. I squinted[32] at it as it drifted past. It looked like a blue condom with strings attached.

"Is it dangerous?" I asked.

"Dangerous? No," Deirdre replied now as we stood looking at the bluebottle. "But don't touch it."

"Why not?"

"Might be a bit uncomfortable."

"Hey, there's another one," said Glenn.

We watched another one drift by. Deirdre was scanning the water.

"Sometimes they come in waves," she said. "Might be an idea to get out of the water."

I didn't have to be told twice.

[23] **astonishment** [ə'stɒnɪʃmənt] = surprise • [24] **to vanish** ['vænɪʃ] = to disappear • [25] **diligently** ['dɪlɪdʒntli] = with a feeling of duty • [26] **to replicate** ['replɪkeɪt] = to copy • [27] **dainty** ['deɪnti] = gentle and ladylike • [28] **merciless** ['mɜːsɪləs] = He's a *merciless* businessman = He's a businessman who will do anything to have success. • [29] **resigned to my fate** [rɪ'zaɪnd tə maɪ 'feɪt] = She's *resigned to her fate (Schicksal)*. = She accepts her fate. • [30] **appalled to discover that ...** [ə'pɔːld] = discovered with horror that ... • [31] **elsewhere** [ˌels'weə] = in other places • [32] **to squint** [skwɪnt] = *here:* to look at sth in a way that shows one isn't happy about sth

⟨Project⟩ English and Art

People have always used pictures to express themselves and their culture, so different parts of the world have different art traditions. This project starts with a look at some western paintings. Then you will find out about Australian Aboriginal art and give an art presentation.

STEP 1: Talk about art from your own culture

a) *Share your ideas about these three paintings.*

b) *What do you know about the artists?*

USEFUL PHRASES
- It's a portrait/self-portrait/religious painting. It shows …
- The first thing you notice is … The style is quite careful/free/…
- The light/colours/ … bold[1]/beautiful/unusual/…
- The atmosphere seems … • I (don't) like the painting because …

▲ Andy Warhol painted Marilyn Monroe in 1962.
◀ This is a Vincent van Gogh self-portrait from 1888.
◀◀ This Madonna was painted by Sandro Botticelli in 1485.

STEP 2: A first look at Australian Aboriginal art

a) *Aboriginals have one of the oldest continuous art traditions in the world, with rock paintings from 20,000 years ago. Use the text an Aboriginal wrote about 'The Dreaming', by modern artist Naiura, to help you talk about what you can see in the picture.*

TIP
Understanding art from a different culture is easier if you know something about that culture.

The Dreaming is the place of our ancestors, our past, and the place that we go to when our short time in this life has come to an end. We tell of the Dreaming in the stories in our art, on a rock, on tree bark[2], or most recently, on canvas[3]. The painting here shows many daily activities – a territory argument, hunting, fishing, cooking and different food sources[4]. It is how Naiura imagines our ancestors in the Dreaming.

b) *Do research to find out more about the Dreaming (also called Dreamtime).*

[1] **bold** [bəʊld] = strong, powerful • [2] **bark** [bɑːk] = the 'skin' of a tree • [3] **canvas** ['kænvəs] = the same thing a ship's sails are made of • [4] **source** [sɔːs] = where sth comes from

STEP 3: A closer look at style and technique

a) *Read this information about Aboriginal art.*

Australian Aboriginal art can be naturalistic or abstract.

- Naturalistic pictures are of people, animals or plants. An 'X-ray[5]' technique is often used to show the internal organs of animals.
- Typical elements in abstract designs are circles, 'U' shapes and lines. These are religious symbols. Circles represent sacred[6] places. Lines represent the paths of ancestors or systems of water or roots[7].
- Both styles, naturalistic and abstract, are often in the form of 'dot[8] paintings', pictures which are created with small dots of paint. This is a very old technique and it is still an important part of Aboriginal culture.

b) *Describe the styles and techniques in the two works of art on this page.*

c) *Now look again more closely at the painting in Step 2. What new or different aspects do you see now that you didn't notice or understand before?*

An Aboriginal shield[9] from the 19th century

STEP 4: Do a project

Work in pairs or groups. Choose ***one*** *of these projects and give a presentation.*

1. Find out about an Aboriginal artist and his/her work.
2. Collect information on old Aboriginal rock paintings like the ones that are mentioned in the 'Time line of Australian history' at the back of your book.
3. Create your own dot painting to show important aspects of your own culture or the world around you.

ART PRESENTATION SKILLS

These ideas can help you to give a good art presentation.

- Present pictures and information in different ways: overhead projector, handouts etc.
- Give details that put the pictures in context: artist, date, subject, style, techniques, background information etc.
- Compare and contrast pictures by the same artist or different artists; also make comparisons with pictures your audience might know.

A bark painting of a kangaroo by Dick Nguleingulei (1975)

[5] **X-ray** ['eksreɪ] = a 'photo' of a body that shows the bones • [6] **sacred** ['seɪkrɪd] = a place with a special religious meaning • [7] **root** [ru:t] = the underground part of a plant/tree • [8] **dot** [dɒt] = a little point • [9] **shield** [ʃi:ld] = sth used for protection in battle (a long time ago)

Unit 2 What next?

Not sure what job you would like to do? Can't decide which is right for you? Our tip is: don't just look at school subjects, think about free-time activities, too. Make your hobby into your job! Here is what three interesting people say about their jobs:

I've always been interested in construction, and I think my job is useful, too, because we need to improve our railway system. So I'm a railway engineer. You see, you can forget about stereotypes when you choose a career!

I turned my love of parties into a party service business! I organise everything, from theme to food to entertainment. It's good to be my own boss, but I have to work long and irregular hours.

When I was studying History, I never dreamt I'd later join the police. I like the fact that no two days are the same. But the reality is different from those TV dramas. Fewer dead bodies and more forms to fill in!

DID YOU KNOW?

- During Year 11, students in English schools reach the age of 16 and must decide whether to continue at school, start a training course or look for a job.
- The most important school exams are taken at the ages of 16 and 18: first GCSEs (General Certificate of Secondary Education) and then A- (Advanced) levels.
- Only 46% of students take a GCSE in a foreign language.
- 43% of young people go on to higher education.
- On average, women in the UK earn 27% less than men.

1 Think about the world of work

a) *What information do the speakers give about the world of work? What is important when you choose a career?*

b) *What questions would you like to ask the speakers about their work?* WB p. 15/1

2 Listening: Work experience

a) *Listen to what students Marco, Pete and Naomi say about the work experience they did in Year 10. Take notes.*

b) *Discuss what you can or can't learn from it.* WB p. 15/2

3 ⟨Comment on the 'Did you know?' facts⟩

a) *Do you find the statistics surprising? What reasons could there be for these facts?*

b) *Research: Find out about the same kind of facts in Germany and comment on them.*

HOW I SEE MYSELF:

Read the following sentences. If you think a sentence describes you, give yourself one point for the colour of that sentence. If there are two colours, give yourself a point for each.

The colour for which you have most points at the end of the questionnaire is the one that suits you best (although other colours may also be important). Find out what this means by reading your colour profile below.

1. I enjoy painting and drawing.
2. I am quick at learning how to use new technical equipment.
3. One of my favourite subjects is Chemistry. (green, blue)
4. I enjoy watching TV commercials. (yellow, red)
5. I like helping people.
6. I am interested in why firms lose money or make money. (red)
7. I write my own computer programmes. (blue)
8. I am good at making my own decisions, but I am also a reliable team member. (green, red)
9. I enjoy making my bedroom look nice. (yellow)
10. I am interested in nature. (yellow, blue)
11. I am good with numbers. (blue, red)
12. Writing stories or plays is fun.
13. I sometimes raise money for charities. (green, red)
14. I love cooking and thinking of my own recipes. (yellow, blue)
15. I would like to make things that I can sell. (yellow, red)
16. I compare prices when I go shopping. (red)
17. I know how much I can earn on money in the bank. (red)
18. I enjoy performing on stage. (yellow, green)
19. I like hanging out with friends. (green)
20. It would be fun to make a machine that uses wind power. (blue)
21. I try to be tactful. (green)
22. I have an idea for a great new invention. (blue, red)
23. I like making guests feel welcome.
24. Music helps me to express my feelings.
25. I enjoy examining things to find out how they work. (blue)
26. I am (would like to be) in a dance group. (yellow, green)
27. I always try to win competitions or races. (red)
28. I am interested in the design and construction of buildings. (yellow, blue)

Green: You are good with people and would enjoy a job in a field like health, social work, education or management, e.g. a nurse, a teacher, a personnel manager. If you prefer animals, you could be a vet or work in a zoo.

Yellow: As a creative person, you would be suited to a job in design or in some form of art or entertainment, e.g. an architect, a cartoon artist, a musician.

Blue: A job where you are involved in science or technology and where you can use your practical skills would suit you, e.g. a research scientist, an engineer.

Red: The business world is full of different opportunities for ambitious, competitive people like you. You could become a banker or a lawyer, or you could even found your own company – if you haven't already done it!

4 Talk about the questionnaire

a) *Do the questionnaire. Do you agree with what it says about you? Say why or why not.*

b) *Think of more jobs and more sentences for each colour.* WB p. 15/3

Information, please!

Students in England wanting careers advice can contact Connexions, an official support service for 13 to 19-year-olds. This morning Marco was at the Peterborough Connexions centre. He did an online questionnaire developed to match teenagers with possible careers, and also talked to the personal adviser helping him. Now he is showing his friend Pete a leaflet given to him by his adviser.

Marco: 'Opportunities with Information Technology', it's called.

Pete: Or in normal English, computer jobs.

Marco: Yeah, why do they have to make it all sound so serious? But look, at least the money's serious, too!

Starting your career, you might earn anything from £15,000+. Later, having worked your way up, this can rise to £50,000+.

Pete: You'll have grey hair by the time you've worked your way up.

Marco: Excuse me, but you're talking to a whiz-kid! Anyway, I want to design computer games. And it says here:

Having grown fast, the world of multimedia offers many good opportunities.

Pete: But have you read the next sentence?

However, being so popular, this area of IT also experiences great competition for jobs.

Pete: Oh, and here's some more bad news for a guy who likes to spend so much time with girls:

Employing mainly men, the industry would like to attract more women.

Marco: Are you trying to put me off, or what?

Pete: Actually, I think IT will really suit you. But I have to laugh reading this – just imagine our History teacher's reaction!

You must be able to meet project deadlines.

Marco: Hey, my last History project was only a week late!

1 Talk about careers in IT

a) *What does the leaflet tell you about work in the field of IT?*

b) *What other kinds of information would you expect to find in the rest of the leaflet?*

2 Find the rule: Participle constructions in place of relative clauses

a) *Compare the participles in these two sentences. What can you say about the forms? Which form is in the active voice, which one in the passive voice?*

1. Students **wanting** careers advice can contact Connexions.
2. Marco is showing Pete a leaflet **given** to him by his adviser.

b) *Rewrite the sentences in a) with relative clauses. Then find the rule about how to make participle constructions in place of relative clauses.*

TIP
Participle constructions like these are often used in written English. They sound more formal than relative clauses.

3 Participles

Find the relative clauses and turn them into constructions with present or past participles.

Example: I'd be great for a firm **that needs** a real whiz-kid. → … **needing** a real whiz-kid.

1. Any idiot who is put in front of a computer can learn how to use it. 2. But only people who are trained in IT can create computer systems. 3. I had a good talk with the Connexions adviser who is helping me. 4. He says clever young people who work in IT can do well. 5. Some of the jobs that are described in this leaflet sound like fun. 6. I like the idea of a job that involves computer games! 7. People who are employed as managers can earn lots of money. 8. I want to find out about universities that offer IT courses. WB p. 16/4

4 Participle constructions to express reasons and time

a) *In factual texts you often see participles in place of clauses with **because** or **when**.*

1. *Look at the participle construction in this sentence from Marco's leaflet.*
   Turn it into a clause expressing the same idea. What conjunction do you need?

   However, being so popular, this area of IT also experiences great competition for jobs.

2. *Now rewrite this sentence with a conjunction and clause:*

   Starting your career, you might earn anything from £15,000 +.

b) *Translate the participle constructions in a) into German.*

TIP
Participle constructions can improve your style in reports etc.

WB p. 16/5

5 Turn a written report on the Connexions website into spoken English

Find the participle constructions and turn them into new sentences.

Start: When I left school, I had … I took … because I wanted … *Go on, please.*

Leaving school, I had no real plans. Wanting to earn money, I took a job in a shoe factory. The low pay was no problem. Living with my parents, I had enough money to spend. Soon the factory no longer needed me. Hearing the news, I stayed calm at first. Then I began to worry, not being able to find another job. Finally I was helped by Connexions to become a nurse. Now my life is great, and learning useful skills, I can look forward to a good future.

6 Write about the students' plans in formal style

Use long forms, and express the reasons for the plans with participle constructions.

Start: 1. **Enjoying** action, Tom would like … 2. **Being** …, Ryan has … *Go on, please.*

1. Tom: I'd like to be a firefighter because I enjoy action!
2. Ryan: I'm interested in machines, so I've decided to become an engineer.
3. Mel: I see my future in fashion because I love clothes!
4. Jake: I plan to start my own company because I have a good business idea.
5. Nicole: I hope to see the world, so I'm going to look for a job in the travel industry.
6. Amy: I might do social work because I want to help people.
7. Ben: I dream of being the next J K Rowling, so I've already started my first book!

WB p. 16/6

7 How to: Talk about personal qualities

a) *Look at what a student tells her personal adviser. Then collect words and phrases to describe your own personal qualities. The Useful phrases can help. You can also use phrases from the questionnaire on page 29.*

USEFUL PHRASES
- I think/I'd say I'm reliable/practical/creative/patient/...
- I'm (not so) good with children/at using words/...
- I find it easy/fun/... to meet people/learn new skills/...
- I (don't) like deadlines/computers/challenges/...
- I prefer to work alone/outside/...

TIP
Ask your teacher or use a dictionary for any new words you need. Collect 'personal vocabulary' in your folder.

b) *In groups, take turns to present yourselves. Tell the truth, but try to stress your good qualities. Listen critically to the others in your group and make helpful suggestions.*

WB p. 17/7

8 Using perfect participles

a) *Look at two more sentences from the IT leaflet. When do you need a perfect participle? What conjunctions can express the same meaning? How are perfect participles formed?*

Later, **having worked** your way up, this can rise to £50,000+.
Having grown fast, the world of multimedia offers many good opportunities.

b) *Use perfect participles to make sentences about a bad day for a young hairdresser.*

Example: **Having been** stuck in traffic, he was late for work.

be stuck in traffic • be late for work; forget to feel the temperature of the water • give a client a nasty shock; collect a pile of clean towels • drop them on the floor; pick up the wrong bottles • mix the wrong hair colour; promise to get a client a cup of coffee • forget to do it; get into trouble all day • glad to go home

c) *Now develop a story with the sentences from b). Choose a name for the boy, and add your own ideas for more problems and details.*

WB p. 17/8

9 Improve the text with participles in place of the underlined phrases

You have to be realistic <u>when you hope</u> for a career in the media. <u>Because you have seen</u> famous stars in the media, you might imagine an exciting lifestyle. Of course most workers <u>who are employed</u> in the industry have nothing to do with celebrities. However, <u>because it is</u> so popular, work in this field is hard to find, and people <u>who want</u> to enter the industry must be ready to take any basic job. For most areas of work <u>that are mentioned</u> in this leaflet qualifications are needed, but <u>when they are looking</u> for their first job, people also need luck. <u>After they have managed</u> to start a career, some work their way up very quickly. <u>Because it has</u> a young image, the world of the media can offer a fast track to the top.

WRITING TEXTS

A letter of application

Beethovenstr. 29
22767 Hamburg
Germany

Webb-Miller Architects
16-18 Rutland Way
Peterborough PE1 5JN
UK

3 March 2011

Application for a work experience placement in summer 2011

Dear Mr Webb

I am writing to apply for a work experience placement with your firm this summer. Your name was given to me by friends in Peterborough.

When I leave school I plan to study architecture. As you will see from the enclosed CV, I spent a month last summer with a firm of architects in Hamburg, so I already have some knowledge of the job. Having learnt English at school for over five years, I would have no language problems.

I hope very much that you are able to offer me a placement. I would work hard for your firm and make myself as useful as possible. Thank you for reading this application. I look forward to hearing from you.

Yours sincerely

Nina Schuster
Nina Schuster

Encl. CV

- Put your address here.
- Put the other person's name and address here or at the end of the letter.
- Show what the letter is about in a heading.
- In the first paragraph, say why you are writing.
- In the second paragraph, add useful information.
- Find/use a friendly ending.
- Print your name under your signature and show what you are enclosing. Do not send a photo.

Curriculum Vitae: Nina Schuster

Personal details

Name:	Nina Schuster
Address:	Beethovenstr. 29 22767 Hamburg, Germany
Tel:	00 49 (0) 40 318 2059
E-mail:	nischu@supermail.com
Nationality:	German
Date of birth:	22 January 1996

Education
2001–2005 Grundschule (primary school)
Since 2005 Martin Luther Gymnasium
In 2013 will take Abitur (like English A-levels)

Work experience
August 2010 Design (architects in Hamburg)
July 2009 volunteer with theatre project

Personal profile
I am creative and reliable, and I have good computer skills. I like travelling because it gives me the chance to meet new people and see different lifestyles. My main hobbies are art and drama. In my free time I also play tennis and swim.

References available if needed

1 Look at the letter

a) *Talk about possible reasons why Nina wants a placement in England.*

b) *Say how the letter is different in style and form from a letter to a friend. Collect phrases that are typical of letters of application.*

2 Talk about the CV

a) *Why is a CV important? What should be in it? Could Nina have added anything to hers?*

b) *Think of other ways to organise a CV.*

3 Your turn: Your own application

Think what kind of firm you would enjoy a placement with. Write your CV and a letter of application in English. Then exchange your application with a partner and compare them.

WB p. 18/10; 11

Just you wait!

Marco sometimes works in his parents' coffee bar, serving the customers. At the moment his friends Naomi and Pete are sitting at a table there, chatting and waiting for their coffee.

Naomi: You'll have to get As at A-level if you want to be a vet, Pete.

Pete: Even then there's no guarantee of a place at uni. The competition is so hot. Hey, did you know Nina wants to come to Peterborough?

Naomi: Oh, the German girl you met on holiday? Yeah, I heard you telling Marco yesterday.

Pete: Talking of Marco, here he is with our espressos.

Marco: Did I hear you mention my name?

Pete: Right! Thanks. Mm. I can feel this coffee waking me up already.

Naomi: You're lucky, Marco. You can always get a job in the family business if your IT plans don't work out.

Marco: Oh, thanks! You don't have much confidence in me, do you? Anyway, what about you? Have you decided on your A-level subjects yet?

Naomi: Well, I'll definitely need Geography for meteorology. And then –

Marco: Oh, are you going to be a meaty – er – a meaty whatsit?

Naomi: Meteorologist, stupid!

Pete: That's why we always see her walking around with her head in the clouds!

Naomi: Laugh if you like, guys, but just you wait! One day I'll be there on TV, doing the weather forecast. And you'll hear me predict a big storm coming in your direction!

1 Think about competition for jobs

a) 1. What kind of jobs are popular career choices? 2. Why do you think the competition is so hot for these jobs? 3. Is competition for jobs a good thing?

b) *Which university courses are hardest to win places on? What would your advice be to someone who dreams of a career for which there is a lot of competition?*

2 Use present participles to link sentences

a) *In written English, when two actions happen at the same time, the second action is often expressed with a present participle. Use this example to explain how to link sentences.*

Marco works in his parents' coffee bar. He serves the customers.
→ Marco works in his parents' coffee bar, **serving** the customers.

TIP
Linking ideas helps to make written texts more fluent.

b) *Use present participles to put these ideas together in one sentence.*

Start: 1. Pete and Nina send e-mails regularly, …

1. Pete and Nina send e-mails regularly. They tell each other their news.
2. Recently Nina contacted Pete. She mentioned her work experience idea.
3. Pete talked to a careers teacher at school. He explained what Nina wanted to do.
4. The careers teacher was very helpful. She gave Pete information about possible firms.
5. Now Nina has written a letter to a firm of architects. She has asked for a placement.
6. She is still waiting to hear from them. She hopes for a positive reply.

WB p. 19/12

3 Participle or infinitive

a) *Verbs of perception (see, hear, feel, etc.) and an object can be followed by a participle or an infinitive without* **to**. *Compare the kinds of action these two forms express. Which action do you see from beginning to end? Which action do you only see part of?*

1. I *saw* Marco **working** in the coffee bar. (= He **was working** there when I saw him.)
2. I *saw* Marco **drop** a cup of coffee. (= He **dropped** a cup of coffee, and I saw this.)

b) *Go through the dialogue on page 34 and find more examples of participles or infinitives after verbs of perception and an object. How do you express these ideas in German?*

WB p. 19/13

4 What Pete saw

Pete sometimes helps the vet he met during his work experience. The vet wants to know why a woman with a cat left before her appointment. Go on with what Pete says he saw/heard/watched etc. Use your own ideas for linking the sentences.

Start: Well, I was outside the waiting room. But I heard … So I went in and saw …

5 Listening: A telephone call for Nina

a) *Listen and take notes about:*

1. what Mr Webb wants to know and what Nina tells him.
2. what will happen next and what Nina should do.

b) *Write an e-mail from Nina to Pete after the phone call from Mr Webb.*

6 ⟨A poem: *Let no one steal your dreams* by Paul Cookson⟩

Let no one steal your dreams
Let no one tear apart
The burning of ambition
That fires the drive inside your heart.

Let no one steal your dreams
Let no one tell you that you can't
Let no one hold you back
Let no one tell you that you won't.

Set your sights and keep them fixed
Set your sights on high
Let no one steal your dreams
Your only limit is the sky.

Let no one steal your dreams
Follow your heart
Follow your soul
For only when you follow them
Will you feel truly whole.

Set your sights and keep them fixed
Set your sights on high
Let no one steal your dreams
Your only limit is the sky.

Write a poem with a nasty speaker who tries to take away people's dreams. Start like this:
Stop dreaming hopeless dreams …

REVISION

⟨Talking about the future⟩

1 Remind yourself of the forms

First look at the information on the right. Then read the dialogue and find examples of how to talk about the future. Explain why the different tenses are used.

GRAMMAR
- **present progressive:** for future arrangements
- **'will' future:** for personal predictions
- **'going to' future:** for plans or when it is already clear what is going to happen
- **simple present:** for 'timetable' information

For more details see → G 5.

Naomi's sister Lucy, a college student, wants to earn some money.

Lucy: Hey, Naomi, have you heard my news?
Naomi: No, but I can see you're going to tell me! So go on.
Lucy: Well, I phoned about a Saturday job in a shoe shop, and I'm going for an interview with the manager tomorrow!
Naomi: Oh, that's cool. Well, good luck!
Lucy: Thanks. The interview starts at 9.45. I don't expect it'll take too long.
Naomi: What are you going to wear?
Lucy: Well, I thought – er – your new skirt? Please, Naomi! It'll be good for you, too, if I get the job. You won't have to pay so much for your shoes!

WB p. 20/15; 16

2 Say what Naomi is doing next week

a) *Use Naomi's notes to give the information.*

Example: On Monday she is having her hair cut. Her appointment is at 4.30.

b) *What arrangements do you and your partner have for next week? Ask and answer questions.*

1. Are you going anywhere special next week?
2. What are you doing after school on …?
3. What time does/is …? …?

WB p. 20/17

Hair appointment Mon 4.30
Tues Geog. project presentation!
Wed 11.15 interview P'borough Regional college
Volleyball Thurs after school
Sat 12.40 meet Grandad at station
Charity Walk Sun – start outside sports centre 10 am
Phone personal adviser Fri

3 Talk about plans for the future

a) *Go on with what Marco tells his friends about his plans for a great life. Find your own verbs.*

"When I leave school, I'm going to study IT at uni. Then I'm going to start …"

b) *Marco's friends want to have a little fun with him. Use your own ideas to make their predictions.*

1. "Sorry, but I don't think your plans will work out!"
2. "I (don't) think you/your business will …"
3. "It's quite possible that/Maybe … will/won't …"

c) *Your turn: How do you see your own future? Write a paragraph describing your plans and predicting what your life will be like. (You needn't be too serious!)*

TALKWISE

Making a good impression at an interview

When you have an interview for a job or for work experience, you are almost always in competition with other people, so it is very important to make a good impression.

1 Talk about how to prepare before the day of the interview

Say what information you should get or what you should do to …

1. … be in the right place by the right time. 2. … look suitable for the job. 3. … have answers ready to give at the interview. 4. … show you are really interested in that company. 5. … feel fresh on the day. WB p. 21/18

2 Comment on the applicants

Your body language and how you look can say as much about you as your words! Look at the two applicants and say what impression you think they make. What might employers find good or not so good? WB p. 21/19

3 Listening: A job in a sports shop

a) *Before you listen, read the interview tips on the right. They are from the Connexions website. Put them in the order needed. Can you think of anything else you should try to remember?*

b) *A boy is being interviewed for a job in a sports shop. Listen and make notes in two lists: 1. Things he does well. 2. Mistakes he makes.*

c) *Listen again, and write down phrases which could be used in other interviews. Start a list of Useful phrases.* WB p. 21/20

A Say why you want the job and why you're suitable for it.
B Wait until you are asked to take a seat.
C Ask how long it will be before you find out whether you've been accepted.
D Answer questions with more than 'yes' or 'no', and don't speak too casually.
E Thank the interviewer when you leave.
F Smile and say good morning/afternoon.
G Ask important questions – about the training, work etc. You can ask about the pay, but don't make it your first question.

4 Team activity: Job interviews

Form groups of four, with two pairs of partners. Each pair acts two dialogues, taking turns to be the interviewer and the applicant. Choose jobs for the interviews and use the ideas on the right to prepare. While one pair does the role play, the other pair watches and listens. Then they can make helpful comments about how to improve.

Interviewer: Write down questions you can ask and information you might have to give about the job or the company.

Applicant: Write down ideas about how to 'sell yourself' and what questions to ask. Think what to say about yourself, and what body language to use.

Now that's what I call living!

The following text is from a British novel about a boy who is trying to discover what kind of person he is. 'Now that's what I call living!' is the title of a little story told by the boy in the novel.

1 Before you read

*What do people mean when they say someone is **weird**? What does the word mean to you?*

Here's a little story.

This guy, let's call him Jimmy, he lives with his family in an old school bus in New Mexico. There's him, his mom and dad and his five brothers and sisters, all in this old bus. They're driving it all around New Mexico and up into California, staying in different places, just bumming around.

Only one day the poor old bus dies. "Dag nabbit," it says, at the end of too many hot and hard days, "I've had enough of ol' Route 66, or wherever we are. I'm off to meet the great bus-builder in the sky."

So when they get to the next corner, Dad turns the wheel and the hippy bus, for the first time in its life, doesn't follow. Yes, for the first time in its long life, it does what it damn well wants. Goes straight on and off the road, down a slope and finally stops upside-down on its roof.

And would you believe it! Mom and Dad and Jimmy and the other five little Brokers all climb out of the doors and windows, every one of them just fine.

And Dad says, after he's counted them all quickly, "OK. That's the last time I live in a bus." And off he goes and buys a tent. A big old army tent. And they're off again, stopping here and there, and life's not so bad until one day the poor old tent is grabbed by a tornado, up into the air and away. And Dad says, "OK. That's the last time I live in a tent."

So they go to the coast, where he buys an old boat. One that's seen better days, of course. And they're planning to live off what they can get from the sea, only none of them has any idea about fishing. Two fishes they catch that first day, two fishes between the seven of them, and Jesus might have been able to feed the five thousand like that, but Mom and Dad, no way.

A storm starts and they can't get back into the harbour. So they're out all night, thrown around by the waves at their most extreme. And Dad doesn't know much about sailing a boat, I'm afraid, not having had much experience because he grew up as far from the sea as anybody can get, but he manages. Just about, he manages.

And when they finally get back to dry land, Mom and Jimmy and the five brothers and sisters all say, like they've been rehearsing it for days, although they haven't actually, "Listen, Dad," they say. "That's the last time we live in a boat. It's time to get your act together, start living in the real world, find yourself a job and us a home!"

And he does, in a way. He gets them a big trailer to live in and he turns himself into a taxi-driving part-time gardener (although he doesn't know a lot about gardens, and he thinks he can drive a cab the way he used to drive that poor old bus, not well at all).

And Jimmy and the rest of the kids have a more normal life after that, with a roof over their heads, and schools, and enough food. But every one of them has been affected by their unusual childhood and so they can never quite match other people's narrow expectations. In other words, they're weird. Real weird.

One grows up to be an artist in Ulan Bator, another becomes a wrestler in Southern Winnipeg and a third is a lion

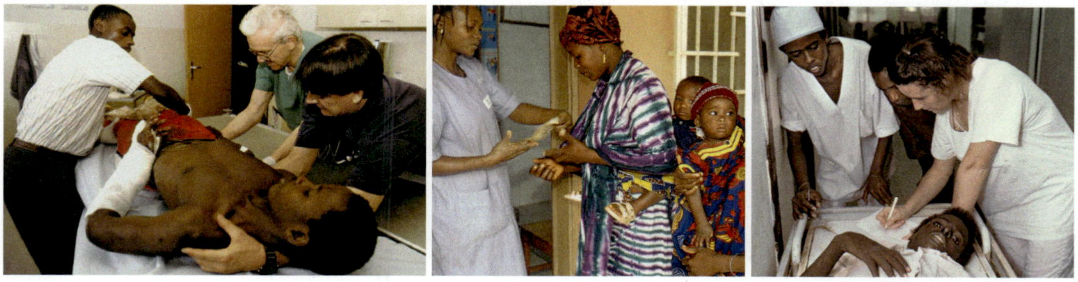

tamer in Outer Mongolia. (I actually haven't any idea what they did – it didn't tell you in the *Sunday Information* where I read about this Jimmy guy, but never mind, I'm sure that's what story-telling is all about, making it up as you go along.) And each one of them goes their own crazy way.

2 Stop and think

*What do **you** think an unusual childhood is?*
How might it affect your later life?

And Jimmy? Well, I can tell you a bit more about Jimmy. Jimmy saves lives. Jimmy studies and passes exams, and passes more exams, and Jimmy becomes a doctor.

And not for Jimmy the nice easy life of a town doctor in the American Midwest, oh no. Jimmy goes to the Congo. Jimmy goes to a village in the middle of Africa, a village of great poverty, a village with lots of disease and no doctors at all. There Jimmy starts a hospital, and there Jimmy saves lives. Lots and lots of lives.

People hear about this, and they come from miles around, on animals, on foot, any way they can get there. They camp outside and wait until Jimmy can help them. As many as his few medicines allow.

And the people love Jimmy because he has a special gift. He can cure with drugs and he can cure with his hands. He's thin and he has white skin and he wears little round John Lennon glasses like his father before him. Well, all those Africans think he's the strangest guy they've ever seen, but they respect him. They respect him and they love him.

For he can cure anything, almost. He comes to your bed when no one else wants to come to your bed, holds your hand when no one else wants to hold your hand, and he talks to you gently, sometimes in your language and sometimes in his. And you don't understand what he's saying and you don't know how holding your hand is going to make you feel better, but it does.

And from time to time Jimmy leaves. He leaves his hospital in the hands of the African doctors and nurses he's trained, and he flies back home to America and he begs for drugs and money to go on with his work.

And he travels all around, talking to businessmen and politicians and church groups and colleges and anyone who'll listen. And he tells them about women dying because there is no clean water, and children dying because they need medicine that costs fifty cents in the United States. And he shows them photos of hungry people and photos of disease and he shows them pictures that would make anyone with even half a heart cry.

And this Jimmy, he shows all these people a photo of a girl who was brought to the hospital one night. She'd been carried twenty miles. She's completely bald and her body is thin and her arms and legs are like sticks. Then, would you believe it! Here's a picture of her a few months later, with a beautiful head of hair, a round face, and a big happy smile!

"So put your hands into your pockets," says Jimmy, "deep, deep down into the large pockets of the west. Because the poor are suffering. All over the world the poor are suffering, and it's up to you to help them."

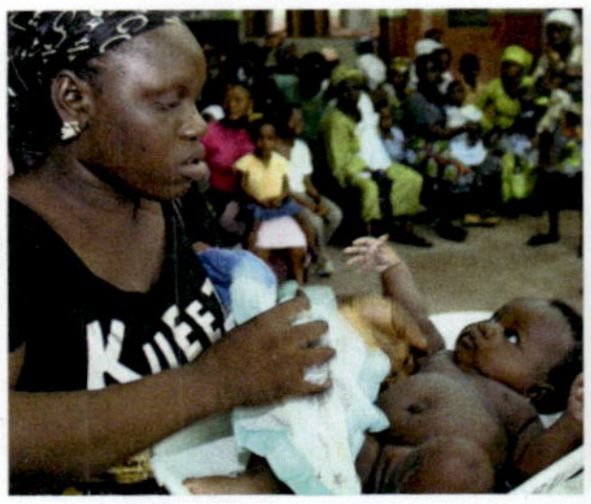
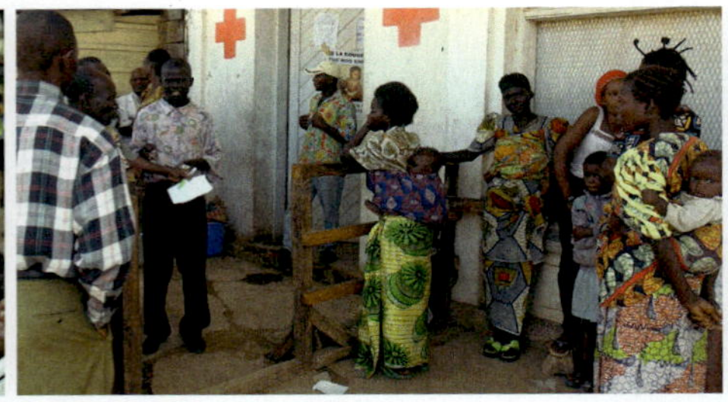
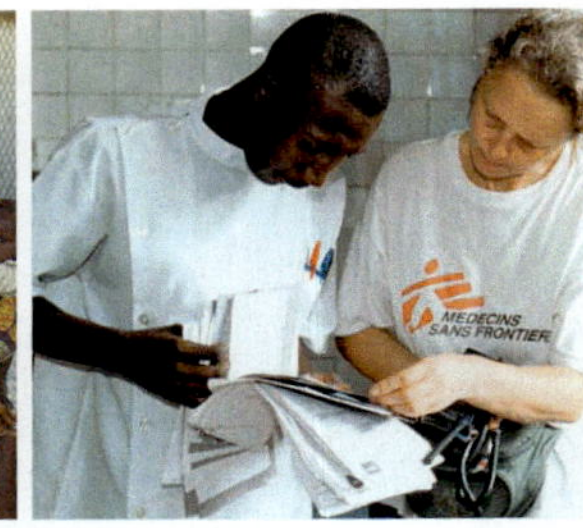

And they do! They take out their wallets, the businessmen. They open their doors, the bankers. They clear out their drug cupboards, the doctors, and they give our Jimmy what he needs to go on for another few months.

And the drugs he gets, he uses to cure people. And the money he gets, he spends on cleaning the water system so there's no more disease. And the rest of the money he spends on schools. Schools to give people an education. And one of the things he makes them teach people in the schools and the villages is how not to get AIDS.

So that's Jimmy. That's what he does, that boy I was telling you about, the one who grew up in a bus, travelling around New Mexico.

And it's all true, because I read it in a Sunday paper some time ago. I've changed the names and the facts a bit, but it's more or less all true.

And if you're still wondering why I'm telling you Jimmy's story, not mine, then you don't understand what I'm talking about at all. I'm talking about life! I'm talking about not just living the same old way everybody else does. I'm talking about getting out there and doing something real.

Because that's what I call living! That's what I call living!

(From *Who is Jesse Flood?* by Malachy Doyle)

3 Talk about Jimmy

1. How is Jimmy's life different from most other people's lives? 2. Why did he become the kind of person he is? WB p. 22/22; 23

5 Examine the text structure

Divide the text into parts. Write down what each part is about.

Start: Childhood: line 1 – …

4 Look at the style

How is a story told in the first person different from one written in the third person? Find typical phrases in the text.

6 ⟨Writing texts: Biographies⟩

Choose one of Jimmy's brothers or sisters. Start at line 82 and write their biography. You can make things up if you want to!

7 Create an ad for Jimmy's campaign for Africa

8 Collaborative writing: Biographies

In groups of four, decide on a person that you all know or admire. It can be someone famous. Make a plan of the person's life, using your text structure from exercise 5 to help you. Then each of you writes one part of the biography. Check and improve your texts together. Is the style of your texts the same? Then read your complete biography to your class.

WB p. 22/24

1 Discuss the qualities needed for different jobs

a) *What kind of person do you need to be for the jobs in the photos?*

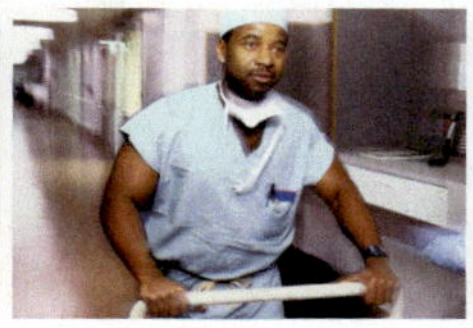

⟨b)⟩ *Think of more jobs and the qualities needed for them.*

WB p. 23/25

2 Compare English and German

a) *Check the meaning of the new phrases on the right. What German adverbs can express the same ideas?*

GRAMMAR

You **are certain to** do it. = You will definitely do it.
You **are likely to** do it. = You will probably do it.
You **happen to** do it. = You do it, but didn't plan to do it.

b) *Complete these exam tips with the new phrases from a). Then put them into German.*

1. When you do revision for your GCSEs, think about what questions you … get.
2. On exam days, get to school early. Then you … be outside the exam room on time.
3. Don't worry if you … forget your watch. You will be able to see the clock in the room.
4. Read the questions carefully so that you … answer them in the right way.
5. Don't get nervous if the exam seems hard. You … do better than you think.
6. If you … need the toilet during an exam, put your hand up. Don't just walk out of the room!

WB p. 23/26

3 Learn to recognise suffixes

a) *A suffix is an added word ending that makes another word. Guess the new words in blue on the right. You already know other words from the same word family.*

b) *Use the words from a) to make lists of typical suffixes for nouns and adjectives. Give at least two examples for every suffix.*

c) *Think of more typical suffixes.*

"I'm not sure what kind of employment is best for me. I'm quite imaginative – I once won a prize with a drawing of an alien. I don't think I'd like to work for a huge organisation. Of course I want an enjoyable job. I need to be successful, too. Money is a weakness of mine. I definitely want a luxurious lifestyle!"

4 ⟨Real English⟩

In casual conversations people often use expressions that can have any meaning. This is because they can't think of the correct word right away or because it's simply easier. Use the context to explain what is meant here:

1. I did the silly **whatsit**'s hair like she said and she hated it!
2. Vets have to carry a lot of **stuff** around in their bags.
3. For safety I had to wear **thingummies** over my eyes.

5 ⟨Book corner⟩

Charles Dickens's famous novel Great expectations *tells the story of Philip Pirrip and what becomes of his hopes and dreams.*

(Klett Easy Classic C)

NOW YOU CAN

- ✔ Talk about choosing a career and making plans for the future.
- ✔ Use participle constructions in place of relative clauses.
- ✔ Use present or perfect participles to express reasons and time.
- ✔ Talk about personal qualities.
- ✔ Write a letter of application and your CV.
- ✔ Use participles to link sentences.
- ✔ Say what you watched people doing or saw them do.
- ✔ Deal with interviews.
- ✔ Write a short biography.

1 Write about careers advice in Germany

An English friend wants to know how teenagers in Germany are helped to make career choices. Write 6–8 sentences explaining how or where you can get information and advice.

2 What does Pete tell Nina? (→ G 4)

Use participle constructions to make the sentences shorter.

TIP
Use present or past participles in place of relative clauses.

1. Year 10 and 11 students who study for GCSEs are under a lot of pressure.
2. People who expect a lot of us, like parents and teachers, are a problem.
3. The good grades that are needed to go on to A-levels are not easy to get.
4. The exams that are taken at the end of Year 11 are really important.
5. All the kids who are waiting for their results in August feel very nervous.
6. Big plans that have been made for the future can be ruined in a minute.

WB p. 24/29

3 Make the style more formal (→ G 4)

Turn the adverbial clauses into participle constructions. Use present or perfect participles.

TIP
If one action happens before the other, use a perfect participle for the first action.

1. After she had seen an advert, Lucy phoned about the job in the shoe shop.
2. Because she wanted to look good, she asked to borrow her sister's (Naomi's) new skirt.
3. Naomi said yes because she hoped to get cheap shoes.
4. Lucy was offered the job because she had made the best impression of all the applicants.
5. When she read her contract, she discovered she could not get cheap shoes right away.
6. After she had worked there for six months, she was finally able to make Naomi happy!

WB p. 24/30

4 Apply for the job in the advert

a) *Write a letter of application for the job in the advert. (You can choose the applicant's name.) Write the letter in the correct form, and use the correct style of language.*

b) *Make a list of six things applicants should always put in a CV.*

Assistant – tourist information centre
Friendly, reliable young person needed to help in busy town tourist information centre. You will have the chance to train at college and in the workplace. At least one European language would be an advantage. Send a letter of application to:
Mrs A Smith, Manager, Tourist Information Centre, 24 High Street, Newtown BD1 8LP

WB p. 24/31

5 Go on with what the boy is thinking (→ G 4)

Think of activities he imagines, using present participles to link the ideas.

Example: 1. Maybe one day I'll be on TV, acting in a soap or reading the news.

1. Maybe one day I'll be on TV, …
2. It would be fun to drive around in a police car, …
3. I might enjoy working in a zoo, …
4. Of course I'd love to be in the England football team, …
5. I don't think I'd like to spend my days in a school, …

WB p. 25/32

6 A girl talks about a guy in the office (→ G 4)

Look at the pictures. Use participles or infinitives after verbs of perception and an object.

1. He always arrives really late for work. This morning I saw him …
2. He clearly prefers magazines to company reports. Today I noticed …
3. A lot of his phone calls from the office are personal ones. Yesterday I …
4. He takes other people's equipment without asking. Yesterday …
5. Our boss isn't too happy with him, of course. This afternoon I …

TIP
Participles for longer actions, infinitives for shorter actions.

arrive — read — talk — take — give

WB p. 25/33

7 Make a good impression at an interview

Imagine you are an applicant for the job advertised in exercise 4 on page 42.
What would you say at these points in the interview?

1. You enter the interview room. 2. You are asked why you think you would enjoy doing the job. 3. You are asked why you think you are the right person for the job. 4. You are given the chance to ask questions yourself. 5. The interview is over. WB p. 25/34

8 Team activity: The six most important things in life

a) *Everyone writes down six things. (1 = most important, etc.).*

b) *You all look at each other's lists and discuss your ideas.*

c) *Together, you agree on a final list for your team.*

⟨Revision for tests⟩ Unit 1–2

Going to school in Australia

A teacher from Manchester is teaching for a year in Australia. She has written this text about the Australian school system for her class back home.

Here in Australia the school year starts at the beginning of February, after the long summer holidays, and there are four terms of 9–10 weeks each. The school day usually starts at about 8 am, Monday to Friday, going on until 2.30 or 3 pm. After that we have extra activities like music and drama. The Australians are crazy about sport, rugby and cricket being especially popular.

Education is organized by the individual states (New South Wales, Queensland, etc.). In each state there are free schools ("government schools") attended by almost 70 % of all Australian students. The other 30–40 % go to fee-paying independent schools. At both types of school the students usually wear uniform. All children must start school by the age of 6 (earlier in some states), and they must stay at school until they are 15 (when they are usually in Year 10), with most Australian students staying on until the end of the final Year 12.

The national curriculum regulates what Australians learn at both government and independent schools in all states. The eight main subject areas are Maths, Society and the Environment, Science, the Arts, Economics, Technology, Health and Physical Education – and English. English is a second language for many students in Australia – for immigrants and Aboriginal families. Special English lessons are very important in the Northern Territory, where there are a large number of Aboriginal students (33 %). This territory is huge, with outback desert, tropical rainforest, few towns, and a very scattered population.

One answer to this problem is the "School of the Air", a radio service offering schooling for younger children in isolated areas. It was started in Alice Springs in the 1950s. This system has developed, and today multimedia IT is an important aspect of distant education for all ages. Now a good education can be given to children in Aboriginal settlements and in isolated small schools and farms in the outback. Not surprisingly, distant learning systems are used in almost all states in Australia.

1 Understanding the text: Australian schools

a) *Are these sentences right or wrong? Or is the information not in the text?*

1. Australian students often spend time in school after normal/official lessons are over.
2. Most students in Australia leave school when they are 15.
3. There are official exams at the end of Year 12.
4. Many immigrant students come from countries where English is not the first language.
5. In the Northern Territory almost all the people live in towns.
6. "Distant learning" is an education system for Aboriginals only.

b) *Correct the sentences that are wrong.*

c) *What is different from schools in Germany? Copy this grid, then make notes about the school year, the school day, and the subjects.*

Australia	Germany
starts – Feb.	...

2 Listening: The film competition

Tyler and Holly are in the film club at their school in Brisbane. They are talking about a competition.

a) *What is the gist of their conversation? Make short notes.*

b) *Listen again and make two lists (note form) of the positive and negative things Holly and Tyler say about taking part in the competition. (Think about the work, the prize(s) …)*

c) *What words and phrases describe Holly and Tyler?*

3 Speaking: Which trip is better?

Two teenagers from Europe are planning a two-week trip to Australia. One of them (A) wants to travel around in the outback. The other one (B) would like to spend the time in a city on the coast.

Make notes for a role play. Think about the ***advantages*** *and the* ***disadvantages*** *of both ideas. Then act out your role play.*

4 Mediation: Sun safety

Your younger brother is crazy about Australia. He has found this text on an official Australian school's website.

a) *Skim the text to get the gist.*

b) *Now answer your brother's questions.*

1. Im Text geht es um Sonne. Was hat denn die Schule damit zu tun?
2. Müssen sich die australischen Schüler anders verhalten als wir?
3. Und die Erwachsenen? Können sie machen, was sie wollen?

All schools in the state must provide education programmes on sun safety. The best possible use of shade must be made for outdoor activities in the school grounds.
In planning these activities schools must try to reduce the time students spend in the sun between 10 am and 2 pm.
Schools should consider planting more trees for shade and take care of trees already in the grounds.
Staff must ensure that students wear protective clothing when in the sun (hats with broad brims, sunglasses, swimming shirts). The use of a Sun Protection Factor 30+ sunscreen on uncovered areas of the skin is to be encouraged.
School staff and parents are extremely important as role models for students.

5 Writing: An e-mail to Australia

Look at the text on page 44 again and at your notes from exercise 1c).

Write to a class at an Australian school and tell the students about your school system. Compare your system with theirs.
Say what you like/don't like about each system. Write about 100 words.

Rhona – the model medic

Read this text from a magazine.

Which kind of work is worse? Dealing with somebody who has fallen under a train? Or wearing fantastic clothes at a fashion show? In this series of articles we look into how people's lives can change. This week's report features Rhona, who now lives in New York.

"When I was a teenager in a small town in Utah, I knew exactly what my dream job was. I wanted to be a model." So Rhona took a big step together with a friend, moved to New York City – and managed to get a job in fashion. As Rhona soon found out, the first step towards becoming a top fashion model is to collect experience in Europe. Models are sent to Paris and Milan where new, fresh faces are wanted every week. "They make you go to France at 17," Rhona says, "and you don't speak French. The people at the agency don't help you because they don't care. You're expected to work hard and earn money for them, in France, Italy or wherever. As a young girl you're very lonely and even in danger. You could get picked up by all the playboys hanging out around the fashion scene." Rhona did not find the work attractive, – and she knew it would not go on for years, anyway. "A model isn't offered a lot of magazine work when she gets to her early 20s and her skin is not as young."

At 28 she knew the work was not going to improve, and she started looking at other possibilities, the first one being medicine. "I had always been interested in medicine since the time I cut my finger badly at the age of 10," Rhona explains. She did an Emergency Medical Training course, followed by paramedical training. "That meant a very intensive course, two years' work pushed into one," she says. Having completed the training Rhona soon found herself in a full-time job. "It can be dangerous, yes – but I love it! Most of us are adrenaline junkies. We love the pressure, and we don't mind taking risks."

The job is very down-to-earth, which she enjoys, but she admits that there are nasty sides to it, and things which make her feel hurt, too. "People get angry with us and even attack us if they think we aren't doing enough to help the patient. I can understand that. They're afraid, and they don't realize that we have all the same equipment as an emergency room."

Rhona says she has no interest in the world of fashion now, none at all. "Being a paramedic is in another class. We're making a difference and helping people. I can see now that I never really liked working as a model. But I could do this job for the rest of my life!"

1 Understanding the text: Which answer is correct?

1. To become a top fashion model in New York you must …
   a) work hard in Manhattan. b) hang out with the playboys. c) collect experience in Europe.
2. A model isn't offered a lot of magazine work when she reaches …
   a) the age of 30. b) her early 20s. c) the age of 40.
3. Rhona loves her new job as a paramedic because …
   a) it's exciting and dangerous. b) she's a junkie. c) it's almost as exciting as being a model.
4. There are other reasons why she loves her new job:
   a) she likes talking to people who are afraid. b) she enjoys using all that interesting equipment. c) she likes medicine and enjoys helping people.

2 Listening: Working for the Royal Flying Doctor Service

A group of British teenagers are interviewing Stephen Webb about his job.

a) *Listen to the text once and find out … 1. where Stephen comes from. 2. what job he trained for. 3. where he lives now. 4. how he helps the doctors.*

b) *Listen to the text again. Make notes about the Royal Flying Doctor Service (what they do, problems, …). Use your notes to write a short text (3–4 sentences).*

3 Speaking: The right person for the job

Which jobs in Unit 2 did you find interesting? Choose one job, and prepare for an interview.

1. *Make notes on these questions and other possible questions the interviewer might ask:*

   What are your qualifications for this job? • Have you had any work experience which might be useful? • How do you see yourself? • What are your strong points? • Tell me something about your interests and hobbies. • …

2. *Use your notes and tell the interviewer about yourself.*

4 Mediation: Job information

Your visitor Karen from Leeds is training to be a hotel manager in the UK. Tell her what the work involves in Germany, how long it takes to become a hotel manager and what the career opportunities are like in Germany.

Hotelfachfrau

Zu den **Arbeitsinhalten** gehören:
- Neigung zu Planung und Organisation
- Neigung zum Umgang mit Zahlen
- Neigung zum Umgang mit Menschen
- Neigung zu praktisch-zupackender Tätigkeit
- Fähigkeit, Stress auszuhalten.

Dauer der Ausbildung: 3 Jahre
Die **Berufsaussichten**, sei es in einem Hotel, einem Restaurant oder in einem Café, sind gut. Ausgebildete Hotelfachfrauen/-männer mit BWL-Studiengang haben ideale Voraussetzungen für die selbständige Führung eines Hotels oder eines großen Restaurants.

5 Creative writing: Developing a story

Look at the pictures of Danny, a builder. Imagine what happened and how the story ended. Make notes first, then write the story. Write about 120 words.

1

2

work • upstairs
repair • wall
downstairs • family
hear • argument •
shout • fight ??
quiet

3

4
? ? ?

⟨Project⟩ English and Politics: the UK

British people are proud that their country has never been invaded since the Normans arrived in 1066. On these two pages you will learn about the British system of democracy and the tradition of political independence in the UK. You can also do your own political survey[1].

STEP 1: Understand the system of government in the UK

a) *Look at the diagram and the information about Parliament today on the 'Political institutions of the UK' page at the back of your book. Find the answers to these questions:*

The House of Commons

1. Why is the House of Commons the most important part of Parliament?
2. What is the title of the person with the top job in British politics?
3. How often must there be elections?
4. How many Members of Parliament are there for each constituency[2]?

b) *Talk about what you can see in the photo of the House of Commons. What is different from the Bundestag?*

STEP 2: Explain a political cartoon

a) *First read this background information.*

The UK has four parts: England, Scotland, Wales and Northern Ireland. Although the UK Parliament represents and makes laws for the whole country, since 1999 Scotland, Wales and Northern Ireland have all had the right[3] to make their own political decisions in areas like education or health. There is a separate Scottish Parliament, and Wales and Northern Ireland each have a National Assembly.

"You're not splitting from[5] us, we're splitting from you."

b) *Now look at the cartoon on the right. Describe what is happening. What do the words below the picture tell you about the British attitude[4] towards political decisions?*

c) *There is no separate parliament for England. Why do you think some English people think this is not fair?*

[1] **survey** ['sɜːveɪ] = a way of finding out information (e.g. asking people questions on the street and/or in a questionnaire) • [2] **constituency** [kən'stɪtjʊənsi] = voting area • [3] **right** [raɪt] = If you have the *right* to do sth, you are allowed by law to do it. • [4] **attitude** ['ætɪtjuːd] = way of thinking • [5] **to split from** ['splɪt frəm] = to break away from

STEP 3: Use survey results to find out British attitudes to the European Union

a) *What do the statistics on this page tell you?*

b) *Comment on what you have found out about British attitudes.*

USEFUL PHRASES

Explaining statistics:
The bar graph shows that …
The table/pie chart …
… % of British people …
A majority[6]/Less than half/…
Compared to other countries …

Commenting on statistics:
I'm (not) surprised that …
I can/can't understand why …
I think it's OK/a pity that …
I think the results of a survey in Germany would be the same/…

How would you describe your national identity?

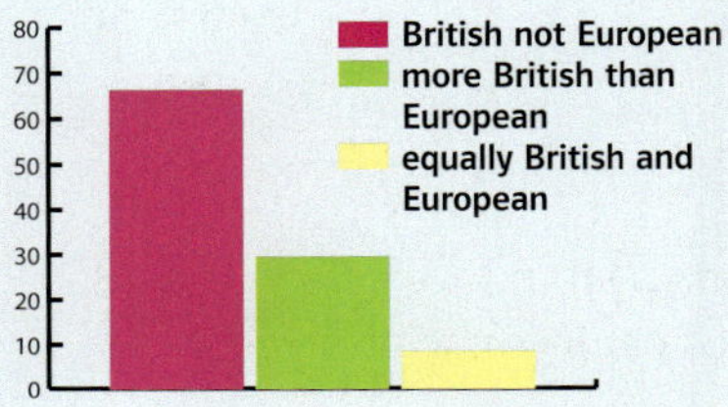

Should the UK join the euro?

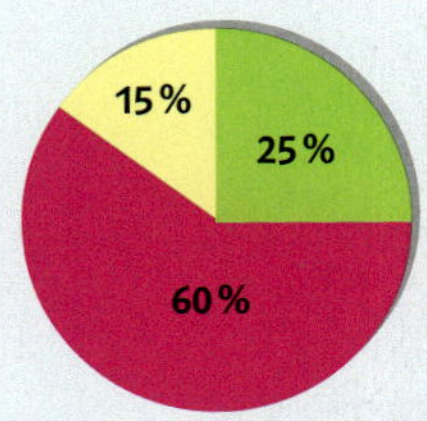

yes 25 % no 60 % don't know 15 %

Is it good to be in the EU? 'Yes' answers of citizens of EU member states:

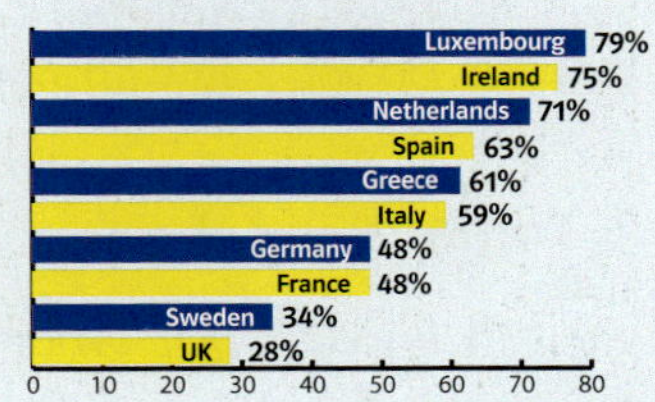

Do you agree with these statements about the EU?	Agree strongly	Agree a little	Disagree a little	Disagree strongly	Don't know
1. It is good for British jobs and trade[7].	24 %	35 %	11 %	10 %	19 %
2. Britain's national identity is being lost.	34 %	24 %	19 %	11 %	12 %
3. The EU makes decisions in an undemocratic way.	21 %	23 %	15 %	10 %	31 %
4. It helps to keep peace in Europe.	26 %	34 %	10 %	12 %	18 %
5. Britain is losing the right to make its own decisions.	34 %	27 %	15 %	11 %	14 %
6. Britain should stay in the EU.	35 %	33 %	6 %	13 %	13 %

c) *What reasons could there be for British people not having a very positive attitude to the EU?*

STEP 4: Do a political survey at your school

a) *Think of* ***one*** *question you want to ask other pupils (e.g. Are you interested in politics? Do you think Europe should become one huge country? Which country has the better system of voting: the UK or Germany? …?). Write the question down and prepare a grid in which you can collect the answers.*

b) *Do your survey. Ask as many pupils as possible so that the statistics will be reliable. Then turn the information you collect into a bar graph or pie chart.*

c) *Make a class display[8] of your diagrams. Comment on the survey results.*

[6] **majority** [məˈdʒɒrɪti] = most people • [7] **trade** [treɪd] = business (between different companies and countries) • [8] **display** [dɪˈspleɪ] = sth to show

Unit 3 Media-mad

First choose with your teacher which of these two texts you want to read:

Text A tells you how to use modern media to become a DIY (Do-It-Yourself) musician.

Text B is from the script of a movie about the power of the media over people's lives.

1 Before you read

1. *What kind of music do you like? Why?*
2. *Do you know anyone who makes music?*

2 Read the text

a) *Read for gist: What are the main points in the text?*

b) *Find headings for the parts of the text.*

c) *Make a flow chart showing what to do to get your music onto the Internet.*

d) *Discuss whether you think the ideas in the text are realistic or not.* WB p. 33/1; 2; 3

3 ⟨Think how to be creative⟩

What other ways can you be creative on the Internet? Collect ideas.

4 Listening: Charlie's video blog

a) *What do you find out about Charlie and his video blog?*

b) *What can be a problem when you put something on the web?*

5 Your turn: Your own blog

With a partner, create a funny conversation (about 50 words) for a video blog. Act or film your dialogue for your classmates. WB p. 33/4

DIY music *(Choice A)*

Go on, admit it – you dream of being a rock or pop star! But sitting in the bath singing to the radio, or applying to be on a reality TV show is not the best way to get people to listen to your music.

Don't give up the dream! Lots of bands now promote and sell their own music. Technology has taken DIY to a whole new level, allowing you to present your songs directly to the people who want to listen to and hopefully buy them.

So let's assume you have a home computer and somewhere in your head you have a melody or lyrics waiting to be heard. Read below to find out how to make a studio in your bedroom/shed/garage and what equipment you need to organise. Then you'll be ready to become a real musician!

First, what about your studio room? You need a relatively empty and extremely quiet space to create a clean recording. So get rid of as much furniture as possible and if there is traffic noise, try to keep it out.

You don't want to spend time editing out sounds you didn't know you had recorded – a washing machine in the distance, or the television or someone's phone. Also, if sounds are being thrown back by furniture and windows, these are likely to be picked up by your recording equipment.

A room with carpet is the best, with curtains or blankets on the windows and walls. Or maybe you ought to start eating lots of eggs. Seriously! Covering the walls with empty egg boxes is another way to stop noise from the outside world coming in.

As lots of DJs, musicians and bands have proved, it is now possible to use a home computer to make a recording of good enough quality. All it takes is your own cool and creative ideas and an Internet connection.

OK, so you might need a little money, too. But not a lot. Number one on your shopping list should be a good microphone. Without one you can't record anything – instruments or vocals – clearly. But there are lots of cheap mikes out there that are good enough.

Then you have to turn your computer into a digital audio workstation. What's that? Well, you want to be able to record, edit and save your music, right? So you need a multi-track audio recorder with audio editing software.

Maybe you're new to this game and all that sounds a bit technical. No problem! There are thousands of tutorials on the web which will teach you how to work with the equipment. You'll soon feel comfortable using it.

Of course before you can make a DIY recording you need a good idea for a song. But what can you do with that idea?

Recording some basic audio and vocal tracks is only the beginning. After you've done that it's time to turn your raw file into killer music that people – yes, your future fans! – will want to buy and download or listen to on the radio.

Almost every song that has ever been released in the history of music has been mixed and mastered. But it's not all hard work. You can have a lot of fun, too. For example, you can use the web to download different sound effects. Or you can create your own sound effects to add to your music. You must have heard songs with noises like an engine roaring or a little kid crying. Well, those effects are all created by building samples into the finished recording.

Be adventurous. You have a raw music file. With that, you can play around as much as you like. Just be careful not to ruin it with something you might not like!

Arctic Monkeys, Lily Allen and almost every musician who has ever heard of MySpace are now using the web to get their music out there. With social networking sites, YouTube and other sites like iTunes and Napster, musicians can offer their own music (whether for money or not) to anyone and everyone who might want to hear it, without the help of a big record label.

These are amazing times. You can easily record a track, even make a video, write your own biography and organise photos, and put all that information on the web. There are lots of online services which will help you do exactly that.

One of the best ways to get tips about how to promote your music online is to look at how successful bands that you like have promoted themselves using the web. The main thing is to be creative and to use the technology that is now available to help you. Sure, there are lots of other people hoping to start a great music career, too. But someone always gets lucky. So go ahead, and who knows? The next one to MAKE IT REALLY BIG could be YOU!

(adapted from: *How to make music in your bedroom* by Nicola Slade)

The Truman Show *(Choice B)*

1 Before you read

Talk about what kind of films you enjoy. Explain why you enjoy watching them.

The movie 'The Truman Show' is about a character called Truman Burbank who has lived his whole life in Seahaven, a fake island town where the other people are all actors. He alone has no idea that his world is a giant studio, where everything is a high-tech illusion controlled by the director Christof. Truman has no idea that he is filmed day and night and is the star of a television reality show. He thinks he is happy but cannot forget a girl called Sylvia who disappeared from his life when he was seventeen. The following extract from the script is a flashback.

FLUSHING MEADOW PARK. EVENING.

Truman and Sylvia sit next to the fountain. They kiss. Truman starts to say something, but she covers his lips with her finger.

Sylvia: In a minute someone's going to come and stop me talking to you.

Truman: *(looking around the empty park)* Who? There's no one here.

Sylvia: *(looking over her shoulder nervously)* There isn't much time. Just listen. Everybody's pretending. Everybody but you. *(pointing to the buildings on the horizon)* Look. You think anybody lives there? It's all for you, Truman. A show. The eyes are everywhere.

Truman: *(protesting)* Eyes? Where?

Sylvia: Everywhere, disguised … Truman, they're going to fill your head with lies. You've got to make yourself deaf.

Suddenly a car roars towards the fountain.

Sylvia: *(scared)* I told you, Truman!

The car stops and a man jumps out. He pulls the frightened Sylvia to her feet.

Truman: *(shocked)* Hey!

Man: *(to Sylvia)* Get in the car!

Truman: *(to the man)* Who are *you*?!

Man: I'm her father!

Sylvia: No he's not! He's just saying that!

The man throws Sylvia into his car. Truman tries to fight the man.

Truman: Leave her alone!

The man pushes Truman away and Truman falls to the ground. The man slams shut the passenger door of the car.

Man: *(to Sylvia)* I told you not to come here anymore!

Sylvia: *(calling out from the car)* Don't listen, Truman. Make yourself deaf. Come find me.

Man: *(to Truman, getting into the car)* Don't bother! We're moving to Australia.

The car roars away. Truman stares after it.

2 Stop and think

a) *What are Truman's feelings during the scene? What words or actions show these feelings? Why do you think he feels like this?*

b) *Why does Sylvia want to warn Truman? Guess: What happens to her?*

This second extract comes later in the movie. The adult Truman now knows his world is fake, but he does not know why. He has just tried to escape from Seahaven, but has been stopped.

A LIVING ROOM SOMEWHERE. NIGHT.

Two old women sit on their sofa. On the television in front of them, a live picture of Truman drinking a cup of coffee at his kitchen table. A message appears on screen: 'FOLGERS Coffee – Good To The Last Drop.' Then a title, "Truman – Total Record Of A Human Life" appears. This is replaced by an interviewer sitting opposite Christof.

STUDIO. NIGHT.

Interviewer: *(to camera)* Welcome to week seventeen hundred and sixty-eight of "Truman". This is "Tru Talk", the forum where we discuss events with the show's award-winning director, Christof. *(to Christof)* Before we start taking calls, what keeps us watching one man twenty-four hours a day?

Christof: The reality. We've become frustrated watching actors give us false emotions. While the world he lives in is fake, there's nothing fake about Truman himself. No scripts. No cue cards. He tells us about *ourselves*. – How about some viewers' calls now?

The Interviewer presses a button on his desk.

Interviewer: Charlotte, North Carolina, for Christof. You're on, caller. Go ahead.

Male Caller: Truman has never been closer. The way he looked directly at us, spoke to us for the first time. Do you think he'll ever work it out?

Christof: Not now. He tested his world, as we all do at times, and it passed the test.

Interviewer: *(pressing another button)* Long Island, you're on "Tru Talk".

Female Caller: How can you say Truman lives a life like any other?

Christof: The only difference between Truman's life and our own is that his is recorded. We all play our roles …

Female Caller: He's not a performer. He's a prisoner.

Christof: He can leave at any time. If he wanted to discover the truth, there's no way we could stop him. I think he feels comfortable in his "cell" …

Female Caller: No, you're wrong! He'll prove you wrong! He can still do it!

Christof: *(directly to camera)* Do I know you, caller? You sound familiar.

3 Talk about the two extracts

a) *Explain the contrast in the way we see Truman in the two extracts.*

b) *How is Truman's life like our own? What is the movie's message about the media?*

c) *Comment on why Christof looks into the camera (line 92). Who might the female caller be and why is her role important?*

WB p. 34/1; 2; 3

4 ⟨Find out the whole plot⟩

Watch a DVD of 'The Truman Show' or research the plot on the Internet. Tell the story in your own words.

5 Listening: Reality shows

a) *Pre-listening: What reality shows do you know?*

b) *Listen to the opinions about reality shows. Write down the positive and negative points.*

c) *Explain why you would or would not take part in a reality show yourself.*

6 Your turn: A magazine page

Create a teen magazine page about a reality show. Write about the show and present opinions for and against it.

WB p. 34/4

READING SKILLS

Reading for research

When you are doing research, especially on the Internet, different reading skills can help you to choose the right texts and then to get the information you need from them.

1 Skim to get the gist

First use the title of this text to guess the topic. Then skim the text to see if you are right.

The MySpace Age
by Jonathan Duffy, BBC News Magazine

In only a couple of years MySpace went from zero to being a top five website which no self-respecting US teenager can ignore. And the same thing has happened in Britain. MySpace is what is known as a social networking site. It's by far the biggest, with over 100 million users around the world. Others include Facebook, Bebo, Friendster and Yahoo 360, all offering users a host of functions – blogging, forums, instant messaging, personal profiles, photo albums. Want to see someone who's into the same music or films as you, or someone you just fancy? Send a message, and if they're interested, hey, you've made a friend. Social networking sites make money out of advertising, and the success of MySpace is being used by companies to target potential customers. For example, anyone who mentions an interest in kite-surfing can expect a mass of e-mails trying to sell them the latest equipment. The easy development of relationships online is also changing the nature of friendship. Briana Dougherty, 25, has 224 "friends" on MySpace, although some are not individuals but bands she likes. Stella Sims, 26, sees a competitive streak among users. "It's a statement of how popular you are," says Stella. Not everyone may understand the idea of setting out one's personal life to an audience of millions. MySpace users, however, show little sign of finding it a problem to deal with their extensive friendship networks.

"Andi"
Girl
17 years old
Birmingham, UK

Andi's quick info:
Hi, my name is Andi and I'm 17 years old. I'm here to find new friends. How about sending me an e-mail?

Andi's friends:
Shirin Lisa Tess [more]

Andi's interests:
Pop music, love stories, movies, my friends [more]

2 Scan to get the facts you want

You are researching the pros and cons for people using social networking sites. Look for what the text above says about this. (Only look up important new words.)

3 Check the source

WB p. 35/5; 6

a) *Why is it important to check the source of information you find on the Internet?*

b) *Look more closely at the text above. Try to answer the questions in the check-list on this page. (It may not always be possible to answer every question, but this list can help you to decide if a text is reliable or not.)*

4 ⟨Use more than one source⟩

Look for more Internet texts about social networking sites. Organise the information you find (facts, pros and cons etc.) and present your results in class.

Check-list for Internet texts
- Which website is the text on?
- What do you know about that website?
- What information is given about the author?
- When was the text written?
- Who is the text written for?
- Does the author give facts or opinions?
- Is the text trying to sell something?

Sorry, you're wrong!

Media and young brains ■ I have no wish to criticize young people themselves. It is not they who have created today's world. However, I do worry about the effect on them of the modern media. Teenagers these days are addicted to technology that feeds them non-stop with messages and pieces of information of no importance at all. Although they may not realize it, this does have a negative effect on their brain power. Not only are they unable to concentrate for more than a minute, but their heads are full of silly gossip. Hardly any young people seem to be interested in thinking critically about serious issues.

Alan Brown, Tunbridge Wells

NEW BRAIN POWER: I am writing in reply to Alan Brown's letter. Sorry, but I think he is wrong. Although, as a typical teenager, I like new technology and use it all the time, this does not mean I cannot concentrate or am only interested in gossip. Scientists are doing new research showing how the younger generation is developing a different kind of brain power. People develop new skills for new situations, and in today's world skills like multi-tasking and filtering information are very important. We teenagers are not using our brains less, just differently.

Laura Bennett (16), by e-mail

1 Think and talk about the letters

a) *How do you think Alan Brown might react to Laura's letter? Explain your answer.*

b) *Summarize Laura's reply. Say why you agree or don't agree with her.*

2 Dynamic and stative verbs

a) *Find the verbs in Laura's letter. Put them in a grid showing whether they are used in the simple form, the progressive form, or both forms.*

Verb	Simple	Progressive
write		X
think	X	
be		

GRAMMAR

- 'Dynamic' verbs express actions. They can be used in the simple or progressive form.
- 'Stative verbs' express a state or quality. They are usually used in the simple form.

b) *Read the Grammar box. Are the verbs in your grid dynamic or stative?*

c) *Try to think of more **stative** verbs.*

(→ G 6) WB p. 36/7

3 Complete the dialogue with the correct forms of the present tense

Dad: Jay, I 1 (need) your help in the garage this morning. Jay! I 2 (talk) to you!

Son: Sorry, it 3 (be) a bit difficult to answer at the moment – I 4 (play) computer tennis.

Dad: You 5 (spend) hours every day on those games. You 6 (become) addicted! I 7 (wish) you would stop. Everybody 8 (know) it 9 (have) a bad effect on young people.

Son: Not true! Scientists 10 (do) research now that proves games like this 11 (train) people to react quickly. Please, Dad. I 12 (try) to win here and you 13 (distract) me. Oh, now my ball 14 (go) into the crowd! It always 15 (happen) when someone 16 (interrupt)!

WB p. 36/8

4 Look at stative verbs in the progressive form

This teletext information uses stative verbs in the progressive form with a dynamic meaning. Explain the meaning with other verbs.

plan · go out with · talk about · enjoy · spend · behave like

Your favourite soap so far: Mike and Ann were **thinking** about getting married, but now she's **seeing** another guy. Kim thinks Ann **is being** an idiot, but Kim has her own problems. She's been **meaning to** put back the money she stole, and now it's too late. Young Sam **is having** a weekend alone at home. He and his friends **are loving** it. But they get a shock …

WB p. 36/9

5 Using unusual word order to give stress

a) *Look at the word order in this sentence. What is unusual? Which phrase is given extra stress by the word order?*

Not for one moment can I imagine life without a mobile phone.

TIP
Inversion is used after adverbials with a "negative" meaning. It is usually only used in written English.

b) *Choose suitable adverbials to complete this written comment.*

1 should using mobile phones be allowed in public places. 2 do they make a noise, but they force others to listen to private conversations. Yesterday a girl on my train talked non-stop. 3 had she finished one call when she started again. 4 have I heard so much silly gossip! I was glad when she got off the train. 5 could I read my book in peace.

Never · No way · Only then · Hardly · Not only

⟨c)⟩ *Turn the text in b) into spoken English. Make the style more casual.*

WB p. 37/10

6 Talk about more ways to add stress

Which of these ad texts has the stronger effect? Which words and phrases add stress?

A You want to look good, right? But you know your hair is letting you down. You need SHINE shampoo! Yes, you've been waiting for SHINE. It really makes your hair shine. The name says it all. SHINE!

WB p. 37/11

B You do want to look good, right? But you know yourself your hair is letting you down. What you need is SHINE shampoo! Yes, it's SHINE that you've been waiting for. It really does make your hair shine. The name itself says it all. SHINE!

7 How to: Argue politely

Act dialogues. One of you starts with one of the statements below, and the other argues against it. Express yourself politely.

- "Most TV is rubbish."
- "The friends you make on social networking sites aren't real friends."
- "Live concerts aren't worth the money."
- "The greatest film of all time is …"
- "…"

WB p. 37/12

USEFUL PHRASES
Disagreeing politely:
Sorry, but I don't agree. • I'm afraid I see it differently. • I have to disagree.
Expressing an argument:
I think/believe … • In my opinion … • The way I see it, …

8 Your turn: Your own opinion

Write a letter expressing your own reaction to Alan Brown's views on teenagers (p. 55 top).

REVISION

⟨Present and past forms⟩

GRAMMAR

- Use **present** forms to talk about regular events or the situation at the moment.
- Use **present perfect** forms for actions in the past that are linked to the present.
- Use **past** forms when actions are completely in the past.
- Use **past perfect** forms to express actions that happened before other actions in the past.
- All tenses can be used in the **simple form** or the **progressive form.**

For more details see → G 8.

1 Simple and progressive forms

Read the dialogue. Find examples of the four tenses above, in the simple form and the progressive form. Explain why these forms are used. What signal words are typical of the tense or the form?

WB p. 38/13

"Hi! I've been trying to call you all morning. I bought this mobile yesterday. I'd been thinking about it for ages. And while I was walking past the shop, I noticed they'd reduced the price. Lucky, eh? So now I'm talking to you on the latest E-phone!"

The latest? Are you sure? They usually reduce the price when they've just developed a new model!

2 Complete the dialogue with the correct past forms or present perfect forms

Mum: Are you still in front of that computer? You've … (sit there all morning).
Kid: Well, I … (do research on new TVs).
Mum: We don't need a new TV! I … (tell you that the other day).
Kid: Oh, Mum! We … (have ours for ages).
Mum: I only … (buy it four years ago).
Kid: Technology … (improve since then). Ed … (get a new TV recently). When I went over, he … (watch it). The picture quality is amazing!
Mum: It's *programme* quality that we need. The level … (go down for years). And a new TV won't help with that!

WB p. 38/14

3 Complete what people say with the past perfect progressive + since/for

1. Movie director: Everyone was glad to go home. We …
2. Author: I finally finished my new book last month. I …
3. TV journalist: Everything in our report was true. We …
4. Singer: I completed my latest album a few days ago. I …
5. Photographer: I took the photo outside the nightclub. I …

wait there • hours
write it • two years
film non-stop • July
research the facts • months
record it • Christmas

WB p. 38/15

4 Tell the story of the taxi driver and the judges

Use past and past perfect forms. Think of a good ending for the story.

WRITING TEXTS

Writing a film script

1 Before you start

What elements do you find in a film script?

2 Read the script on the right

a) *What kind of film is the script for? What elements make this clear?*

b) 1. *Why are some parts of the script in normal type and other parts in italics?*
2. *What tense is used for the directions?*
3. *What information is given in brackets?*
4. *What do you notice about the form of the verbs in the brackets?*

c) *Make a list of the phrases about camera work. Explain the effect of these shots.*

3 Plan and write your own script

a) *Choose **one** product. Think of a good name for it. Then collect ideas for a scene for a commercial. Think of a funny or unusual situation people will remember.*

TIP

Commercials often end with a "catch phrase". Writing this first can help to give you ideas.

b) *Now write your script. Keep the scene short, but give clear directions for the atmosphere and action. Don't forget to mention important camera shots, too.*

4 ⟨Turn your scripts into films⟩

Film your scripts and show them in class. Maybe your drama teacher can help.

***SCENE:** A living room with soft lighting and romantic background music. A wide shot shows a **GIRL** and **BOY** sitting on a sofa. On a table in front of the **BOY** is an open bag of **MELTERS** sweets. The camera zooms in for a close-up of the bag. We see the **BOY** take out two sweets and put one in his own mouth and the other in the **GIRL**'s. They speak while sucking their sweets.*

Girl: I'm mad about you.
Boy: Mm. And I'm mad about you, too.
Girl: Do you really love me?
Boy: *(finishing his sweet)* Of course I do.

He puts two more sweets in their mouths.

Girl: What would you do to prove it?
Boy: I'd do anything at all.

*The **BOY** feels in the bag a third time, but only pulls out one sweet. The music stops.*

Boy: *(shocked)* It's my last Melter!

*A medium shot shows the **GIRL** nervously watching the **BOY**. After a short pause he turns away from her and quickly puts the sweet in his own mouth. She jumps up.*

Girl: *(running out of the room)* I hate you!
Boy: *(shrugging, looking into the camera)* Now she's mad *with* me instead of *about* me. But well, sometimes you have to make a choice. *(sucking his sweet)* Mm …

*A close-up shows a new bag of **MELTERS**. The romantic music starts again.*

Voice-over: Would *you* give anyone *your* last Melter? Mm. Simply mad about Melters.

WB p. 39/16; 17

1 Collect personal media vocabulary

Choose two forms of media that you personally use a lot. Make a word web for each of them.

Internet? magazines? TV? radio? ...?

2 Express cause and effect

Check how the words and phrases in yellow link ideas. Do they express cause or effect?

1. Susie often busks because she enjoys singing to an audience. 2. As she is a big fan of Lily Allen, she always sings Lily's songs. 3. She has a good voice and therefore lots of people usually stop to listen. 4. Last Saturday Susie suddenly noticed Lily Allen at the back of the crowd, with the result that she stopped singing. 5. Because of the shock she forgot the words of the song. 6. Lily Allen had been enjoying Susie's singing, so she came to the front and sang with her. 7. Since Lily was so sweet and friendly, Susie is now an even bigger fan of hers.

WB p. 40/18

3 Watch out for 'false friends'

a) *Make a grid showing the real meanings of the pairs of 'false friends' below. Use a dictionary to find any new words you need.*

German	English	German	English
Kunst	art	Art	kind
...	to become	bekommen	...

art – *Art* • to become – *bekommen* • meaning – *Meinung* • rock – *Rock* • note – *Note* • floor – *Flur* • brave – *brav* • to spend – *spenden* • gift – *Gift* • actually – *aktuell*

⟨b)⟩ *Choose six pairs from a) and write sentences showing the English words in context.*

WB p. 40/19

4 Make adjectives with past participles

Complete this local radio news.

steal close want break improve expect shock fight

1. Police are looking for a gang who tied up the 1 owner of a shop in North Street and grabbed jewellery. They warn that the 2 men, who are driving a 3 car, are dangerous.
2. Work has started behind the 4 doors of the main library. The 5 date for reopening is March, when the library will be able to offer 6 services for all age groups.
3. It was bad luck for United today. Although they won a hard-7 match against City, their star player had to be carried off the field with a 8 leg.

WB p. 40/20

5 ⟨Real English⟩

Find examples of words made shorter in casual speech.

I'd love to be a celeb! • What's on telly? • I found the info on the web. • This sofa is really comfy. • The silly ref's lost his whistle! • This paper is just gossip.

6 ⟨Book corner⟩

Newsflash! by Nicola Brown

This is the story of Sarah's work experience placement at a newspaper in the UK. It is full of excitement – and tragedies.

NOW YOU CAN

- ✔ Talk about different media.
- ✔ Use reading skills to research information.
- ✔ Use dynamic/stative verbs.
- ✔ Add stress, using inversion and other constructions.
- ✔ Argue politely.
- ✔ Write a film script for a commercial.

1 Your turn: Media in your life

Describe how you use different media during a typical day in your life. Write 6–8 sentences, using your word webs from exercise 1 on page 59 to help you.

2 Complete this interview with the correct forms of the present tense (→ G 6)

Interviewer: We 1 (be) in the television centre, just outside Studio B. Right now I 2 (talk) to fourteen-year-old Lucy Freeman, and if she 3 (seem) a little nervous, well, she 4 (have) a good reason. Right, Lucy?

Lucy: Yes, I 5 (wait) to take part in Junior Mastermind. I 6 (think) I'm crazy!

Interviewer: You 7 (see), viewers, Studio B 8 (be) where every week four young people 9 (get) the chance to appear in the famous quiz. We 10 (film) this interview just before the show 11 (start). So tell us what 12 (go) through your head now.

Lucy: Well, I 13 (try) to think how to control my hands because they 14 (shake) so much. I just 15 (hope) I can control my voice, too. I 16 (get) very nervous now, and when that 17 (happen), my voice always 18 (disappear)!

Interviewer: Don't worry. You 19 (speak) just fine. Your voice 20 (sound) quite normal. What about your parents? I 21 (expect) they 22 (look) forward to seeing you in the quiz.

Lucy: Yes, they 23 (sit) in the studio audience already. – Oh, someone 24 (call) me now!

WB p. 41/22

3 Find the right order to complete the sentences with added stress (→ G 7)

1. "YouTube is OK, but it's ..." (I use • Facebook • the most • that)
2. "Wow, look at your shelves! You ..." (an amazing number • do • of DVDs • have)
3. "Look at the price! No way ..." (for a mobile • I pay • that much • would)
4. "It's a fantastic book. I'd love ..." (to write stories • myself • like that • to be able)
5. "Well, he isn't good-looking, but he ..." (know • sing and dance • does • how to)

WB p. 41/23

4 Rewrite this Internet argument to make it more polite

Dave: I predict that twenty years from now there won't be any books.
Penny: Rubbish! People are never going to stop reading.
Dave: Who said anything about not reading? But all words will be on screen, not paper.
Penny: That's a silly prediction. For many people there'll still be a place for books.
Dave: You're so wrong! The only place for books will be in museums.
Penny: You can't be serious! What about reading in bed? You can't use a computer for that.

WB p. 41/24

⟨Uglies⟩

The novel "Uglies" takes place three hundred years in the future. Tally Youngblood is about to turn 16, and she can hardly wait for her birthday. All teenagers get operated on when they turn 16: They are turned from an Ugly – a normal person – into a Pretty with a perfect face and body. All they do after their operation is have fun. But then Tally meets Shay, and Shay doesn't want to be operated on. She disappears to the Smoke where unoperated people live, out in the wild and far away from New Pretty Town. Tally is forced to find Shay for Dr. Cable of Special Circumstances[1] (the secret police) – or she won't get her own operation. So Tally goes on a long journey to the Smoke and finally finds her friend Shay.

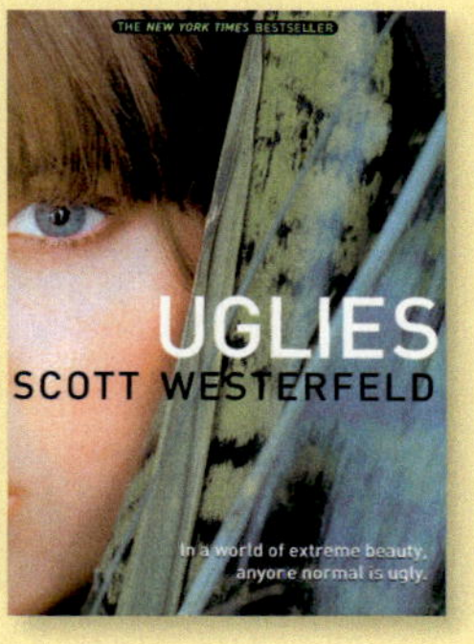

"Come on, I'll take you down to the library. You've got to meet the Boss," Shay said.

The Boss wasn't really in charge[2] here, Shay explained. He just acted like it, especially to newbies. But he was in command of the library, the largest of the buildings in the settlement's central square.

The familiar smell of dusty books overwhelmed[3] Tally at the library door, and as she looked around, she realized that books were pretty much all the library had. No big airscreen, not even private workscreens. Just mismatched desks and chairs and rows and rows of bookshelves.

Shay led her to the center of it all, where a round kiosk was inhabited by a small figure talking on an old-fashioned handphone. As they drew closer, Tally felt her heart starting to pound. She'd been dreading[4] what she was about to see.

The Boss was an *old* ugly. Tally had spotted a few from a distance on the way in, but had managed to turn her eyes away. But here was the wrinkled[5], veined[6], discolored, shuffling, horrific truth, right before her eyes. His milky eyes glared at them as he berated[7] whoever was on the phone, in a rattling voice, and waved one claw[8] at them to go away.

Shay giggled[9] and pulled her toward the shelves. "He'll get to us eventually. There's something I want to show you first."

"That poor man …"

"The Boss? Pretty wild, huh? He's, like, *forty*! Wait until you talk to him."

Tally swallowed, trying to erase the image of his sagging[10] features[11] from her mind. These people were insane to tolerate that, to *want* it. "But his face …," Tally said.

"That's nothing. Check these out." Shay sat her down at a table, turned to a shelf, and pulled out a handful of volumes in protective covers. She plonked them in front of Tally.

"Books on paper? What about them?"

"Not books. They're called 'magazines'," Shay said. She opened one and pointed. Its strangely glossy pages were covered with pictures. Of people.

Uglies.

Tally's eyes widened as Shay turned the pages, pointing and giggling. She'd never seen so many wildly different faces before. Mouths and eyes and noses of every imaginable shape, all combined insanely on people of every age. And the *bodies*. Some were grotesquely fat, or weirdly overmuscled, or uncomfortably thin,

[1] **circumstance** ['sɜːkəmstæns] = I usually don't do this but there are special *circumstances.* = I usually don't do this, but it's a special situation. • [2] **to be in charge** [ˌbi‿ɪn 'tʃɑːdʒ] = to be the boss • [3] **to overwhelm** [ˌəʊvə'welm] = The perfume *overwhelmed* me. = I found the perfume extremely strong. • [4] **to dread** [dred] = to not look forward to at all • [5] **wrinkled** ['riːŋkld] = full of wrinkles *(Falten)* • [6] **veined** [veɪnd] = full of veins *(Venen)* • [7] **to berate sb** [bɪ'reɪt] = to tell sb (loudly) that they did sth wrong • [8] **claw** [klɔː] = People have hands; many animals (e.g. cats) have *claws.* • [9] **to giggle** ['gɪgl] = to laugh quietly • [10] **to sag** [sæg] = to hang (too) low • [11] **features** ['fiːtʃəz] = the parts of a face

and almost all of them had wrong, ugly proportions. But instead of being ashamed of their deformities, the people were laughing and kissing and posing, as if all the pictures had been taken at some huge party.

"Who are these freaks?"

"They aren't freaks," Shay said. "The weird thing is, these are famous people."

"Famous for what? Being hideous[12]?"

"No. They're sports stars, actors, artists. The men with stringy hair are musicians, I think. The really ugly ones are politicians, and someone told me the fatties are mostly comedians."

"That's funny, as in strange," Tally said. "So this is what people looked like before the first pretty? How could anyone stand to open their eyes?"

"Yeah. It's scary at first. But the weird thing is, if you keep looking at them, you kind of get used to it."

Shay turned to a full-page picture of a woman wearing only some kind of formfitting underwear, like a lacy swimsuit.

"What the …," Tally said.

"Yeah."

The woman looked like she was starving[13], her ribs thrusting out from her sides, her legs so thin that Tally wondered how they didn't snap[14] under her weight. Her elbows and pelvic bones looked sharp as needles. But there she was, smiling and proudly baring her body, as if she'd just had the operation and didn't realize they'd sucked out way too much fat. The funny things was, her face was closer to being pretty than any of the rest. She had the big eyes, smooth skin, and small nose, but her cheekbones were too tight, the skull practically visible beneath her flesh. "What on earth is she?"

"A model."

"Which is what?"

"Kind of like a professional pretty. I guess when everyone else is ugly, being pretty is sort of, like, your job."

"And she's in her underwear because …?" Tally began, and then a memory flashed into her mind. "She's got that disease! The one the teachers always told us about."

"Probably. I always thought they made that up to scare us."

Back in the days before the operation, Tally remembered, a lot of people, especially young girls, became so ashamed at being fat that they stopped eating. They'd lose weight too quickly, and some would get stuck and would keep losing weight until they wound up like this "model". Some even died, they said at school. That was one of the reasons they'd come up with the operation. No one got the disease anymore, since everyone knew at sixteen they'd turn beautiful. In fact, most people pigged out just before they turned, knowing it would all be sucked away.

Tally stared at the picture and shivered. Why go back to *this*?

"Spooky, huh?" Shay turned away. "I'll see if the Boss is ready yet."

Before she disappeared around a corner, Tally noticed how skinny[15] Shay was. Not diseased skinny, just ugly skinny – she'd never eaten much. Tally wondered if, here in the Smoke, Shay's undereating would get worse and worse, until she wound up starving herself.

Tally fingered the pendant[16]. This was her chance. Might as well[17] get it over with[18] now.

These people had forgotten what the old world was really like. Sure, they were having a great time camping out and playing hide-and-seek, and living out here was a great trick on the cities. This starving almost-pretty was only one of them. Why go back to that?

[12] **hideous** ['hɪdɪəs] = terribly ugly • [13] **to starve** [stɑːv] = to die from not eating • [14] **to snap** [snæp] = to break • [15] **skinny** ['skɪni] = very thin • [16] **pendant** ['pendənt] = sth that hangs from a piece of jewellery around your neck • [17] **Might as well …** [ˌmaɪt‿əz 'wel] = Why not … • [18] **to get sth over with** [ˌget‿'əʊvə] = to do sth unenjoyable now so that you don't have to worry about it later

Tally popped open the heart pendant, looking down into the little glowing aperture[19] where the laser waited to read her eye-print. She brought it closer, her hand shaking. It was foolish to wait. This would only get harder.

And what choice did she have?

"Tally? He's almost –"

Tally snapped closed the pendant and shoved it into her shirt.

Shay smiled slyly[20]. "I noticed that before. What gives?"

"What do you mean?"

"Oh, come on. You never wore anything like that before. I leave you alone for two weeks and you get all romantic?"

Tally swallowed, looking down at the silver heart.

"I mean, it's a really nice necklace. Beautiful. But who gave it to you, Tally?"

Tally found she couldn't bring herself[21] to lie. "Someone. Just someone."

Shay rolled her eyes. "Last-minute fling[22], huh? I always thought you were saving yourself for Peris."

"It's not like that. It's …"

Why not tell her? Tally asked herself. She'd figure it out when the Specials came roaring in, anyway. If she knew, Shay could at least prepare herself before this fantasy world came tumbling down. "I have to tell you something."

"Sure."

"My coming here is kind of … the thing is, when I went to get my –"

"What are you *doing*?"

Tally jumped at the craggy voice. It was like an old, broken version of Dr. Cable's, a rusty razor blade[23] drawn across her nerves.

"Those magazines are over three centuries old, and you're not wearing gloves!" The Boss shuffled over to where Tally was sitting, producing white cotton gloves and pulling them on. He reached around her to close the one she was reading.

"Your fingers are covered with very nasty acids, young lady. You'll rot away these magazines if you're not careful. Before you go nosing around[24] in the collection, you come to me!"

"Sorry, Boss," Shay said. "My fault."

"I don't doubt it," he snapped, reshelving the magazines with elegant, careful movements at odds with his harsh words. "Now, young lady, I suppose you're here for a work assignment."

"Work?" Tally said.

They both looked down at her puzzled expression, and Shay burst into laughter.

The heart pendant that Tally has around her neck is a "finder". Dr. Cable of Special Circumstances gave it to her so she and Shay could be located in the Smoke. Will Tally betray[25] her friend or not? Her decision changes her life forever …

adapted from: *Uglies* by Scott Westerfeld

[19] **aperture** ['æpətʃə] = opening (e.g. in a camera lens) • [20] **slyly** ['slaɪli] = in a way that shows you know there's a secret • [21] **to bring oneself to do sth** [brɪŋ] = to force oneself to do sth • [22] **fling** [flɪŋ] = short love affair • [23] **razor blade** ['reɪzə ˌbleɪd] = *Razor blades* are used to get rid of body hair (e.g. on legs, on one's face). • [24] **to nose around** [ˌnəʊz‿ə'raʊnd] = to try to find out more about sth that is none of your business • [25] **to betray** [bɪ'treɪ] = to go against a deal/plan you had with a friend

⟨Revision for tests⟩ Unit 3

That's stealing, too

Read this article from the BBC news website.

Virtual thief caught

In the Netherlands a teenager has been arrested for stealing virtual furniture from "rooms" in Habbo Hotel, a 3D website.

The 17-year-old is suspected of stealing 4,000 euros (£2,840) worth of virtual furniture, bought with real money. Five 15-year-olds have also been questioned by the police who were contacted by the website's owners. The six teenagers are suspected of moving the stolen furniture into their own Habbo rooms.

A spokesman for Sulake, the Habbo Hotel company, said: "The accused found out members' Habbo passwords by creating fake Habbo websites. In Habbo, as in many other virtual worlds, stealing people's user names and other personal information has been happening for some time now. We've had much of this stealing going on in many countries, but this is the first time that the police have taken legal action."

Habbo users can create their own characters, buy their own furniture, play a number of games and talk to other users in chatrooms. The virtual furniture (known as "furni" by the website's members) is bought with Habbo Credits, which have to be paid for with real money. And as in real life, the coolest things are often the most expensive.

"What is happening here is not just part of a PC game. It's serious stealing because the furniture is paid for with real money," the company spokesman said. "The thief must have invented a fake Habbo website on the Internet – and Habbo users thought it was real and visited it. This criminal was then able to get these people's user names, log into the real Habbo Hotel and steal their furniture!"

This is becoming a serious problem for the company because more and more people log into fake Habbo Hotel websites and get their personal information stolen.

Six million people in more than 30 countries play Habbo Hotel. So there is a lot of virtual furniture which could be stolen if Habbo members aren't more careful.

1 Understanding the text: Internet thieves

a) *Finish the sentences.*

1. The police found out about the thieves when … 2. The missing furniture is now probably … 3. The police have never … before. 4. Habbo Hotel members use Habbo Credits to … 5. They need real money … 6. The people at Sulake are worried about …

b) *Make a list in note form of what the 17-year-old did, finishing with what the police did.*

Start like this: • became Habbo Hotel user • …

2 Listening: Two interviews in the street

Sally, a radio reporter, is recording interviews with teenagers in Brighton.

a) *Listen to the two interviews. Is this right, wrong or not in the text?*

1. The boy uses his phone for texting more than for talking. 2. He often sends music to his friends. 3. Sally tells him that he has more numbers in his phone than the average teenager. 4. The girl uses her mobile when she wants to talk to her friends. 5. The results of the survey last year show that she spends less time online than the average teenager. 6. She often visits a sports chatroom.

b) *Correct the sentences that are wrong.*

c) *Listen to the interviews again. Write Sally's notes for her report. You could organise her notes in a grid.*

3 Speaking: A new cell phone

With a partner, act the role of Ryan, a US teenager, and one of his parents. Ryan wants his parents to buy him a new cell phone, but they are against it:
Think of the advantages a new cell phone might have, e.g. you can do more things with it, it looks better than the old one, … and the disadvantages, e.g. the price, you spend even more time phoning and texting, …

4 Mediation: Tracking

Your brother has heard of "Handy-Ortung", or "Tracking", and he would like to know more. Read this text and tell him in German how it works and how you can keep your privacy.

New technology known as mobile tracking allows worried parents to track your mobile phone, locating your position at any time of the day. Not so good for teenagers who prefer to keep their leisure activities private. How does it work? Mobile phone tracking is set up using the SIM card. When a tracker (e.g. a parent) has registered as a user, he or she can make searches online from a computer or a mobile. How do you avoid being tracked? Tracking companies are legally obliged to ask permission from the tracked person, and then to offer alternatives. For instance, a tracked teenager can stop the tracking company operating at weekends. If you suspect you're being tracked, look out for suspicious text messages, and keep your mobile switched off when you don't need to receive any calls.

5 Writing: Using the Internet

Judy helps to organise her school's Computer Club. Everybody wants younger students to use the Internet the right way, so Judy has started to prepare a list of "Dos and don'ts for the Internet". Finish her list, then write her article for the club website. Write about 100 words.

Dos …	Don'ts …
• surf for info	• use real name
• watch for viruses	• steal
• …	• …

The redwar saga by Justin B. Leroy

Read this book review written by journalist Jeff Pinto.

The redwar saga is the latest book by the Canadian writer Justin B. Leroy. Like his earlier science-fiction novels, it takes us into an unknown world where human beings must fight alien enemies to survive. The environment can be friendly or dangerous – something our heroes must find out and use to their advantage before they can hope to win. I don't want to give you too many details here, and nobody will expect me to tell you what the ending is. That's a secret! Readers hoping for a surprise to finish with will not be disappointed – but getting to the end is not always easy.

Many of Leroy's fans think *The redwar saga* is his best book so far. I can't say I share this opinion. I loved his *Off to the future*, published two years ago. Not only was it action-packed, but it was a great story, too. It was simply one of the most exciting science-fiction novels I have ever read. But in my opinion Leroy's *Redwar saga* is nowhere near as good. It has quite a good storyline as far as the main plot is concerned. But less than halfway through the novel Leroy introduces a few sub-plots which do not connect well and are in fact very boring. (I found myself wondering whether Alec's search for blue sand was important or exciting for me. It wasn't!) But the main idea, fighting the aliens, is taken up again towards the end, and I was interested enough to make it to the last page.

The book is not all disappointing. One thing Leroy does very well is describe the landscape and surroundings. You can really smell the smoke in the cold air and hear the sound of heavy boots on the dry sand. Great stuff! Then there are the parts which are seen through the eyes of young Pip. The language very cleverly fits the boy's character, and we can feel both his fear and his growing anger. But unfortunately most of the other characters do not develop with their experiences. They're just stereotypes. In a good novel the author should let the reader get to know the main characters and form a picture of them. Sadly, Leroy just doesn't do that for me here. I'm looking forward to his next book and hoping that it will be as good as *Off to the future*.

1 Understanding the text: Summary

Complete this book review summary on Jeff's homepage.

Justin B. Leroy is a writer of [1], whose latest [2] is *The redwar saga*. In the main [3] the heroes must fight aliens to [4]. Unfortunately there are a few sub-plots which are very [5]. Most of the characters are uninteresting, too, because they're just [6]. On the positive side, the writer creates one good [7], and Leroy does [8] the landscape well. The ending? That's a [9]!

2 Speaking: Talking about a book

Tell a group of American students about a book (English or German) which made an impression on you. Make notes on its good points and then on its bad points. Think of plot development, characterization, setting, perspective, foreshadowing, turning point and climax.

3 Listening: The future of print media

a) *Listen to Jane Morgan's talk and find the right answers.*

1. Jane Morgan
   a) writes books. b) works for a radio station. c) works for a newspaper.
2. Surveys show that young people
   a) used to read more books. b) don't read anything.
   c) now read more books than last year.
3. With digital media readers can
   a) read more quickly. b) store a lot of information. c) buy cheap laptops.
4. Jane says modern media are
   a) getting less expensive. b) no longer anything special.
   c) becoming old-fashioned.
5. She thinks that maybe print media will
   a) become fashionable. b) not survive. c) be used more for advertising.

b) *Listen again. What is said about 1. print media and 2. modern digital media? Make two lists. You will need your notes for exercise 4.*

4 Writing: A letter to a newspaper

You have just listened to Jane Morgan's talk about the future of print media. Write a letter to the "The Daily World" and say why you agree or disagree with her, and mention your own use of the media. Use your notes from exercise 3b). Write about 100 words.

5 Mediation: A very popular writer

Carl from America is visiting you and sees this article in one of your magazines. He is interested because he read "Inkworld" and "Inkheart" when he was younger. Read the article, then answer his questions in English.

1. So she's German! Where does she live now?
2. Did she become a writer as soon as she left school?
3. How does she create the great atmosphere in her books?
4. Does the article say what she's doing right now?

Für Cornelia Funke ist das Erzählen immer wichtig gewesen. Sie hat es früher genossen, wenn ihre Großeltern oder ihre Eltern ihr vorlasen, und schon als Kind hat sie selber gerne Geschichten erzählt. Nach der Schulzeit wurde sie aber trotzdem nicht gleich Schriftstellerin. Zuerst studierte sie Pädagogik und arbeitete mit Jugendlichen. Den Weg zu eigenen Büchern fand Cornelia Funke durch Bilder. Sie studierte an einer Kunsthochschule und arbeitete anschließend einige Zeit als Buchillustratorin. Erst mit 35 fing sie an, eigene Bücher zu schreiben. Ihr Erfolg als Autorin kommt zum Teil sicherlich daher, dass sie es so gut versteht, die Bilder in ihrem Kopf in Wörter umzusetzen und die Welt durch andere Augen zu sehen. Vor einigen Jahren ist sie nach Los Angeles gezogen, wo manche ihrer Bücher verfilmt wurden.

6 Speaking: The book first, or the DVD?

Kelly has just bought the DVD of "Dracula", and she wants to watch it with Dean now. But he is reading the novel and thinks the movie would ruin it for him. Kelly disagrees. You and your partner make notes with Kelly's/Dean's arguments. Then act the dialogue.

Unit 4 Human rights

Are there enough women in positions of power?

White males still dominate business in North America and Europe. For how much longer?

Child labour: a continuing problem especially in the developing world

1 The different faces of human rights

Look at the images on these pages. Which ideas do they represent? (There can be more than one answer.) Explain.

- equal opportunity
- freedom of speech/religion
- the right to an education
- tolerance
- racial equality
- the right to protest
- equality of the sexes
- protection of children

WB p. 47/1

2 Values as the basis of human rights

The United Nations Universal Declaration of Human Rights states the following:

'All human beings are born free and equal in dignity and rights.
They [...] should act towards one another in a spirit of brotherhood.'

Say whether these values are important to you and why:

freedom | equality | spirit of brotherhood

Should living and expressing a different lifestyle be a basic right?

It isn't possible to be so open about same-sex relationships in every country. In some places just being gay or lesbian is illegal.

DID YOU KNOW?

- In 1997, the proportion of women in national parliaments around the world was 11.2%. Ten years later it had risen to only 17.2%.
- In the US, there are equal opportunity laws that make it illegal for an employer to ask a job applicant to send a photo with his/her CV.
- In a recent 'Democracy Index', only 16% of the world's countries qualified as full democracies, while 32% were considered to be authoritarian regimes. First place went to Sweden, as the most democratic country, while last place went to North Korea as the world's least democratic society.

Authoritarian regimes think little of human rights and do not tolerate protest, as can be seen in the way China treats Tibet.

3 Listening: In the news

a) *Listen to a news story and say what the subject is. What human rights are being talked about?*

b) *What do you know about the situation in Tibet at the moment?* WB p. 47/2

4 Your turn: Your rights, your values

a) *For your English folder, make a list with the ideas from exercise 1. Organize them in two categories: 'Mostly satisfactory' (when you feel enough is being done around the world), and 'Still much to be done' (for the opposite).*

b) *Which rights and values important to you and your lifestyle are not mentioned here? Discuss: Is enough being done about those rights in your country? Add them to your list.*

Dignity for all?

1 Ask a group of children what they feel like doing at the weekend, and "going to the cinema" or "going to the shops" would be typical replies. But "working as a slave"? In 2007, British police freed a group of Romanian children who had been smuggled into the country as slaves. Some of them were as young as four and had been recruited for pick-pocketing in London. It may be difficult for many people in the UK or the US to imagine slavery in their own countries – to most this is a problem found only in Africa or Asia – but it is still a reality. The Romanian children are just one example of modern slavery in the western world, a problem many are happy to ignore.

2 Slavery goes against human dignity. But dignity for all – as the basis for the right to freedom – is a relatively new concept. In ancient Egypt or Rome and during the Middle Ages, people were used to seeing slavery. Then, in 18th century Europe and America, the ideas of dignity and democracy started to spread. Even then, however, only white male landowners enjoyed rights like voting or receiving an education.

3 In authoritarian societies, the individual and human dignity have little meaning. Basic rights like free speech or the freedom to protest do not exist. There is no need for the dictator to tolerate more than one opinion because there *is* only one opinion: the dictator's. He and his secret police know how to make their system work – if necessary by force.

4 Many people cannot imagine losing rights which have already been won. Perhaps they should be more interested in keeping them. After terrorists attacked the US on 11 September 2001, the US Congress passed President Bush's Patriot Act. The act cut deeply into privacy rights and gave the police, FBI and CIA easier access to personal information. Human rights activists were the first to protest the loss of privacy, one of the most basic aspects of personal dignity. Instead of protesting, however, most Americans decided to accept the Patriot Act: they were more afraid of terror attacks than losing their rights.

1 The concept of dignity

a) *Identify the rights mentioned in each text.*

b) *Text 4 is about losing rights. Which rights would **you** miss most if the state/your parents/ your school suddenly decided that you could no longer have them?*

Example: "I wouldn't want to lose the right to a free school education."

c) *With a partner, write a definition for 'dignity'. Compare your definitions.*

2 Revision: Gerunds

see | grow up | own | be | change | ask | make | think

Complete the sentences below. Use the verbs on the right.

Mike: I can't imagine [1] a slave-owner. I mean, who could ever think of [2] another person?
Zoe: Well, back in ancient Egypt human life didn't mean much. [3] slaves build new pyramids or whatever was normal. Everyone just accepted it. That was life back then.
Mike: Not even the normal people seemed to be interested in [4] things.
Zoe: Right, and when you've stopped [5] yourself how people in the past could possibly have been slave-owners, you can start [6] about the child slaves in Asia or Africa today, now.
Mike: [7] as a child slave must be terrible. What do their parents think?
Zoe: Well they were slaves, too; they're used to [8] it. They don't know it any other way.

WB p. 48/3

3 A new gerund construction

a) *Look at the new construction on line 45/46 on page 70 and the phrases in the Grammar box. Then match up the sentences below.*

GRAMMAR

Gerunds after prepositions

instead of	protesting …
without	thinking …
by	helping others …

(→ G 10)

1. People in democratic countries often enjoy their rights **without**
2. Many think they will always have their rights, **in spite of**
3. But **apart from**
4. That changes when people really want to change something *themselves* **instead of**
5. People will learn about human rights and democracy most directly **by**

a) seeing people on TV who have to fight for their rights in authoritarian states.
b) just watching other people protest.
c) realizing there is a cause worth fighting for and then trying to make changes themselves.
d) thinking of where those rights came from.
e) spending a few minutes watching the news on TV every day, few people think about the danger of losing their own rights.

b) *Translate the sentences into German to show you understand the new construction.* WB p. 48/4

4 Revision: Infinitives with *to*

go out | stay out | do | help | be | get | marry | be | give | get

a) *Read what a London girl says about teenage rights. Finish her sentences with the verbs on the right.*

"My parents know how [1] very strict. They expect me [2] good marks and start [3] angry when I'm in front of the TV and not at my desk doing English or Maths. I'm only allowed [4] with friends one weekend per month. And when I go out, I always need [5] home by 11.30 pm. When I'm 16, I'll be able [6] later, they say. My parents are happy [7] me pocket money, but it's never much. But when they want me [8] them with something, they ask in a nice voice. I know that other kids have more freedom [9] what they want, but still, I really can't complain. Especially when I think of poor girls in other countries whose parents force them [10] men they don't even know or like!"

⟨b)⟩ *Discuss: How strict should parents be? How much freedom do teenagers need?* WB p. 48/5

5 New infinitive form with *to*: infinitives after *for* + noun

a) *Make sentences with the new infinitive construction. Start with these ideas.*

Example: There is a **need for governments to create** more democracy.

There is There are It is	+ a need reasons important not easy hard dangerous wrong …	+ for +	teenagers schools governments the media everyone parents …	+ to give teens enough freedom. to report human rights problems. to have an open mind. to take away rights. to listen to others' point of view. to accept different lifestyles. to make the world a better place. to create more democracy. to fight for rights. …

b) *With a partner, think of five things you could do in the area of human rights.*

Start like this: "It's important/wrong/… for teenagers to …"

WB p. 49/6

6 Gerund or infinitive?

a) *Complete this statement made by an American girl in a discussion.*

TIP
Remember:
to stop doing sth ≠ to stop to do sth

"My parents had some friends over for dinner. Two of them kept on (say), 'Oh, all those *poor* people in Africa. I just can't *stand* (hear) about all their problems! It makes me so sad when I think about it all.' Now, I'm not very good at (keep) my mouth shut, so I told them: 'The best thing for people like you (do) would be to look in the mirror. Instead of (worry) about Africa all the time, start (think) about all the problems here in *America*.' My mom wanted me (shut up), of course. And I really meant (stop) it, but I just couldn't. 'When are we going to stop (look) at the problems everywhere but here? But that's impossible for people like you (do). It would mean (admit) that America isn't perfect! Instead of (think) about the poor children in Africa, think of how (make) a university education affordable for Americans who aren't rich. Or do you *really* think every US family is able (pay) $20,000 or more a year for university?!'"

b) *Do you agree with the girl?*

c) *Listen to the rest of what the girl says about the dinner with her parents' friends.*

1. Which topics does she mention? Pages 68–69 can give you some ideas.
2. Can you imagine having this conversation at a dinner with your family and their guests? Why/why not?

WB p. 49/7

7 Your turn: Your views and where they came from

*How did you get **your** views about human rights? What influences have there been?*

TALKWISE

Tolerance and respect

Tolerance of and respect for others, even in simple everyday situations, are main ingredients in a society which takes human dignity seriously. So it is important to be able to express tolerance and respect in words, too.

1 Who should respect whom?

a) *Listen to a scene in a Los Angeles café. What is going wrong in your opinion? Who should be more tolerant, who should be more respectful?*

b) *Now listen to a different version of the same scene. Which phrases are more appropriate?*

c) *Listen to the third version. Which phrases are more appropriate? Make a list.*

2 Think before you talk

Listen to the beginning of another conversation. With a partner, rewrite the situation so that the people show more tolerance and respect. The Useful phrases can help you.

USEFUL PHRASES

- I really don't think it's fair …
- I'm terribly sorry, but …
- Do you really think it's appropriate to … ?
- Would you mind … ?
- Could you show a little more respect for … ?
- I'd really appreciate it if you could …

WB p. 50/9

3 Role play: Show tolerance and respect

With a partner, choose one of the situations on this page (or a different one). Use the Useful phrases in a role play. Then act it out for the rest of the class. After that the class gives each pair points (1 to 10) for their acting and for how much tolerance and respect is shown. Make sure that ***you*** *show tolerance and respect when you criticize the other pairs!* WB p. 50/10

4 Survey: Different people, different tolerance levels

Read both opinions on tolerance levels below. Everyone gives them each a rating:
Agree strongly, Agree, No opinion, Disagree *or* ***Disagree strongly.***
Collect the results for the whole class in a grid. Then discuss the results.

- "Some people are too sensitive. Somehow their feelings *always* get hurt, even when you think you've said something nice to them. They should work on getting a thicker skin."
- "I don't know why some people show others so little respect in what they say and do. It can really hurt. Why not just be as nice as possible to each other?"

WB p. 50/11

Heroes

1 The power of pictures

a) *Before you read the text, look at the photo. It has become a symbol of the American civil rights movement. Why do you think that is?*

b) *What emotions can you see on the faces in the photo? What do you think could have caused them?*

Elizabeth Eckford was 15 when this photo was taken of her trying to get into Little Rock's Central High School in September 1957. She and eight other black students that year were the first to integrate an all-white school in Arkansas after the US Supreme Court had decided in 1954 that racial segregation was illegal. On the day of her famous walk to school, Elizabeth, like the other eight black students who wanted the chance to attend their city's best high school, showed great courage. Anyone who saw the black students start their famous walk towards the angry mob would have smelled trouble.

"For a moment all I could hear was the shuffling of their feet," Elizabeth remembers. "Then someone shouted, 'Here she comes, get ready!'. The mob came closer and began to follow me, calling me names. I still wasn't afraid. Just a little bit nervous. Then suddenly my knees started to shake and I wondered whether I could make it to the center entrance a block away." She tried different entrances, but nobody let her pass. Elizabeth didn't know where to go. She finally found a bench at a bus stop and sat there in shock. Weeks later, the US government – with the help of the army – finally made Central High accept integration. The 'Little Rock Nine' could now attend school. But it was not easy to get through each day that first year. Josh McHughes, a white student at Central, remembers how Elizabeth's "terrified look never went away, from the first day to the last day of that year. She would have no reason to remember me. I was just another white face. She just wanted to get down the hall and get *away* from me."

Now, it is easier for Elizabeth to talk to students about her experiences. Those talks have made her stronger, she says. She advises students to get the best education they can and not to be silent observers of any kind of racism and bullying.

(by Elizabeth Kelleher, from *america.gov*, Sept. 2007; adapted)

2 Heroes

The concept of the 'hero' is a very positive one in the English-speaking world. Heroes, whether famous people or 'just' ordinary people, are admired as role models. What makes Elizabeth Eckford a hero? Work in groups and discuss what the qualities or actions of a hero are, and think of other people who could be called heroes.

3 ⟨Internet project: 'The mean girl'⟩

Find out about 'the mean girl' (as she has been called) with the dark hair in the photo, screaming at Elizabeth. How did the famous photo change her life? Write a short report.

4 Revision: Infinitives with and without *to*

a) *There are many different infinitive constructions in the text on page 74. Find the different constructions and organize them in two lists: with* **to** *and without* **to**.

b) *For each example, add the translation of the examples in German to your lists.*

GRAMMAR

Infinitive with 'to'	Infinitive without 'to'
after question words: → *Elizabeth didn't know* ***where to go.***	**after modals:** → *The Little Rock Nine* ***could attend school.***

(→ G 11, 14)

5 Craig Kielburger: The children's hero

a) *Read about the Canadian human rights hero Craig Kielburger. Decide whether you need* **to** *or not.*

When he was still in school in 1995, Craig Kielburger read about a 12-year-old boy in Pakistan, Iqbal Masih, who had been murdered. Iqbal had been trying [1] bring the world's attention to the awful child-labour system in Pakistan's carpet industry. Craig saw Iqbal as a hero for speaking out about child labour. He understood that a young person can [2] make a difference.

Craig was eager [3] learn all about human rights. And he was sure he knew how [4] do it properly: He wanted the chance [5] see the problem of child labour for himself in Asia. His parents weren't happy about his plans. They didn't want [6] see him [7] go, but finally they let him [8] join Canadian human rights workers on a trip through Asia.

When Craig arrived and started [9] talk to child workers in the Asian sweatshops, it was easy for him [10] see why Iqbal Masih had been protesting: The sweatshops were like scenes out of hell. They made Craig [11] want [12] change the world more than ever. WB p. 51/12; 13

b) *Who is the bigger hero to you: Craig or Iqbal?*

6 ⟨Book corner: Free the children⟩

Read about Craig's experiences as a very young person in Asia, fighting for the rights of other young people.

7 How to: Show everyday courage and support

a) *What could you say in the following situations? Look at the phrases on the right for ideas.*

1. At a party: All the guests are white. Someone tells a racist joke. You don't think it's funny.
2. In an expensive shop: You have just been treated very well by a shop assistant. She then turns to a poor-looking girl your age and tells her that maybe she should try one of the cheaper shops down the street. You think this is awful.

⟨b)⟩ *Think of how these situations could continue and then act them out.* WB p. 51/14

USEFUL PHRASES

- Do you think that's appropriate?
- It's not right to judge people by their looks/skin colour.
- Don't you think that's a bit unfair/racist/nasty?

REVISION

⟨Equal opportunity⟩

1 Modals and their substitutes

a) *Leo wants an after-school job at the new London Abercrombie & Fitch shop. Complete the dialogue with the correct past or future substitute forms.*

GRAMMAR

Remember: Modal verbs like *must, can, needn't* have no past tense or future forms. Use their substitute forms like *to have to, to be able to, to be allowed to.*

For more details see → G15.

Dad: I'm afraid you (**must**) look for another after-school job. I'd already told you 'no' – so why were you back at A&F yesterday?

Leo: I was back in the shop because they said they simply (**must**) talk to me again: I'd be *perfect* as a store model. They hope I (**can**) start soon.

Dad: Leo, when I was your age, shops (**needn't**) worry about 'store models'. They only (**must**) have shop assistants. And when I was 16, teens (**can't**) just walk into a shop and talk about working there. They (**must**) talk to their parents *first*. I'm sure you (**can**) find a company that isn't known for employing good-looking white people.

Leo: But that was *years* ago. Now, it's all good-looking whites, blacks *and* Asians. It's real equal opportunity!

⟨b)⟩ *In his last two sentences, what point is Leo missing about equal opportunity?* WB p. 52/15

GRAMMAR

- Remember: When you report something in **indirect speech** and you start with a verb in the past, you need a **tense shift** for the rest of the sentence.
- If there is no question word in a direct **question**, you need 'if' or 'whether' to report it.
- You use 'to' or 'not to' in **indirect commands**. You introduce these with *ask, tell* or *warn*.

For more details see → G16.

2 Indirect speech

Read the rest of Leo's conversation with his dad. Later Leo writes an e-mail to his friend Tariq and reports the conversation. Use statements, questions and commands.

Example: "You're missing the point." → **My dad said (that) I was missing the point.**

Dad: Real equal opportunity'? Leo, you're missing the point. I mean, it's great if people of all races work at A&F as 'store models'. But employing only good-looking people, whether black or Asian, is still discrimination. It's not a healthy environment. And remember, I've heard bad stories about A&F. They had real problems in America.

Leo: But Dad, give the place a second chance. And what's 'good-looking' anyway? Everybody has a different opinion. And don't most shops want good-looking shop assistants? What shop employs the winner of the Mr Ugly Competition?! Abercrombie & Fitch is just a cool place to be. And they asked Tariq to work there, too. Oh come on, Dad, it'd be so much fun there with my best friend. And don't forget that I can buy everything there for 30 % off!

Dad: Hm, I hadn't thought about the discount. But why do you need to work in such a cool place? Stop trying to be *so* cool all the time, Leo. WB p. 52/16

WRITING TEXTS

Short biographies

On page 40 you practised biographical writing. Here you will take this a step further, learning to focus more on a person's character. Being able to write a short biography (or 'bio') is a useful skill, e. g. for your school newspaper, a company's website, *your* website, etc.

1 Gandhi: A human rights hero

Read about the Indian human rights leader Mohandas Gandhi, later called 'Mahatma' ('Great Soul'). These ideas are useful if you want to write a bio.

Gandhi as a young man

Gandhi in later life

Mohandas Gandhi, loved and respected by people around the world as one of the great human rights activists, did not really match the hero cliché. He was thin and poor-looking in his simple white robes. But Gandhi proved that fine clothing and status symbols were not necessary to achieve one's goals. Fighting for the rights and dignity of the poor, the uneducated and the homeless of India would not be easy. To some people, moving mountains might have seemed simpler. But where other people think about having more material things in their lives, Gandhi did not need any of that. His mind was free to concentrate on what his heart told him to do. And his heart told him to make the world a fairer and more peaceful place. Nobody is one-dimensional, though: There was a big difference, like night and day, between Gandhi's public image as the symbol of peaceful protest and the private man who could be a tyrant to family members.

Participles can create a more adult tone and flowing style.

References to **appearance** help to paint a clearer picture.

Adjectives as nouns keep your text short and make it flow better.

Sometimes **symbols** are colourful and can help to make your language stronger.

Mentioning **a person's mind, heart, body, etc.** helps you to understand the person's feelings, thoughts and actions better.

Everyone's character features **contradictions**. Bringing this out makes your writing better.

2 Collect ideas

With a partner, make a short list of interesting people you could imagine writing a bio about, e. g. heroes of yours. Your bios should have at least two of the following elements:

- high / low points
- contradictions in character
- an interesting appearance

3 Write a short bio

a) *Now write your own short bio about one of the people you thought of in exercise 2. Look at the person's character and not just the historical facts. Use the ideas from exercise 1.*

⟨b)⟩ *Exchange texts with a partner. How well has he/she developed his/her bio? Be critical (but respectful!).* WB p. 53/17; 18

Protest songs

1 Before you listen: The sound of protest

a) *Which words on the right do you think describe typical characteristics of protest songs? Give reasons.*

b) *What protest songs do you already know? Which of the adjectives here best describe them?*

emotional, fun, poetic, loud, gentle, harmonious, aggressive, idealistic, dissonant, obnoxious

Bob Dylan: *Blowin' in the wind* (1963)

How many roads must a man walk down
Before you call him a man?
How many seas must a white dove sail
Before she sleeps in the sand?
Yes, how many times must the cannon balls fly
Before they're forever banned?
The answer my friend is blowin' in the wind
The answer is blowin' in the wind.

Yes, how many years can a mountain exist
Before it's washed to the sea?
Yes, how many years can some people exist
Before they're allowed to be free?
Yes, how many times can a man turn his head
Pretending he just doesn't see?
The answer my friend is blowin' in the wind
The answer is blowin' in the wind.

Yes, how many times must a man look up
Before he can see the sky?
Yes, how many ears must one man have
Before he can hear people cry?
Yes, how many deaths will it take till he knows
That too many people have died?
The answer my friend is blowin' in the wind
The answer is blowin' in the wind.

Christina Aguilera: *Can't hold us down* (2003)

So what am I not supposed to have an opinion
Should I be quiet just because I'm a woman
Call me a bitch cos I speak what's on my mind
Guess it's easier for you to swallow if I sat and smiled

When a female fires back
Suddenly the target don't know how to act
So he does what any little boy will do
Making up a few false rumors or two

That for sure is not a man to me
Slanderin' names for popularity
It's sad you only get your fame through controversy
But now it's time for me to come and give you more to say

Chorus:
This is for my girls all around the world
Who've come across a man who don't respect your worth
Thinking all women should be seen, not heard
So what do we do girls?
Shout louder!
Letting them know we're gonna stand our ground
Lift your hands high and wave them proud
Take a deep breath and say it loud
Never can, never will, can't hold us down

Nobody can hold us down
Nobody can hold us down
Nobody can hold us down
Never can, never will

So what am I not supposed to say what I'm saying
Are you offended by the message I'm bringing
Call me whatever cos your words don't mean a thing
Guess you ain't even a man enough to handle what I sing

If you look back in history
It's a common double standard of society
The guy gets all the glory the more he can score
While the girl can do the same and yet you call her a whore

I don't understand why it's okay
The guy can get away with it and the girl gets named
All my ladies come together and make a change
Start a new beginning for us everybody sing

2 First reactions

a) *Which song did you like better, and why?*

b) *Look back at exercise 1. Which adjectives there best describe 'Blowin' in the wind' and 'Can't hold us down'? What other adjectives can you think of to describe the two songs?*

3 The message

a) *Say what the basic message in each song is and which words/lines tell you this.*

b) *Think about the role of human dignity and human rights in these songs. Which song is more specific about some rights, and which is more general? Which phrases tell you this?*

c) *Can you relate to the songs' messages? Why or why not?*

d) *Discuss whether songs should offer solutions to problems or if 'just' protesting is enough.*

WB p. 54/19; 20

4 The lyrics

a) *Describe the style of the lyrics in each song. Example:* poetic – realistic.

b) *Identify the refrain in each song. Explain why this part of the song is important.*

5 The music

Do you feel that the music in each song helps to present the message? Imagine 'Blowin' in the wind' with louder, faster and more aggressive music, and 'Can't hold us down' as a slow, gentle song. Would the messages stay the same? Why or why not?

6 Protest songs: Timeless or dated?

In which ways are the songs' messages timeless, in which ways are they dated? Then talk about what makes a song timeless or not.

7 ⟨Internet project: Protest songs⟩

These artists have all had big hits with protest songs. Find out more about the artists, which protest songs they sang, and what the songs' messages were.

Aretha Franklin

John Lennon

Pink

8 Your turn: Write your own protest song

What problems do you feel like bringing to people's attention? Try writing a protest song.

1 The message behind the photo

Look at the picture "Mimic" (1982) by the Canadian photographer Jeff Wall.

1. *Describe the scene: what are the people doing?*
2. *What could they be thinking?*
3. *Why do you think Wall wanted to create this scene?*
4. *How well does this photograph express Wall's message?*

2 Word building

Build your 'human rights' vocabulary by learning more forms of the words you see below (verbs, adjectives, opposites). Start with the dictionary in your book and then use an English dictionary for more words.

Example: 1. **tolerance** → tolerant, to tolerate (*found in* Green Line); • intolerance (*found in an English dictionary)*

2. race 3. equality 4. democracy 5. protest 6. slavery 7. integration WB p. 55/23

3 Adjectives as nouns

You know that some adjectives can be used as nouns to describe groups of people. Use the following adjectives to complete these comments from a TV guide about TV shows:

sick brave young intolerant homeless famous sensitive

1. 'On the street': discussion about the problems of the ___ in New York City.
2. 'Heroes': a close look at the ___ of this world.
3. 'Health hour': How can the ___ in poor countries survive with so few hospitals?
4. 'Teen talk': afternoon discussion for the ___
5. 'Just give me a chance': Where do the ___ get their narrow views of people and society?
6. 'Starwatch': A look at how the ___ use their fame to fight for children's rights.
7. 'I've got feelings, too!': The ___ and their easily hurt feelings.

4 ⟨Real English⟩

Can you say what these two American girls mean with their slang expressions?

Stacy: Oh no. The look on your face tells me somebody's just been workin' your nerves again big-time. – Amanda and her 'Free the children' project again?

Tanya: God, she sure knows how to push *all* my buttons! I'm so tired of her shit. I mean, she's always in my face about all these things she wants done and goes *completely* ballistic when I don't do them in two seconds!

Stacy: Oh, come on, don't be hatin' on her just because she wants the project to be a success. She wants to lend a hand to the kids in those Indian sweatshops just as much as you do.

NOW YOU CAN

- ✔ Talk about human rights issues.
- ✔ Judge when to use gerunds and infinitive forms.
- ✔ Discuss tolerance/respect.
- ✔ Write short biographies.
- ✔ Understand the art of the protest song.

1 Gerund or infinitive? (→ G13)

"It's not always easy for people 1 (agree on) what human rights are exactly. Should 2 (wear) extreme outfits and make-up be a right, even if by 3 (do) this you might offend others? Some people would be quick 4 (say) that the freedom to express oneself is part of one's dignity. Others wouldn't dream of 5 (consider) wild make-up a form of freedom: To them dignity means 6 (look) like a 'normal' person. And what about freedom of speech? Wouldn't most people in a democratic society expect everyone 7 (be able) to say what they want? Yes and no: 8 (express) an opinion would be considered by many 9 (be) a basic right. But how appropriate is it 10 (shout) dirty words in public? *Leo, 17, London*"

WB p. 56/25

2 More practice with gerunds and infinitives (→ G13)

1. Craig Kielburger wanted (make) life better for children in Asia.
2. He couldn't stand (hear) about the awful sweatshops in the developing world.
3. The children were the reason for him (do) something about their problems.
4. So he decided (become) active himself.
5. He didn't stop (think) that he might be too young himself to help anyone.
6. His parents finally stopped (tell) him not to go.
7. They allowed him (travel) to Asia with a group of Canadian human rights activists.
8. Craig didn't mind (be) the world's youngest human rights activist.
9. Actually, people were interested in (find) out about him because he was so young.

3 Different ages, different rights (→ G11, 14)

*Decide which verbs are missing, and also whether the verbs need **to** or not.*

work | drink | understand | attend | do | take | quit | show | vote | be

1. What things do teenagers in western nations have the right ___ while they're still under 18?
2. In most countries they can't ___ in elections until they're 18.
3. But they are allowed ___ part-time at 16.
4. In the US, most states let teenagers ___ their drivers' tests at the age of 16.
5. Teens older than 16 in most western countries needn't ___ school anymore.
6. But any personal adviser would advise them not ___ school too soon.
7. It isn't easy for many European teens ___ America's laws about alcohol.
8. If you want ___ alcohol in the US, you must be 21.
9. If you look young, bars will make you ___ that you are over 18.
10. But most teens are just happy ___ 18: Then they can do what they want (but not drink) without asking their parents.

WB p. 57/27

4 Tolerance levels

a) *Look at the three situations. What is happening? You are sitting at the next table. When would you say something to make the people stop? When wouldn't you? Talk about it with a partner.*

⟨b)⟩ *Now act the situations. Make sure you both have at least one chance to be the person who is reacting to one of the situations.* WB p. 57/29

5 ⟨Your turn: Your taste in music⟩

a) *Everyone likes music. But have you ever stopped to think why? Think about your favourite music artists (groups, singers, DJs, …) and make a grid. Give the artists ratings in different categories (1 =* ***not at all****, 10 =* ***very much****).*

	I like the lyrics.	I like the music.	I like the image/looks.	I like the videos.
Artist 1	4	8	10	10
Artist 2	10	8	4	*This artist has no videos.*

b) *Has anyone else in your class named the same artists? Compare your results.*

6 ⟨Team activity: Your end-of-book quiz⟩

- *Make five groups. Two people aren't in groups; they are the referees.*
- *Each group chooses a unit in this book (including 'Zoom-in') and writes seven quiz questions about it. Each question must be about a* ***fact*** *and have one clear answer. First, every person writes three questions. Then the group must agree on the seven best questions.*

  Example from Unit 1: → What are witchetty grubs?

- *The referees check to make sure each question is a fact and that the same question isn't asked twice.*
- *After all the questions are answered, each group looks at the questions of the other groups.*
- *Now you can see which group studied best during the school year!*

⟨Project⟩ English and Politics: the US

This project deals with the second oldest modern democracy after England. It can help you to think about the ways in which politicians communicate their ideas to people. At the end you get the chance to communicate your own ideas about issues that are important to YOU.

STEP 1: Learn how American democracy began

a) *Before you listen: Talk about why governments make people pay taxes[1].*

b) *Check that you know where Boston is. Then listen to a talk by a tourist guide. Take notes.*

c) *Explain why the British colonies in America decided to fight for their independence.*

d) *Look at the back of your book to find out the system of government Americans created for their new country.*

STEP 2: Listen to a famous speech

Although after 1865 there was no more slavery in the United States, the law did not stop racial segregation until 1964. One of the people who helped to change the law was the civil rights leader Martin Luther King Jr. In 1963 he gave a famous speech in Washington.

> I have a dream that one day this nation will rise up and live out the true meaning of its creed[2]: "We hold these truths to be self-evident[3]: that all men are created equal."
> I have a dream that one day on the red hills of Georgia the sons of former[4] slaves and the sons of former slave owners will be able to sit down together at the table of brotherhood.

a) *Before you listen: Read the words from the speech above. Explain what the 'dream' is.*

b) *Now listen to part of the speech. What do you think makes the speech so inspiring[5]?*

c) *Think of other famous or important political speeches (in your own country, too). Who gave the speech? When? What was it about?*

LISTENING SKILLS

When you listen to a talk or a speech with a political theme, it is important to think carefully about who and what you hear.

1. Who is speaking? What do you know about his/her background?
2. Is the speaker trying to inform/inspire/persuade[6] you?
3. What kind of language does the speaker use: factual[7] or emotional?

[1] **tax** [tæks] = money the government collects from the people • [2] **creed** [kri:d] = all the main things one believes in (values, etc.) • [3] **self-evident** [self‿'evɪdnt] = obvious • [4] **former** ['fɔ:mə] = used to be • [5] **to inspire** [ɪn'spaɪə] = to give sb positive ideas about sth • [6] **to persuade** [pə'sweɪd] = to convince • [7] **factual** ['fæktʃʊəl] = having to do with facts

STEP 3: Talk about how politicians communicate

a) *Make a list of different methods of communication used by politicians to express their views and persuade people to vote for them. The photos below will help you to start.*

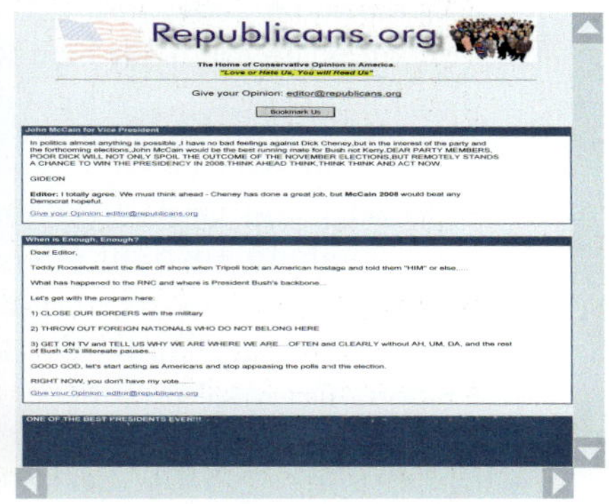

b) *Look again at the methods of communication shown in the photos. Say which you think are most effective and least effective. Explain your opinion.*

c) *Talk about changes through the ages in the way in which politicians communicate with people. How do you think political communication will develop in the future?*

STEP 4: Do a project: Communicate your views on a political issue

a) *First choose an issue that is relevant or important to you, e.g. homeless people in your town • drugs • an environmental problem • …*

b) *Discuss what you want to say about the issue. Make a big word web with phrases you can use to express the problem and your ideas about how to solve it. Think of a good slogan that sums up[8] your message.*

TIP
Use the different strengths[9] of different members of your group. Think who is good at writing/drawing/speaking/…

c) *Now plan how you can communicate your views and ideas to other people. Choose at least three different methods: poster, leaflet, speech etc. Decide who is going to do what.*

d) *Put your plan into action!*

[8] **to sum up** [sʌm‿ˈʌp] = to summarize • [9] **strength** [streŋθ] = sth one is good at (or: sth one is strong at)

Mediation

UNIT 1 Misunderstandings

After school you see Drew, the Australian foreign exchange student living with you, and Hannes, a younger boy from 8th grade, talking excitedly. You go to find out what's up.

Translate back and forth between Drew and Hannes.

MEDIATION SKILLS

Especially when cultural differences play a role, it's important to think of people's feelings. So be polite. Should you really translate everything that someone says, or are some things best left out or changed a bit? Being polite can really help to solve problems.

Drew: Thank God you're here. Hannes doesn't seem to know anything about Australia or else he's just having trouble understanding.

Hannes: Ich verstehe ganz gut, danke. Er ist es, der nichts versteht und kein Deutsch kann. Ich hab' ja nur ein paar harmlose Fragen gestellt.

You: Drew, he says ...

Drew: Innocent questions? It started with "G'day mate". He thinks that's all that Australians say to each other. And that all we do is fight crocodiles and have barbies all the time. He's just full of preconceptions.

You: Hannes, hast du ...

Hannes: Ja, OK, aber ...

Drew: And he thinks that if we're not at the beach then all Australians are running around in the outback, talking to kangaroos.

Hannes: Es gibt doch nichts anderes in Australien.

Drew: What did he say?

You: ...

Drew: Tell him he's wrong. Ask him if he's ever been to Australia or talked to an Aboriginal – now that would be really interesting!

You: ...

Hannes: Natürlich nicht, aber man weiß doch wie die Eroberer die Einheimischen behandelt haben. Frag ihn doch wie es den Aborigines geht. Ich möchte zu gern hören, was er dazu sagt.

You: ...

Drew: It's true that they used to be treated very badly and that there are still a lot of problems, but things are changing. For example, where I come from, Cairns, the Aboriginals help with the protection of the Great Barrier Reef. We know that for thousands of years they lived with the reef, respected it and took good care of it. In fact, they still use the reef for their traditions.

You: …
Hannes: Das wusste ich nicht. Ist ja interessant.
Drew: What?
You: …
Drew: I'm glad he's interested in Australia, but next time he should be a bit more careful about what he says. I've never believed that all Germans wear Lederhosen and drink beer all day. Maybe he's got some more *real* questions about Australia.
You: Er sagte …
Hannes: Hab' schon verstanden – Lederhosen und Bier. – Ja, ich hab'noch ein paar Fragen.
You: …
Drew: Kein Problem! He can watch my presentation tomorrow night at school here. Guess what the title is: *G'day, Down under!*

UNIT 1 Australian TV

a) *In a video chat, your Australian pen-friend has told you about her favourite TV shows. You are going to visit her soon, so she has sent you this e-mail pdf that tells you even more about her favourite shows.*

Explain to your younger brother what the shows are about (2–3 sentences for each show).

Blue Water High

Anna decides it's time to be a normal teenager and goes on a date with Bec's brother while the others are making a video presentation to win some new surfboards. She forgets the closing date and almost ruins the presentation.

☆ *Genre: Drama*

The Real Seachange

The dream of leaving city life. It's a vision for millions of people, yet the risk is great. Is the challenge too much? Follow 16 brave families, couples and singles leaving the big cities behind and risking it all in search of a better life.

☆ *Genre: Reality*

Blood, Sweat and Gears

Advanced Drivers Course. After a long search all over Australia for the country's best cars and drivers, the top 10 will take part in challenges that will find Australia's best car and driver in the wild outback.

☆ *Genre: Entertainment*

Bondi Rescue

Bondi Rescue follows the work of the best lifeguards controlling the world's busiest beach. With people's lives in their hands, these lifeguards make sure safety is their number one job.

☆ *Genre: Reality*

b) *Write an e-mail back to your pen-friend and describe your favourite shows on German TV.*

UNIT 2 Working in England

You are 15 years old and your friend is 14. Together you want to go to England and earn some money in the holidays. You have already found some information on the Internet.

Scan the text for information and answer your friend's questions as completely as possible in German.

MEDIATION SKILLS

Sometimes official information is difficult to understand because of the style or difficult words. If you don't know all the words, use the context to help you. Often you can guess what a word means when you look at the rest of the sentence or paragraph.

Who can work in the UK?
Citizens of a country of the European Union (EU), the European Economic Area (EEA) or the European Free Trade Area (EFTA) can live and work in the UK without a visa or a work permit because of their membership in the Free Movement of Workers Agreement.

Regulations for minors
Children are not legally allowed to work until they are 13. During school holidays, 13 and 14-year-olds may work up to a maximum of 25 hours per week and 5 hours per day. 15 and 16-year-olds may work up to 35 hours per week during school holidays.

Wages
The minimum hourly wage for 16-17-year-olds is £3.53 and for 18-21-year-olds £4.77. Teenagers under 16 can earn up to £3 per hour, but the National Minimum Wage does not apply to workers under 16.

Job suggestions
Many teenagers are paperboys or girls and deliver newspapers to houses in their local area before school. From the age of 14, teenagers may help the milkman deliver milk to houses on his round. There are also summer jobs available in agriculture or at riding stables, shops, cafés, restaurants, hotels or offices, as a hairdresser or at a car wash.

UNIT 2 Instructions for use

You are visiting your English exchange partner and have brought the family a present. You know that the whole family is very interested in fitness, so you have chosen a special kind of scales that weigh and compare your body fat to the water in your body. The instructions are only in German.

MEDIATION SKILLS

If you don't know the exact words, you can explain what something looks like, what it is made of, what it is used for. Relative clauses are very useful here.

Example: This is a machine that …
The part which shows the numbers is …

Mit dieser Körper-Analyse-Waage leisten Sie einen entscheidenden Beitrag zur Ihrer Gesundheit.
Sie hat folgende Funktionen:
Die Körper-Analyse-Waage ermittelt anhand Ihrer persönlichen Daten Ihren Körperfett- und Körper-wasser-Anteil sowie Ihr Gewicht.

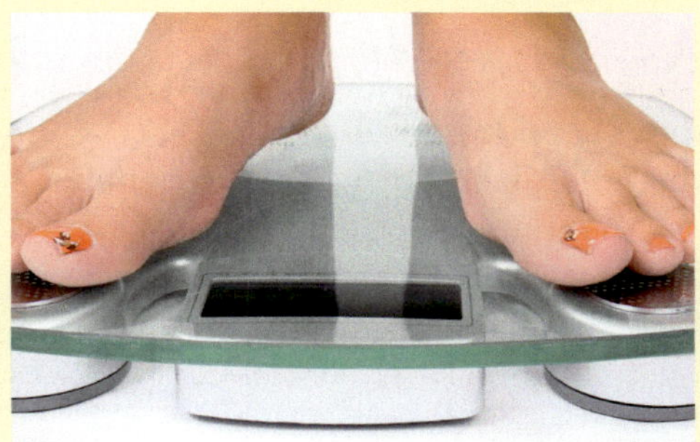

Vorbereitung

1. Batteriestrip entfernen.
2. Für alle Messungen Waage eben und auf festem Untergrund aufstellen.
3. Achtung! Rutschgefahr bei nasser Oberfläche.

Dateneingabe

1. Waage zum Einstellen auf einen Tisch stellen.
2. Waage durch Drücken der ↵-Taste einschalten und warten bis "0.0" angezeigt wird.
3. Dateneingabe durch 2 Sekunden langes Drücken der ↵-Taste starten.
4. Speicherplatz (01 … 10) auswählen (▼ = minus, ▲ = plus) und bestätigen (↵).
5. Geschlecht auswählen (▼ = ♂ männlich oder ▲ = ♀ weiblich) und bestätigen (↵).
6. Alter einstellen (▼ = minus, ▲ = plus) und bestätigen (↵).
7. Körpergröße einstellen (▼ = minus, ▲ = plus) und bestätigen (↵).
8. Die Waage zeigt erneut den aktiven Speicherplatz. Sie können weitere Daten eingeben. Ansonsten schaltet die Waage nach viermaligem Blinken ab.

Körperanalyse

Analyse nur barfuß möglich. Persönliche Daten müssen vorher eingegeben sein.

1. Waage einschalten und warten bis 0.0 angezeigt wird.
2. Speicherplatz auswählen und bestätigen (↵). Die letzten ermittelten Werte werden hintereinander angezeigt.
3. Zeigt die Waage 0.0 zusammen mit dem Geschlechtssymbol (♂ oder ♀) an, Waage betreten. Gewicht wird angezeigt. Danach startet die Körperanalyse. Bitte ruhig stehen bleiben bis zum Ende der Analyse.
4. Körperfettanteil in Prozent, der Körperwasseranteil in Prozent und das Körpergewicht werden 3 Mal im Wechsel angezeigt.
5. Sie können die Waage verlassen.

Answer the family's questions about their new scales:

1. "I can't turn the scales on."
2. "Why do I have to give my age and tell the scales if I'm a man or woman?"
3. "How can I begin putting in my personal information?"
4. "Can more than one person put their information into the scales?"
5. "I just want to find out my weight. Is that possible, too?"

UNIT 3 A podcast

You and your father are listening to a podcast, but your father's English isn't very good and he doesn't really understand the topic.

MEDIATION SKILLS

First listen for gist: find out what the text or dialogue is about.
Listen for the main points and note them down. You can leave a line or two between each main point.
After that find out what the person wants to know.
If you can't answer all of the person's questions, listen again for details. If necessary, fill in the lines between the main points with any details you still need.

After you have listened to the podcast, tell your father …

1. what the podcast is about.
2. what YouTube is and why it's so popular.
3. how YouTube started.
4. how YouTube makes money.
5. what Chad's job at YouTube is now.

UNIT 3 Anglicisms

An *anglicism* is an English word that is used in another language. The original English word is often changed a bit to fit the other language – which sounds funny to a British person!

a) *Read the definitions in an English PC magazine and guess any new words. Then explain them in German.*

BLOG ■ Short for "weblog", an online diary kept by someone who thinks other people will be interested in their activities and opinions.

FILE-SHARING ■ A way of downloading music and videos from other computer users worldwide. There is a risk, however, of being infected with viruses. Careful! The music and the videos that you download may be illegal copies.

INSTANT MESSAGING (IM) ■ Enables friends to chat with each other by typing messages. Because there is a list of contacts, it is safer than using a chatroom.

WIKI ■ Open-access web pages that anyone can help to create. The best-known example is Wikipedia, an encyclopedia written by its readers.

b) *Bob25 is chatting with CathyCat. The chat is full of words that aren't German. Help your parents to understand them by using German words.*

1. Ich hab' schon 153 Hits auf mein neues Video auf YouTube!
2. Aber als ich gestern ein neues uploaden wollte, musste ich meinen Computer 3 Mal rebooten, weil er gecrasht ist.
3. Wenn ich mehr Kohle hätte, um die Programme upzudaten, wär' das nicht passiert.
4. Und ein USB-Stick wär' auch nicht schlecht, um meine Files mitzunehmen.
5. Ich muss jetzt gehen. Da steigt ein Event im Chatroom, das ich nicht verpassen will.

UNIT 4 Explaining a song

Your cousin in the US has asked you for an example of a modern German protest song. After listening to the song you suggested, "Schrei nach Liebe" by *Die Ärzte*, your cousin writes an e-mail that all he understood was 'Schrei' and 'Liebe'. He thinks it's a love song and asks for more help. *Your partner in class takes the role of your cousin.*

First listen for gist: listen to the lyrics without translating every word.

MEDIATION SKILLS

1. Ask your partner what he/she has understood and start from there. Once you start explaining what the song deals with and what it is protesting about, you can ask the other person whether they have any ideas on the subject.
2. Then look at page 80 for help: What is the style of the lyrics? Is the refrain important for the message of the song? Does the song use lots of symbols?

Die Ärzte: *Schrei nach Liebe*

Du bist wirklich saudumm, darum geht's dir gut.
Hass ist deine Attitüde, ständig kocht dein Blut.
Alles muss man dir erklären, weil du wirklich gar nichts weißt.
Höchstwahrscheinlich nicht einmal, was Attitüde heißt.

Deine Gewalt ist nur ein stummer Schrei nach Liebe,
Deine Springerstiefel sehnen sich nach Zärtlichkeit.
Du hast nie gelernt, dich zu artikulieren,
Und deine Eltern hatten niemals für dich Zeit.
Oh oh oh Arschloch!

Warum hast du Angst vorm Streicheln, was soll all der Terz?
Unterm Lorbeerkranz mit Eicheln, weiß ich, schlägt ein Herz,
Und Romantik ist für dich nicht bloß graue Theorie,
Zwischen *Störkraft* und *DEN ANDEREN* steht 'ne Kuschelrock-LP.

Deine Gewalt ist nur ein stummer Schrei nach Liebe,
Deine Springerstiefel sehnen sich nach Zärtlichkeit.
Du hast nie gelernt, dich zu artikulieren,
Und deine Eltern hatten niemals für dich Zeit.
Oh oh oh Arschloch!

Weil du Probleme hast, die keinen interessieren,
Weil du Schiss vorm Schmusen hast, bist du ein Faschist.
Du musst deinen Selbsthass nicht auf andere projizieren,
Damit keiner merkt, was für ein lieber Kerl du bist.

Deine Gewalt ist nur ein stummer Schrei nach Liebe,
Deine Springerstiefel sehnen sich nach Zärtlichkeit.
Du hast nie gelernt, dich zu artizukulieren,
Und deine Freundin, die hat niemals für dich Zeit …

⟨Going home⟩ by "JB" (after Unit 1)

1 Going home

What do you think of when someone talks about "going home"?

This short story was written by "JB" (his name is a secret) from Wulagi, Northern Territory, Australia. JB writes about a girl from the "Stolen Generations". The "Time line of Australian history" at the back of this book explains what the Stolen Generations are.

The girl was standing off the road on the edge of the spear grass. She didn't signal me to stop in any way, but when I saw her shoulders slump as I passed, my foot just slipped off the accelerator and the car slowed.

I reversed[1] and wound down the passenger window.

"Are you OK?"

"Pretty tired, mister, come 'long way."

I motioned her foward until her head was at the door. She looked dirty and exhausted.

"You need a lift[2] somewhere?"

Her face brightened and with a nod of her head she indicated the way I was traveling.

"Near the crossing, big fallin' rock lying in the creek[3]. That place."

"I know the rock," I said. It was about a half hour's drive.

"Get in, I'll take you home." I didn't usually offer lifts and don't know why I did this time.

"Thank you, mister."

Gingerly lifting her sore, bare feet, she sat next to me, slowly sank into the backrest and put her hands together in her lap. The posture reminded me of nuns, so as we rejoined the road I spoke.

"Have you been in school?"

"Yes, mister."

"Where?"

She turned her head to the window and watched the endless spear grass whip by. When she replied, it was in a faltering[4] voice.

"Don't matter now, long way from here, finished now, goin' home."

She turned back to watch as in the distance the country was changing from flat floodplain to rocky outcrops. She looked to the approaching hills and seemed to brighten with recognition.

"That's my mother's country there, mister."

She fell quiet again with a frown[5]. Her hands found each other back in her lap and began to churn.

"Does anyone know you're coming home?" I asked.

She shrugged. "My little brother said he'd wait for me there."

We swept around a sprawling mesa and came across the creek. A large chunk of rock face had broken away eons ago[6] and rested like a huge arrowhead pointing down the waterway that had little billabongs[7] dotted along its well-worn course.

The girl was excited now as the car left the road and came to a gravelly stop on the other side of the little bridge. She hopped out, and bowed her head toward me.

"Bin traveling long time, mister, thanks for the ride home."

She waved and I couldn't help but smile as she disappeared from view.

Days later on my return journey I stopped again to look at the rock. An old blackfella appeared as I stood lost in thought.

[1]**to reverse** [rɪˈvɜːs] = to go in the opposite direction • [2]**lift** [lɪft] = I offered her a *lift.* = I asked her if I could take her somewhere. • [3]**creek** [kriːk] = a very little river • [4]**faltering** [ˈfɔːltərɪŋ] = becoming weaker • [5]**frown** [fraʊn] = *frown* ↔ smile • [6]**eons ago** [ˈiːɒnz‿əˌɡəʊ] = a long, long time ago • [7]**billabongs** [ˈbɪləbɒŋz] = little pools of water along a river/creek that are left over from a time when the river had more water in it

"G'day, mate," he said with a strong voice as he offered his hand.

A little spooked[8], I shook hands.

"Bin waiting for you to come back, mate," he said, nodding in the direction of a small camp under the bridge. A campfire sent wisps of smoke barely noticeable into the air which for me had suddenly become oppressive[9] with heat, and what little breeze there was seemed reluctant[10] to stir.

"Knew you'd have to stop, mate. Her spirit wanted you to know."

I was a little uneasy and wondered again what it was that made me stop here today.

"How is she?" I asked.

The old man looked around and a smile came to his cheeky eyes.

"She's home now. She rests with her real people."

A cooling breeze along the creek coincided[11] with the numbing[12] of every hair on my body.

"You're her brother, aren't you?" I said.

The man grinned and nodded. "They took her away because she was part whitefella. She said she would come back in a motor car. I said I would wait for her at the fallen rock. She died fifty years ago where you found her. She ran away from that place, got hit by a car … so close to home after walking thousan' miles. Thank you for bringing my sister home, mate."

2 The story

a) *Why did the author call this story "going home"?*

b) *Characterization: Analyze the changes in the way the girl acts. What do these changes tell the reader?*

3 A closer look

a) *What is the turning point and what is the climax of the story? The ideas on page 20 can help you. Compare your ideas with a partner.*

b) *In what ways do you think this story is typical of the Aboriginal world?*

4 Writing texts: A newspaper report

With a partner, write a newspaper report about the car accident the girl had 50 years earlier. Two years ago in Green Line 3 you learned how to write a newspaper report. Don't forget to use the elements "headline," "basic information" and "background information".

5 Internet project: The Aboriginal world

a) *First look at pages 26/27: Collect the information you have there about the Aboriginal spiritual world.*

b) *Then research the Aboriginal spiritual world. Start with the word "songlines".*

[8] **spooked** [spu:kt] = feeling surprised and a bit afraid • [9] **oppressive** [ə'presɪv] = so heavy to make a person not feel well • [10] **reluctant** [rɪ'lʌktnt] = He's *reluctant* to help me. = He doesn't want to help me. • [11] **to coincide** [ˌkəʊɪn'saɪd] = to happen at the same time • [12] **to numb** [nʌmb] = to take the feeling away from sth (e.g. a body part)

⟨Stone cold⟩ by Robert Swindells (after Unit 2)

1 Personal qualities

What personal qualities are important for a job? Exercise 7 on page 32 can help you. You will need your notes for exercise 6.

"Stone cold," a novel by Robert Swindells, tells the story of Link, a teenager from Bradford. Link's dad has left Link's mum, and Link can't get along with his mum's new boyfriend. So he runs away to London. He is glad to find a little room that a rat-faced man lets him rent. After setting himself up in his new room, Link goes out to find a job.

I'd applied for loads of jobs in the months since I'd left school. Office work. Supermarkets. Catering[1]. Filling stations – you name it. Most employers wanted experience, and some ads actually said unemployed persons need not apply, which is criminal, in my opinion. I'd started applying in August and I'd had a couple of interviews, but as I said before, sleeping in your clothes makes you look scruffy[2], and by Christmas I looked like a tramp. I knew nobody was going to take me on looking like that, and I started getting really depressed.

I'd seen lots of movies where the character who's on the road picks up casual work in towns he's passing through. Washing dishes. Cutting firewood. Sweeping[3]. I couldn't believe that in a city the size of London it might be impossible for a guy to find that sort of work. I mean, the place is packed with[4] restaurants, caffs and kebab houses, not counting all the pubs. During my two weeks in Wharfedale Road I must've tried two hundred of them, starting with those in the King's Cross area. I got nowhere. Nowhere at all. As the days passed I widened the area of my search, and by half-way through the second week I'd been as far north as St John's Wood and south into Lambeth. I'd tramped the narrow little streets of Soho and the boulevards of South Kensington from early morning (I thought potential[5] employers might be impressed by my willingness[6] to be out and about[7] early) till late at night. I'd offered my services in sleazy greasy caffs[8] and posh[9] hotels and everything in between till my feet felt bruised[10] and I could hardly drag myself out of bed in the morning. I walked everywhere to save money. I lived on cheese rolls and tea, but I was down to nine quid[11] and some change when rat-face came for his rent.

2 Stop and think

a) *Collect information about Link: his age, what he is trying to do, where he lives etc.*

b) *Why do you think Link calls the man who comes to collect his rent "rat-face"?*

It was Friday night. Eight o'clock. I'd just got in. The room was freezing cold and I was treating myself to a quick burst of the cash-gobbling[12] electric fire before bed when there was this knock on the door. I opened up and it was him. He said two words, "Evening," and "Rent".

I looked at him. "It's only Friday," I said. "And I paid for two weeks."

[1] **catering** ['keɪtərɪŋ] = food service • [2] **scruffy** ['skrʌfi] = dirty and untidy • [3] **to sweep** [swi:p] = to clean with a broom • [4] **packed with** ['pækt wɪð] = full of • [5] **potential** [pə'tentʃl] = possible • [6] **willingness** ['wɪlɪŋnəs] = When you show *willingness*, you show that you really want to do sth. • [7] **out and about** [aʊt‿n‿ə'baʊt] = out in the streets • [8] **sleazy greasy caffs** ['sli:zi ˌgrɪsi 'kæfs] = cheap cafés • [9] **posh** [pɒʃ] = expensive • [10] **bruised** ['bru:zd] = hurt • [11] **quid** [kwɪd] = pounds • [12] **burst ... cash-gobbling** [bɜ:st ... 'kæʃgɒblɪŋ] = a bit that costs a lot

He shook his head. "Friday's rent day, sunshine."

"But I moved in on a Monday," I protested. "And paid two weeks. That makes the room mine till Sunday night."

He moved so quickly I hadn't time to step back. One second there was a yard of space between us, and the next he had a bunch of my shirt in his fist and his face was an inch from mine. "Listen, sunshine," he hissed[13]. "The room's mine. I make the rules around here and the rent's due. If you've got it, pay up. If you haven't I'll give you five minutes to pack your stuff and get out." He shoved me and followed me in, leaving the door open.

I tried to reason with him – told him I was waiting for a decision by the DSS. He laughed.

"You're waiting, son," he snarled[14]. "I'm not."

I said I was looking for work and pointed out that I'd been quiet and kept the room tidy. I didn't know what I was saying, really, I was that desperate[15], but it was no good. He told me to pack my bag and stood there with his arms folded while I did it.

When I'd finished I brushed past him on my way to the door and said, "I'll have you for this. Sooner or later, one way or another I'll have you." His laughter rang in my ears as I went down the stairs.

And that's how I came to join them – the homeless kids I'd seen everywhere on my travels. The kids I'd given change to a week ago when I'd thought things were bound to work out[16]. I was one of them now – poised[17] at the top of that downward spiral[18].

After he is forced out of his room, Link has got to live on the streets of London. He is jobless and homeless. His new friend Ginger helps him to survive. But then Ginger disappears. Somewhere in London there is a killer who believes he must "clean" the streets of homeless kids by killing them …

adapted from: *Stone cold* by Robert Swindells

3 Think about the novel

a) *Do you think this story could really happen?*

b) *How are Link and "rat-face" characterized? Were your ideas from ex. 2 b) correct?*

c) *What do you think about the way "rat-face" acts?*

4 Story elements

What are the setting, turning point and climax in this text?

5 Perspective

Tell the story from the perspective of "rat-face". Write about 150 words.

6 Collaborative writing: A letter of application

In groups, write a letter of application for Link. Think of a job he could do. Add a CV. Page 33 can help you.

[13] **to hiss** [hɪs] = to make the sound of a snake • [14] **to snarl** [snɑːl] = to make the sound of a lion • [15] **desperate** [ˈdesprɪt] = having no hope • [16] **bound to work out** [baʊnd‿tə wɜːk ˈaʊt] = would surely be good in the end • [17] **poised** [pɔɪzd] = *here:* ready • [18] **downward spiral** [ˌdaʊnwəd ˈspaɪrəl] = *here:* the way down

⟨A history of rock and pop music⟩ (after Unit 3)

There is no clear boundary[1] between rock 'n' roll and popular music (or simply *rock* and *pop*). The fact that rock music can also become very popular makes it impossible to separate the two. But generally, one can say that rock has always been more extreme than pop. Rock musicians are also associated with playing instruments on stage, and many pop artists have become famous as "just" singers.

The term *popular music,* in contrast to classical music, is much older than rock 'n' roll. But rock was something really new in the 1950s.

Rock 'n' roll's first star: Bill Haley

The 1950s: How rock 'n' roll started

When Bill Haley's 1954 song "Rock around the clock" *(◎ – You can listen to the songs with the ◎ symbol.)* came out, teenagers knew this was something new. In fact, it was more than something new: it was a *revolution*. Songs like "Rock around the clock" had a stronger beat than any music before, while the lightning[2]-fast electric guitar riffs created a whole new sound. Most parents in the 1950s hated rock 'n' roll. They were still living in the saxophone sweetness of 1940s big bands and their soft swing music. Teenagers had had enough of big bands and the 1940s. Rock 'n' roll was the perfect expression of a fast society and the way teenagers felt.

Bill Haley had none of the charisma of Little Richard ("Tutti frutti") ◎ or Elvis Presley ("Hound dog") ◎ who quickly took the new music genre of rock 'n' roll to the next level of success. The relatively new medium of television played a major role, too, doing what radio never could have: it gave the new sound a *look*. Elvis in particular shocked parents (and thrilled[3] teenage girls) with his provocative hip swings and pelvic thrusts[4]. "Elvis the Pelvis[5]" would go on to become "The King" and one of biggest stars the planet has ever known.

Little Richard singing "Tutti frutti"

Elvis Presley

[1] **boundary** ['baʊndri] = border • [2] **lightning** ['laɪtnɪŋ] = the flashes of light you see in the sky during a storm at night • [3] **to thrill** [θrɪl] = to excite • [4] **thrust** [θrʌst] = a forward movement *(Stoß)* • [5] **pelvis** ['pelvɪs] = the area from one hip to the other is the *pelvis*

The 1960s: "The times they are a-changin'"

Society was changing fast in the 1960s. Young people felt more distant than ever from the older generation. Everything about their parents bothered them: their clothes (business suits and nice dresses), their ideals (a house in the suburbs), their conservative politics (wars in places like Vietnam), their morals (no sex before marriage) – it was all so *yesterday*. It soon became clear that the teenagers of the 60s wanted a new, alternative society. And they wanted it now. So out with the old, in with the new. That often meant provocatively long hair and loose and comfortable clothing with wild patterns[6]. The "hippie" look was born.

Jimi Hendrix at Woodstock in 1969

The music of the 60s matched this hunger for change, for protest, for alternative lifestyles. Jimi Hendrix ("Purple haze"), the Rolling Stones ("Satisfaction") and Janis Joplin ("Piece of my heart") went for a hard, aggressive sound, while Joan Baez ("We shall overcome") and Bob Dylan ("The times they are a-changin'") explored more poetic approaches[7] to change. Whatever one's taste in music, it was something the younger generation wanted to *share*, and rock festivals were the place to be. The huge Woodstock festival in 1969, for example, became an instant legend.

But no overview of the 60s would be complete without the Beatles! Starting in the early 60s, the four friends from Liverpool introduced the world to their catchy[8] pop tunes and to their cool haircuts. But while the early songs like "I want to hold your hand" were fun, this was not the kind of music to influence future composers. The later songs ("Lucy in the sky with diamonds", "Revolution", "A day in the life") with their kaleidoscope of sounds and feelings made the Beatles the most influential music group ever.

The Beatles' greatest album: "Sgt. Pepper's Lonely Hearts Club Band"

The 1970s: Arena rock, Punk and Disco

Arena rock was more theatrical and much louder than anything in the 60s. Groups like Queen ("Bohemian rhapsody"), Led Zeppelin ("Stairway to heaven") or David Bowie ("Suffragette city") showed in very different ways how special effects and dramatic stage antics[9] could create new musical experiences in huge arenas.

Those who wanted their music *much* more aggressive, faster and more chaotic, found it in the punk-rock scene of New York and London. Groups like the Ramones ("Teenage lobotomy") or the Sex Pistols ("Anarchy in the UK") were alienated from society and preferred anarchy to the way most people lived. The punk movement may not have lasted long, but the era is still influential today in both music and fashion trends.

Those who weren't at a punk-rock concert or a big arena show were probably at the disco. The DJs made sure the music went on all night: Donna Summer ("I feel love"), the Bee Gees ("Stayin' alive"), Gloria Gaynor ("I will survive"), Chic ("Le freak") …

[6] **pattern** ['pætən] = Flower *patterns* on clothing were popular in the 60s. • [7] **approach** [ə'prəʊtʃ] = way of doing sth • [8] **catchy** ['kætʃi] = A *catchy* song is one which is one that is easy to remember. • [9] **stage antics** ['steɪdʒ‿æntɪks] = things that are typical for a performer on stage (e.g. special way of jumping around, etc.)

The 1980s: The MTV generation

On 1 August, 1981, the world of pop and rock changed forever: MTV went on the air. For the first time, one could watch one's favourite singers and bands 24 hours a day! Selling an artist's image became as important as selling their music, and record companies invested heavily in video productions. It is no coincidence[10] that masters of the video genre like Michael Jackson ("Thriller") or Madonna ("Like a virgin") became the decade's greatest stars.

Together with the Beatles and Elvis the biggest pop stars of all time: Michael Jackson and Madonna

1980s and 1990s: Big-voiced divas

Whitney Houston ("I will always love you") and later Mariah Carey ("Vision of love") were the biggest singing stars with countless No. 1 hits. These singers proved that videos and music styles may come and go, but big, soulful voices somehow never go out of fashion.

1990s: Rock is back

Rock was big in the 90s: Seattle grunge groups like Nirvana ("Smells like teen spirit") were successful with their hard rock/Punk mix, while Oasis ("Wonderwall") proved that the UK was still a world-player in rock.

The 21st century

Who among the current generation of young artists will be able to stand up alongside all the superstars mentioned above? Christina Aguilera has proved she can sing like Whitney and Mariah – but will anybody know who she is 10 or 20 years from now? Or Amy Winehouse? Only time will tell.

Amy Winehouse: Still a name in 10 years?

1 Other kinds of music

What kinds of music are not mentioned here? Example: Techno.
Why are they important?

2 Present and future

Complete this history of rock and pop to the present, and guess who you think will be tomorrow's great stars.

3 A project: Music through the decades

In groups, divide up the decades between the 1950s and now. Find out more about the artists and the music of that decade. Do a multimedia presentation for each decade.

[10] **coincidence** [kəʊˈɪnsɪdns] = *Zufall*

⟨Slam poetry⟩ (after Unit 3)

In 1984 Marc Smith, a Chicago construction worker and poet, decided that poems should not only be written but also performed. So he started performing his poems – and the poetry slam was born. Now poetry slams are held all over the world, from the US to the UK, from Nepal to the Netherlands, and in Germany, too.
A poetry slam has been described as the "competitive art of performance poetry". Competitors perform their original work, using a wide variety of styles. The topics – love, politics, religion – are just as varied as the performers.
The members of the audience at a poetry slam take part actively. The five judges are chosen from the audience. The audience is encouraged to boo or cheer after or even during a poem. A poet may even be jeered off the stage before completing his or her poem.
Remember, a poem doesn't have to rhyme. It should express feelings and emotions, using colourful language.

a) *Read the poem on the right.*

1. *What emotions are expressed there?*
2. *In pairs, read parts of the poem and decide which sounds best: slow or fast; loud or quiet; with a lot of or very little expression.*

b) *Now read the beginning of one more poem and discuss how to perform it.*

1. *Try out ways of performing it.*
2. *Can you continue the poem?*

Do, make, manufacture, produce.
What have you done today? Made today?
Show me what you've done and I'll show you what you're worth.
I'm talking about my generation. The sensation!

He asked me for the time and I told him it was five to twelve.
He said he had time to wait for his bus, so how about us, Babe.
He was a charmer, a talker, a real smooth man.
He said he was all, all mine, "I'll show you a good time, Babe."
I followed him, believed him, wanted to be charmed by him.
He promised me love and love and love and demanded, "All of your time, Babe."
The promises turned vague, the love never came.
He kept me waiting and praying and watching the clock.
I spat and screamed and hissed and cursed.
Then the charmer walked in and said, "What are you doing? Look at the time, Babe."
The talker, the real smooth man and his babe.
I never should have given him the time of day.

c) *Here are the general rules for a poetry slam:*

1. Poets perform their own original poems.
2. There are five judges who give scores between 0 and 10. The lowest and highest scores that judges give are not counted, meaning a poet can score between 0 and 30.
3. No props, music or costumes are allowed.
4. There is a three minute time-limit for performing a poem.
5. Rules may be changed to fit your needs or your event. How about a slam with a theme?

Examples: Love poems through the ages. Or: Poems about sports.

Visit a slam near you and then organize one at your school!

⟨Deportation at breakfast⟩ by Larry Fondation (after Unit 4)

1 Deportation

Explain the word "deportation". Then look at the title of the short story. What do you think could happen in the story?

The signs on the windows lured[1] me inside. For a dollar I could get two eggs, toast, and potatoes. The place looked better than most – family run and clean. The signs were hand-lettered and neat[2]. The paper had yellowed some, but the black letters remained bold. A green-and-white awning was over the door, where the name 'Clara's' was written.

Inside, the place had an appealing[3] and old-fashioned look. The air smelled fresh and homey, not greasy. The menu was printed on a chalkboard. It was short and clear. It listed the kinds of toast you could choose from.

Because I was alone, I sat at the counter, leaving the empty tables free for other customers that might come in. At the time, business was quiet. Only two tables were occupied, and I was alone at the counter. But it was still early – not yet seven-thirty.

Behind the counter was a short man with dark black hair, a moustache, and a youthful beard. He was dressed immaculately[4], all in chef's white – pants, shirt, and apron, but no hat. He had a strong accent. The name 'Javier' was stitched on his shirt.

2 Stop and think

Were your ideas from exercise 1 correct? Explain.

I ordered coffee, and asked for a minute to choose between the breakfast special for a dollar and the cheese omelette for $1.59. I selected the omelette.

The coffee was hot, strong, and fresh. I spread my newspaper on the counter and sipped at the mug[5] as Javier went to the grill to cook my meal.

The beaten eggs were spread out on the grill, the bread was inside the toaster, when the authorities[6] came in. They grabbed Javier quickly and without a word, forcing his hands behind his back. He, too, said nothing. He did not resist, and they pushed him out the door and into their waiting car.

3 Stop and think

a) *Why do you think Javier gets arrested[7]?*

b) *Do you think this is fair?*

On the grill, my eggs bubbled. I looked around for another employee – maybe out back somewhere, or in the washroom. I leaned over the counter and called for someone. No one answered. I looked behind me toward the tables. Two elderly men sat at one; two elderly women at the other. The two women were talking. The men were reading the paper. They seemed not to have noticed Javier's exit.

I could smell my eggs starting to burn. I wasn't quite sure what to do about it. I thought about Javier and stared at my eggs. After some hesitation, I got up from my red stool and went behind the counter.

[1] **to lure** [lʊə] = If a place *lures* you inside, then sth about it is attractive to you. • [2] **neat** [ni:t] = *neat* ↔ messy • [3] **appealing** [ə'pi:lɪŋ] = attractive, inviting • [4] **immaculately** [ɪ'mækjələtli] = perfectly, neatly, cleanly • [5] **mug** [mʌg] = (big) coffee cup • [6] **the authorities** [ði‿ɔ:'θɒrətiz] = the police (or: other official people from the government) • [7] **to arrest** [ə'rest] = He *was arrested*. = He was taken away by the police.

I grabbed a spare apron, then picked up the spatula[8] and turned my eggs. My toast had popped up, but it was not browned, so I put it down again. While I was cooking, the two elderly women came to the counter and asked to pay. I asked what they had had. They seemed surprised that I didn't remember. I checked the prices on the chalkboard and rang up their order. They paid slowly, fishing through[9] large purses, and went out, leaving me a dollar tip. I took my eggs off the grill and put them onto a clean plate. My toast had come up. I buttered it and put it on my plate beside my eggs. I put the plate at my spot at the counter, right next to my newspaper.

As I began to come back from behind the counter to my stool, six new customers came through the door. "Can we pull some tables together?" they asked. "We're all one party[10]." I told them yes. Then they ordered six coffees, two decaffeinated. I thought of telling them I didn't work there. But perhaps they were hungry. I poured their coffee. Their order was simple: six breakfast specials, all with scrambled eggs and toast.

I got busy at the grill. Then the elderly men came to pay. More new customers began arriving. By eight-thirty, I had my hands full. With this kind of business, I couldn't understand why Javier hadn't hired a waitress. Maybe I'd put a 'help-wanted' ad in the paper tomorrow. I had never been in the restaurant business. There was no way I could run this place alone.

4 Reactions

a) *Describe what happens in the second half of the story (after line 43). How do the customers react? How does the narrator react?*

b) *Do you understand the way they react? Explain.*

5 Short stories

Short stories often start unusually ("medias in res" – right in the middle of the action) and end with a surprise. Look at "Deportation at breakfast" again: find these elements and say why they are important here.

6 An American short story

a) *How do Javier and the narrator try to live the American Dream?*

b) *Write about 150 words on how the story could continue: will the narrator's business be a success or not?*

[8] **spatula** ['spætjələ] = a kitchen tool used for turning eggs or omelettes • [9] **to fish through sth** [fɪʃ] = to dig through sth • [10] **party** ['pɑːti] = a word used at restaurants for 'group of people' ('a *party* of four').

⟨Battle of the books⟩ (Throughout the school year)

All over the world, the **Battle of the books** is an event held at a growing number of schools and universities. At the end of the school year, you can have one, too – maybe even together with other schools in your town or area.

What is the "battle"?

You take part in the competition by reading from the book list given to you by your teacher at the beginning of the school year. In the battle, you answer questions about the books you have read. Because the battle is held during the last two weeks of the school year, you have lots of time to read the books. The reading list may include books you have read before. It is a good idea to summarize each book which you can then reread before the battle.

How does the competition work?

In some countries, the day begins with a meeting in the cafeteria, a morning snack and what the teams must do that day. Then students become team members and are sent to their first round of the "Battle." They play several rounds, each against a different team. One teacher (or group of teachers) gives the points. At the end of the morning, points are added up and the two teams with the most points are invited to a "Grand battle" after lunch, with the other teams as their audience.
Other versions of the competition are played in the afternoon only, with teams from one class or from different classes playing each other.
In the version presented here, there are **three different sections**. Each section features tasks that look at different aspects of the books. Here are some example questions about the novel *Silver fin* by Charlie Higson, a great book about the childhood days of James Bond.

Section one: Questions

In this section, you will be asked specific questions about the contents of a book. For example:

- ? How did James's parents die?
- ? Describe Randolph Hellebore.
- ? Who is Red Kelly?

Section two: Interpretation

In this section, you have to do more than just repeat facts: You have to show your understanding of the characters, of their motives, and talk about the book itself. For example:

- ? Name some of James's special talents. What does he learn as a boy that he can use later in the three adult novels?
- ? Describe parts of the novel that are very exciting.
- ? At the end of the novel, George decides to help James. Do you find this believable?

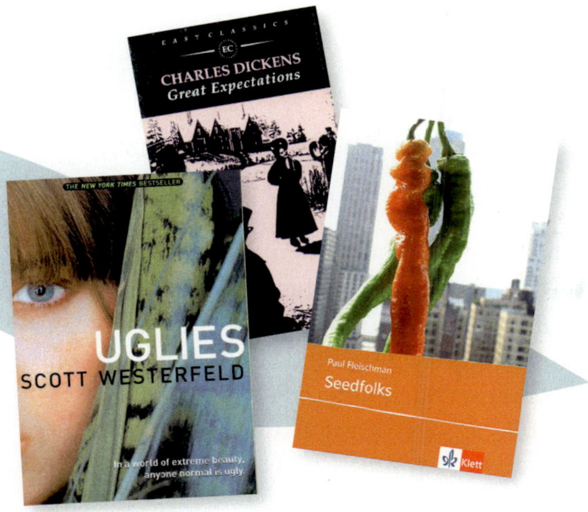

Section three: Creative writing

In this final section, you will have to write your own texts. This can be in writing, but sometimes you might also be asked to do a role play with the characters in one of the books you've read. For example:

- **?** Write the plot for another Young James Bond novel, based on a James Bond movie.
- **?** Write the plot for a similar novel based on another fictitious (female?) character.
- **?** Imagine James meets George during the competition. What could happen between them? What could they say to each other? Act out their dialogue.

Here are some of the books you have seen in ***Green Line*** **2–5**. You have only read parts of these books. Your teacher might like to add or take away some of the titles, depending on what kind of books you (and your teacher) are interested in:

Abrahams, Peter: *Down the rabbit hole* (in *Green Line* 4)
Colfer, Eoin: *Benny and Omar* (in *Green Line* 3)
Dickens, Charles: *Oliver Twist* (in *Green Line* 2)
Doyle, Sir Arthur Conan: *The speckled band* (in *Green Line* 2)
London, Jack: *The call of the wild* (in *Green Line* 4)
Oates, Joyce Carol: *Big mouth and ugly girl* (in the Workbook of *Green Line* 3)
Pullman, Philip: *The ruby in the smoke* (in *Green Line* 3)
Rowling, J.K.: *Harry Potter and the philosopher's stone* (in *Green Line* 2)
Snicket, Lemony: *A series of unfortunate events* (in the Workbook of *Green Line* 3)
Stevenson, Robert Louis: *Treasure Island* (in *Green Line* 3)
Swindells, Robert: *Stone cold* (in *Green Line* 5)
Westerfeld, Scott: *Uglies* (in *Green Line* 5)

FAQS

Here are the answers to some frequently asked questions (FAQs):

1. **Do I have to read all the books on the list?**
   No, you don't. Most students read only about half of the books. The more you read, the easier it is to win the competition. In your team, there will be other students who have read only some of the books, too.
2. **Do we need to have prizes for the winning teams?**
   Absolutely! But keep them to a minimum. The idea is to read a lot, not to win big prizes.
3. **Do we need other schools to have a battle or can we have one only at my school?**
   It is best to start small. The first time you fight a battle, it is best to do it alone at your school. It is always good, however, to have other schools in your area "fight" their own battle. In the second year, plan on having an area-wide battle.

Enjoy reading the books, have a good "battle" and good luck!

Grammar

Liebe Schülerin, lieber Schüler,
dieser Grammatikteil ist dir mittlerweile vertraut.
Er fasst die Regeln zusammen, die dir helfen können,
- wenn du etwas nicht verstanden hast
- wenn du ein paar Stunden gefehlt hast
- wenn du etwas wiederholen möchtest
- wenn du Hausaufgaben machst
- wenn du für eine Klassenarbeit übst.

Jedes Grammatikkapitel hat eine Nummer, z. B. **G 2**, und eine große Überschrift.
Die Seitenangabe rechts neben dieser Überschrift zeigt dir, auf welcher Seite der neue Grammatikstoff in der Unit eingeführt wird.
Wo ein **!** steht, musst du besonders aufpassen.
Dieses Kästchen ist nun auf Englisch.

Bei **Revision** wird bekannte Grammatik wiederholt.

Da du Englisch schon gut beherrschst, ist die Unitübersicht **In this Unit you will learn** nur noch auf Englisch.
Aus demselben Grund sind die Zusammenfassungen nach jedem Pensum **ENGLISH SUMMARY** auch auf Englisch. Sie helfen dir, im Unterricht auf Englisch über Grammatik zu sprechen. Die **ENGLISH SUMMARY** ist nun um Beispielsätze erweitert worden. Neben Beispielsätzen findest du auch idiomatische Wendungen und weniger gebräuchliche grammatische Phänomene, die über das hinausgehen, was im Kern der jeweiligen Unit behandelt wird. Diese Phänomene sind in blauer Schrift beschrieben.

Unter **Grammatical terms** findest du wieder eine Liste der grammatischen Begriffe, die in diesem Buch vorkommen.

Grammatical terms

English term	English example	Deutsche Bezeichnung / Übersetzung
dynamic verbs G 6	They **are playing** computer games.	Tätigkeitsverben
emphasis G 7		Hervorhebung
inversion	Only then **did he realize** that he had gone the wrong way.	– durch Inversion
emphatic *do*	I **do** like your new pullover.	– mit *do*
it is/it was	**It was** Pete who saw them first.	– mit *it is/it was*
what	**What** I'm looking forward to is a break.	– mit *what*
R: *-self/-selves* pronouns	She believes it **herself**.	– mit den Pronomen auf *-self/-selves*
R: adverbs of degree	This is **really** nice.	– Gradadverbien

English term	English example	Deutsche Bezeichnung / Übersetzung
R: future tenses G5		Futurzeiten
going to	I'**m going to have** something to eat.	– *Going to* Futur
will future	She'**ll** be 17 next year.	– *Will* Futur
present progressive	We'**re playing** against Peterborough on Saturday.	– Verlaufsform der Gegenwart (mit futurischer Bedeutung)
simple present *(time-table future)*	The concert **starts** at 7.30.	– Einfache Form der Gegenwart (mit futurischer Bedeutung)
R: gerund G9	She enjoys **playing** football.	Gerundium/Gerund
gerund after prepositions G10	**In spite of working hard**, Pete did poorly in the test.	Gerund nach Präpositionen
R: gerund or infinitive G13	She's **stopped talking** to him. She's **stopped to talk** to him.	Gerund oder Infinitiv
have something done G2	We **have our car checked** regularly.	etwas machen lassen
R: indirect speech G16	He told us **that he'd arrive on Sunday**.	Indirekte Rede
R: infinitive with *to* G11, G14	I would like you **to read** the first chapter.	Infinitiv mit *to*
infinitive with *to* after *for* + (pro)noun G12	It's **difficult for them to understand** this.	Infinitiv mit *to* nach *for* + Pro(Nomen)
R: infinitive without *to* G14	I really must **go** now.	Infinitiv ohne *to*
R: modal auxiliaries and their substitutes G15	You **needn't** worry about it.	Modale Hilfsverben und ihre Ersatzverben
object + infinitive		Objekt + Infinitiv
after verbs of perception G4	We **saw Marco** suddenly **drop** two cups of coffee.	– nach Verben der sinnlichen Wahrnehmung
after ***let*** G2	My mother often **lets me have** her car.	– nach *let* + Objekt + Infinitiv
after ***make*** G2	The new coach **makes the team work** very hard.	– nach *make* + Objekt + Infinitiv
past participle G4	The people **injured** in the accident were taken to hospital.	Partizip der Vergangenheit
perfect participle G4	**Having read** the leaflet, Marco had a better idea about possible careers.	Partizip Perfekt

English term	English example	Deutsche Bezeichnung / Übersetzung
present participle G4		Partizip Präsens
instead of relative clause	The girl **sitting** at the table over there works in my parents' shop.	– anstelle eines Relativsatzes
shortening adverbial clauses	**Knowing** that the roads would be icy, they went by train.	– zur Verkürzung adverbialer Nebensätze
after verbs of perception	I **heard him talking** to you for some time.	– nach Verben der sinnlichen Wahrnehmung
R: present and past tenses G8		Gegenwarts- und Vergangenheitsformen
simple present	I always **go** to school by bus.	– Einfache Form der Gegenwart
present progressive	Look, my bus **is coming** round the corner now.	– Verlaufsform der Gegenwart
simple past	I **saw** him yesterday.	– Einfache Form der Vergangenheit
past progressive	He **was** just **writing** an e-mail when she called.	– Verlaufsform der Vergangenheit
present perfect (simple)	We **haven't been** to Australia yet.	– Einfache Form des Perfekt
present perfect progressive	They **have been waiting** for ages.	– Verlaufsform des Perfekt
past perfect (simple)	When they **had finished** the job they went home.	– Einfache Form des Plusquamperfekt
past perfect progressive	They **had** only **been playing** for half an hour when it started to rain.	– Verlaufsform des Plusquamperfekt
R: relative clauses G3		Relativsätze
defining	Is that the Australian actor **that** played Romeo?	– notwendige
non-defining	Sydney, **which** has 4 million inhabitants, is Australia's largest city.	– nicht-notwendige
contact clauses	It is the great white shark swimmers worry about most.	– notwendige Relativsätze ohne Relativpronomen
stative verbs G6	You **look** much better now.	Zustandsverben
used to G1	I **didn't use to like** vegetables when I was small.	*Used to* (gewohnheitsmäßige Handlung)

Unit 1

IN THIS UNIT YOU WILL LEARN

- ✓ that you can use *used to* + the infinitive to express that something often happened in the past or was true in the past. G1
- ✓ how to express different meanings of German "lassen": *to let* someone do something, *to make* someone do something and *to have* something *done*. G2
- ✓ how to use *defining* and *non-defining relative clauses* and *contact clauses* (Revision). G3

G1 Used to

Seite 17

Mit ***used to*** + Infinitiv kannst du ausdrücken, dass früher etwas Bestimmtes geschah oder dass ein bestimmter Zustand existierte.

Mum and Dad always used to take us to the seaside when we were small.

We always **used to go** on holiday with our parents.	**Früher** machten wir immer Urlaub mit unseren Eltern.
Where **did** you **use to go** ?	Wo seid ihr (**immer**) hingefahren?
There **didn't use to be** any cheap flights then, so we **used to go** to the seaside every summer.	**Damals** gab es keine Billigflüge. Daher sind wir jeden Sommer ans Meer gefahren.
We **never used to fly** anywhere in those days.	**Damals** sind wir nie irgendwohin geflogen.

- Von ***used to*** gibt es nur die ***past tense***-Form, keine ***present tense***-Form.
- Im Deutschen kannst du ***used to*** mit **früher** oder (**damals**) **immer** wiedergeben. Häufig wird es auch gar nicht übersetzt.
- Fragen werden mit ***did … use to*** gebildet.
- Die Verneinung kann mit ***didn't use to*** oder ***never used to*** gebildet werden. Weniger gebräuchlich ist ***used not to***.

ENGLISH SUMMARY

- **Used to + infinitive** expresses that something often happened or was true in the past: He **used to do** a lot of sport when he was younger.
- Questions are made with **did ... use to**: **Did** you **use to** go to Manly Beach in Sydney?
- Negation can be expressed with **didn't use to** or **never used to**: No, we **didn't use to** go there. / We **never used to** go there. We went to Bondi Beach.

G2 Englische Entsprechungen für das deutsche *lassen*

Seite 17–18

English equivalents for *lassen* in German

„Lassen" kann im Deutschen unterschiedliche Bedeutungen haben und wird je nachdem im Englischen unterschiedlich wiedergegeben.

a) *Let* and *make* + object + infinitive

Das deutsche „lassen" + Objekt + Infinitiv kann sowohl „etwas zulassen" (= *to allow*) wie auch „etwas veranlassen" (= *to force*) bedeuten. Im Englischen werden diese gegensätzlichen Bedeutungen durch ***let*** und ***make*** ausgedrückt.

Blake's parents let him have rooftop barbies.

But they make him clean everything up after the barbies.

Zulassen: *let* **someone do something**	**Veranlassen:** *make* **someone do something**
Blake's parents often let him have **rooftop barbies**. But they **don't let the guests drink any alcohol** at his parties. His mother always **lets him use** her car to take the guests home.	After the party they **make Blake clean** everything **up**. Blake **makes his guests bring** their own food. Last time the thick fog **made him drive** extremely slowly.

- ***Let*** *someone* ***do*** *something* bedeutet „jemandem erlauben, etwas zu tun"; „etwas zulassen".
  Vergleiche: *Blake's parents* ***don't allow the guests to drink*** *any alcohol.*
- ***Make*** *someone* ***do*** *something* bedeutet „jemanden dazu bringen oder zwingen, etwas zu tun"; „veranlassen, dass etwas geschieht".
  Vergleiche: *The thick fog* ***forced him to drive*** *slowly.*

b) to have something done

Wenn man veranlasst, dass etwas von jemand anderem gemacht wird, kann man ***to have something done*** verwenden.

	Have	Direct object	Past participle		
She always	**has**	**her hair**	**dyed**	at Gino's.	Sie **lässt** sich immer bei Gino die Haare färben.
Next time we	**won't have**	**pizzas**	**delivered.**	We'll cook something ourselves.	Nächstes Mal **lassen** wir uns keine Pizzen bringen.
I	**had**	**my bike**	**repaired**	last week.	Ich habe letzte Woche mein Fahrrad reparieren **lassen.**

- ▶ Mit ***have something done*** kannst du ausdrücken, dass jemand veranlasst, dass etwas gemacht wird. Es ist nicht wichtig, wer das tut.
- ▶ Du darfst ***have something done*** nicht mit dem ***present perfect*** oder dem ***past perfect*** verwechseln. Beachte die unterschiedliche Stellung der Objekte in den Beispielen unten:

Have	Direct object	Past participle	Present perfect	Direct object	
Normally she **has**	**her hair**	**dyed** at Gino's.	But this time **she has dyed**	**her hair**	herself.

Normalerweise **lässt sie** sich bei Gino die Haare **färben.**

Aber diesmal **hat sie** sich die Haare **selbst gefärbt.**

!

If „lassen" means „zurücklassen", „belassen" or „sein lassen", you can't use ***let*** or ***make*** in English. You must use ***leave***:

Meine Mutter hat ihren Schirm im Bus liegen **lassen.** → My mother **left** her umbrella on the bus.
Lass mich in Ruhe! → **Leave** me alone!
Er lässt sein Auto immer am Bahnhof (stehen). → He always **leaves** his car at the station.
Ich fürchte, ich habe das Licht brennen lassen. → I'm afraid I've **left** the lights on.

ENGLISH SUMMARY

- You can use **let** to say that someone allows someone to do something, or allows something to happen:
  Our French teacher always **lets us use** dictionaries in tests.
- You can use **make** to say that someone forces someone to do something, or makes something happen:
  Yesterday our coach **made us run** round the court five times.
- German ***lassen*** can also be expressed by **to leave**.
  I'**ve left** my keys at home. – **Leave** me in peace!

G3 Wiederholung: Notwendige und nicht-notwendige Relativsätze
Revision: Defining and non-defining relative clauses

Seite 19

Du kennst schon notwendige und nicht-notwendige Relativsätze. Hier findest du zur Wiederholung noch einmal ihre wichtigsten Eigenschaften und die Unterschiede zwischen ihnen.

Defining relative clause	Non-defining relative clause
James Cook was the British explorer **who discovered the east coast of Australia.**	Captain Cook, **who sailed from England in 1768**, reached Australia in April 1770.
	The kangaroo, **which can only be found in Australia and Tasmania**, is a marsupial.
Marsupials are the only animals **which/that carry their young around in pouches.**	Australia, **whose animal world is unique**, is visited by millions of tourists every year.

- Notwendige Relativsätze bestimmen ihr Bezugswort *(the English explorer, the only animals)*.
- Sie legen fest, wer oder was gemeint ist. Ohne sie wäre der Hauptsatz unverständlich.
- Zwischen Hauptsatz und notwendigem Relativsatz steht **kein Komma**.
- Die Relativpronomen im notwendigen Relativsatz sind ***who*** oder ***that*** für Personen, ***which*** oder ***that*** für Dinge.
- ***Whose*** kann für Personen und Dinge verwendet werden und bezeichnet eine Beziehung oder Zugehörigkeit (Australien, dessen Tierwelt …).

- Nicht-notwendige Relativsätze enthalten zusätzliche Informationen.
- Der Hauptsatz wäre auch ohne diese Informationen verständlich.
- Zwischen Hauptsatz und nicht-notwendigem Relativsatz stehen **Kommas**.
- Für Personen verwendet man ***who***, für Dinge ***which***.
- ***Whose*** kann für Personen und Dinge verwendet werden und bezeichnet eine Beziehung oder Zugehörigkeit (Australien, dessen Tierwelt …).

Contact clause

The ranger **we met at the the Marine Park** took us out in a glass-bottom boat.
The crocodiles **I saw in the river** didn't look very friendly.

- Ist das Relativpronomen **Objekt** des notwendigen Relativsatzes (*The ranger **who/that** we met* ... Der Ranger, **den** wir ... trafen ...), kann es entfallen. Notwendige Relativsätze ohne Pronomen werden als ***contact clauses*** bezeichnet.

ENGLISH SUMMARY

- There are two types of relative clauses: **defining relative clauses** and **non-defining relative clauses**.
- A **defining relative clause** gives important information about a noun. Without the relative clause it is impossible to understand who or what is meant:
  This is the man **who saw the accident**.
- A **non-defining relative clause** gives extra information. (The main clause is complete without it.) It can make the sentence more interesting:
  The kangaroo, **which can jump as high as three meters**, can only be found in Australia and Tasmania.
- There is **no comma** between the main clause and a **defining relative clause**.
  There are **commas** between the main clause and a **non-defining relative clause**.
- In **non-defining relative clauses** you use **who** and **whose** for people and **which** and **whose** for things. You mustn't use **that**.
- When the relative pronoun is the **object** of the relative clause, you can leave it out. These relative clauses are called **contact clauses**:
  Here's a photo of the ranger who/that we met at the Great Barrier Reef.
  → Here's a photo of the ranger **we met** at the Great Barrier Reef.
- There is a special type of **non-defining relative clause**: You can use a **which-clause** to **comment** on the main clause: Large areas of the continent are very hot and dry, which makes it difficult to live there. (... , was der Grund dafür ist, dass ...).

Unit 2

IN THIS UNIT YOU WILL LEARN

- ✓ how to use *present participles, past participles* and *perfect participles* to link sentence parts and make texts more fluent. G4
- ✓ how to use the *present participle* or the *infinitive* after verbs of perception (*to hear, to see, to watch* etc.) and an object. G4
- ✓ how to express the future in different ways **(Revision)**. G5

G4 Partizipien Participles

Seite 30–32

Du kennst sowohl das ***present participle*** als auch das ***past participle*** und zwei häufige Verwendungsmöglichkeiten:

Bildung von Verbformen

Das ***present participle*** wird zur Bildung der ***progressive form*** gebraucht:
Marco and Pete are **looking** at a leaflet.
Das ***past participle*** dient zur Bildung der Perfektformen:
Marco has **done** an online questionnaire.

Adjektive

Außerdem weißt du, dass ***present*** und ***past participle*** auch als Adjektive verwendet werden können:
The **winning** team waved to their fans. *(active meaning)*
The **defeated** team left the field sadly. *(passive meaning)*

Daneben gibt es eine Reihe weiterer Verwendungsmöglichkeiten von ***present*** und ***past participles***.

a) Das Partizip anstelle eines Relativsatzes
Participles in place of relative clauses

Seite 30–31

In Unit 1 hast du die Relativsätze wiederholt. Nun lernst du, dass du mit Hilfe von Partizipien Relativsätze umformen kannst.

Relative clause	Participle construction
active	
The man **who is talking** to Marco is his personal adviser.	The man **talking** to Marco is his personal adviser.
Most of the students **that take** A-levels go on to university.	Most of the students **taking** A-levels go on to university.
passive	
He was given a questionnaire **which was** specially **written** for Year 11 students.	He was given a questionnaire specially **written** for Year 11 students.
Marco is showing Pete a leaflet **that was given** to him by his adviser.	Marco is showing Pete a leaflet **given** to him by his adviser.

- Für Relativsätze kann man auch Partizipialkonstruktionen verwenden, wenn das Relativpronomen Subjekt des Relativsatzes ist. Das Relativpronomen entfällt dann. Genau wie der entsprechende *defining relative clause* wird auch die Partizipialkonstruktion nicht durch ein Komma vom Hauptsatz getrennt.
- Dabei tritt das ***present participle*** für Relativsätze im **Aktiv** *(The adviser who is talking …)* und das ***past participle*** für Relativsätze im **Passiv** ein *(The leaflet which was written …)*.
- Das ***present participle*** kann sowohl die ***progressive form*** *(The adviser who is talking …)* wie auch die ***simple form*** *(The students that take the …)* ersetzen.
- Bei der Übersetzung dieser Partizipialkonstruktionen ins Deutsche verwendet man meist Relativsätze: *The woman **talking** to Marco …* – Die Frau, **die** mit Marco spricht …

b) Partizipialkonstruktionen an Stelle von adverbialen Nebensätzen
Participle constructions in place of adverbial clauses

Seite 30–32

Adverbiale Nebensätze geben wie adverbiale Bestimmungen einen Zeitpunkt, einen Grund oder eine Bedingung an.
Vergleiche:
Adverbiale Bestimmung: *in the rain*
Adverbialer Nebensatz: *... when it rains.*
Adverbiale Nebensätze werden durch Konjunktionen wie *when, because, if, as* etc. eingeleitet.
Anstelle von adverbialen Nebensätzen können auch Partizpialkonstruktionen stehen. Dies gilt besonders für adverbiale Nebensätze der **Zeit** und des **Grundes**.

Die Partizipialkonstruktionen wirken fast immer förmlicher als die entsprechenden adverbialen Nebensätze und werden vorwiegend in der Schriftsprache verwendet.

Adverbial clause of time

Adverbial clause of time	Participle construction
When he read the leaflet, Pete had lots of new ideas.	**Reading the leaflet**, Pete had lots of new ideas.
While she was looking for a seat on the bus, Naomi suddenly saw Marco on the other side of the street.	**Looking for a seat on the bus**, Naomi suddenly saw Marco on the other side of the street.

- Adverbiale Nebensätze der Zeit werden häufig durch *when, while* oder *after* eingeleitet.
- Werden sie zu Partizipialkonstruktionen umgewandelt, entfällt das Subjekt des Nebensatzes *(he, she)*, da es mit dem Subjekt des Hauptsatzes identisch ist (Pete, Naomi).

Adverbial clause of reason

Adverbial clause of reason	Participle construction
Some young people don't go to university right away after A-levels **because they want to see the world first**.	**Wanting to see the world first**, some young people don't go to university right away after A-levels.
Lots of people look for jobs in other countries **because they are attracted by better pay.**	**Attracted by better pay,** lots of people look for jobs in other countries.

- Adverbiale Nebensätze des Grundes werden sehr oft durch *because* eingeleitet.
- Die Reihenfolge Hauptsatz – Nebensatz kann verändert werden, so dass die Partizipialkonstruktion am Anfang des Satzes steht.
- Konstruktionen mit dem ***present participle*** entsprechen **Aktivsätzen** (*Wanting to ...* entspricht *Because they want to ...*).

▶ Konstruktionen mit dem ***past participle*** entsprechen Passivsätzen (*Attracted by …* entspricht *They are attracted by …*).

Perfect participle

Adverbial clause of time or reason	Perfect participle
After they had found out that houses in France were much cheaper, they decided to move to Normandy.	**Having found out that houses in France were much cheaper**, they decided to move to Normandy.
They found living in France difficult at first **because they hadn't learned any French at school**.	**Not having learned any French at school**, they found living in France difficult at first.
After he had been employed by a computer firm for five years, he started his own business.	**Having been employed by a computer firm for five years**, he started his own business.

▶ Die Perfektformen des Partizips werden verwendet, um auszudücken, dass eine Handlung vor einer anderen geschah:
1. *They found out …* 2. *So they decided …* → *Having found out …, they decided …*
(In adverbialen Nebensätzen der Zeit wird die Konjunktion *after* häufig verwendet.)

▶ Hierbei entspricht ***having + past participle*** *(Having found out/Not having learned …)* aktiven Verbformen *(had found out, hadn't learned)*.

▶ ***Having been + past participle*** *(Having been employed)* entspricht passiven Verbformen *(had been employed)*..

ENGLISH SUMMARY

▶ You can use **present** and **past participles** to link sentence parts.

▶ With the help of **participles** you can make **relative clauses** shorter:
Most people who work for the firm have IT qualifications.
→ Most people **working** for the firm have IT qualifications.

▶ You can also change **adverbial clauses of reason and time** into participle constructions:
They went by train because they knew that the roads would be full of traffic.
→ **Knowing** that the roads would be full of traffic, they went by train.

▶ You can use the **perfect participle** to say that something happened before another action in the past began:
Having played for the team for 10 years, he decided to leave and join another club.

▶ You can also use the **present participle** to describe things happening at the same time as things described in the main clause:
The tourists walked along the Thames, **taking** photos of all the famous sights.
In German you can use a main clause *(… und sie machten …)* or a clause with *indem* or *wobei (… wobei sie … machten)*.

c) Das Partizip und der Infinitiv nach Verben der Wahrnehmung und einem Objekt Seite 34–35
The participle and the infinitive after verbs of perception and an object

Verben wie *to feel, to hear, to listen to, to notice, to see* und *to watch* sind Verben der sinnlichen Wahrnehmung.

Participles after verbs of perception and an object

***Present participle:* Ablauf einer Handlung**

Verb of perception		Direct object	Present participle	
We	**watched**	**Marco**	**serving**	his customers for a time.
We	**heard**	**him**	**arguing**	with a young man. (… streiten)
We	**saw**	**the man**	**getting**	angry.

- ▶ Das ***present participle*** nach einem Verb der sinnlichen Wahrnehmung beschreibt eine Handlung, die gerade abläuft. Es wird besonders dann verwendet, wenn der (oder die) Beobachter das Ende der Handlung nicht wahrnimmt.
- ▶ Das ***present participle*** entspricht hier gewöhnlich der ***progressive form:***
  The man was getting angry.
- ▶ Im Deutschen kannst du diese Konstruktion mit einem Infinitiv oder mit einem Nebensatz mit **wie** wiedergeben. (Wir sahen ihn ärgerlich werden. → Wir sahen, **wie** er ärgerlich wurde.)

The infinitive after verbs of perception

Infinitiv: Handlung als Ganzes

Verb of perception		Direct object	Infinitive without *to*
Then we	**heard**	**the man**	**swear** at Marco.
We	**saw**	**him**	**leave** the coffee bar, **get** into his car and **drive** away.

- ▶ Der **Infinitiv** nach Verben der sinnlichen Wahrnehmung drückt aus, dass eine Handlung als Ganzes vom Beginn bis zum Ende wahrgenommen wird.
- ▶ Häufig handelt es sich dabei um Handlungen von kurzer Dauer *(swear)* oder um eine Folge von Handlungen *(… leave …, get … and drive).*
- ▶ Der Infinitiv entspricht hier der ***simple form***: *The man swore.*

ENGLISH SUMMARY

- You can use the **present participle** or the **infinitive without *to*** after **verbs of perception** (to hear, to see, to watch etc.) **+ direct object**.
- The **present participle** describes an action that is continuing. Only part of the action is seen or heard: We watched the boys **playing** football for a time.
- The **infinitive** describes a completed action. This action is often short. The infinitive is also used when one action after another is described:
  Suddenly we heard a boy **shout** and we saw him **fall** from the window. A few minutes later we saw an ambulance **arrive**, and then we saw the paramedics **put** the boy in the ambulance and **drive** away.

G5 Wiederholung: Die Wiedergabe der Zukunft

Seite 36

Revision: Talking about the future

Du kennst schon eine Reihe verschiedener Möglichkeiten, mit denen man auf Englisch die Zukunft wiedergeben kann. Für welche von ihnen du dich entscheidest, hängt davon ab, was du ausdrücken möchtest. Zur Wiederholung sind hier noch einmal die wichtigsten Formen zusammengestellt.

Going to future	
Marco has decided what he wants to do after his GCSEs. **He is going to stay** on at school.And he**'s going to take** some A-levels.	▶ Das ***going to future*** verwendest du, wenn du sagen möchtest, dass jemand vorhat, in der Zukunft etwas zu tun. Es drückt einen **Plan** oder eine **Absicht** aus.
Lucy hasn't seen that bag on the floor. She**'s going to fall over** it. It's raining heavily. **We're going to get** terribly wet.	▶ Mit dem ***going to future*** kannst du ausdrücken, dass etwas sicher eintreten wird, weil es schon **Anzeichen** dafür gibt (z.B. der starke Regen).

Will future	
By the time Naomi has finished school she **will be** 18.	▶ Mit dem ***will future*** drückst du aus, dass etwas **sicher in der Zukunft** geschieht, auf das der Sprecher/die Sprecherin keinen Einfluss hat.
I expect **she'll go on** to university. She**'ll** probably **do** very well.	▶ Das ***will future*** steht auch nach bestimmten Verben wie *to think, to expect, to be sure* und nach Adverbien wie *probably, perhaps* etc. In diesem Fall drückt es eine **Vermutung** aus.
Hey, Zach, this is hard. - OK. **I'll help you** with the exercise. The books are terribly heavy. **Will** you **carry** some of them, please?	▶ Mit dem ***will future*** kannst du **spontane Entscheidungen** ausdrücken, z.B. um jemandem Hilfe anzubieten oder auch selbst um Hilfe zu bitten.
If Pete wants to be a vet, he**'ll have to do** well in his A levels.	▶ In Konditionalsätzen (Typ 1) drückst du mit dem ***will future*** eine **Folge für die Zukunft** aus.

Present progressive

Naomi: What **are** you **doing** this weekend, Pete?
Pete: Well, on Saturday **I'm helping** at the dogs' home. But I'**m not doing** anything special on Sunday.

- Mit dem ***present progressive*** drückst du aus, dass du für die Zukunft etwas **fest geplant** oder **vereinbart** hast.
- Es steht häufig mit Zeitbestimmungen der Zukunft wie *this weekend, on Sunday, tomorrow, next week* etc., damit man nicht glaubt, es gehe um eine Gegenwartshandlung.

Simple present

Marsha: When **does** your interview in Leicester **start**, Jason?
Jason: It **begins** at 10.30.
Marsha: And when **does** your train **leave**?
Jason: It **leaves** Peterborough at 8.54 and **gets** to Leicester at 9.51. So I'll have lots of time.

- Du kannst das ***simple present*** verwenden, wenn es um feste Termine in der Zukunft geht, auf die du selbst keinen Einfluss hast. Meist sind dies genaue Zeitangaben aus **Fahrplänen, Programmen** usw. Deshalb wird diese Verwendung des *simple present* auch als ***timetable future*** bezeichnet.

ENGLISH SUMMARY

You use different forms when talking about the future in English:

- You use the **going to future** when you have a **plan** to do something in the future:
  Naomi is going to do meteorology at university.
- You use the **will future** to talk about **events** in the future that you cannot influence:
  I'll be 18 next year.
- You also use the **will future** when you **ask for help** or **offer to help**:
  It's cold in here. Will you shut the window, please? – Yes, sure. I'll get you a pullover, too.
- You use the **present progressive** when you talk about **arrangements** for the future (often with future adverbials like *tomorrow, next week* etc.):
  I'm playing tennis with Marco tomorrrow.
- You use the **simple present** for **timetable information** in the future (train times, programmes etc.):
  The rock concert starts at 7.30.

!

In German you often use **Präsens** when you talk about future events:

- Morgen spielen wir Tennis.

In English the **simple present** is very rarely used when expressing future events. Normally you use different future forms:

- We'**re going to** play tennis tomorrow. *(That's what we've decided.)*
- We'**re playing** tennis tomorrow. *(I have it in my calendar.)*
- We'**ll play** tennis tomorrow *(if the weather is nice).*

But: The train **leaves** at 10.54 tomorrow. (**timetable future**)

Unit 3

IN THIS UNIT YOU WILL LEARN

- ✓ the difference between *dynamic verbs* and *stative verbs*. G6
- ✓ how to use *emphasis* **(partially Revision).** G7
- ✓ how to talk about the *present* and the *past* and how to use *simple* and *progressive forms* correctly **(Revision).** G8

G6 Tätigkeitsverben und Zustandsverben

Dynamic verbs and stative verbs

Seite 55-56

Im Englischen gibt es zu jeder Zeitform eine ***simple form*** und eine ***progressive form***.
Alle englischen Verben können in der ***simple form*** gebraucht werden.
Die ***progressive form*** kann dagegen nur bei den Verben verwendet werden, die einen Ablauf oder eine Tätigkeit beschreiben. Solche Verben bezeichnet man als ***dynamic verbs***.
Verben, die normalerweise nur in der ***simple form*** stehen, nennt man ***stative verbs***.

a) Dynamic verbs

Simple form	Progressive form
Marco **plays** for the school team almost every week.	He**'s playing** well today, isn't he?
My sister **reads** lots of travel books.	At the moment she**'s reading** a book about Australia.
Everybody **gets** tired after working for hours.	By the time the bell rang for lunch, I **was getting** very tired.

▶ Die ***simple form*** und die ***progressive form*** sind möglich:
→ bei Verben, die eine Tätigkeit beschreiben wie *to play, to read, to eat, to work* etc.

→ bei Verben, die einen Vorgang beschreiben wie *to become, to get, to grow* etc.

b) Stative verbs

Simple form
Have you **noticed** that Naomi has dyed her hair? **I didn't see** her yesterday. I'm glad you've got rid of your awful cold. You **look** much better now. And your voice **sounds** normal again.
How long **have** you **known** him? – I **think** I first met him at Laura's party.

▶ Die ***progressive form*** ist normalerweise nicht möglich:
→ bei Verben, die eine Sinneswahrnehmung beschreiben – wie *to notice, to see, to hear, to sound, to smell, to look* (= aussehen) etc.

→ bei Verben, die Wissen, Vermutungen oder Meinungen ausdrücken – wie *to think, to believe, to know, to mean* (= bedeuten), *to realize, to seem* etc.

Simple form	
Most young people **like** new technology. They **want** to use the most modern equipment.	→ bei Verben, die Vorliebe, Abneigung oder einen Wunsch ausdrücken – wie *to like, to love, to hate, to want, to wish* etc.
That CD **isn't** mine. It **belongs** to Laura.	→ bei Verben, die einen Zustand, Besitz oder eine Zugehörigkeit bezeichnen – wie *to be, to have, to belong* (= gehören) etc.

c) Verben mit statischen und dynamischen Bedeutungen
Verbs that can be used statively and dynamically

Es gibt eine Gruppe von Verben, die im Allgemeinen einen Zustand beschreiben (*stative meaning*). Sie können jedoch auch eine Tätigkeit ausdrücken (*dynamic meaning*). Die folgenden Bedeutungsunterschiede musst du beachten:

Simple form: Zustand *(stative)*	Progressive form: Tätigkeit *(dynamic)*
Their new house **has** three bedrooms. … hat …	We **were having** lunch when he rang. … waren gerade beim Mittagessen … (ebenso: *to have a bath, to have fun, to have a party* etc.)
He **is** often in a bad mood. … hat oft schlechte Laune …	Today he **is being** very critical again. … ist/verhält sich …
Your hair **looks** great. … sieht … aus.	Why **are** you **looking** at me in that funny way? … schaust … an?
What **does** 'multi-tasking' **mean**? … bedeutet …	I**'ve been meaning** to visit them for ages. … habe ... die Absicht …
Marco **loves** football. … liebt … /mag …	He's team captain now. And he**'s loving** every minute of it. … genießt …
I **see** that you like Naomi a lot. Wie ich sehe …	When **are** you **seeing** her again? … triffst du dich … mit ihr?
I **think** History is a very interesting subject. … glaube/denke …	I**'m** even **thinking** of doing it at university. … überlege …, ob …

▶ Manche Verben können sowohl statisch als auch dynamisch verwendet werden. Dadurch ergeben sich Bedeutungsunterschiede. Welche Verben das sind, musst du auswendig lernen.

G7 Hervorhebung
Emphasis

Seite 56

Es gibt im Englischen verschiedene Möglichkeiten, Aussagen hervorzuheben.

a) Die Inversion Inversion

Du weißt, dass die übliche Satzstellung im englischen Aussagesatz **Subjekt – Verb** (oder **Prädikat**) – **Objekt** ist. Nur in wenigen Fällen kann man von dieser Satzstellung abweichen, um Texten eine besonders dramatische Wirkung zu geben.

Adverbiale Bestimmung	Hilfs-verb	Subjekt	Vollverb	Restlicher Satz
Not for a moment	**could**	**I**	**think of**	my grandmother as old-fashioned.
Not only	**does**	**she**	**surf**	the Internet for hours, **but** she also uses the latest mobile to call her friends.
Hardly	**has**	**she**	**finished**	a call **when** she is back at her computer writing e-mails.

- Wenn eine negative oder einschränkende adverbiale Bestimmung (*not only, hardly*) am Satzanfang steht, so werden (wie im Fragesatz) Subjekt und Hilfsverb umgestellt. Diese Umstellung nennt man **Inversion**.
- Ist kein Hilfsverb vorhanden, so wird eine Form von *do* gebraucht. (*Not only does she …*)
- Solche negativen bzw. einschränkenden adverbialen Bestimmungen sind:

hardly had I (… **when**) kaum (… als)	**not only** had I (… **but**) nicht nur (sondern)	**never** had I noch nie, niemals
no sooner had I (… **than**) kaum (… als)	**not for a moment** could I keine Sekunde (lang)	**no way** had I auf keinen Fall
		only then had I erst dann

b) Hervorhebung mit *do* Emphatic *do*

Du weißt, dass du mit ***do/does*** und ***did*** verneinte Sätze bilden und Fragen stellen kannst. ***Do***, ***does*** und ***did*** können aber auch verwendet werden, wenn bejahte Sätze stärker betont werden sollen.

Betonung eines Gegensatzes	
Young people **don't** read books any more. – I think you're wrong there. They **do** still read books. … sie lesen **doch** noch …	Why didn't you do your homework, Darren? – But I **did** do it. I just can't find it anywhere. … habe sie **wirklich/doch** gemacht …

- Mit ***do*/*does*/*did* + *infinitive*** kannst du jemandem widersprechen.
- Diese Sätze folgen häufig auf Verneinungen (*Young people* ***don't*** *read* …).

Verstärkung einer Aufforderung – Ausdruck einer spontanen Gefühlsreaktion	
1. Oh, **do** have another piece of cake, Mrs Robinson.	… nehmen Sie **doch** noch …
2. **Do** hurry up with that exercise – and **do** be quiet over there.	Beeilt euch **doch** … und seid **doch bitte** still …
3. Your hair **does** look nice, Naomi.	… sieht **wirklich** gut aus …
4. I **did** enjoy the party last night. It was fantastic.	… habe mich … **so sehr** amüsiert …

- Mit ***do* + *infinitive*** kannst du Aufforderungssätze verstärken. Diese können je nach Zusammenhang entweder besonders höflich (Beispiel 1) oder besonders ungeduldig (Beispiel 2) klingen.
- Mit ***do/does/did*** kannst du spontane Gefühle ausdrücken (Beispiele 3 und 4).
- In jedem Fall wird die Form von ***do*** stark betont ausgesprochen.
- Im Deutschen entsprechen dieser Konstruktion Adverbien wie **doch**, **wirklich**, **so** (**sehr**), **tatsächlich** oder **ganz**.

c) Hervorhebung mit *it is*/*it was* Emphasis with *it is*/*it* was

	Subject	Verb	Object	Adverbial	Adverbial
Aussagesatz:	Pete	saw	Lucy	at the disco	**on Saturday**.

It was **Pete** who saw Lucy … (and not Marco).
It was **Lucy** that Pete saw … (and not Naomi).
It was **at the disco** that Pete saw Lucy … (and not at the cinema).
It was **on Saturday** that Pete saw Lucy … (and not on Friday).

- Mit ***it is*** oder ***it was*** kannst du jeden Satzteil – außer dem Verb – hervorheben. Die restlichen Satzteile werden mit einem Relativsatz (… *who saw Lucy* …) oder mit einem *that*-Satz angeschlossen (… *that Pete saw Lucy* …).
- Die Singularform ***it is*/*it was*** wird auch dann verwendet, wenn ein Nomen im Plural folgt: ***It is*** *good* ***friends*** *that are most important in life.*
- Meistens werden ***it is*/*it was*** verwendet, wenn etwas richtig gestellt werden soll.

d) *What*-Sätze zur Hervorhebung Emphasis with *what*

What I need now **is** a cup of coffee.
What Laura wrote in her e-mail **was** very interesting.
What Laura did **was (to) send** the newspaper an e-mail.

- Mit ***what*** + einer Form von ***be*** (*is, was*) als Hervorhebung können Dinge klargestellt werden.
- Wenn man das direkte Objekt betonen möchte, steht es nach einer Form von ***be*** (*... is a cup of coffee.*)
- Wenn das Verb betont werden soll, wird es im ersten Teil des Satzes durch eine Form von ***do*** (*What Laura did ...*) vertreten und im zweiten Teil durch einen Infinitv mit oder ohne *to* ausgedrückt (*... was (to) send ...*). (Im Deutschen gibt es diese Konstruktion ebenso, sie ist jedoch weniger häufig: **Was** ich jetzt brauche, ist eine Tasse Kaffee. **Was** sie tat, war einen Leserbrief zu schreiben.)

e) Wiederholung: Hervorhebung durch Pronomen auf *-self/-selves*
Revision: Emphasis with *self*-pronouns

Du kennst schon die Pronomen auf ***-self/-selves*** und weißt, dass sie sowohl reflexiv (*I can't see **myself** in the photo.*) wie auch verstärkend (*I'm going to do it **myself**.*) verwendet werden können.

Perhaps Mr Brown doesn't use any new technology **himself**.
But scientists **themselves** say that modern technology lets you develop your brain power.

- Mit den Pronomen auf ***-self/-selves*** kannst du betonen, dass jemand etwas selbst tut. In diesem Fall sprichst du das Pronomen stark betont aus.

f) Wiederholung: Hervorhebung durch Gradadverbien
Revision: Emphasis through adverbs of degree

Wie du schon weißt, können Gradadverbien (*adverbs of degree*) ein anderes Wort im Satz (ein Adjektiv, ein Verb oder ein Adverb) hervorheben.

I was **extremely shocked** when I read Mr Brown's letter.
Does he **really believe** that young people are like that?
I think he sees modern technology and young people **much too negatively**.

- Zu den Gradadverbien gehören: ***extremely, really, (much) too, completely, only, very, terribly, even*** und ***quite***. Sie verstärken das Wort, vor dem sie stehen.

ENGLISH SUMMARY

- There are two types of verbs in English – **dynamic verbs** and **stative verbs**.
- **Dynamic verbs** (*play, swim, eat* etc.) describe an activity and can be used in the simple and also in the progressive form:
  → Lucy always **swims** a lot in the summer. Look, she**'s swimming** over there now.
- **Stative verbs** (*have, own, love* etc.) describe a state and can normally only be used in the simple form: The royal family **has owned** Buckingham Palace since 1762.
- There are a number of stative verbs that can also express a dynamic meaning and can be used in the progressive form: We**'re having** a really good time. I**'m loving** every minute of it.
- You can **stress sentence parts** in a number of ways:
  → **Inversion: Hardly** **had the people seen** the Queen when she waved goodbye.
  → **Emphatic *do*: Do sit** down.
  → ***It is/it was***: And **it is** England that has scored!
  → ***What*: What** we are all looking forward to is the holidays.
  → ***Self*-pronouns:** It was the King **himself** who opened the new theatre.
  → **Adverbs of degree:** It is **really** amazing that there aren't more bike accidents.

G 8 Wiederholung: Gegenwarts- und Vergangenheitsformen

Revision: Talking about the present and the past

Seite 57

Du kennst jetzt alle Zeitformen des Englischen. Hier zur Wiederholung noch einmal die wichtigsten Regeln zum Gebrauch des ***present tense***, des ***past tense***, des ***present perfect*** und des ***past perfect***. Sie haben alle eine ***simple form*** und eine ***progressive form***.

a) Simple present, present progressive

Simple present	
Marco **goes** to school in Peterborough. He sometimes **works** in his parents' coffee bar.	▶ Das ***simple present*** drückt aus, dass jemand etwas regelmäßig, häufig oder nie tut. ▶ Häufig handelt es sich hierbei um Hobbys oder berufliche Tätigkeiten (*Marco goes to school.* = *Marco is a pupil.*). ▶ Sätze mit dem ***simple present*** enthalten oft die Signalwörter *every day, always, often, sometimes, never, regularly* etc.
Kangaroos **live** in Australia and in Tasmania. Wet wood **doesn't burn** well.	▶ Das ***simple present*** beschreibt allgemein gültige Tatsachen, z.B. Naturgesetze, typische Fähigkeiten und Eigenschaften.
In 'Romeo and Juliet' Romeo **meets** Juliet at a party. They **fall** in love at once. But they **find** it difficult to meet because their families are enemies.	▶ Mit dem ***simple present*** kann man Handlungsabfolgen beschreiben und Zusammenfassungen und Inhaltsangaben verfassen. (Zur Verwendung des ***simple present*** als *timetable future* vgl. G 5)

Present progressive	
Smile, please. I'**m taking** a photo of you! My sister **is watching** something on TV at the moment.	▶ Das ***present progressive*** beschreibt Handlungen, die im Moment des Sprechens gerade ablaufen und noch nicht beendet sind. ▶ Typische Signalwörter sind: *at the moment, just now, right now* etc.
Our school team **is doing** very well this year. Marco **is training** a lot these days.	▶ Mit dem ***present progressive*** kann man auch Handlungen beschreiben, die über einen längeren Zeitraum ablaufen (*this year, these days*). (Zur Verwendung des ***present progressive*** zur Beschreibung von zukünftigen Ereignissen vgl. G5)

b) Present perfect, simple past, past perfect

Es gibt im Englischen drei Zeitformen, die sich auf die Vergangenheit beziehen: ***present perfect***, ***simple past*** und ***past perfect***.

Present perfect	
I'**ve** *already* **seen** the film. So I know how it ends.	▶ Das ***present perfect*** drückt eine vergangene Handlung aus, die eine spürbare Auswirkung in der Gegenwart hat. Signalwörter: *already, just.*
We **haven't had** the results of the test *yet*. **Have** you *ever* been to Australia?	▶ Es wird auch verwendet, um auszudrücken, dass etwas bisher noch nicht geschehen ist bzw. um zu fragen, ob etwas bisher schon einmal geschehen ist. Signalwörter: *(not) yet, ever, never, so far.*

Present perfect progressive	
You'**ve been watching** TV *for hours*. I'**ve been working** hard *since* I got up this morning.	▶ Das ***present perfect progressive*** beschreibt eine Handlung, die in der Vergangenheit angefangen hat und noch nicht beendet ist. Hierbei wird die Dauer des Vorgangs betont. ▶ ***For*** bezieht sich auf den Zeitraum, den eine Handlung andauert (*for hours*). ▶ ***Since*** bezieht sich auf den Zeitpunkt, an dem die Handlung begann (*since I got up*).

Simple past	
We **read** 'Romeo and Juliet' at school last year.	▶ Das ***simple past*** drückt aus, dass ein Ereignis in der Vergangenheit stattfand und vorbei ist. Signalwörter: *last year, yesterday, when, a few years ago, in 1595* etc.
I **didn't** like it at first because I **thought** it **was** so difficult. But then I **watched** it on DVD and at last I **understood** the story.	▶ Es wird auch verwendet, um eine Abfolge von Ereignissen in der Vergangenheit wiederzugeben und ist daher die typische Zeitform für Berichte und Erzählungen.

Past progressive	
I called Naomi last night. She didn't answer the phone because she **was having** a bath.	▶ Das ***past progressive*** drückt aus, dass etwas zu einem bestimmten Zeitpunkt in der Vergangenheit stattfand und noch nicht abgeschlossen war.
We **were** just **getting** ready to go when it started to rain.	▶ Häufig wird das ***past progressive*** verwendet, um zu betonen, dass ein Vorgang noch andauerte, während sich etwas Neues ereignete. In diesem Fall steht das neue Ereignis im ***simple past*** (*started to rain*).
I **was preparing** lunch while my brother **was playing** computer games and my sister **was practising** for the school concert.	▶ Es wird auch verwendet, um auszudrücken dass mehrere Handlungen in der Vergangenheit gleichzeitig abliefen. Solche gleichzeitig ablaufenden Handlungen werden oft durch Nebensätze mit *while* miteinander verbunden.

Past perfect	
After we **had visited** our relations in Sydney, we flew back home. We **had been** to the Great Barrier Reef before we went to Sydney.	▶ Das ***past perfect*** wird verwendet, um zu betonen, dass ein Ereignis in der Vergangenheit im Vergleich zu einem anderen noch früher stattgefunden hat (Vorzeitigkeit). Daher steht es praktisch immer in der Nähe von Formen des simple past (*flew, went*).

Past perfect progressive	
Darren **had been reading** 'Walkabout' *for three hours* when his girlfriend rang and asked him to go surfing with her. They**'d** only **been surfing** *for a few minutes* when they suddenly saw a shark.	▶ Das ***past perfect progressive*** drückt aus, dass eine Handlung schon andauerte, bevor sich eine andere Handlung in der Vergangenheit ereignete (*rang ... asked, saw*). ▶ Zeitangaben mit *for* und *since* geben Dauer und Ablauf der Handlung an.

ENGLISH SUMMARY

R: Simple present, present progressive

- You use the **simple present** when you talk about things that happen **regularly** or when you talk about **facts**: → I **don't often** help my parents in the kitchen. Lots of people **like** a cup of tea in the afternoon.
  It is often used with adverbs like *often*, *regularly*, *never* etc.
- You use the **present progressive** to describe something that is happening **at the moment**: → Don't move. I**'m taking** a picture of you.

ENGLISH SUMMARY

R: Present perfect, simple past, past perfect

- The **present perfect** stresses the **result** of an activity. It is often used with *already, (not) yet, so far* etc.: → I'**ve mended** the garden gate. It's OK now.
- The **present perfect progressive** describes an activity that began in the past and has continued until now: → It **has been raining** for days now. It is often used with *for* and *since*. ***For*** is used for a **period of time** (*for days*); ***since*** is used for a **point in time** (*since three o'clock*).
- You use the **simple past** when you want to say that something happened in the past and is **over**. It is often used with *ago, yesterday, when, in 2007* etc.: → I **didn't go** to school yesterday because I felt sick.
- The **past progressive** describes an activity that **was happening** in the past. It is often used with *while*: → While we **were watching** the news, our TV suddenly stopped working.
- The **past perfect** describes an activity that happened **before** another activity in the past: → After she **had bought** the book, she started reading it at once.
- The **past perfect progressive** describes an activity that was **in progress before** another activity in the past happened: → She **had been reading** for only a few minutes when she fell asleep.

Unit 4

IN THIS UNIT YOU WILL LEARN

- ✓ how to use the *gerund* in different ways **(Revision)**. G9
- ✓ how to use the *gerund* after prepositions like *without, by, instead of* etc. G10
- ✓ how to use the *infinitive* with *to* and the *infinitive* without *to* **(Revision)**. G11 G14
- ✓ how to use the *infinitive* after ***for*** + a noun or a pronoun. G12
- ✓ that a number of verbs can be followed by a gerund or an infinitive **(Revision)**. G13
- ✓ how to use *modal auxiliaries* and their substitutes **(Revision)**. G15
- ✓ how to use indirect speech **(Revision)**. G16

G9 Wiederholung: Das *gerund* Revision: The gerund

Seite 70–71

Du kennst schon die meisten Funktionen und Verwendungsmöglichkeiten des *gerund*. Diese Zusammenstellung gibt dir noch einmal einen Überblick.

The gerund	
Fighting for one's rights **isn't** always easy. (Das) Kämpfen … ist nicht …	▶ Das ***gerund*** kann wie ein Nomen **Subjekt** des Satzes sein.
People in democratic countries can't **imagine living** without basic rights and freedoms. … können sich nicht vorstellen, ohne … zu leben.	▶ Das ***gerund*** steht häufig als **Objekt** nach bestimmten Verben wie *to enjoy, to finish, to imagine, to keep, (not) to mind, to suggest* etc.
My friends always **talk about organizing** a protest march. But so far they haven't done anything. … sprechen immer darüber, … zu organisieren. …	▶ Das ***gerund*** steht nach **Verben mit Präpositionen**. Zu ihnen gehören *to dream of, to feel like, to look forward to, to talk about, to think of* etc.
Perhaps they are **afraid of getting** into trouble at school. … haben sie Angst, Schwierigkeiten … zu bekommen.	▶ Eine Reihe von Verbindungen aus **Adjektiv + Präposition** werden mit dem ***gerund*** gebraucht. Dazu gehören: *to be afraid of, to be famous for, to be good/bad at, to be interested in, to be keen on, to be/ get used to* etc.
Most people think that the **idea of living** in an authoritarian society is awful. Für die meisten Leute ist die Vorstellung, in … zu leben, …	▶ Zu den Verbindungen von **Nomen + Präposition**, denen ein ***gerund*** folgt, gehören *a/the chance of, in danger of, an/the idea of, practice in, a/the way of.*

G10 Präpositionen + *gerunds* als adverbiale Bestimmung

Prepositions + gerunds as adverbials

Seite 70–71

In spite of living in luxury, some people still aren't happy.	Obwohl sie im Luxus leben, …
They should enjoy their lives **instead of worrying** all the time.	Anstatt sich … Sorgen zu machen, …
We hear about child labour and slavery **without realising** it exists in our country, too.	… ohne dass wir uns bewusst sind, dass …

- Zusammen mit den Präpositionen *apart from, by, in spite of, instead of* und *without* kann das ***gerund*** Teil einer adverbialen Bestimmung sein. (*In spite of living in luxury, ... = Although they live in luxury, ...*)
- Im Deutschen werden **Präposition + *gerund*** durch einen adverbialen Nebensatz (**Obwohl** sie im Luxus leben, ...) oder eine Infinitivkonstruktion (Anstatt sich Sorgen **zu machen** ...) wiedergegeben.

G11 Wiederholung: Der Infinitiv mit *to*

Revision: The infinitive with *to*

Seite 70–71

Die meisten Verwendungsmöglichkeiten des Infinitivs sind dir schon bekannt. Die folgende Zusammenschau soll dir zur Erinnerung dienen.

We've **decided to do** a project on child labour. ... haben uns entschlossen, ... zu machen.	Nach **Verben** wie *to decide, to expect, to want* und *to wish* beschreibt der Infinitiv etwas, das noch geschehen soll.
Our teacher **wants us to collect** as much material as possible. ... möchte, dass wir ... sammeln.	Nach *to allow, to expect, to want, to wish, would like* etc. kann ein **direktes Objekt** (*us*) **zwischen Verb und Infinitiv** stehen.
It isn't **difficult to find** enough information. ... nicht schwierig, ... zu finden.	Der Infinitiv kann nach **Adjektiven** stehen.
At first we didn't know **how to start**. ... , wie wir anfangen sollten.	Nach den **Fragewörtern** *how, what, which, who, when, where* und *whether* kann der Infinitiv verwendet werden.
Of course we aren't the **only ones to do** a project like that. ... die einzigen, die ein Projekt ... machen.	Der Infinitiv kann nach *the first, the last* und *the only one/person* gebraucht werden.
We have the **chance to present** our project to the whole school. ... die Möglichkeit/Gelegenheit, unser Projekt ... zu präsentieren.	Nach **Nomen** wie *chance, decision, freedom, plan, wish* etc. kann der Infinitiv stehen. (Nach *chance of* folgt jedoch ein ***gerund***: *We had no **chance of winning** the game.* = Wir hatten keine **Chance**, das Spiel zu gewinnen.)

!

If you want to express „Ich möchte, dass ..." or „Ich will, dass ..." in English, you must use an infinitive:

Unser Lehrer **möchte/will, dass** wir als Team arbeiten. → Our teacher **wants us to work** as a team.

Ich **möchte, dass** ihr bis zum Wochenende fertig seid. → I'd **like you to finish** by the weekend.

Do not use *that* after *want* or *would like*.

G12 Die Infinitivkonstruktion mit *to* nach *for* + (Pro)Nomen

Seite 70, 72

The infinitive with *to* after *for* + (pro)noun

	Adjective/ Noun	For + Noun/ Pronoun	Infinitive with *to*	
It is	**difficult**	**for children**	**to imagine**	what adult life is like.
It is	**important**	**for them**	**to grow up**	in a safe environment.
It is often a	**problem**	**for young people**	**to find**	the right job.
But there is no	**need**	**for us**	**to worry**	about that yet.

- Der Infinitiv mit *to* steht häufig nach *it is/ it was* + Adjektiv + *for* + Nomen oder Pronomen.
- Der Infinitiv mit *to* kann auch nach Nomen + *for* + Nomen/Pronomen stehen.
- Im Deutschen wird für diese Konstruktion häufig ein dass-Satz verwendet:

It isn't **unusual for teenagers to have** different opinions from their parents. →
Es ist nicht ungewöhnlich, dass Teenager andere Meinungen als ihre Eltern haben.

G13 Wiederholung: Gerund oder Infinitiv?

Seite 72

Revision: Gerund or infinitive?

Wie du schon weißt, gibt es manche Verben, die man sowohl mit dem ***gerund*** als auch mit dem **Infinitiv** verwenden kann. Bei einigen gibt es keinen Bedeutungsunterschied, bei anderen ändert sich die Bedeutung. Die folgende Übersicht stellt noch einmal das Wichtigste zusammen.

a) Infinitive = gerund

Seite 72

Verb + infinitive	Verb + gerund
We**'ve started to collect** material for our human rights project.	I**'ve started cutting** pictures out of magazines.

- Du kannst eine große Anzahl von Verben sowohl mit dem **Infinitiv** als auch mit dem ***gerund*** verwenden. Es gibt praktisch keinen Bedeutungsunterschied.
  Zu diesen Verben gehören: *to begin, to continue, to start, to like, to love, to hate* und *to prefer.* (Zu den Verben, die nur mit dem ***gerund*** gebraucht werden, vgl. G9 .)

b) Infinitive ≠ gerund

Seite 72

Verb + infinitive	Verb + gerund
I **mean to do** what I can for peace in the world. Ich **habe die Absicht/habe vor**, … zu tun.	That **means fighting** for human rights and **taking part** in the big protest march here. Das **bedeutet,** dass ich … kämpfen … teilnehmen muss.
Let's **stop to think** what values are important for us. Lass uns mal anhalten, **um** darüber **nachzudenken,** …	I'm afraid that some people **stopped thinking** about human rights long ago. Ich fürchte, manche Leute haben … **aufgehört**, über Menschenrechte **nachzudenken**.
I must **remember to send** some money to Amnesty International this year. Ich muss daran denken, … **zu schicken.**	I can't **remember sending** them any money last year. Ich kann mich nicht daran erinnern, … **geschickt zu haben.**
I mustn't **forget to show** you the photos we took of the protest march. Ich darf nicht vergessen, euch … **zu zeigen**.	I'll never **forget seeing** all those people who took part. Ich werde nie vergessen, wie ich … **gesehen habe**, …

- Der **Infinitiv** nach *to mean, to stop, to remember* und *to forget* weist auf eine Handlung hin, die beabsichtigt ist und noch bevorsteht.
- Das ***gerund*** nach *to remember* und *to forget* beschreibt dagegen eine Handlung, die schon stattgefunden hat.
- Das ***gerund*** nach *to mean* bezeichnet eine logische Folge.

ENGLISH SUMMARY

The use of the gerund

- **R:** You can use the **gerund**
  - → as the subject of a sentence: **Swimming** is fun.
  - → after certain verbs: I **enjoy swimming** very much.
  - → after verbs + prepositions: We'**re looking forward to going** to Australia.
  - → after certain adjectives + prepositions: In the 18th and 19th centuries people were still **used to seeing** slavery.
- The **gerund** can also be used **after prepositions** like **by**, **in spite of**, **without** etc.: I can't really judge this **without knowing** all the facts.

ENGLISH SUMMARY

The infinitive with *to*

- **R:** You can use the **infinitive with *to***
  - → after certain verbs: He **expected to do** well in the test.
  - → after certain verbs + direct object: I **would like you to finish** the job by the weekend.
  - → after adjectives: It's **nice to see** you again.
  - → after question words: They didn't know **what to do**.
  - → after **the first**, **the last**, **the only one/ones**: The Americans were **the first to land** on the moon.
  - → after certain nouns: A hundred years ago women didn't have the **right to vote**.
- **R: infinitive or gerund?**

There are a number of verbs that can be followed by an **infinitive** or a **gerund**:

- After **to like**, **to love**, **to hate**, **to prefer**, **to begin**, **to continue** and **to start** you can use an **infinitive** or a **gerund** **without any difference** in meaning: She **started to ski** when she was five. → She **started skiing** when she was five.
- There is a **difference in meaning** between the **infinitive** and the **gerund** after **to mean**, **to stop**, **to forget** and **to remember**.

G14 Wiederholung: Der Infinitiv mit *to* und ohne *to*

Seite 74–75

Revision: The infinitive with *to* and without *to*

Nachdem du in G11 und G12 die Funktionen des Infinitivs mit *to* wiederholt hast, werden hier noch einmal die Verwendungsmöglichkeiten des Infinitivs mit *to* und ohne *to* gegenübergestellt.

Infinitive with *to*	Infinitive without *to*
after certain verbs: I **would like to go** to university.	**after modal auxiliaries**: **Can** you **see** Elizabeth in the picture?
after certain verbs + direct object: My parents **want me to get** a good education.	**after *let* and *make*:** Before 1954, white people in the South **didn't let black students attend** 'white' schools. They **made them go** to all-black schools.
after adjectives: It's **difficult for us to understand** what racial segregation meant.	**after verbs of perception + direct object:** Josh **saw the black students start** their walk to the school and **heard someone** behind him **shout** a nasty word.
after certain nouns: Everybody should have the **chance to go** to the school they choose.	
after *the first/the last/the only one/ones*: Elizabeth Eckford was **not the only black student to try** to get into an all-white school.	
after question words: I really don't know **what to do** after I've finished school.	

G15 Wiederholung: Die modalen Hilfsverben und ihre Ersatzverben

Seite 76

Revision: Modal auxiliaries and their substitutes

Du kennst die modalen Hilfsverben und weißt, wie sie verwendet werden. Die am häufigsten verwendeten modalen Hilfsverben sind *can* und *must*. *May* und *must* können nur im ***simple present*** verwendet werden, *can* hat noch die ***simple past***-Form *could*. Für alle anderen Zeiten musst du die Ersatzverben *to be able to*, *to be allowed to* oder *to have to* gebrauchen.

Modal auxiliaries			Substitutes	How to use them
can können	↔ ↔	**can't/cannot** nicht können	**to be able to**	I **can** speak English, but I **can't** speak Spanish. When we were in Spain last year I **couldn't** understand very much. I **wasn't** even **able to** order things in a restaurant. But next year I'm going to Australia. I'**ll be able** to talk to everybody there.
can/may dürfen	↔ ↔	**can't/ may not/ mustn't** nicht dürfen	**to be allowed to**	**May** we bring the dog in here? – No, I'm afraid you **can't**. Sorry, but you **mustn't** bring him in. When pets **were allowed** to come into the restaurant, lots of guests didn't like it. And I don't think you'**ll be allowed** to take him into any other restaurant in town.
must müssen	↔ ↔	**needn't** nicht müssen/ nicht brauchen	**to have to**	I really **must** start on that human rights text now. I still **have to** do some reading first. Luckily I **needn't** write more than four pages. Last week I **had to** do a lot of work. This week I'll **have to** do some revision, too.

!

Be careful with **must**, **mustn't** and **needn't.**

Ich **muss** das tun. → I **must** do that.
Ich **darf** das **nicht** tun. → I **mustn't** do that.
Ich **brauche** das **nicht** zu tun. → I **needn't** do that.

Must wird benutzt, wenn man etwas besonders betonen will. **Have to** in Aussagesätzen ist aber gebräuchlicher.

G16 Wiederholung: Die indirekte Rede

Seite 76

Revision: Indirect speech

Du kennst schon die indirekte Rede im Englischen und weißt, dass sich die Zeiten gegenüber denen in der direkten Rede ändern, wenn das einführende Verb in der **Vergangenheit** steht *(He **told** me… They **said**…)*.
Hier sind noch einmal die wichtigsten Regeln in einer Übersicht zusammengefasst.

Achte in dieser Übersicht neben der Verschiebung der Zeiten auch auf
- die Veränderung der Pronomen *(you → I, your → my* etc.*)*.
- die Veränderung von Zeit- und Ortsangaben *(here → there, last week → the week before)*.

Direct speech	Indirect speech
"We **like** the way you **walk** and **wear** your clothes." present tense →	The manager told me that they **liked** the way I **walked** and **wore** my clothes. past tense
"We'**ve been looking** for someone like you." present perfect →	He said they **had been looking** for someone like me. past perfect
"We **had** a very nice student here, but he **left** us last week." past tense →	He said that they **had had** a very nice student there, but that he **had left** them the week before. past perfect
"We'**ll pay** you 10 pounds an hour." will →	He told me that they **would** pay me 10 pounds an hour. would
"When **can** you start?" question word →	He wanted to know when I **could** start. question word
"Do you live in the city?" no question word →	He asked me **whether** I lived in the city. *whether* or *if*
"**Try** to get here as early as possible." "And **don't believe** the stories you've heard about us." command →	He told me **to get** there as early as possible. And he told me **not to believe** the stories I had heard about them. infinitive with *to*/*not to*

!

In modern English the shift of tenses in indirect speech is used less and less. People often don't change the tenses when they report what someone said.

"We'll pay you 10 pounds an hour."

Instead of hearing this …
→ The manager said they would pay me 10 pounds an hour.
… you might hear this:
→ The manager said they'll pay me 10 pounds an hour.

ENGLISH SUMMARY

R: The infinitive without *to*

- You can use the infinitive without *to* after
  - → modal auxiliaries: **Can** I **call** you this afternoon?
  - → after *let* and *make* + direct object: Our English teacher **makes us do** a lot of homework. But at least she **lets us use** dictionaries in tests.
  - → after verbs of perception + direct object: Didn't you **hear the doorbell ring** just now?

R: Modal auxiliaries and their substitutes

- **Can**, **may**, **must** and **needn't** are modal auxiliaries. **May**, **must** and **needn't** can only be used in the present tense; **can** has the past tense form **could**. For all the other tenses you must use substitutes:

→ **to be able to** for **can**:	Sorry, I **wasn't able to** do my homework yesterday.
→ **be allowed to** for **may** and **can**:	I don't think I'**ll be allowed to** sit next to Pete in the test tomorrow.
→ **to have to** for **must**:	We **didn't have to** copy the exercise, did we?

R: Indirect speech

- When direct speech is turned into indirect speech with a reporting verb in the simple past (He said that … She asked whether …), all the tenses are shifted one tense further back into the past (present → past, present perfect → past perfect, will → would etc.) "I'**ll come** on Friday." → My mother said that she **would come** on Friday.
- If you report questions with a question word , you use *ask/want to know* + question word: **When** does the concert start? → Josh wanted to know **when** the concert started.
- The personal pronouns and the adverbs of time and place must also be changed.

Vocabulary

Im ***Vocabulary*** sind die Vokabeln dieses Bandes in der Reihenfolge ihres Vorkommens aufgelistet und erklärt. In der linken Spalte stehen die englischen Wörter und Sätze sowie die Lautschrift. In der Mitte ist die deutsche Übersetzung aufgeführt. Die rechte Spalte enthält Beispiel- oder Erklärungssätze und Hinweise auf Besonderheiten sowie Verweise auf verwandte Wörter in Französisch oder Latein.

Die **fett** gedruckten Wörter gehören zum Lernwortschatz, du musst sie verstehen und anwenden können. Normal gedruckte Wörter sind nur zum Verständnis bestimmter Texte und Übungen nötig. Wenn darunter Wörter sind, die du für besonders interessant und nützlich hältst, kannst du sie in dein ***Personal vocabulary*** übertragen.

Neu in diesem Band sind folgende Elemente:
Zu Beginn jeder Unit gibt eine **Landeskunde-Box** interessante Hintergrundinformationen zum Thema der Unit.
Die ***Vocabulary skills*** enthalten neben nützlichen Lerntipps kleine Übungen, so dass du den Tipp gleich anhand des gelernten Wortschatzes umsetzen kannst. Auch sonst findest du hin und wieder solche Übungen zum gelernten Wortschatz.
In ***Linking old and new vocabulary*** wird bereits bekanntes und neues Vokabular zum Thema übersichtlich zusammengefasst. So kannst du den Wortschatz zu einem bestimmten Thema gezielt wiederholen und erweitern.
An das ***Vocabulary*** schließt sich ab Seite 175 das alphabetische ***Dictionary*** an, in dem du die Wörter aller Bände nachschlagen kannst.

Abkürzungen und Zeichen

pl	*plural*	*coll*	*colloquial* (= ugs.)	***n***	neutrum
sing	*singular*	*ugs.*	umgangssprachlich	*Fr.*	Französisch
sth	*something*	*vulg*	*vulgar* (= ordinär; derb)	*Lat.*	Latein
sb	*somebody*	jmdm.	jemandem	5	In dieser Übung kommen die Wörter vor.
adj	*adjective*	jmdn.	jemanden	!	Achtung!
AE	*American English*	etw.	etwas	↔	ist das Gegenteil von
BE	*British English*	***f***	feminin	→	ist verwandt mit
e.g.	*for example* (= z. B.)	***m***	maskulin	=	entspricht

Englische Laute

Konsonanten

[ŋ]	morning
[r]	red
[s]	this
[z]	is
[ʒ]	television
[dʒ]	page
[ʃ]	she
[tʃ]	chair
[ð]	the
[θ]	thanks
[v]	video
[w]	wow, one

Vokale

[ɑː]	father
[ʌ]	but
[e]	pen
[ə]	a sister
[ɜː]	girl
[æ]	flat
[ɪ]	it
[i]	happy
[iː]	teacher, she
[ɒ]	got
[ɔː]	ball
[ʊ]	book
[u]	January
[uː]	too, two

Doppellaute

[aɪ]	I, my
[aʊ]	now, house
[eə]	there, pair
[eɪ]	name, they
[ɪə]	here, idea
[ɔɪ]	boy
[əʊ]	hello
[ʊə]	sure

Zusätzliche Zeichen

[ˈ]	Hauptakzent auf der nachfolgenden Silbe
[ˌ]	Nebenakzent auf der nachfolgenden Silbe
[‿]	Bindebogen zwischen zwei Wörtern

Alle anderen Zeichen werden genauso ausgesprochen, wie sie geschrieben werden, z. B. [b], [j], [l] usw.

Zoom-in: The world speaks English

order ['ɔ:də]	Bestellung →	*order* → to order
to **record** [rɪ'kɔ:d]	aufnehmen; aufzeichnen →	Musical artists *record* their songs in studios.
banker ['bæŋkə]	Banker, Bankier →	When people think of Manhattan's Wall Street, they think of *bankers*.
to **call in** [kɔ:l‿'ɪn]	bei laufender Sendung/ während einer Sendung anrufen →	Don't you love it when people *call in* with really strange stories on radio shows?
by [baɪ]	um →	The world population has grown *by* about 12 per cent over the last ten years.
foreign ['fɒrɪn]	ausländisch; fremd →	*foreign* = not from your own country
regulation [ˌregjə'leɪʃn]	Regelung; Regulierung; Vorschrift →	Some people say languages need *regulation*, e.g. not to allow too many foreign words.
to **break up** [breɪk‿'ʌp]	(sich) auflösen; auseinandergehen →	The British Empire really started to *break up* after World War II, when more and more British colonies became independent.
influence ['ɪnfluəns]	Einfluss →	How people behave has a big *influence* on whether you like them or not.
superpower ['su:pəˌpaʊə]	Supermacht →	Will China and India be the next *superpowers*?
pop culture ['pɒp ˌkʌltʃə]	Popkultur →	*pop culture* → pop music, pop star
status ['steɪtəs]	Status →	English enjoys the *status* as the main language of pop culture in the world.
to **lead**, **led**, **led** [li:d, led, led]	führen →	The US plays a *leading* role in science and technology.
to **dominate** ['dɒmɪneɪt]	dominieren; jmdn./etw. beherrschen →	Business *is dominated* by English words. = English words play a very big role in business.
to **take a tour** [ˌteɪk‿ə 'tʊə]	sich auf eine Rundreise begeben →	*to take a tour* = to go on a trip
sq. *(= square)* [skweə]	Quadrat *(Flächeneinheit)* →	The area of Canada is 9.9 million *sq.* km.
Namáste! [nʌ'mʌsteɪ]	Guten Tag. *(Begrüßung in Indien)* →	In India, when people greet each other they put both hands together and say *Namáste*.
democracy [dɪ'mɒkrəsi]	Demokratie →	! Watch the spelling and the pronunciation
Indian ['ɪndiən]	Inder/-in; indisch →	People from India are *Indians*.
dialect ['daɪəlekt]	Dialekt →	Both India and Britain are countries with many regional *dialects*.
Hindi ['hɪndi:]	Hindi →	'Pyjama', 'caravan' and 'guru' are all *Hindi* words which have become part of the English language.
possibility [ˌpɒsə'bɪləti]	Möglichkeit →	*possibility* → possible
change [tʃeɪndʒ]	(Ver)Änderung →	*change* → to change
poverty ['pɒvəti]	Armut →	*poverty* → the poor → poor
survey ['sɜ:veɪ]	Umfrage; Studie →	With a *survey* you can find out about people's opinions, how they behave, etc.
dish [dɪʃ]	Gericht →	Many Britons love Indian food. Their favourite Indian *dish* is chicken tikka masala.
Bollywood ['bɒliwʊd]	Bollywood *(indische Filmindustrie: Bombay + Hollywood)* →	*Bollywood* films are best known for their love stories and their colourful song-and-dance scenes.
independence [ˌɪndɪ'pendəns]	Unabhängigkeit →	*independence* → independent
forest ['fɒrɪst]	Wald →	It would be hard to imagine Canada without all its *forests*.
tundra ['tʌndrə]	Tundra →	! Watch the pronunciation

monarch ['mɒnək]	Monarch/-in →	*monarchs* = kings and queens
portrait ['pɔ:trɪt]	Portrait; Konterfei →	! Watch the pronunciation
Canadian [kə'neɪdiən]	Kanadier/-in; kanadisch →	*Canadians* = people from Canada
reminder [rɪ'maɪndə]	Erinnerung; Mahnung →	*reminder* → to remind (about)
head of state [ˌhed‿əv 'steɪt]	Staatsoberhaupt →	The *head of state* of a country can be a president, a monarch, etc.
Howzit! ['haʊzɪt]	Hallo. *(Begrüßung in Südafrika)* →	*Howzit!* = Hello!
election [ɪ'lekʃn]	Wahl →	*election* → to elect
civil rights [ˌsɪvl 'raɪts]	Bürgerrechte	
leader ['li:də]	Führer/-in, Anführer/-in →	*leader* → to lead
president ['prezɪdnt]	Präsident/-in →	! Watch the pronunciation
figure ['fɪgə]	Persönlichkeit; Gestalt →	Are there any important *figures* in world history you'd like to read about?
racist ['reɪsɪst]	rassistisch; Rassist/-in →	Before 1994, South Africa was a *racist* country; people who weren't white didn't enjoy full civil rights.
apartheid [ə'pɑ:taɪt]	Apartheid →	The South African *apartheid* system ended with the first free elections in 1994.
separateness ['seprətnəs]	Getrenntheit; Isolation	
system ['sɪstəm]	System →	! Watch the pronunciation
minority [maɪ'nɒrəti]	Minderheit →	Before 1994, a rich white *minority* was in control of a country which was mostly non-white.
police state [pə'li:s ˌsteɪt]	Polizeistaat →	In a *police state*, nobody can ever really feel free.
society [sə'saɪəti]	Gesellschaft →	*society* → social
wealth [welθ]	Wohlstand; Reichtum →	*wealth* ↔ poverty
black (person) [blæk]	Schwarze/-r	
crowded ['kraʊdɪd]	überfüllt →	*crowded* → crowd
township ['taʊnʃɪp]	Township *(von Schwarzen und Farbigen bewohnte, abseits der Städte gelegene Siedlungen in Südafrika)* →	South Africa's best-known *township* is Soweto (= South Western Townships) in Johannesburg.
middle class [ˌmɪdl 'klɑ:s]	Mittelschicht →	During apartheid, there was no black *middle class* in South Africa. There is one now, although it is still quite small.
G'day! *(= Good day!)* [gə'daɪ]	Guten Tag./Hallo./Hi. *(Begrüßung in Australien)* →	This is how Australians say hello.
endlessness ['endləsnəs]	Weite; Unendlichkeit →	Visitors from crowded places like Europe often like the *endlessness* of the landscape in countries like Australia or Canada.
outback ['aʊtbæk]	Outback *(australisches Hinterland)* →	The *outback* is the wild, empty country away from Australia's towns and cities.
rainforest ['reɪnˌfɒrɪst]	Regenwald →	The world's *rainforests* are important for our climate.
settlement ['setlmənt]	Siedlung →	*settlement* → settler
Aussie *(coll)* ['ɒzi]	Australier/-in; australisch *(ugs.)* →	*Aussie* = Australian
indigenous [ɪn'dɪdʒɪnəs]	einheimisch →	The Native Americans are the *indigenous* population of the USA.
Aboriginal [ˌæbə'rɪdʒnl]	Aborigine, Ureinwohner/-in Australiens →	The *Aboriginals* are the indigenous population of Australia.

continent ['kɒntɪnənt]	Kontinent, Erdteil →	❗ Watch the pronunciation region – country – *continent*
unique [ju:'ni:k]	einzigartig →	When something is *unique* there is nothing else like it.
systematic [ˌsɪstə'mætɪk]	systematisch; gezielt →	*systematic* → system
forced [fɔ:st]	erzwungen	
relocation [ˌri:lə'keɪʃn]	Umsiedlung →	*Relocation* means that people are moved from one place to another.
to **tear apart, tore apart, torn apart** [teər‿ə'pɑ:t, tɔ:r‿ə'pɑ:t, tɔ:n‿əpɑ:t]	auseinanderreißen; zerreißen →	Families *were torn apart* during the forced relocation of Aboriginals.
Aboriginal [ˌæbə'rɪdʒnl]	der Aborigines →	*Aboriginal* culture = the culture of the Aboriginals
to **destroy** [dɪ'strɔɪ]	zerstören →	Too much settlement and development *destroys* natural environments.
relations *(pl.)* [rɪ'leɪʃnz]	Verhältnis; Beziehungen →	If you have good *relations* with your neighbours, it means you get on well with them.
ozone layer ['əʊzəʊn ˌleɪə]	Ozonschicht	
skin cancer ['skɪn ˌkænsə]	Hautkrebs →	People who spend too much time in the sun risk getting *skin cancer.*
cancer ['kænsə]	Krebs	
separated ['sepreɪtɪd]	getrennt →	*separated* → separateness
platypus pl. **platypi** ['plætɪpəs, 'plætɪpaɪ]	Schnabeltier →	The *platypus* is an odd-looking animal which is unique to Australia.
koala [kəʊ'ɑ:lə]	Koala	
kangaroo [ˌkæŋgr'u:]	Känguru	
roo *(coll)* [ru:]	Känguru *(ugs.)*	
down under [ˌdaʊn‿'ʌndə]	*Spitzname für Australien*	

Unit 1: Australia

Australia

Australia is the smallest continent – and at the same time the largest island in the world. It is very often called by its nickname 'Oz', and another popular name for it is 'down under'. Although in area it is the world's sixth largest country, it has a population of only about 20 million; on average, there are only two people per square kilometre! Although about 90% of Australians are from families that once came from Europe, most new immigrants today come from Asia and the Pacific. Only about one in a hundred people are Aboriginals. The first settlers came from Britain, so Australia became an English-speaking country, and the Australians drive on the left – just like the British. The Australian flag shows a group of stars called the Southern Cross – but it also has the British flag in one corner, which shows that Australia was once a British colony.

Australia is the hottest and driest continent, and much of it is desert. Most Australians live in cities around the coast. The outback is huge and lonely, and not many people choose to live there, apart from those who work there as farmers. In some parts of the outback there is sometimes no rain for months and even years, and bush fires are often a big problem.

50 million years ago, the Australian continent was cut off from the other continents. This meant that plants and animals developed that were unique to Australia. The kangaroo and the koala, both marsupials that carry their young in a pouch, are well-known examples.
Some of the world's most dangerous animals can be found in Australia. But each year many more Australians are killed by the red-back spiders that live in the cities than by crocodiles or sharks!

Text A: Walkabout

walkabout ['wɔ:kəbaʊt]	*eine rituelle, sechsmonatige Wanderung durch das Outback, auf die die Aborigines ihre dreizehnjährigen Jungen schicken*	
survivor [sə'vaɪvə]	Überlebende/-r →	*survivor* → to survive
human being [ˌhju:mən 'bi:ɪŋ]	Mensch →	Can you imagine living all alone, with no other *human beings* around? I can't.
to appear [ə'pɪə]	auftauchen; erscheinen →	*to appear* = to be there suddenly
to be terrified (of sth) [bi 'terəfaɪd‿əv]	(große) Angst (vor etw.) haben →	*to be terrified* = to be really afraid
1 to overreact [ˌəʊvri'ækt]	überreagieren →	He always *overreacts.* = His reaction is always too extreme.
impulse ['ɪmpʌls]	Impuls →	! Watch the spelling and the pronunciation
stranger ['streɪndʒə]	Fremde/-r →	I don't know that man – he's a *stranger.*
to die away [ˌdaɪ ə'weɪ]	schwinden; nachlassen →	Her feelings for him *died away.* = Her feelings for him went away.
weapon ['wepən]	Waffe →	Guns and knives are *weapons*.
inquisitive [ɪn'kwɪzətɪv]	neugierig; wissbegierig; fragend →	*inquisitive* = curious
threatening ['θretnɪŋ]	bedrohlich →	That dog looks very *threatening*. I'm really afraid of it.
motionless ['məʊʃnləs]	reg(ungs)los, bewegungslos →	When you don't move at all, you're *motionless*.
length [leŋθ]	Länge →	*length* → long
pre-digested [ˌpri:daɪ'dʒestɪd]	vorverdaut	
to provide sb/sth with [prəʊ'vaɪd wɪð]	jmdn./etw. mit etw. versorgen; jmdm./etw. etw. bieten →	We'll *provide* you *with* money. = We'll give you the money you need.
continuous [kən'tɪnjuəs]	ununterbrochen, dauernd; kontinuierlich →	I'm really tired of his *continuous* comments about how much better everything was at his old school with his old friends. He talks about it all the time!
push-button ['pʊʃˌbʌtn]	Druckknopf-	
among [ə'mʌŋ]	unter; inmitten →	! Watch out: *among* ≠ under He stood *among* the trees. = in the middle of the forest, but not under a tree
unchanging [ʌn'tʃeɪndʒɪŋ]	unveränderlich, gleich bleibend →	She's very *unchanging* in her opinions. = Her opinions never change.
to be devoted to sb/sth [bi dɪ'vəʊtɪd‿tə]	jmdm./etw. (treu) ergeben sein; in etw. (völlig) aufgehen →	He doesn't just like sport; he's completely *devoted to* it, doesn't think of anything else.
purpose ['pɜ:pəs]	Ziel; Absicht; Zweck →	He's devoted to one *purpose* for the next year: training hard to be on the Olympic team.
to be dedicated to sth [bi 'dedɪkeɪtɪd‿tə]	etw. verschrieben sein; (nur) für etw. leben →	She's completely *dedicated to* her work. = The most important thing in her life is her job.
death [deθ]	Tod →	life ↔ *death*
weakness ['wi:knəs]	Schwäche →	*weakness* → weak
face to face [ˌfeɪs tə 'feɪs]	Auge in Auge; von Angesicht zu Angesicht →	Some people say the best way to deal with one's fears is to come *face to face* with them.

lion [laɪən]	Löwe	
to stare sb/sth down [steə 'daʊn]	jmdn./etw. zum Wegsehen zwingen →	I don't think I could *stare* a lion or bear *down*; I'd be too afraid, and the animal would feel it.
to slink away [ˌslɪŋk ə'weɪ]	davonschleichen	
shame [ʃeɪm]	Scham; Schande, Schmach →	It was so embarrassing, we all felt the *shame* of the situation.
nakedness ['neɪkɪdnəs]	Nacktheit	
strategy ['strætədʒi]	Strategie →	! Watch the spelling and the pronunciation
rock wallaby [ˌrɒk 'wɒləbi]	Wallaby *(austral. Beuteltier)* →	*Rock wallabies* are night animals.
creature ['kri:tʃə]	Kreatur, Lebewesen; Geschöpf →	! Watch the spelling and the pronunciation
movement ['mu:vmənt]	Bewegung →	*movement* → to move
to intrigue sb [ɪn'tri:g]	jmdn. faszinieren →	When something *intrigues* you, you want to know more about it.
lack (of) [læk‿əv]	Mangel (an); Fehlen (von) →	Politeness is extremely important in English-speaking countries, so showing a *lack of* it in those countries is not a good idea.
harmless ['hɑ:mləs]	harmlos, ungefährlich →	Kangaroos aren't as *harmless* as they might look; they can kill with a hard kick to the head.
to dislike [dɪs'laɪk]	nicht mögen →	*to dislike* ↔ to like
examination [ɪgˌzæmɪ'neɪʃn]	Untersuchung; Prüfung →	*examination* → to examine
to intensify [ɪn'tensɪfaɪ]	intensivieren; verstärken →	When you *intensify* what you're doing, then you put more work into it.
stare [steə]	Starren, starrer Blick →	*stare* → to stare
bush [bʊʃ]	Busch *(Buschlandschaft)*; Wildnis →	*Bush* is the word you use to describe open country in e.g. Australia or southern Africa; for Australia, you can also say 'the outback'.
to fidget ['fɪdʒɪt]	(herum)zappeln →	People who are nervous often *fidget*.
train of events [ˌtreɪn‿əv‿ɪ'vents]	Reihe von Vorfällen/ Ereignissen	
waggle ['wægl]	wackeln; fuchteln	
to raise [reɪz]	*(hier:)* strecken →	*to raise* = to lift (up)
to hold one's breath [ˌhəʊld wʌnz 'breθ]	den Atem anhalten, die Luft anhalten →	What's the world record for *holding one's breath* under water?
breath [breθ]	Atem; Atemzug →	She's got really bad *breath*, it's awful. But how do you tell somebody something like that?
to sneeze [sni:z]	niesen	
sneeze [sni:z]	Nieser →	*sneeze* → to sneeze
disaster [dɪ'zɑ:stə]	Katastrophe, Unglück; Desaster →	*disaster* = a terrible event
spell [spel]	Zauber, Bann; Zauberspruch →	Do you believe in *spells* and witches and things like that?
silence ['saɪləns]	Stille; Schweigen; Ruhe →	*silence* → silent(ly)
the heavens *(lit)* [ðə 'hevnz]	das Firmament *(literarisch)*, der Himmel *(literarisch)* →	*The heavens* is a more creative expression for 'the sky'.
the gods *(lit)* [ðə 'gɒdz]	die Götter *(literarisch)* →	*The gods* must be angry with me at the moment because *everything* went wrong today!
force [fɔ:s]	Kraft; Gewalt, Stärke	
to whirl around [ˌwɜ:l‿ə'raʊnd]	sich abrupt umdrehen, herumfahren →	While she was walking through a Sydney shopping centre she suddenly heard her name and *whirled around*. It was a friend from London!

gust of laughter [ˌgʌst‿əv ˈlɑːftə]	Lachanfall	
laughter [ˈlɑːftə]	Gelächter, Lachen →	*laughter* → to laugh
melodious [məˈləʊdiəs]	melodiös, wohlklingend	
uncontrolled [ˌʌnkənˈtrəʊld]	unkontrolliert →	*uncontrolled* → to control
amazement [əˈmeɪzmənt]	Erstaunen, Verwunderung →	*amazement* → amazing
infectious [ɪnˈfekʃəs]	ansteckend →	Their laughter was so *infectious* that you just had to laugh, too, even if you didn't know what they were laughing about.
instant [ˈɪnstənt]	sofortige/-r/-s	
appreciation [əˌpriːʃiˈeɪʃn]	Verständnis; Wertschätzung; Anerkennung →	My boyfriend never shows any *appreciation* for all the things I do for him. Well, one day he'll wish he had …
ludicrous [ˈluːdɪkrəs]	lächerlich; absurd, grotesk →	The situation was so *ludicrous* that we just didn't know whether to laugh or cry.
guilt [gɪlt]	Schuld; Schuldgefühl	It was obvious that he had done something wrong. You could see the *guilt* in his face.
in the twinkling of an eye [ɪn ðə ˌtwɪŋklɪŋ‿əvn‿ˈaɪ]	im Nu; im Handumdrehen	
adapted [əˈdæptɪd]	adaptiert; angepasst →	Something that has been *adapted* has been changed in some way.
abridged [əˈbrɪdʒd]	gekürzt →	An *abridged* text is one that has been made shorter.
2 preconception [ˌpriːkənˈsepʃn]	vorgefasste Meinung →	Not all *preconceptions* turn out to be true.
3 **characterization** [ˌkærəktraɪˈzeɪʃn]	(Personen)Beschreibung, Charakterisierung →	*characterization* → character
protective [prəˈtektɪv]	fürsorglich	
overprotective [ˌəʊvəprəˈtektɪv]	überfürsorglich →	*Overprotective* parents don't let their kids do much on their own.
confident [ˈkɒnfɪdnt]	selbstsicher, selbstbewusst →	*confident* → confidence
direct [dɪˈrekt]	direkt, offen →	Telling the truth in conversations is fine, but being too *direct* is not always a good thing.

Linking old and new vocabulary: Feelings

You have already learnt a lot of words with which you can express your own feelings or describe how someone else feels. So it is useful to do some revision and add the new words you have learnt in this unit. Here you go!

Words you already know		New words
to love	to be angry	to dislike
to like	to be aggressive	shame
to hate	to be grumpy	(to be) confident
to laugh	to be lonely	to be terrified of sth
to cry	to be shy	
to be happy	to be scared	
to be glad	to be worried	
to be excited	to be tired of sth	
to be relaxed	to feel good	
to be sad	to feel bad	
to be nervous		

Text B: Angela

	part-Aboriginal [ˌpɑːt æbəˈrɪdʒnl]	teils Aborigine →	A *part-Aboriginal* child might have a white father and an Aboriginal mother or an Aboriginal father and a white mother.
	politically active [pəˌlɪtɪkli ˈæktɪv]	politisch engagiert →	*Politically active* people are interested in politics and want to change things.
	uni(versity) [ˈjuːnɪ, juːnɪˈvɜːsəti]	Uni(versität) →	Cambridge is one of the world's most famous *universities*.
	rally [ˈræli]	(Massen)Versammlung →	Only about 30 people came to the *rally*.
	cause [kɔːz]	Sache →	One *cause* I feel strongly about is the environment.
	point of view [ˌpɔɪnt‿əv‿ˈvjuː]	Ansicht, Einstellung; Standpunkt →	Your *point of view* is your way of seeing things.
1	to regret sth [rɪˈgret]	etw. bedauern →	When you feel sorry about something you said or did, then you *regret* it.
	shopper [ˈʃɒpə]	(Ein)Käufer/-in →	*shopper* → shopping
	buzz [bʌz]	geschäftiges Treiben; Durcheinander →	Some people like the *buzz* of big cities, others prefer quieter places.
	slob *(coll)* [slɒb]	Assi *(ugs.)* →	Mike, we're going to a nice restaurant for dinner, so why are you still in those dirty old jeans and trainers? You look like a *slob*!
	thongs *(pl.)* [θɒŋz]	Flip-Flops *(AE; Aus)* →	I like your *thongs* with the Australian flag on them, cool!
	footy *(Australian rules football) (coll)* [ˈfʊti]	*ugs. für die Sportart 'Australian rules football'* →	Who can tell me the difference between rugby and *footy*?
	shorts *(pl.)* [ʃɔːts]	Shorts, kurze Hose →	! Your *shorts* **are** nice.
	to strut [strʌt]	herumstolzieren →	She always *struts* around school like she's a model or something.
	catwalk [ˈkætwɔːk]	Laufsteg; Catwalk →	Models have to have a lot of confidence to be up on a *catwalk* with everyone's eyes on them.
	negligence [ˈneglɪdʒəns]	Nachlässigkeit; Fahrlässigkeit →	Drivers' *negligence* is the reason for many bad traffic accidents each year.
	to be on edge [bi ɒn‿ˈedʒ]	nervös sein; gereizt sein →	Why *has* Derek *been* so *on edge* the past few days? I know he's worried about something, but what?
	booth [buːð]	Stand; Bude	
	no sign of [nəʊ ˈsaɪn‿əv]	keine Spur von; kein Anzeichen von	We waited and waited but there was still *no sign of* a bus.
	to slouch off [slaʊtʃ ˈɒf]	davonzockeln →	She *slouched off*. = She walked away slowly and lazily.
	overalls *(pl.)* [ˈəʊvrɔːlz]	Overall →	! Where **are** my *overalls*?
	to hesitate [ˈhezɪteɪt]	zögern →	He *hesitated* for a few seconds, but then he went up to the most popular girl at school and started a conversation.
	hotly [ˈhɒtli]	hitzig, erregt	
	blouse [blaʊz]	Bluse →	A *blouse* is a shirt for women.
	swept-back [swept ˈbæk]	zurückgekämmt →	I think your hair would look nicer if you wore it *swept-back*.
	confident [ˈkɒnfɪdnt]	selbstsicher, selbstbewusst →	*confident* → confidence

stance [stɑːns]	Haltung →	Monarchs often have a very confident *stance* which comes from years of being in public.
to spell sth [spel]	*(hier:)* etw. bedeuten →	The look on the bully's face *spelt* 'trouble'.
to look the part [ˌlʊk ðə ˈpɑːt]	danach aussehen →	People always think she's a model, but she's not. She sure *looks the part*!
to hurry [ˈhʌri]	sich beeilen →	*to hurry* → hurry
handful [ˈhænfʊl]	Handvoll →	a *handful* of words = not many words; just a few words
to turn to sb [ˈtɜːn‿tə]	sich an jmdn. wenden; sich jmdm./etw. zuwenden →	I *turned to* him to say something but he wasn't there any more.
instead [ɪnˈsted]	stattdessen →	If the weather is too cold for swimming, we could go for a walk *instead*.
incredulously [ɪnˈkredjələsli]	ungläubig; fassungslos →	I told my boss I wasn't going to do what he wanted. He just looked at me *incredulously*; you should have seen his face.
rage [reɪdʒ]	Wut, Zorn →	He felt so much *rage* that his face started to get red while he was screaming at us.
fucking *(vulg)* [ˈfʌkɪŋ]	Scheiß- *(derb)* →	*Fucking* is very strong language and it would be extremely rude to use it in public (e.g. in a train, restaurant, shop, etc.).
nearby [ˌnɪəˈbaɪ]	in der Nähe →	*nearby* = not far away
to get lumped in with [ˌget lʌmpt‿ˈɪn wɪð]	in einen Topf geworfen werden →	Because people know his brother is in jail, he *gets lumped in with* the bad guys. But he has never been in trouble with the police.
to draw [drɔː]	anlocken, anziehen →	The buskers were so good that they really started to *draw* a big crowd.
to form [fɔːm]	bilden, formen →	*to form* → form
semicircle [ˈsemɪˌsɜːkl]	Halbkreis →	*semicircle* = half circle
to pause [pɔːz]	(eine kurze) Pause machen; innehalten →	*to pause* → pause
breath [breθ]	Atem; Atemzug; Luft →	She's got really bad *breath*, it's awful. But how do you tell somebody something like that?
generous as can be [ˌdʒenrəs əz kən ˈbiː]	so großzügig, wie man nur sein kann →	He's *generous as can be* with his money, but not with his time.
on one's own terms [ɒn wʌnz ˌəʊn ˈtɜːmz]	unter den eigenen Bedingungen →	OK, I'll do the job. But only *on my own terms*. That means you'll have to pay me more.
to be in tears [ˌbi‿ɪn ˈtɪəz]	weinen →	*to be in tears* = to cry
to colonise [ˈkɒlənaɪz]	kolonisieren →	*to colonise* → colony
to move in [muːv ˈɪn]	*(hier:)* Kontrolle übernehmen	
to hold back [həʊld ˈbæk]	(zurück)halten →	When my friends and I go to the clubs there's no *holding back*: We don't stop dancing all night!
frustration [frʌsˈtreɪʃn]	Frust; Enttäuschung; Frustration →	My biggest *frustration* right now is not having enough time to see my friends.
to bottle up sth [ˌbɒtl‿ˈʌp]	etw. unterdrücken →	Don't keep everything *bottled up* inside you; let it out.
to throw sth back in sb's face [θrəʊ ˌbæk in ˌsʌmbədiz ˈfeɪs]	jmdm. etw. wieder auftischen	
to care about sb [ˈkeər‿əˌbaʊt]	Zuneigung für jmdn. empfinden; sich für jmdn. interessieren; sich um jmdn. kümmern →	*to care about sb* = to like sb; to be interested in sb; to look after sb

Linking old and new vocabulary: Feelings

You have already learnt a lot of words with which you can express your own feelings or describe how someone else feels. So it is useful to do some revision and add the new words you have learnt in this unit. Here you go!

Words you already know		New words
to love	to be angry	to be in tears
to like	to be aggressive	to be on edge
to hate	to be grumpy	rage
to laugh	to be lonely	frustration
to cry	to be shy	to care about sb
to be happy	to be scared	
to be glad	to be worried	
to be excited	to be tired of sth	
to be relaxed	to feel good	
to be sad	to feel bad	
to be nervous		

to step out of line [ˌstep aʊt‿əv ˈlaɪn] — aus der Reihe tanzen → — His parents are very strict, there's no *stepping out of line* in their home!

to turn on sb/sth [ˈtɜːn‿ɒn] — sich gegen jmdn./etw. wenden → — I thought she was my friend, but one day she just *turned on me*.

to storm away [ˌstɔːm‿əˈweɪ] — davonstürmen → — Every time he gets mad he doesn't talk about it; he just *storms away*.

to part [pɑːt] — sich teilen; auseinandergehen

adapted [əˈdæptɪd] — adaptiert; angepasst → — Something that has been *adapted* has been changed in some way.

abridged [əˈbrɪdʒd] — gekürzt → — An *abridged* text is one that has been made shorter.

3 **characterization** [ˌkærəktraɪˈzeɪʃn] — (Personen)Beschreibung, Charakterisierung → — *characterization* → character

direct [dɪˈrekt] — direkt, offen → — Telling the truth in conversations is fine, but being too *direct* is not always a good thing.

ungrateful [ʌnˈgreɪtfl] — undankbar → — I don't think I heard you say 'thank you' to grandma for her present. Don't be so *ungrateful*.

hypocritical [ˌhɪpəˈkrɪtɪkl] — heuchlerisch, scheinheilig → — You tell everyone they have to do this or think that, and then you do the exact opposite! Sorry, but that's really *hypocritical*.

4 discrimination [dɪˌskrɪmɪˈneɪʃn] — Diskriminierung

Skills: Listening skills – Taking notes

to **depend (on)** [dɪˈpend‿ɒn] — abhängen (von) → — *Fr. dépendre (de); Lat. de + pendere*

point of view [ˌpɔɪnt‿əv‿ˈvjuː] — Ansicht, Einstellung; Standpunkt → — Your *point of view* is your way of seeing things.

1 **glass-bottom** [ˈglɑːs ˌbɒtm] — Glasboden-

2 **shorthand** ['ʃɔ:thænd]	Kurzschrift, Stenografie →	b/c (= because) is an example of *shorthand*.
to **interest** ['ɪntrəst]	interessieren →	*to interest* → interested in → interesting
4 **World Heritage Site** [wɜ:ld 'herɪtɪdʒ saɪt]	Welterbestätte; *von der UNESCO anerkanntes Weltkulturerbe* →	There are more *World Heritage Sites* in Spain than in any other country.

Language: First time in 'Oz'

Oz *(coll)* [ɒz]	Oz *(Spitzname für Australien)* →	*Oz* = nickname for Australia
to **post** [pəʊst]	online stellen; posten →	He's sad because his favourite band *hasn't posted* anything new on their website for days.
bit of information [ˌbɪt‿əv‿ɪnfə'meɪʃn]	eine Information →	There's always some interesting *bit of information* on Blake's travel website.
first-time [ˌfɜ:s'taɪm]	erstmalig →	*First-time* outback travellers often don't realize just how big the outback is; the nearest shop is often hundreds of miles away.
used to *(+ infinitive)* ['ju:s‿tə]	früher; pflegte(n) zu →	! *used to* + infinitive can only be used in the past tense: We *used to* live in Munich. = Wir wohnten früher in München.
penal colony ['pi:nl ˌkɒləni]	Strafkolonie →	White Australia began as a *penal colony*.
shipload ['ʃɪpləʊd]	Schiffsladung →	*Shiploads* of illegal immigrants from Africa often die as they try to cross the sea to Europe.
to **make sb do sth** [meɪk]	jmdn. veranlassen, etw. zu tun →	I can't believe your parents don't *make you clean* the house, that's not fair. Mine *make me do* everything!
convict ['kɒnvɪkt]	Sträfling →	A *convict* is somebody who has been sent to prison.
criminal ['krɪmɪnl]	Kriminelle/-r; Verbrecher/-in →	*criminal* → crime → criminal *(adj)*
ancestor ['ænsestə]	Ahne/Ahnin; Vorfahre/Vorfahrin →	Most of my *ancestors* come from Scotland, but I have Italian *ancestors*, too.
to **let sb do sth** [let]	jmdm. erlauben, etw. zu tun; etw. zulassen →	Are your parents going to *let you come* to Ibiza with us?
version ['vɜ:ʃn]	Version →	! Watch the pronunciation I enjoyed the book much better than the film *version* of the story.
Asian-Pacific [ˌeɪʒn pə'sɪfɪk]	asiatisch-pazifisch →	He's very interested in *Asian-Pacific* culture and wants to spend time in Hawaii and then in Australia.
nearby [ˌnɪə'baɪ]	in der Nähe →	*nearby* = not far away
yummy *(coll)* ['jʌmi]	lecker →	This cake is *yummy*! = This cake is delicious!
coat of arms [ˌkəʊt‿əv‿'ɑ:mz]	Wappen →	Germany has a black eagle on its *coat of arms*.
preconception [ˌpri:kən'sepʃən]	vorgefasste Meinung →	Not all *preconceptions* turn out to be true.
to **have sth done** [ˌhæv 'dʌn]	etw. machen lassen →	She *had* an outfit *made* for the 'Down under' party.

lassen

to **let** sb **do** sth	My parents **let** me **stay** in bed longer on Sundays.	jmdm. erlauben, etw. zu tun; etw. zulassen
to **make** sb **do** sth	My mum sometimes **makes** me **tidy up** my room.	jmdn. veranlassen, etw. zu tun
to **have** sth **done**	We **have** our newspaper **delivered.**	etw. machen lassen

Choose the right word in these sentences:

1. Matt is such a bully! Don't … him tell you what to do! 2. My camera doesn't work. – Can't you … it mended? 3. You can't … me go to that party if I don't want to. 4. That fish was awful! It … me feel sick! 5. Do you … your dog sleep on your bed? 6. Your hair looks great. Where did you … it cut? 7. Please … me cut the cake! 8. Sad films always … me cry!

	exotic [ɪg'zɒtɪk]	exotisch →	I love *exotic* dishes, but I don't always want to know exactly what I'm eating. It's probably better that way …
	to **deliver** [dɪ'lɪvə]	liefern →	If pizza is brought to your house by a pizza service, it is *delivered* to your house. *Fr. délivrer*
	green ant [ˌgri:n‿'ænt]	grüne Ameise	
	witchetty grub [ˌwɪtʃəti 'grʌb]	Witchetty-Made; Holzbohrerlarve →	I'm not sure I could eat *witchetty grubs*; they look so awful!
	emu ['i:mju:]	Emu →	An *emu* is a bird but it can't fly.
	crocodile ['krɒkədaɪl]	Krokodil →	! Watch the spelling and the pronunciation You can find *crocodiles* not just on some of Australia's coasts, but in many lakes and rivers, too.
1	**aspect** ['æspekt]	Aspekt, Gesichtspunkt, Blickwinkel →	! Watch the pronunciation
5	**barbie** *(= barbecue) (coll)* ['bɑ:bi]	Grillen; Grillparty	
	rooftop terrace [ˌru:ftɒp 'terɪs]	Dachterrasse →	If I lived in Sydney, I'd want a flat with a big *rooftop terrace* and a view of Harbour Bridge and all the skyscrapers.
	all kinds of [ɔ:l 'kaɪndz‿əv]	allerhand, vielerlei; alle möglichen →	*all kinds of* food = a lot of different kinds of food
6	**form** [fɔ:m]	Formular →	When you fill out *forms*, it's important to read each line very carefully.
	consulate ['kɒnsjʊlət]	Konsulat →	! Watch the spelling and the pronunciation

USEFUL PHRASES

When you travel, it's always good to know how to explain a problem to the police.

Hello there, may I help you?
My passport and a few other things have been stolen.
Would you let me use/May I use your telephone?
Please fill out these forms so that I can help you.
Could you describe exactly what happened?
The German consulate can give you a passport for your flight home.

Revision: Using relative clauses

	necessary ['nesəsri]	nötig, notwendig, erforderlich →	It won't be *necessary* to book tickets. = You won't need to book tickets.
	followed by ['fɒləʊd baɪ]	gefolgt von	
1	teddy bear ['tedi ˌbeə]	Teddybär	
	pouch [paʊtʃ]	Beutel →	She took a great photo of a baby kangaroo in its mother's *pouch*.
	marsupial [mɑː'suːpiəl]	Beuteltier →	Kangaroos and koalas are probably the best-known *marsupials*.
	to bite, bit, bitten [baɪt, bɪt, 'bɪtn]	beißen; stechen →	Koalas may look like sweet little teddy bears, but they can *bite*.
2	symbol ['sɪmbl]	Symbol →	! Watch the pronunciation
	to die out [daɪ 'aʊt]	aussterben →	Many animals *have died out* over the last few hundred years.
	contagious [kən'teɪdʒəs]	ansteckend →	Cancer is usually not *contagious*, but the Tasmanian devil's form of cancer is.
3	protection [prə'tekʃn]	Schutz →	Part of environmental protection is the *protection* of animals.
	to lay, laid, laid [leɪ, leɪd, leɪd]	legen →	! Some animals ***lay*** eggs. ↔ The eggs are **lying** in the grass.
	dingo ['dɪŋgəʊ]	Dingo *(austral. Wildhund)* →	*Dingoes* look like pet dogs, but they are wild animals which kill other animals for food.
	laughing kookaburra [ˌlɑːfɪŋ 'kʊkəˌbʌrə]	Kookaburra, Lachender Hans →	*Kookaburra* is an Aboriginal word.
	red-back (spider) [ˌredbæk 'spaɪdə]	Rotrückenspinne →	What's worse: tiny animals that can kill you like the *red-back spider*? Or big ones that can kill you? Australia has lots of both kinds.

VOCABULARY SKILLS

Remembering words

a) *Look at the words below and give yourself 2-3 minutes to remember them. Then close your book and write down as many of them as you can.*

kangaroo	rainforest	platypus	convict
ozone layer	yummy	prison	emu
skin cancer	form	dingo	shark
exotic	protection	continent	Asian-Pacific
apart	marsupial	Aboriginal	criminal

b) *Compare your list of words with those above. Why did you remember some words and not others?*

Tip: It can be easier to remember • unusual words • words that can be used in the same context or are connected in some way • the first word in a list.

c) *Find a partner and compare your lists. Were there any words you both forgot? Think why that probably happened. Did you write down any words that were not in the list above? What might the reason be?*

d) *It is easier to remember words if you learn them in groups. Put as many words from the list as you can into groups, and find a heading for each (e.g. Group 1: Animals).*

e) *Choose words from Unit 1 and write your own list. Give it to a partner and test what he/she – and you! – remembers.*

Writing Texts: Elements of a story

1	**road trip** ['rəʊd trɪp]	Tour, Trip →	A *road trip* is about just being on the road. It is not that important to know exactly where you are going.
	perspective [pə'spektɪv]	Perspektive, Blickwinkel →	! Watch the pronunciation
	princess-like [prɪn'ses,laɪk]	prinzessinenhaft →	She's too *princess-like* for him; he likes girls who are more natural and aren't afraid of getting their hands dirty.
	worry-wart ['wʌriwɔ:t]	*jmd., der sich ständig Sorgen macht*; Grübler/-in →	Don't be such a *worry-wart*! Why are you always so afraid something terrible is going to happen?
	foreshadowing [fɔ:'ʃædəʊɪŋ]	Vorahnung →	A good writer uses *foreshadowing* to make the reader wonder what will happen.
	hint [hɪnt]	Hinweis, Tipp; Andeutung →	Can't you give me just a little *hint* about my birthday present? Please!
	red-herring [,red'herɪŋ]	Ablenkungsmanöver →	A good writer can lead the reader down a false path for a long time with the help of *red-herrings*.
	to **return** [rɪ'tɜ:n]	zurückkehren, zurückkommen →	*to return* = to go or come back
2	**turning point** ['tɜ:nɪŋ ,pɔɪnt]	Wendepunkt →	A point (usually in a story) when the situation suddenly changes.
	climax ['klaɪmæks]	Höhepunkt →	The *climax* is the most exciting point in a story, the story's highlight.
4	**peer editing** ['pɪər‿edɪtɪŋ]	*Kritik/Kontrolle durch Gleichaltrige*	

Wordwise

2	surfie *(coll)* ['sɜ:fi]	Surfer/-in *(ugs.)* →	*surfie* = surfer
	to mark [mɑ:k]	markieren; kennzeichnen →	*Mark* the short forms, please.
	to miss sth [mɪs]	etw. verpassen; etw. versäumen →	Hey, you *missed* a great party! Where were you?
3	**formal** ['fɔ:ml]	formell; förmlich; formal →	Spoken English is almost always much less *formal* than written English.
	to **be said to** *(+ infinitive)* [bi 'sed‿tə]	gelten als →	French cooking *is said to* be the world's best. = Die französische Küche gilt als die beste der Welt.
	to **be supposed to** *(+ infinitive)* [bi sə'pəʊzd‿tə]	(etw. tun) sollen →	French cooking *is supposed to* be the world's best. = Die französische Küche soll die beste der Welt sein.
4	the time has come [ðə ,taɪm həz 'kʌm]	die Zeit ist gekommen	
	to belong (to) [bɪ'lɒŋ tə]	gehören (zu)	
	to turn [tɜ:n]	(sich) drehen	

Unit 2: What next?

Leaving school and choosing a career in Britain

Most British students go to comprehensive schools, which are a bit like *Gesamtschulen* in Germany. At the age of 15 or 16 they take exams called GCSEs (General Certificate of Secondary Education). Teachers help students to decide which subjects – and how many – to take for their exams. Almost all students take GCSEs in English, Maths and General Science, and many also take English Literature, a foreign language, IT (Information Technology), Art and Design, or Business Studies. Grades are given from A (the top grade) to G (the lowest).

After GCSEs most students leave school and go on with their education at vocational or technical colleges, or start a training course. Some look for a job right away. But it is also possible to stay on at school for two more years, to prepare for A-Level exams. If you want to go to university, you usually need good grades in at least two or three subjects as qualifications.

The right choice of A-Level subjects is very important in Britain. It is usual to choose subjects that 'go together' (and which will also be useful in your later career). For example, if you plan to study French and Spanish at university, good A-Level results in these subjects will be expected when you apply for a place.

Choosing a career is one of the most important decisions in life, and most schools have a careers teacher who helps to advise pupils. He/She explains the advantages and disadvantages of different careers the students might be interested in, and what qualifications they will need.

Check-in

construction [kən'strʌkʃn]	Bau →	Skyscrapers and huge bridges must be dream projects for people who are interested in *construction*.
railway system ['reɪlweɪ ˌsɪstəm]	Eisenbahnnetz →	The *railway system* in Europe is much more developed than in North America.
stereotype ['steriəʊtaɪp]	Klischee, Stereotyp →	! Watch the pronunciation A *stereotype* is an (often wrong) idea about a type of person or thing.
career [kə'rɪə]	Beruf; Laufbahn →	There are many possibilities for a *career* in music: performing, writing, teaching, …
to **study** ['stʌdi]	studieren; lernen →	I want to *study* a subject that will give me a chance of a good career later.
dead body [ˌded 'bɒdi]	Leiche →	When you work for the police, you usually don't see *dead bodies* every day. That's only on TV or in films.
exam [ɪg'zæm]	Prüfung; Examen →	Do you get nervous before *exams*, too?
to **take an exam** [ˌteɪk‿ən‿ɪg'zæm]	eine Prüfung schreiben; ein Examen schreiben →	People have to *take exams* to show that they really know their subject.
to **reach** [ri:tʃ]	erreichen →	You can't buy alcohol in the USA until you *reach* the age of 21.
GCSE (= General Certificate of Secondary Education) [ˌdʒi: si: es 'i:; ˌdʒenrl se'tɪfɪkət‿əv ˌsekəndri edʒʊ'keɪʃn]	*allg. Abschluss der weiterführenden Schulen in GB*	
A-levels ['eɪlevlz]	*britische Abiturprüfung*	
foreign language [ˌfɒrɪn 'læŋgwɪdʒ]	Fremdsprache →	A lot of British schools teach French as the first *foreign language*.

higher education [ˌhaɪə edʒʊ'keɪʃn]	Hochschulbildung; Hochschulwesen →	If you decide to go to university after school, you go on to *higher education*.
questionnaire [ˌkwestʃə'neə]	Fragebogen →	I like *questionnaires* because I like giving information and/or my opinion.
to **suit sth** [su:t]	passen zu →	I hate seeing blood, so I don't think a career as a doctor would *suit* me well.
technical ['teknɪkl]	technisch →	I'm not good with machines, so I guess I wouldn't be so great at a *technical* job.
reliable [rɪ'laɪəbl]	verlässlich, zuverlässig; vertrauenswürdig →	He is very *reliable*. He always does what he says he will do.
bank [bæŋk]	Bank →	*bank* → banker
tactful ['tæktfl]	taktvoll →	If you are *tactful*, you make sure you don't say or do things which would hurt people's feelings.
social work ['səʊʃl ˌwɜ:k]	Sozialarbeit →	If you like *social work*, you enjoy helping people.
nurse [nɜ:s]	Krankenschwester, Krankenpfleger →	My mother works at the hospital. She's a *nurse*.
personnel manager [pɜ:sn'el ˌmænədʒə]	Personalchef/-in →	A good *personnel manager* helps his/her firm to find the right people for the right jobs.
practical ['præktɪkl]	praktisch →	*Practical* fields like business are better suited to me than music or art.
architect ['ɑ:kɪtekt]	Architekt/-in →	! Watch the spelling and the pronunciation
musician [mju:'zɪʃn]	Musiker/-in →	*musician* → music → musical instrument
opportunity [ˌɒpə'tju:nəti]	Gelegenheit; Chance →	*opportunity* = chance
competitive [kəm'petɪtɪv]	konkurrenzfähig, wettbewerbsfähig	
lawyer ['lɔɪə]	Anwalt/Anwältin, Jurist/-in →	*lawyer* → law
2 **work experience** ['wɜ:k‿ɪkˌspɪəriəns]	Praktikum; Berufserfahrung	
3 statistics *(pl.)* [stə'tɪstɪks]	Statistik →	! The *statistics* **show** that …

Language 1: Information, please!

support service [sə'pɔ:t ˌsɜ:vɪs]	*(hier:)* Beratungsstelle →	*support service* → to support
adviser [əd'vaɪzə]	Berater/-in →	*adviser* → to advise → advice
leaflet ['li:flət]	Broschüre; Informationsblatt; Prospekt →	What information does the *leaflet* give about jobs in fashion?
plus (+) [plʌs]	aufwärts →	A really cool new club has just opened, but I can't get in: It's for the 21+ age group.
to **work one's way up** [ˌwɜ:k wʌnz weɪ 'ʌp]	sich hocharbeiten →	Their parents own the company, so Mark and Theresa didn't have to *work their way up* to management level.
to **rise** [raɪz]	(an)steigen →	*to rise* = to go up
whiz-kid ['wɪzkɪd]	kluger Kopf →	Jamie and his sister are really good with computers. They're real computer *whiz-kids*.
to **design** [dɪ'zaɪn]	entwerfen; gestalten →	*to design* → a design
it says … [ɪt 'sez]	hier steht … →	Can you read what this sign *says*?
multimedia [ˌmʌlti'mi:diə]	Multimedia; multimedial →	! Watch the pronunciation
competition [ˌkɒmpə'tɪʃn]	Konkurrenz →	There is always lots of *competition* for the best and/or most interesting jobs because a lot of people would like to get them, of course.

	to **employ sb** [ɪm'plɔɪ]	jmdn. beschäftigen; jmdn. einstellen, jmdn. anstellen →	When you *employ* people, you pay them to work for you.
	mainly ['meɪnli]	hauptsächlich, in erster Linie; vorwiegend →	*mainly* = mostly
	to **put sb off** [pʊt‿'ɒf]	jmdn. von etw. abbringen; jmdm. etw. verleiden →	I know you don't want me to go to Scotland for a year, but stop trying to *put me off*. I'm going!
	deadline ['dedlaɪn]	(Abgabe)Termin →	Your *deadline* for the article is 11.00 pm tonight. If I get it later than that, it won't be in the newspaper tomorrow.
	to **meet a deadline** [ˌmi:t‿ə 'dedlaɪn]	einen (Abgabe)Termin einhalten →	Journalists have to be able to *meet a deadline*.
2	**in place of** [ɪn 'pleɪs‿əv]	(an)statt, anstelle von →	You can use apples *in place of* bananas for the cake.
3	to **train sb (in sth)** ['treɪn‿ɪn]	jmdn. (in etw.) ausbilden →	After I've *been trained in* the restaurant business, my cousin and I want to open a café.
	university [ˌju:nɪ'vɜ:səti]	Universität →	Cambridge is a very famous British *university*.
5	**pay** [peɪ]	Lohn; Gehalt →	Which famous model once said she wouldn't get up in the morning if the *pay* was less than $20,000 that day?
7	**quality** ['kwɒləti]	Eigenschaft, Merkmal →	In job interviews, it is important to concentrate on your positive *qualities*.
8	**hairdresser** ['heədresə]	Friseur/-in →	*hairdresser* → hair
9	**image** ['ɪmɪdʒ]	Image, Ruf →	Different jobs have different *images*, but the *image* isn't always the same thing as reality.

USEFUL PHRASES

What are your personal qualities? These Useful phrases help you to describe yourself postitively.

I think/I'd say I'm
reliable/practical/creative/patient/ …
I find it easy/fun/interesting/… to meet people/learn new skills/ …
I'm interested in technology/fashion/ …
I prefer to work alone/in a team/outside/ …
I'm (not so) good with children/animals…
I'm (not so) good at explaining things/learning new things/ …
I (don't) like
deadlines/computers/challenges/languages/ writing stories/ …

Writing texts: A letter of application

letter of application [ˌletər‿əv‿æplɪ'keɪʃn]	Bewerbungsschreiben →	There should never be spelling mistakes in a *letter of application*.
application [ˌæplɪ'keɪʃn]	Bewerbung →	If you want a job, you first have to send in an *application*.
placement ['pleɪsmənt]	Praktikum →	A *placement* lets you work for a firm for a short time to give you experience in that field.
to **apply (for)** [ə'plaɪ fə]	sich bewerben (für) →	Do you think I should *apply for* a job in that new shop at the shopping centre?
architecture ['ɑ:kɪtektʃə]	Architektur →	! Watch the spelling and the pronunciation *architecture* → architect

CV *(= Curriculum Vitae)* [ˌsiː'viː]	Lebenslauf →	A *CV* describes what jobs and activities you have done in your life so far, what exams you have taken, etc.
knowledge ['nɒlɪdʒ]	Kenntnisse; Wissen →	! Watch the pronunciation: *knowledge* [ɒ] ↔ to know [əʊ]
Yours sincerely [jɔːz sɪn'sɪəli]	Mit freundlichen Grüßen →	*Yours sincerely* can be used at the end of a formal letter, e.g. a letter of application.
Encl. [ɪn'kləʊzd]	Anlage →	When you send something with a letter, you write *Encl.* at the bottom of the page and write down what you are sending.
to **print** [prɪnt]	(etw. in Druckschrift) schreiben; drucken	
signature ['sɪgnətʃə]	Unterschrift →	*signature* → to sign *Fr. signature f; Lat. signare*
to **enclose** [ɪn'kləʊz]	beifügen, beilegen →	When you *enclose* something, you put it in with the letter you want to send.
date of birth [ˌdeɪt‿əv 'bɜːθ]	Geburtsdatum →	*date of birth* → birthday → birthplace
volunteer [ˌvɒlən'tɪə]	Freiwillige/-r; ehrenamtliche/-r Helfer/-in →	Being able to show *volunteer* work on a CV is often very important in the USA.
reference ['refrns]	Referenz(schreiben) →	A *reference* is a letter written by somebody who knows you and recommends you for a job.
available [ə'veɪləbl]	verfügbar, zur Verfügung stehen; erhältlich →	If something is *available*, you can get it or buy it.

Language 2: Just you wait!

Just you wait! [dʒʌst ju‿'weɪt]	Wart's (nur) ab!/Wirst schon sehen! →	I don't think you'll get the job. – Oh yes I will, *just you wait!*
to **serve** [sɜːv]	(be)dienen; servieren →	In a restaurant or in a café a waiter/waitress *serves* the customers.
hot [hɒt]	*(hier:)* groß →	The competition is *hot*. = There are a lot of other very good people who want the same job.
to **work out** [ˌwɜːk‿'aʊt]	funktionieren, klappen →	*to work out* = to get the result you hope for
to **decide on sth** [dɪ'saɪd‿ɒn]	sich für etw. entscheiden →	*to decide on* a career = to choose a career
meteorology [ˌmiːtir'ɒlədʒi]	Meteorologie	
whatsit *(coll)* ['wɒtsɪt]	Dingsda, Dings *(ugs.)*	
meteorologist [ˌmiːtir'ɒlədʒɪst]	Meteorologe/-in →	*meteorologist* → meteorology
stupid ['stjuːpɪd]	Blödmann, Dummkopf →	*Stupid!* = Silly!
to **have one's head in the clouds** [həv wʌnz ˌhed‿ɪn ðə 'klaʊdz]	über den Dingen schweben; in höheren Regionen schweben	
weather forecast ['weðə ˌfɔːkɑːst]	Wettervorhersage →	What will the weather be like tomorrow? Have you seen the *weather forecast* yet?
to **predict** [prɪ'dɪkt]	vorhersagen, voraussagen →	When you say "I think the weather will be good tomorrow", you *predict* what the weather will be like.
direction [dɪ'rekʃn]	Richtung →	Which *direction* is the museum? – It's that way.
2 **fluent** ['fluːənt]	fließend →	If you are *fluent* in French, you can speak it easily and well.

3	**verb of perception** [ˌvɜːb‿əv pəˈsepʃn]	Verb der Wahrnehmung →	Verbs like 'see', 'watch', 'hear', 'feel' are *verbs of perception.*
4	**appointment** [əˈpɔɪntmənt]	Termin →	I have an *appointment* at the bank at 9 am tomorrow morning.
	waiting room [ˈweɪtɪŋ ˌrʊm]	Wartezimmer →	When you are at the doctor's, you usually have to wait in the *waiting room* until it is your turn.
6	ambition [æmˈbɪʃn]	Ehrgeiz; Streben; Ambitionen; Ziel	
	to fire [faɪə]	*(hier:)* antreiben; anspornen	
	to hold sb back [ˌhəʊld ˈbæk]	jmdn. zurückhalten	
	to set one's sights [ˌset wʌnz ˈsaɪts]	sich Ziele stecken	
	fixed [fɪkst]	fest, unbeweglich	
	limit [ˈlɪmɪt]	Limit; Grenze; Beschränkung	
	soul [səʊl]	Seele	
	truly [ˈtruːli]	wirklich, wahrhaftig	
	to take away [teɪk‿əˈweɪ]	wegnehmen	

Revision: Talking about the future

1	prediction [prɪˈdɪkʃn]	Vorhersage, Voraussage →	*prediction* → to predict
	interview [ˈɪntəvjuː]	Vorstellungsgespräch →	I applied for a job last month. I've been invited for an *interview* on Thursday.

Talkwise: Making a good impression at an interview

	to **make a good/bad impression (on sb)** [ˌmeɪk‿ə gʊd ɪmˈpreʃn‿ɒn]	einen guten/schlechten Eindruck (auf jmdn.) machen →	What do you think of him? Did he *make a good impression on* you?
1	**suitable** [ˈsuːtəbl]	geeignet; passend →	Food without fish or meat in it is *suitable* for vegetarians.
2	**applicant** [ˈæplɪkənt]	Bewerber/-in →	In a letter of application, the *applicant* applies for a job.
	body language [ˈbɒdi ˌlæŋgwɪdʒ]	Körpersprache →	You don't always need words to express something. Sometimes your *body language* says a lot, too.
	employer [ɪmˈplɔɪə]	Arbeitgeber/-in →	*employer* → to employ
3	to **be interviewed for a job** [bi‿ˈɪntəvjuːd]	ein Vorstellungsgespräch haben →	*to be interviewed for a job* → interview
	interviewer [ˈɪntəvjuːə]	Leiter/-in eines Vorstellungsgesprächs; Interviewer/-in →	*interviewer* → interview → to be interviewed

Words to do with work

Qualifications

to study
(to take an) exam
GCSEs
A-Levels
higher education
to train / do a training course
(to do) work experience
university

Applying for a job

to apply (for)
personnel manager
opportunity
application
letter of application
placement
CV
knowledge
reference
appointment
interview
applicant
to accept

The working world

career
employer
to employ
to be out of work
to work one's way up
deadline
to meet a deadline
pay
part-time
workplace

Text: Now that's what I call living!

to bum around [bʌm əˈraʊnd]	herumziehen →	*to bum around* = to travel or move around without really knowing where you are going
'dag nabbit' [dæg ˈnæbɪt]	*(sinngemäß:)* Verflixt nochmal!	
ol' *(= old)* [əʊl]	alt	
to **be off** [bi‿ˈɒf]	gehen →	*I'm off!* = I'm leaving!
builder [ˈbɪldə]	Bauarbeiter/-in →	*builder* → building → to build
to **turn** [tɜːn]	(herum)drehen →	He *turned* the wheel and the car turned around.
It does what it damn well wants. [ˈdæm wel]	Es macht genau das, was es will.	
upside-down [ˌʌpsaɪd ˈdaʊn]	umgedreht; auf den Kopf gestellt →	My little brother doesn't know how to read. Yesterday he looked at a book *upside-down*.
Would you believe it! [ˌwʊd ju bɪˈliːv‿ɪt]	Kaum zu glauben! →	*Would you believe it!* = It's hard to believe.
tent [tent]	Zelt →	The campsite was so full that there was almost no space between the *tents*.
to **grab** [græb]	(er)greifen; schnappen →	The mother *grabbed* her daughter's arm to stop her from running into the road.
tornado [tɔːˈneɪdəʊ]	Tornado →	! Watch the pronunciation
to **throw around** [ˌθrəʊ‿əˈraʊnd]	hin und her werfen; herumwerfen →	The children *threw* the ball *around*.
just about [dʒʌst‿əˈbaʊt]	gerade noch (so)	
to **get one's act together** [ˌget wʌnz‿ˈækt təˌgeðə]	sich am Riemen reißen, sich zusammen reißen →	*to get one's act together* = to behave in the right way
trailer [ˈtreɪlə]	Wohnwagen →	In the USA a lot of people don't live in houses, they live in big *trailers*.
part-time [ˌpɑːtˈtaɪm]	Teilzeit-, Halbtags- →	My new job is a *part-time* job. I only work half-days.

gardener ['gɑ:dnə]	Gärtner/-in →	*gardener* → garden
to **be affected by** [bi ə'fektɪd baɪ]	beeinflusst sein von →	*to be affected by sth* = sth has an influence on you
childhood ['tʃaɪldhʊd]	Kindheit →	When I was young, I was a happy child. I had a very happy *childhood*.
to **make sth up** [ˌmeɪk‿'ʌp]	etw. erfinden; sich etw. ausdenken →	What she told us isn't true. She *made it* all *up*.
to **pass an exam** [ˌpɑ:s ən‿ɪg'zæm]	eine Prüfung bestehen →	We did very well in our exams. We *passed* all of them.
in the middle of [ɪn ðə 'mɪdl‿əv]	mitten in →	I live in the centre of San Francisco. = I live *in the middle of* San Francisco.
disease [dɪ'zi:z]	(Infektions)Krankheit →	AIDS is a terrible *disease* which kills millions of people each year.
medicine ['medsn]	Medizin, Medikamente →	! Watch the spelling and the pronunciation When you are ill your doctor may give you *medicine*.
gift [gɪft]	Talent, Gabe →	If you have a special *gift*, you are very good at something.
to **cure** [kjʊə]	heilen; kurieren →	*to cure* sb = to help a sick person to get better/ well
drug [drʌg]	Medikament, Arznei(mittel) →	*drug* = medicine
round [raʊnd]	rund	
African ['æfrɪkən]	Afrikaner/-in; afrikanisch →	*Africans* = people from Africa
to **beg (for)** [beg fə]	betteln (um) →	The child was *begging for* money.
politician [ˌpɒlɪ'tɪʃn]	Politiker/-in →	*Politicians* are people who work in politics.

Linking old and new vocabulary: Jobs/Careers

You have already learnt a lot of words connected to the field of "Jobs/Work". Having dealt with more words from the same field in this unit, you will find it useful to look at them all again.

Words you already know		New words
actor/actress	dancer	architect
athlete	DJ	builder
baker	doctor	electrician
banker	(taxi) driver	gardener
captain	editor	hairdresser
caretaker	(fashion) model	lawyer
cook	firefighter	meteorologist
craftsperson	teacher	musician
		nurse
		politician

bald [bɔ:ld]	glatzköpfig, kahl →	*bald* = having no hair
stick [stɪk]	Stock; Zweig; *(hier:)* sehr dünne Arme und Beine, wie Stöckchen	
to **suffer** ['sʌfə]	leiden →	*to suffer* = to experience pain *Fr. souffrir; Lat. sufferre*
It's up to you. [ɪts‿ʌp tə 'ju:]	Es ist an dir (zu entscheiden)./Wie du willst.	

	wallet ['wɒlɪt]	Brieftasche; Geldbörse →	I can't buy anything. I forgot my *wallet*.
	paper *(= newspaper)* ['peɪpə]	Zeitung →	*paper* = newspaper
7	**campaign** [kæm'peɪn]	Kampagne; Aktion →	! Watch the spelling and the pronunciation
8	**collaborative** [kə'læbrətɪv]	zusammenarbeitend	

Wordwise

2	to **be certain to do sth** [bi 'sɜːtn]	etw. sicher tun →	*to be certain to do sth* = to definitely do sth
	to **be likely to do sth** [bi 'laɪkli]	etw. wahrscheinlich tun →	*to be likely to do sth* = to probably do sth
3	**suffix** ['sʌfɪks]	Suffix, Nachsilbe →	-ment, -tion, -ive, -able etc. are *suffixes*.
4	expression [ɪk'spreʃn]	Ausdruck, Wendung; Äußerung →	*expression* → to express
	thingummy *(coll)* ['θɪŋəmi]	der/die/das Dings(da) *(ugs.)* →	*thingummy* = whatsit

VOCABULARY SKILLS

Word families

New words and phrases are often made from parts of words and phrases you already know. To remind yourself, write them all down in word families.
Examples:
to train: • trainer • training • training course
application: • to apply (for) • applicant • letter of application

Think of word families for the words below (from Unit 2) and collect more word families while you work through this book.

Tip: It can help you also to write down what kind of word it is e.g. noun or verb.

questionnaire	technical	social work	adviser	management	interviewer
out of work	competition	practical	to employ	to decide on	architect

Check-out

3	**adverbial clause** [əd'vɜːbiəl ˌklɔːz]	Adverbialsatz	
	advert ['ædvɜːt]	Anzeige; Werbespot →	! Watch the pronunciation: *advert* ↔ ad**vert**isement
4	**workplace** ['wɜːkpleɪs]	Arbeitsplatz; Arbeitsstätte →	*workplace* → work → worker → to work

Unit 3: Media-mad

The Media

Every day more and more information is brought to the public by 'the media' – by newspapers and magazines, television and radio, the Internet, and by advertising. Many people hardly realize how great the power of the media is over their lives. Have you ever thought about the effect the media can have on your own ideas and opinions?

Daily newspapers, which started appearing in Britain in the 18th century, were the first 'media form'. These days they are read by millions of people. There are 'quality' (or 'serious') newspapers, like *The Times*, and 'popular' ones, like *The Sun*, which offer the latest gossip, and have more pictures and shorter articles.

Before the days of TV, radio was the main form of entertainment in most people's homes. First started by the BBC in 1922, radio today still offers regular news and information, and also music, sport, plays, etc.

Today the average person in Britain or the USA spends four or more hours a day in front of the TV. When TV first began to find its way into more and more people's homes in the 1950s, the picture was black and white, and everyone watched the same programmes because there was only one channel! These days, of course, viewers can choose between lots of different channels, with all kinds of programmes, from Hollywood films and soap operas to chat shows. Thanks to video and DVD, people can also watch their favourite films at home whenever they want, without having to go to the cinema.

The influence of advertising on our lives is huge. Advertisements are everywhere – in newspapers and magazines, on the radio, in TV commercials and on the Internet and, of course, everywhere you go – in towns, in buses, on the underground …

Finally, there is the Internet, which can be used in so many different ways, firstly as a source of information, and for communication by e-mail, etc. It didn't take long for social networking sites, like MySpace and Facebook, to become a favourite hobby for millions of people of all ages. The amazing development of mobiles, too, which have become so much more than just phones, has made them so attractive that it is difficult to imagine what life would be like without them.

media-mad ['mi:diəmæd]	medienverrückt →	Is somebody *media-mad* just because they watch TV and use the Internet, e-mail and a mobile every day?
power ['paʊə]	Macht →	A lot of parents worry about the *power* of TV over their children.

Text A: DIY music

bath [bɑ:θ]	Badewanne →	! Watch the difference: The towels are in the bathroom. (= im Bad/ Badezimmer) ↔ John is in the *bath*. (= in der Badewanne)
to promote sth [prə'məʊt]	für etw. werben →	*to promote sth* = to advertise sth
directly [dɪ'rektli]	direkt, ohne Umwege →	Many bands promote their music *directly*, e.g. with concert tours.
to assume sth [ə'sju:m]	annehmen →	If you *assume* something, you think it is true although you don't really know. *Lat. assumere*
melody ['melədi]	Melodie →	! Watch the spelling and the pronunciation
lyrics *(pl.)* ['lɪrɪks]	Liedtext →	Are the *lyrics* of songs important to you, or just the music?

relatively ['relətɪvli]	relativ →	If you know French, then other languages in the same family like Italian or Spanish are *relatively* easy to learn.
recording [rɪ'kɔ:dɪŋ]	Aufnahme; Aufzeichnung →	*recording* → record
to edit (out) [ˌedɪt 'aʊt]	etw. herausschneiden →	Some musicians don't like to *edit out* every little mistake in a recording so that things don't sound too perfect.
washing machine ['wɒʃɪŋ məˌʃi:n]	Waschmaschine →	*washing machine* → to wash
television ['telɪvɪʒn]	Fernsehapparat, Fernseher; Fernsehen →	My parents didn't let me watch *television* until I was 13.
likely ['laɪkli]	wahrscheinlich →	Are you sure you want to spend your holiday in Majorca in August? It's *likely* to be very crowded.
to pick up [pɪk‿'ʌp]	aufschnappen →	Animals can *pick up* sounds that people can't.
carpet ['kɑ:pɪt]	Teppich →	Please take your shoes off before you walk on our new *carpet*, thanks.
blanket ['blæŋkɪt]	(Bett)Decke →	In winter I sleep under two *blankets*.
Seriously! ['sɪəriəsli]	Im Ernst! →	I've just seen Prince William, at Harrods! *Seriously!*
to **cover** ['kʌvə]	bedecken; abdecken →	She has *covered* the walls of her room with holiday photos, it's cool.
to **prove** [pru:v]	beweisen →	*to prove* = to show that sth is true
creative [kri'eɪtɪv]	kreativ →	! Watch the spelling and the pronunciation
connection [kə'nekʃn]	Verbindung →	Something is wrong with my Internet *connection* again and it's driving me crazy!
microphone (mike) ['maɪkrəfəʊn, maɪk]	Mikrofon →	! Watch the pronunciation
vocals ['vəʊklz]	Gesang →	The *vocals* on your recording are great. I love the way you use your voice.
digital ['dɪdʒɪtl]	digital →	! Watch the pronunciation
workstation ['wɜ:kˌsteɪʃn]	Arbeitsplatzrechner; Workstation	
to save [seɪv]	speichern →	Oh no, I forgot to *save* the letter on the computer! Now I have to write it again.
multi-track ['mʌltitræk]	mehrspurig	
recorder [rɪ'kɔ:də]	Aufnahmegerät →	*recorder* → recording
tutorial [tju:'tɔ:riəl]	Anleitung	
to **feel comfortable** [ˌfi:l 'kʌmftəbl]	sich wohl fühlen →	I don't *feel comfortable* driving this car yet; I'll need a few weeks to get used to it.
comfortable ['kʌmftəbl]	bequem; behaglich; angenehm →	This sofa is really *comfortable*.
track [træk]	(Ton)Spur →	Many musicians record the drum *track* first, and then add the *tracks* for other instruments and the vocals later.
raw [rɔ:]	roh; unbehandelt →	*raw* meat = meat that has not been cooked
file [faɪl]	Datei →	Don't forget to save the *file*!
killer *(coll)* ['kɪlə]	Killer-, Wahnsinns- →	That song is always the highlight on every dancefloor. No wonder, it's got a *killer* beat.
to release [rɪ'li:s]	veröffentlichen; herausbringen →	Some artists only *release* songs on the Internet.
sound effect ['saʊnd‿ɪˌfekt]	Geräuscheffekt, Toneffekt →	What would films be like without music and *sound effects*?

to **roar** [rɔ:]	(auf)heulen, dröhnen; brüllen →	The lions *have been roaring* all night.
adventurous [əd'ventʃrəs]	experimentierfreudig; abenteuerlustig, risikofreudig →	*adventurous* → adventure
social networking site [ˌsəʊʃl 'netwɜ:kɪŋ ˌsaɪt]	Online-Netzwerk →	You can chat with all kinds of people on *social networking sites*.
Go ahead. [gəʊ‿ə'hed]	Nur zu!, Mach' nur! →	Can I use your mobile? – No problem, *go ahead!*
to make it big [ˌmeɪk‿ɪt 'bɪg]	groß (he)rauskommen →	I'm going to *make it big* as a musical star; in a few years, you'll see my name in lights on Broadway!

Text B: The Truman Show

illusion [ɪ'lu:ʒn]	Trugbild, Illusion; Täuschung	
television ['telɪvɪʒn]	Fernsehapparat, Fernseher; Fernsehen →	My parents didn't let me watch *television* until I was 13.
extract ['ekstrækt]	Auszug; Exzerpt →	An *extract* from a book or script is just a small part of the whole story.
flashback ['flæʃbæk]	Rückblende, Flashback →	What's wrong? – Oh, I just had a *flashback* about something really awful that happened once.
to **cover** ['kʌvə]	bedecken; abdecken →	She has *covered* the walls in her room with holiday photos, it's cool.
lip [lɪp]	Lippe	
to stop sb doing sth [stɒp]	jmdn. davon abhalten, etw. zu tun →	You can't *stop me doing* what I want, so don't even try.
to pretend (sth) [prɪ'tend]	(etw.) vortäuschen, (etw.) vorgeben →	Stop *pretending* you're someone you're not, OK? Just be yourself!
but [bʌt; bət]	außer →	Everybody *but* John has a profile on MySpace.
horizon [hə'raɪzn]	Horizont →	! Watch the spelling and the pronunciation
to protest [prəʊ'test]	protestieren →	! Watch the pronunciation: *to protest* [prəʊ'test] ↔ a protest ['prəʊtest]
disguised [dɪs'gaɪzd]	verborgen; verkleidet, maskiert	
to fill [fɪl]	füllen →	He really can't sing, so stop *filling* his head with the idea that he can become a star.
deaf [def]	taub →	My grandfather is quite *deaf*, so I have to speak loudly to him.
to **roar** [rɔ:]	(auf)heulen, dröhnen; brüllen →	The lions *have been roaring* all night.
frightened ['fraɪtnd]	verängstigt →	*frightened* = scared
ground [graʊnd]	(Erd)Boden, Erde →	When you go camping, you usually sleep in a tent on the *ground*.
to slam shut [slæm 'ʃʌt]	zuschlagen, zuknallen →	Please don't *slam* the door *shut*. Close it quietly.
to escape (from) [ɪ'skeɪp]	(ent)fliehen, entkommen →	*to escape* = to run away from a prison or an enemy
drop [drɒp]	Tropfen →	Oh, I think that was a *drop* of rain. Let's go before it really starts to rain.
total ['təʊtl]	gesamt →	! Watch the pronunciation
record ['rekɔ:d]	Bericht; Dokumentation	
human ['hju:mən]	menschlich →	It's only *human* to make mistakes, we all do.

to replace sb/sth (by sb/sth) [rɪ'pleɪs]	jmdn./etw. (durch jmdn./etw.) ersetzen →	If you break a window it has to be *replaced*.
forum ['fɔ:rəm]	Forum →	I'm sorry, but this is the wrong *forum* for that kind of discussion. Another time, OK?
frustrated [frʌs'treɪtɪd]	frustriert →	*frustrated* = not happy
emotion [ɪ'məʊʃn]	Gefühl, Emotion →	Some people like to show their *emotions*, some don't.
cue card ['kju: ˌkɑ:d]	Stichwortkarte →	I don't like it when TV people always read from their *cue cards*; it's so boring.
viewer ['vju:ə]	(Fernseh)Zuschauer/-in →	*viewer* → view → to view
to press [pres]	drücken →	Oh, your mobile's totally different from mine. What do I *press* if I want to call the same number again?
button ['bʌtn]	Knopf →	To turn off the machine, press this *button*.
to be on [bi‿'ɒn]	auf Sendung sein	
Go ahead. [gəʊ‿ə'hed]	Nur zu!, Mach' nur! →	Can I use your mobile? – No problem, *go ahead!*
male [meɪl]	männlich →	There are only men in a *male* choir.
directly [dɪ'rektli]	direkt, ohne Umwege →	Many bands promote their music *directly*, e.g. with concert tours.
to work out sth [ˌwɜ:k‿'aʊt]	etw. verstehen, hinter etw. kommen →	*to work out* = to find out
at times [ət 'taɪmz]	ab und zu; hin und wieder; zeitweise	
female ['fi:meɪl]	weiblich →	Male voices are usually deeper than *female* voices.
performer [pə'fɔ:mə]	Darsteller/-in; Künstler/-in →	*performer* → to perform
no way [nəʊ 'weɪ]	keine Möglichkeit; kein Weg	
to **feel comfortable** [ˌfi:l 'kʌmftəbl]	sich wohl fühlen →	I don't *feel comfortable* driving this car yet; I'll need a few weeks to get used to it.
comfortable ['kʌmftəbl]	bequem; behaglich; angenehm →	This sofa is really *comfortable*.
cell [sel]	Zelle →	I think a prison *cell* would drive me crazy. So little space!
to **prove sb wrong** [ˌpru:v 'rɒŋ]	beweisen, dass jmd. Unrecht hat →	They all say my English isn't good enough to work in the UK, but *I'll prove them wrong*.
to **prove** [pru:v]	beweisen →	*to prove* = to show that sth is true

Skills: Reading skills – Reading for research

source [sɔ:s]	Quelle →	What was the *source* of your information? = Where did you get your information from?
2 **social networking site** [ˌsəʊʃl 'netwɜ:kɪŋ ˌsaɪt]	Online-Netzwerk →	You can chat with all kinds of people on *social networking sites*.

Language: Sorry, you're wrong!

brain(s) [breɪn, breɪnz]	Gehirn; Verstand →	1. Your *brain* is the part of your head that controls your feelings and how you think and move. 2. A clever person has *brains*.
effect [ɪ'fekt]	Effekt; Wirkung →	Every action has some kind of *effect* on somebody or something.
these days ['ði:z deɪz]	heutzutage →	In the 1980's, nobody had a mobile. *These days*, you can't imagine life without one.

	of no importance [əv ˌnəʊ ɪm'pɔːtns]	ohne Bedeutung →	Why does he spend all his time on things *of no importance* when his A-levels are only a few weeks away?
	importance [ɪm'pɔːtns]	Bedeutung, Wichtigkeit →	*importance* → important
	brain power ['breɪn paʊə]	Intelligenz	
	to **be unable to do sth** [bi ʌn'eɪbl tə]	unfähig sein, etw. zu tun; nicht in der Lage sein, etw. zu tun →	I'*m unable to concentrate* on my homework when it's a nice sunny day.
	unable [ʌn'eɪbl]	unfähig, außerstande →	*unable* ↔ able
	gossip ['gɒsɪp]	Klatsch; Tratsch; Gerede →	Want to hear some hot *gossip*? You're not going to believe what I heard about Julie!
	hardly ['hɑːdli]	kaum →	! You're working hard. = Du arbeitest hart. ↔ I can *hardly* believe it. = Ich kann es kaum glauben.
	issue ['ɪʃuː, 'ɪsjuː]	Angelegenheit, Thema, Problem →	Violence on television is a serious *issue*.
	in reply to [ɪn rɪ'plaɪ tə]	als Antwort auf, als Reaktion auf →	The phrase *'in reply to'* is formal and is typical of formal letter-writing.
	to **multi-task** ['mʌltiˌtɑːsk]	mehrere Dinge gleichzeitig tun →	They say women are better than men at *multi-tasking*; what do you think?
	to **filter sth** ['fɪltə]	etw. filtern →	You *filter* information to sort it and find out what is important for you.
1	to **summarize sth** ['sʌmraɪz]	etw. (kurz) zusammenfassen →	Who can *summarize* for the class what the author was trying to say in chapter 2?
2	**dynamic** [daɪ'næmɪk]	dynamisch	
	stative ['steɪtɪv]	statisch →	*stative* ↔ dynamic
4	**teletext** ['teliˌtekst]	Videotext →	*Teletext* is a useful TV service for quick information on TV programmes, sports, the weather, etc.
	to **get married** [get 'mærid]	heiraten →	You're thinking of *getting married*? But you're only 19!
	to **see sb** [siː]	mit jmdm. zusammen sein →	My parents don't like the guy I'*m seeing* right now, but that's their problem.
5	**inversion** [ɪn'vɜːʃn]	Inversion →	When you use *inversion*, you change the order of the subject and verb.
	adverbial [əd'vɜːbiəl]	Adverbialbestimmung →	'Hardly … ' and 'not only … ' are examples of *adverbials*.
	written ['rɪtn]	schriftlich →	*Written* language is often quite formal.
	no way [nəʊ 'weɪ]	auf keinen Fall; keineswegs →	*No way* should using mobiles be allowed during flights.
	spoken ['spəʊkn]	gesprochen →	His *spoken* English is better than his written English.
6	**shampoo** [ʃæm'puː]	Shampoo →	! Watch the pronunciation
7	to **argue** ['ɑːgjuː]	argumentieren →	In a discussion, you use arguments to *argue* for or against something.
8	**view** [vjuː]	Ansicht, Einstellung; Standpunkt →	*view* = point of view

USEFUL PHRASES

Always argue politely in a discussion – even when you disagree!

I think/believe …	Sorry, but I don't agree.
In my opinion …	I'm afraid I see it differently.
The way I see it, …	I have to disagree.

Revision: Present and past forms

1 for ages [fə 'eɪdʒɪz]	seit einer Ewigkeit →	*for ages* = for a very long time
to reduce [rɪ'dju:s]	reduzieren; verringern →	There was a small hole in the sweatshirt so they *reduced* the price for me.
the latest ['leɪtɪst]	der/die/das neueste →	! *the latest* news = die neuesten Nachrichten
model ['mɒdl]	Modell →	! Watch the spelling and the pronunciation
2 to go over [gəʊ 'əʊvə]	hinübergehen →	Come on, let's *go over* to your house. – No, my parents are at home, let's go somewhere else.
to go down [gəʊ 'daʊn]	sinken; nachlassen →	*to go down* = to get worse
4 judge [dʒʌdʒ]	Juror/-in →	The *judges* at that competition said such awful things about my singing! – Well, you can't sing, so it's no surprise.

Writing Texts: Writing a film script

2 **normal type** ['nɔ:ml taɪp]	Normalschrift →	Do you want to print the poem in *normal type*, or should it be bigger, smaller, or in a special colour?
italics [ɪ'tælɪks]	Kursivschrift →	The word *'shocked'* is written in *italics*.
direction [dɪ'rekʃn]	Anweisung, Instruktion →	In a script, it is usually clearer to have the *directions* in a different type from the one used for the actors' words.
bracket ['brækɪt]	Klammer →	These are *brackets*: ( ).
shot [ʃɒt]	(Kamera)Einstellung	
soft lighting [sɒft 'laɪtɪŋ]	Dämmerlicht	
romantic [rə'mæntɪk]	romantisch →	If I ever get married, I don't want any of that *romantic* stuff. I just want a big party in a very cool place.
wide shot ['waɪd ʃɒt]	Totale *(Kameraeinstellung)* →	Let's use a *wide shot* for this scene so we can see everything that's going on.
to **zoom in** [zu:m'ɪn]	heranzoomen, heranfahren →	After we get the wide shot of the man and woman in the living room, let's *zoom in* on the letter.
close-up ['kləʊsʌp]	Nahaufnahme →	OK, let's zoom in for a *close-up* of her face.
to **suck** [sʌk]	lutschen	
to **be mad about sb/sth** [bi 'mæd‿əˌbaʊt]	verrückt nach jmdm./etw. sein →	He *is mad about* old films from the 1930s and 1940s.
medium shot ['mi:diəm ʃɒt]	Halbnahe *(Kameraeinstellung)*	
to **turn away from sb/sth** [ˌtɜ:n‿ə'weɪ frəm]	sich von jmdm./etw. abwenden →	Don't *turn away from* me when I'm talking to you!
to **shrug** [ʃrʌg]	mit den Achseln/Schultern zucken →	When I asked him if he wanted to be in the play, he just *shrugged* and didn't look interested.
to **be mad with sb** [bi 'mæd‿wɪθ]	auf jmdn. böse sein; auf jmdn. sauer sein →	He's *mad with* me and I have no idea why.

instead of [ɪn'sted‿əv]	(an)statt, anstelle von →	We're going to have a holiday in the winter *instead of* the summer.
to **make a choice** [ˌmeɪk‿ə tʃɔɪs]	eine Wahl treffen →	*to make a choice* = to choose
voice-over ['vɔɪsəʊvə]	Offkommentar; Hintergrundkommentar	
3 **catch phrase** ['kætʃ freɪz]	Slogan →	A *catch phrase* is supposed to be easy to remember.

VOCABULARY SKILLS

Which preposition?

Knowing which preposition to use in English isn't always easy. Try to learn new words together with the preposition they take. Which one is correct here?

about • in • of • on • over • to • with

1. How great is the power of the media ... your life? 2. Watching too much TV can have a negative effect ... young children. 3. I am writing ... reply ... your letter of 2nd March. 4. Anyone can see she's in love – she's mad ... that guy! 5. Tom's had an accident in Mum's car – no wonder she's mad ... him! 6. Did you check the source ... that information you found on the Internet?

Wordwise

2 **cause** [kɔːz]	Grund, Ursache →	*cause* → to cause
to **busk** [bʌsk]	Straßenmusik machen →	*to busk* → busker
as [æz; əz]	da, weil →	I wasn't really mad that my order took so long *as* I wasn't really hungry anyway.
therefore ['ðeəfɔː]	deshalb, deswegen, daher →	You came home late again last night and *therefore* you're going to have to stay at home next weekend.
because of [bɪ'kɒz‿əv]	wegen →	We couldn't sleep *because of* the noise.
since [sɪns]	da →	! *since* I was little = seit ... ↔ *since* it's too late = da ...

False friends

Careful! English and German words that look (almost) the same don't always have the same meaning!

Put these words in a grid to show the real meanings. (Use a dictionary if necessary.)

gang – *Gang* • brand – *Brand* • chips – *Chips* • director – *Direktor* • fast – *fast* • gymnasium – *Gymnasium* • loch – *Loch* • action – *Aktion* • still – *still* • photograph – *Fotograf* • map – *Mappe*

German	English	German	English
schnell	fast	*fast*	...
...	brand	*Brand*	...

4 **local** ['ləʊkl]	hiesig, örtlich, lokal →	! Watch the pronunciation The schools in your area are your *local* schools.
to **tie up** [taɪ‿'ʌp]	fesseln	
6 excitement [ɪk'saɪtmənt]	Aufregung →	*excitement* → exciting → excited

tragedy ['trædʒədi]	Tragödie →	a *tragedy* = sth very terrible that happens to a person

A word quiz

Find words or phrases (all new in Unit 3) that mean …

1. the part of your head you think and feel with 2. talk or information (often shocking!) about other people 3. doing two or three things at the same time 4. to make lower (e.g. the price of something) 5. to explain the gist (e.g. of a story) in a few words or sentences 6. one of the people that decides who is best (e.g. in competition) 7. a picture taken when you zoom in with the camera 8. something you say (especially when you give facts or express an opinion)

Check-out

2 **viewer** ['vju:ə]	(Fernseh)Zuschauer/-in →	*viewer* → to view
X to **appear** [ə'pɪə]	auftreten →	He is a very successful actor. He *has appeared* in lots of films.
from now [frəm 'naʊ]	in →	50 years *from now* I'm sure there'll be lots of high-tech things we can't even imagine yet.

Linking old and new vocabulary: The Media

You have already learnt a lot of media words in *Green Line* 3. Having dealt with more words in this unit, you will find it useful to look at them all again. Here you go!

Words you already know	New words
medium pl. media	power
quality newspaper / popular newspaper	source
headline	issue
advertising / ad(vertisement) / to advertise	catch phrase
the public	viewer
programme	television
entertainment	gossip
director	direction
assistant	lighting
script	voice-over
to film	camera shot
to photograph	to zoom in / close-up
couch potato / bookworm	media-mad

Unit 4: Human rights

Human rights

Oxfam, one of the best-known charities in the UK, states that every person has a basic right to a safe environment, food and clean water, a home, an education, equal chances, and doctors to look after their health. To people living in democratic societies today, this doesn't seem too much to expect. But the idea of dignity for all and of living in a spirit of brotherhood and freedom is actually quite modern. Until 1865, for example, slavery was legally accepted in the USA, and even after it came to an end, racial discrimination and segregation still made life hard for blacks in America for a very long time.

At the beginning of the 20th century women in Britain started to fight for the right to vote in elections. In those days it was unusual for women to go to university, and women were often expected to give up their jobs when they got married. Girls these days would find such old-fashioned ideas impossible to accept. Many have no idea how much life has improved for women over the years.

Many countries in the world today have laws to protect them from discrimination. In the USA, for example, there are laws against discrimination connected with race, sex, religion or colour. But many people are still treated unfairly and discriminated against.

However, although life in our western-style democracies is still far from perfect, the situation in the world's many authoritarian regimes, where protest is not tolerated at all and human rights have little meaning, is definitely much more difficult for the people there than most of us can ever imagine.

Check-in

human rights [ˌhju:mən 'raɪts]	Menschenrechte →	In many parts of the world, people haven't got even the most basic *human rights*.
human ['hju:mən]	menschlich	
right [raɪt]	Recht →	All children should have the *right* to an education.
position of power [pəˌzɪʃnˌəv 'paʊə]	Machtposition →	I wonder what it would be like to be in a *position of power*, like the leader of a country.
position [pə'zɪʃn]	Position →	! Watch the pronunciation My two best friends aren't speaking to each other and it's really putting me in a difficult *position*.
male [meɪl]	Mann →	*Male* is a more formal word for 'man' (e.g. for talking about statistics): "50 % of all *males* born in the year 1990 are ..."
child labour [ˌtʃaɪld 'leɪbə]	Kinderarbeit →	*Child labour* goes against the rights of children.
labour ['leɪbə]	Arbeit →	*labour* = work
continuing [kən'tɪnjuɪŋ]	ständig; andauernd →	*continuing* problems = problems which don't stop
developing world [dɪ'veləpɪŋ ˌwɜ:ld]	Entwicklungsländer; Schwellenländer →	Workers in countries of the *developing world* don't often enjoy the protection of labour laws.
same-sex ['seɪmseks]	gleichgeschlechtlich →	Europe does more than any other part of the world for *same-sex* rights.
relationship [rɪ'leɪʃnʃɪp]	Beziehung →	What's the longest *relationship* you've ever had? Mine was six months.

	gay [geɪ]	schwul; Schwuler →	If a guy says another guy is good-looking, he must be *gay*. – Oh please, you don't actually believe that cliché, do you?!
	lesbian ['lezbiən]	lesbisch; Lesbe →	Carrie and Tony want to start a gay-*lesbian* club at school; what do you think?
	authoritarian [ˌɔ:θɒrɪ'teəriən]	autoritär →	In *authoritarian* societies, people are not free to do/say/be what they want.
	regime [reɪ'ʒi:m]	Regime →	*Regime* is usually the word used to describe the government of an authoritarian country.
	to **tolerate sth** ['tɒlreɪt]	etw. tolerieren; etw. dulden →	In a free country, it is expected that society *tolerates* different opinions and lifestyles.
	protest ['prəʊtest]	Protest →	! Watch the pronunciation
	proportion [prə'pɔ:ʃn]	Anteil →	What's the *proportion* of women to men in technical jobs?
	parliament ['pɑ:ləmənt]	Parlament →	! Watch the spelling and the pronunciation
	equal opportunity [ˌi:kwəl‿ɒpə'tju:nəti]	Chancengleichheit →	Before the USA had *equal opportunity* laws, women and non-white people found it difficult to get (good) jobs.
	equal ['i:kwəl]	gleich	
	recent ['ri:snt]	kürzlich; neueste/-r/-s; letzte/-r/-s →	*Recent* events are things that happened only a short time ago.
	democracy [dɪ'mɒkrəsi]	Demokratie →	People in a *democracy* are free to elect their government.
	to **qualify** ['kwɒlɪfaɪ]	die (nötigen) Voraussetzungen/ Bedingungen erfüllen →	*Qualifying* for that exchange programme in Paris isn't going to be easy; the test I have to take is really hard.
	to **be considered (to be) sth** [bi kən'sɪdəd]	als etw. gelten →	Germany *is considered to be* one of the most democratic countries in the world.
	democratic [ˌdemə'krætɪk]	demokratisch →	! Watch the pronunciation: *democratic* [ˌdemə'krætɪk] ↔ democracy [dɪ'mɒkrəsi]
	least [li:st]	am wenigsten →	*least* ↔ most
1	to **represent** [ˌreprɪ'zent]	repräsentieren; darstellen →	The same photo can *represent* different things to different people.
	freedom of speech [ˌfri:dəm‿əv 'spi:tʃ]	Redefreiheit →	People who enjoy *freedom of speech* know that they can criticize their government without fear of going to prison – or worse.
	religion [rɪ'lɪdʒn]	Religion →	*religion* → religious → R.E. (Religious Education)
	tolerance ['tɒlrns]	Toleranz →	*tolerance* → to tolerate
	racial equality [ˌreɪʃl‿ɪ'kwɒləti]	Rassengleichheit	
	to **protest** [prəʊ'test]	protestieren →	! Watch the pronunciation: *to protest* [prəʊ'test] ↔ a protest ['prəʊtest]
	sex [seks]	Geschlecht	
2	**basis** ['beɪsɪs]	Basis, Grundlage	
	to **state** [steɪt]	erklären; aussagen; nennen →	*to state* → statement
	dignity ['dɪgnəti]	Würde	
	spirit ['spɪrɪt]	Geist →	In the true *spirit* of sport, taking part is more important than winning.
	brotherhood ['brʌðəhʊd]	Brüderlichkeit →	*brotherhood* → brother
4	**satisfactory** [ˌsætɪs'fæktri]	zufriedenstellend →	If you get *satisfactory* grades at school, then it means they are 'OK', but not great.

Language 1: Dignity for all?

slave [sleɪv]	Sklave/Sklavin →	*Slaves* are not paid for their work, and they must do what their owners tell them.
to free [fri:]	befreien →	Don't you wish you could *free* those poor kids who work as slaves? – Yes, what an awful life it must be.
Romanian [rʊ'meɪniən]	Rumäne/Rumänin; rumänisch, aus Rumänien; Rumänisch →	*Romanians* = people from Romania
to smuggle ['smʌgl]	schmuggeln →	*to smuggle* sth into a country = to bring sth into a country illegally
to recruit sb [rɪ'kru:t]	jmdn. rekrutieren →	Soldiers *are recruited* to the army.
pick-pocketing ['pɪkˌpɒkɪtɪŋ]	Taschendiebstahl →	*Pick-pocketing* is a real problem in some big cities, esp. in crowded places like trains.
slavery ['sleɪvri]	Sklaverei →	*slavery* → slave
western ['westən]	westlich →	The *western* world is Europe, North America and other parts of the world with a strong European influence.
to be happy to do sth [bi 'hæpi tə ˌdu:]	etw. gerne tun; etw. tun können →	Excuse me, could you take a picture of us, please? – Of course, I'*d be happy* to.
relative ['relətɪv]	relativ →	Whether something is good or bad is *relative*; it depends on whose point of view it is.
concept ['kɒnsept]	Vorstellung, Idee; Konzept →	! Watch the spelling and the pronunciation
ancient ['eɪnʃnt]	alt; antik →	In the *ancient* world of Rome and Egypt, only very few people enjoyed rights.
Middle Ages ['mɪdlˌeɪdʒɪz]	Mittelalter →	the *Middle Ages* = the time in history from about 500 to 1500
to spread, spread, spread [spred, spred, spred]	(sich) verbreiten →	The disease *spread* very quickly.
landowner ['lændˌəʊnə]	Grundbesitzer/-in →	In some countries like Brazil or the USA, there are *landowners* who own areas the size of countries like Belgium or Holland.
to **vote** [vəʊt]	wählen; (für/gegen jmdn.) stimmen →	Who are you going to *vote* for in the election? I can't decide.
to **receive** [rɪ'si:v]	erhalten, bekommen →	*to receive* = to get
individual [ˌɪndɪ'vɪdʒuəl]	Einzelperson; Einzelne/-r; Individuum →	Each *individual* is a unique person.
need [ni:d]	Notwendigkeit; Bedarf →	*need* → to need
dictator [dik'teɪtə]	Diktator/-in →	German history shows what awful things a *dictator* and his regime can do.
secret police [ˌsi:krət pə'li:s]	Geheimpolizei	
necessary ['nesəsri]	nötig, notwendig, erforderlich →	It won't be *necessary* to book in advance. = You won't need to book in advance
by force [baɪ 'fɔ:s]	gewaltsam, mit Gewalt →	Dictators often reach their goals *by force*.
Congress ['kɒŋgres]	Congress *(Parlament der USA)* →	*Congress* makes the laws in the United States, not the president.
to **pass** [pɑ:s]	*(ein Gesetz)* verabschieden →	A new law *was passed* in Congress yesterday.
patriot ['peɪtriət]	Patriot/-in →	! Watch the pronunciation
act [ækt]	Gesetz →	*act* = law
activist ['æktɪvɪst]	Aktivist/-in →	*activist* → activity → active
loss [lɒs]	Verlust →	*loss* → to lose
1 to **identify** [aɪ'dentɪfaɪ]	aufzeigen; identifizieren →	*to identify* → identification
2 **pyramid** ['pɪrəmɪd]	Pyramide →	! Watch the spelling and the pronunciation

3	**in spite of** [ɪn ˈspaɪt‿əv]	trotz →	*in spite of* the rain = although it was raining
	by *(+ gerund)* [baɪ]	indem →	The world will never become a better place *by* just ignoring problems.
	cause [kɔːz]	Sache →	What *cause* do you think it'd be worth fighting for? – That's difficult, there are so many.
4	**mark** [mɑːk]	Note →	*mark (BE)* = grade *(AE)*
	to **complain** [kəmˈpleɪn]	sich beschweren, sich beklagen →	My coffee was cold, so I *complained* to the waiter.
6	**mirror** [ˈmɪrə]	Spiegel →	She is looking at herself in the *mirror.*
	affordable [əˈfɔːdəbl]	bezahlbar; erschwinglich →	Living in the centre of London isn't *affordable* for many people; flats are extremely expensive.

Talkwise: Tolerance and respect

	everyday [ˈevrideɪ]	alltäglich →	My favourite part of French class is when we practise *everyday* situations, like talking on the phone or making small talk.
	ingredient [ɪnˈɡriːdiənt]	Zutat →	Something is missing in this cake; what *ingredient* did I forget?
1	**tolerant** [ˈtɒlrnt]	tolerant →	! Watch the pronunciation *tolerant* → tolerance → to tolerate
	respectful [rɪˈspektfl]	respektvoll →	*respectful* → respect → to respect
	appropriate [əˈprəʊpriət]	angemessen →	Do you really think it's *appropriate* to wear such short shorts to a nice restaurant?
2	**I'd appreciate it if ...** [aɪd‿əˈpriːʃieɪt‿ɪt ɪf]	Könnten Sie/Könntest du ...; Ich wäre Ihnen sehr verbunden, wenn ... →	Excuse me, *I'd* really *appreciate it if* you could play your music more quietly on your mp3 player; it's very loud. Thanks.
4	**sensitive** [ˈsensɪtɪv]	empfindlich →	A *sensitive* person gets angry or worried easily if somebody says the wrong thing.
	thick [θɪk]	dick →	*thick* ↔ thin

Language 2: Heroes

1	**movement** [ˈmuːvmənt]	Bewegung →	*movement* → to move
	to **cause** [kɔːz]	verursachen	
	to **integrate** [ˈɪntɪɡreɪt]	(sich) integrieren; (sich) einfügen; *(hier:) Schulen für Schwarze zugänglich machen* →	The 'Little Rock Nine' had a very difficult time *integrating* an all-white school.
	segregation [ˌseɡrɪˈɡeɪʃn]	(Rassen)Trennung →	When people use the term *segregation*, they are usually talking about racial segregation.
	courage [ˈkʌrɪdʒ]	Mut, Tapferkeit, Courage →	! Watch the pronunciation
	mob [mɒb]	Mob, (Menschen)Menge; Pöbel →	*mob* = a large crowd that is ready to cause trouble or violence
	to **shuffle** [ˈʃʌfl]	schlurfen →	Don't *shuffle* like that – lift your feet when you walk!
	to **call sb names** [ˌkɔːl ˌsʌmbɒdi ˈneɪmz]	jmdn. beschimpfen →	*to call sb names* = to use nasty words/names to describe sb
	block [blɒk]	(Häuser)Block →	A *block* is an area of land (in a town) with streets on each side.
	to **pass** [pɑːs]	vorbeigehen; vorübergehen; vorbeikommen →	It took 20 minutes before the crowd let the film star *pass*; everyone wanted to have their picture taken with her.

bench [benʃ]	(Sitz)Bank →	I wish there were more *benches* to sit on in this park.
integration [ˌɪntɪˈɡreɪʃn]	Integration, Integrierung; Eingliederung →	! Watch the pronunciation *integration* → to integrate
to **get through sth** [ɡet θruː]	etw. überstehen →	He's not looking forward to his first day at the new school, but he'*ll get through* it, don't worry.
terrified [ˈterəfaɪd]	erschrocken; verängstigt →	*terrified* = very, very frightened
silent [ˈsaɪlənt]	still; ruhig; schweigsam →	If you don't say anything, you stay *silent*.
observer [əbˈzɜːvə]	Beobachter/-in; Zuschauer/-in →	When I see a bully hurting someone, I want to help and not be a silent *observer*. But at the same time I'm afraid that I could be hurt.
racism [ˈreɪsɪzm]	Rassismus →	*racism* → racist → racial
to **bully** [ˈbʊli]	jmdn. tyrannisieren; jmdn. drangsalieren →	*to bully* → a bully

VOCABULARY SKILLS

The same ideas – less formally expressed

When you learn new words or phrases, try to think of synonyms or how you can express them differently.

Many of the words and phrases in this unit sound quite formal. They would not always be used in everyday conversation. Can you express these ideas in less formal language?

Example:
Males still dominate the business world. – There are many more men than women in the business world.

1. Child labour is a continuing problem in the developing world. – In poorer countries … 2. Human beings should act towards one another in a spirit of brotherhood. 3. Freedom of speech is a basic human right. 4. Dictators do not tolerate protest. 5. In 1954 the Supreme Court decided that racial segregation in schools was illegal. 6. Some people have a lower tolerance level than others. 7. Do you believe in the equality of the sexes? 8. A large proportion of the population of India lives in extreme poverty.

2 **ordinary** [ˈɔːdnri]	gewöhnlich, normal →	I thought he was just an *ordinary* boy from school. I had no idea he was a drug dealer.
role model [ˈrəʊl ˌmɒdl]	Vorbild →	What qualities do you think a *role model* has?
3 **mean** [miːn]	gemein →	He was really *mean* to me. = He treated me badly.
5 to **murder sb** [ˈmɜːdə]	jmdn. ermorden, jmdn. umbringen →	*to murder sb* = to kill sb
to **bring sb's attention to sth** [brɪŋ əˈtenʃn tə]	jmds. Aufmerksamkeit auf etw. lenken →	We'll never change anything if we don't *bring people's attention to* the human rights problems.
carpet [ˈkɑːpɪt]	Teppich →	We need a new *carpet* for the living room floor.
to **speak out (about sth)** [ˌspiːk‿ˈaʊt]	seine Meinung deutlich vertreten; sich zu etw. äußern →	He's always the first to *speak out about* things he thinks are wrong or unfair.
to **make a difference (to sth)** [ˌmeɪk‿ə‿ˈdɪfrns]	etw. verändern →	Some schools have 'Make a difference' days where all the pupils start projects to *make a difference* in their town and make it a better place.

to **be eager to do sth** [bi 'i:gə tə]	etw. unbedingt tun wollen, darauf erpicht sein, etw. zu tun; eifrig bemüht sein, etw. zu tun →	She's always so *eager* to be the first or the best in everything she does; it really drives me crazy.
properly ['prɒpli]	richtig; anständig →	He can speak a little French, a little Spanish and a little Greek, but he can't speak any foreign language *properly*.
sweatshop ['swetʃɒp]	Ausbeuterbetrieb →	*Sweatshops* are clothes factories where workers – often children – have to work long hours in an unhealthy environment for very low pay.
hell [hel]	Hölle →	It was a terrible time for me – I went through *hell*.
7 to **judge sb/sth by sth** ['dʒʌdʒ baɪ]	jmdn./etw. beurteilen; jmdn./etw. einschätzen →	People who *judge by* looks are only concentrating on one aspect of a person and his/her lifestyle.

USEFUL PHRASES

Express tolerance, respect, courage and support in different everyday situations.

I really don't think it's fair …
I'm terribly sorry, but …
Would you mind …?
Could you show a little more respect for …?
I'd really appreciate it if you could …
Do you think that's appropriate?
I don't think it's right to judge by people's looks/appearance/skin colour.
Don't you think that's a bit unfair/racist/nasty?

Revision: Equal opportunity

1 substitute ['sʌbstɪtju:t]	Ersatz →	Can you play tennis for me on Sunday? I need a *substitute*.
to miss a point [ˌmɪs ə 'pɔɪnt]	nicht verstehen, worum es geht →	You're *missing the point*, Paul. Listen, I'll explain it again …
tense shift ['tens ʃɪft]	Zeitverschiebung *(gramm.)*	
2 race [reɪs]	Rasse →	*race* → racial → racism → racist
discrimination [dɪˌskrɪmɪ'neɪʃn]	Diskriminierung →	How many times have you seen situations in which someone (maybe even yourself) was experiencing *discrimination*?
off [ɒf]	reduziert →	If you get 30 % *off* a pair of shoes, you pay 30 % less.
discount ['dɪskaʊnt]	Rabatt, Preisnachlass →	Let's buy this mp3 player, it's really cheap. There's a 50 % *discount*!

Writing Skills: Short biographies

biographical [baɪəʊ'græfɪkl]	biographisch →	She likes *biographical* writing because she thinks stories about real people are the most interesting.
further ['fɜ:ðə]	weiter →	far → *further*

	↻ **focus (on)** ['fəʊkəs‿ɒn]	sich konzentrieren (auf) →	You missed another party, Rachel! – I know, but I have to *focus on* my exams right now, no time for parties.
	bio *(= biography)* ['baɪəʊ]	Biografie →	*bio* → biography → biographical
1	**soul** [səʊl]	Seele →	I just feel in my *soul* that I should help people in the developing world.
	robe [rəʊb]	Gewand →	People in ancient Rome used to wear *robes*.
	clothing ['kləʊðɪŋ]	Kleidung →	*clothing* → clothes
	status symbol ['steɪtəs ˌsɪmbl]	Statussymbol →	There are lots of different *status symbols*: expensive watches, cars, …
	to **achieve** [ə'tʃi:v]	erreichen; erfolgreich sein →	If you work hard and are ambitious, you can *achieve* a lot.
	uneducated [ʌn'edʒʊkeɪtɪd]	ungebildet →	Giving *uneducated* people the chance to go to school is an important cause to fight for.
	homeless ['həʊmləs]	obdachlos →	*homeless* → home
	material [mə'tɪəriəl]	materiell →	I'm not really interested in *material* things. Who needs another mp3 player, more clothes, another computer?
	mind [maɪnd]	Geist, Verstand →	You think and feel with your *mind*.
	peaceful ['pi:sfl]	friedlich →	*peaceful* → peace
	one-dimensional [wʌndaɪ'menʃnl]	eindimensional →	All you think about is your career; don't be so *one-dimensional*!
	though [ðəʊ]	(je)doch →	Even then, *though* … = But even then …
	tyrant ['taɪrənt]	Tyrann/-in →	Our neighbour is a terrible *tyrant*, shouting commands at his wife all the time.

Linking old and new vocabulary: Characterization

You have already learnt a lot of words to describe people. Having dealt with more words in *Green Line* 5, you will find it useful to look at them all again. Here you go!

Words you already know			New words
aggressive	funny	predictable	authoritarian
ambitious	gentle	quiet	competitive
angry	good	realistic	confident
annoying	heartless	reckless	eager
brilliant	helpful	relaxed	emotional
calm	hot-headed	rude	exotic
clever	impolite	sad	idealistic
crazy	independent	scary	one-dimensional
criminal	interesting	selfish	ordinary
curious	kind	shy	peaceful
dangerous	lazy	special	reliable
difficult	lonely	strange	respectful
disappointing	mean	strict	romantic
embarrassing	nasty	strong	sensitive
extreme	nervous	stupid	serious
fair	nice	violent	successful
fake	odd	weak	tactful
famous	patient	weird	tolerant
friendly	popular	wise	
frightening	polite	worried	

	to **flow** [fləʊ]	fließen; strömen →	Rivers *flow* into the sea.
	reference ['refrns]	Anspielung; Erwähnung, Bezugnahme →	There are a lot of *references* to discrimination in pop music. = A lot of songs are about discrimination.
	thought [θɔ:t]	Gedanke →	*thought* → to think
	to **feature (sth)** ['fi:tʃə]	(etw.) aufweisen →	Everyone's character *features* special qualities. = There are always special qualities in everyone's character.
	contradiction [ˌkɒntrə'dɪkʃn]	Widerspruch; Widersprüchlichkeit →	Don't you think it's a *contradiction* for you to eat chocolate cake while you tell other people it's bad to eat stuff like that?
3	**historical** [hɪ'stɒrɪkl]	historisch, geschichtlich →	*historical* → history

Text: Protest songs

1	**emotional** [ɪ'məʊʃnl]	emotional; gefühlsmäßig →	He gets *emotional* when he hears sad songs on the radio.
	harmonious [hɑ:'məʊniəs]	harmonisch, wohlklingend →	Most people would agree that Mozart's music is *harmonious*.
	dissonant ['dɪsnənt]	dissonant, nicht harmonierend →	*dissonant* ↔ harmonious
	poetic [pəʊ'etɪk]	poetisch, dichterisch →	*Poetic* language uses beautiful words.
	obnoxious [əb'nɒkʃəs]	unausstehlich; unmöglich; widerwärtig →	It's so *obnoxious* the way she always has to be the centre of attention, I hate it!
	idealistic [aɪˌdɪə'lɪstɪk]	idealistisch →	*Idealistic* people dream of creating a better world.
	to blow [bləʊ]	wehen, blasen →	A cold wind began to *blow* and it started to snow.
	dove [dʌv]	Taube →	The white *dove* is a symbol of peace.
	cannon ball ['kænən bɔ:l]	Kanonenkugel	
	forever [fə'revə]	für immer; ewig →	Nobody lives *forever.*
	to **ban** [bæn]	bannen; sperren; verbieten →	Some countries *have banned* child labour, it is no longer allowed there.
	to wash [wɒʃ]	wegschwemmen, wegspülen	
	to **pretend (sth)** [prɪ'tend]	(etw.) vorgeben; (etw.) vortäuschen →	Stop *pretending* you're someone you're not, OK? Just be yourself!
	death [deθ]	Tod →	*death* → dead *death* ↔ life
	till [tɪl]	bis →	*till* = until
	to hold sb down [ˌhəʊld 'daʊn]	jmdn. niedrig halten; jmdn. unterdrücken →	*to hold sb down* = to stop sb from achieving sth
	bitch *(vulg)* ['bɪtʃ]	Miststück; Schlampe; Zicke *(derb)* →	You mustn't call anyone a *bitch*; it is not the kind of word people use in public.
	cos *(coll)* [kʌz]	weil →	*cos* = because
	to **be on one's mind** [bi‿ən wʌnz 'maɪnd]	jmdn. beschäftigen, jmdn. umtreiben →	What's *on your mind*? You look like you're worried about something.
	to swallow ['swɒləʊ]	(hinunter)schlucken →	With babies and little kids, you have to be careful that they don't *swallow* things they shouldn't.
	to fire back [faɪə 'bæk]	zurückschlagen →	I said some things I shouldn't have said, and she *fired back* with some awful things, too.
	target ['tɑ:gɪt]	Ziel(scheibe)	

	rumor ['ru:mə]	Gerücht →	Have you heard the new *rumor* about Daniel? – No, and I'm not interested in your gossip.
	to slander (sb/sth) ['slɑ:ndə]	(jmdn./etw.) verleumden →	*to slander sb* = to spread false rumors/stories about sb
	popularity [ˌpɒpjə'lærəti]	Popularität; Beliebtheit →	*popularity* → popular *Fr. popularité*
	controversy ['kɒntrəvɜ:si]	Kontroverse; Auseinandersetzung →	*controversy* = a public discussion featuring very different and often emotional opinions
	worth [wɜ:θ]	Wert →	Every person has *worth* and dignity.
	to stand one's ground [ˌstænd wʌnz 'graʊnd]	sich behaupten →	*to stand one's ground* = not to give up
	to take a deep breath [teɪk‿ə ˌdi:p 'breθ]	tief einatmen, tief Luft holen →	I don't know if I can sing in front of all those people! – Just *take a deep breath*, concentrate and go out there!
	to **offend** [ə'fend]	beleidigen; verletzen →	Topics like religion or politics aren't good for starting small talk; people can be easily *offended* by other people's views.
	to **handle** ['hændl]	umgehen mit; handhaben; bedienen →	*to handle* = to deal with
	common ['kɒmən]	üblich, gewöhnlich; (weit) verbreitet →	*common* = everyday
	double standard [ˌdʌbl 'stændəd]	Doppelmoral →	When you buy something expensive it's OK, but when I do it, it's not. What a *double standard*!
	glory ['glɔ:ri]	Ruhm; Ehre →	It was a moment of *glory* to win the gold medal for my country.
	to score *(coll)* [skɔ:]	jmdn. ins Bett kriegen *(ugs.)* →	He's very popular with girls and *scores* every night he goes out.
	whore *(vulg)* [hɔ:]	Nutte; Flittchen *(derb)* →	You mustn' call anyone a *whore*; it is not the kind of word people use in public.
	to get named *(coll)* [get 'neɪmd]	beschimpft werden →	*to get named* = to have your name connected with sth bad (e.g. a bad rumor)
3	**message** ['mesɪdʒ]	Botschaft; Message →	I don't understand this song! What's the singer trying to tell us? What's his *message*?
	specific [spə'sɪfɪk]	genau →	*specific* = clear and exact
	general ['dʒenrl]	allgemein →	Do you need details or just *general* information?
	to **relate to (sb/sth)** [rɪ'leɪt‿tə]	eine Beziehung/Zugang zu jmdm./etw. finden →	I just can't *relate to* him. I don't understand him at all
	solution [sə'lu:ʃn]	Lösung →	Find a *solution*! = Solve the problem!
4	**lyrics** *(pl.)* ['lɪrɪks]	Liedtext →	Are the *lyrics* of songs important to you, or just the music?
	refrain [rɪ'freɪn]	Refrain →	! Watch the pronunciation The song is OK, but the *refrain* is repeated too often.
6	**timeless** ['taɪmləs]	zeitlos →	*timeless* fashion ≠ trendy fashion
	dated ['deɪtɪd]	veraltet, überholt →	When you talk to people who are much, much older than you, some of the words they use might sound a bit *dated*.

Human rights

activist
authoritarian regime
basic rights
child labour
civil rights (movement)
courage
death
democracy
democratic country
(the) developing world
dictator
dignity
discrimination
(to) dominate
double standard
equal opportunities
freedom of speech
freedom; (to) free
gay
harmonious
health
homeless
integration; (to) integrate
landowner
lesbian
(to) murder
parliament
(to) pass a law
peaceful
position of power
poverty
privacy; private
protection of children
(to) protect
protest march
protest; (to) protest
racial equality
racism
religion
race
respect; respectful
(to) respect
role model
same-sex relationship
secret police
segregation
sex
slavery; slave
(to) speak out about sth
spirit of brotherhood
sweatshop
terror; terror attack
terrorist
tolerant; (to) tolerate
tyrant
uneducated
(to) vote (in an election)
(the) western world

Adjectives as nouns

Some adjectives can be used as nouns – to describe people you think of as a 'group', not as individuals.

a) Which could you use instead of these descriptions?

the disabled • the homeless • the very young • the famous • the rich • the uneducated
the hungry • the poor • the unemployed • the brave • the lonely • the sick

1. people who have never been to school
2. those who have very little money
3. children under the age of three
4. people with lots of money, or too much
5. people who are ill
6. those without a job

b) Now find your own descriptions for the ones you didn't use in a).

Dictionary

In dieser alphabetischen Liste ist das gesamte Vokabular von *Green Line* 1 bis 5 enthalten mit Ausnahme der Wörter, die nicht zum Lernwortschatz von Band 1 bis 4 gehören. Namen werden in gesonderten Listen am Ende des ***Dictionary*** aufgeführt. Die mit * gekennzeichneten Verben sind unregelmäßig (siehe auch S. 214–215).
Die Fundstellen verweisen auf das erstmalige Vorkommen der Wörter, z. B.
a [ə; ən] ein/-e **I** kommt zum ersten Mal vor in Band I
actor ['æktə] Schauspieler **II** kommt zum ersten Mal vor in Band II
advert ['ædvɜ:t] Anzeige; Werbespot **V U2**, 42 kommt zum ersten Mal vor in Band V, Unit 2, Seite 42
Die Wörter, deren Fundstellen in Spitzklammern stehen, gehören nicht zum aktiv zu beherrschenden Lernwortschatz.
U = Unit, ZI = Zoom-in

A

a(n) [ə; ən] ein/-e **I**
a bit [ə 'bɪt] ein wenig, ein bisschen **II**
a day [ə 'deɪ] pro Tag **II**
a lot of [ə 'lɒt‿əv] viel/-e, eine Menge **I**
a pair of [ə 'peər‿əv] ein Paar **III**
aargh! [ɑ:g] Grrrr! **I**
*to be **able to (do sth)** [bi‿'eɪbl tə] können, fähig sein (zu) **III**
Aboriginal [ˌæbə'rɪdʒnl] Aborigine, Ureinwohner/-in Australiens **V ZI**, 11
Aboriginal [ˌæbə'rɪdʒnl] der Aborigines **V ZI**, 11
part-Aboriginal [ˌpɑ:t æbə'rɪdʒnl] teils Aborigine ⟨**V U1**, 14⟩
about [ə'baʊt] ungefähr, circa, etwa **II**
about [ə'baʊt] über **I**
to be about [bi ə'baʊt] gehen um, handeln von **III**
above [ə'bʌv] oben, über, oberhalb **III**
abridged [ə'brɪdʒd] gekürzt **V U1**, 13; **V U1**, 15
abseiling ['æbseɪlɪŋ] Abseilen **II**
abstract ['æbstrækt] abstrakt **III**
accent ['æksnt] Akzent **III**
to **accept** [ək'sept] akzeptieren, hinnehmen; annehmen **IV**
access *(no pl.)* ['ækses] Zugang, Zutritt **IV**
accident ['æksɪdnt] Unfall **II**
It was **ace!** *(coll)* [ˌɪt wəz‿'eɪs] Es war geil! *(ugs.)* ⟨**V U1**, 21⟩
to **achieve** [ə'tʃi:v] erreichen; erfolgreich sein **V U4**, 77
across [ə'krɒs] über; hinüber; herüber; querdurch **III**
act [ækt] Gesetz **V U4**, 70
to get one's act together [ˌget wʌnz‿'ækt təˌgeðə] sich zusammenreißen **V U2**, 38
to **act** [ækt] spielen **I**
action ['ækʃn] Handlung; Action **III**
active ['æktɪv] Aktiv **III**
politically **active** [pəˌlɪtɪkli 'æktɪv] politisch engagiert ⟨**V U1**, 14⟩
activist ['æktɪvɪst] Aktivist/-in **V U4**, 70
activity [æk'tɪvəti] Aktivität **I**
actor ['æktə] Schauspieler **II**
actress ['æktrəs] Schauspielerin **III**
actually ['æktʃuəli] tatsächlich, wirklich; eigentlich **III**
AD *(= Anno Domini)* [eɪ'di:] nach Christus **III**
adapted [ə'dæptɪd] adaptiert; angepasst **V U1**, 13; **V U1**, 15
to **add** [æd] etw. (zu etw.) hinzufügen **II**
addicted (to) [ə'dɪktɪd tə] süchtig **II**
addiction [ə'dɪkʃn] Sucht; Abhängigkeit **IV**
address [ə'dres] Adresse **I**
address book [ə'dres ˌbʊk] Adressbuch **I**
adjective ['ædʒɪktɪv] Adjektiv, Eigenschaftswort **I**
to **admire** [əd'maɪə] bewundern **IV**
to **admit** [əd'mɪt] zugeben **III**
adrenaline [ə'drenlɪn] Adrenalin **IV**
adult ['ædʌlt] Erwachsene/-r **III**
adult ['ædʌlt] erwachsen; reif, vernünftig **IV**
advantage [əd'vɑ:ntɪdʒ] Vorteil **IV**
adventure [əd'ventʃə] Abenteuer **I**
adventurous [əd'ventʃrəs] experimentierfreudig; abenteuerlustig, risikofreudig ⟨**V U3**, 51⟩
adverb ['ædvɜ:b] Adverb **II**
adverb of degree [ˌædvɜ:b‿əv dɪ'gri:] Gradadverb **IV**
adverbial [əd'vɜ:biəl] Adverbialbestimmung **V U3**, 56
adverbial clause [əd'vɜ:biəl ˌklɔ:z] Adverbialsatz **V U2**, 42
advert ['ædvɜ:t] Anzeige; Werbespot **V U2**, 42
to **advertise** ['ædvətaɪz] Werbung machen (für), werben; anpreisen; inserieren **III**
ad(vertisement) [əd'vɜ:tɪsmənt] Anzeige; Werbespot **III**
advertising *(no pl.)* ['ædvətaɪzɪŋ] Werbung, Reklame **III**
advice [əd'vaɪs] Rat, Ratschlag **III**
giving advice [ˌgɪvɪŋ əd'vaɪs] einen Rat geben **III**
to **advise (sb to do sth)** [əd'vaɪz] (jmdm.) raten (etw. zu tun) **III**
adviser [əd'vaɪzə] Berater/-in **V U2**, 30
aerobics [eə'rəʊbɪks] Aerobic **II**
*to be **affected by** [bi ə'fektɪd baɪ] von etw. beeinflusst sein **V U2**, 38
affordable [ə'fɔ:dəbl] bezahlbar; erschwinglich **V U4**, 72
I'm **afraid** [aɪm ə'freɪd] leider **III**
to be afraid (of) *(+ gerund)* [bi‿ə'freɪd‿əv] (sich) fürchten (vor), Angst haben (vor) **IV**
African ['æfrɪkən] Afrikaner/-in; afrikanisch **V U2**, 39
after ['ɑ:ftə] nach; nachdem **I**
after that ['ɑ:ftə ðæt] danach **I**
afternoon [ˌɑ:ftə'nu:n] Nachmittag **I**
again [ə'gen] wieder, noch einmal, nochmal **I**
again and again [ə'gen‿ənd‿ə'gen] immer wieder **II**
against [ə'genst] gegen **I**
age [eɪdʒ] Zeitalter; Alter **III**
ages ago ['eɪdʒɪz əˌgəʊ] vor einer Ewigkeit **IV**
for ages [fə 'eɪdʒɪz] seit einer Ewigkeit ⟨**V U3**, 57⟩
legal driving age [ˌli:gl 'draɪvɪŋ eɪdʒ] *(Mindestalter für den Führerscheinerwerb)* **IV**
Middle Ages ['mɪdl‿eɪdʒɪz] Mittelalter **V U4**, 70
travel **agency** ['trævl ˌeɪdʒnsi] Reisebüro **III**
agent ['eɪdʒnt] Agent/-in **III**
aggressive [ə'gresɪv] aggressiv **II**
ages **ago** ['eɪdʒɪz əˌgəʊ] vor einer Ewigkeit **IV**
ago [ə'gəʊ] vor *(zeitlich)* **II**

agony aunt ['æɡəni ˌɑ:nt] Kummerkastentante **III**
to **agree** [ə'ɡri:] zustimmen **III**
Go **ahead.** [ɡəʊ‿ə'hed] Mach nur! **V U3,** 51; **V U3,** 53
air [eə] Luft **I**
to end in thin air [ˌend‿ɪn θɪn‿'eə] im Nichts enden **II**
airport ['eəpɔ:t] Flughafen **II**
alarm clock [ə'lɑ:m ˌklɒk] Wecker **I**
alcohol *(no pl.)* ['ælkəhɒl] Alkohol **IV**
alien ['eɪliən] Außerirdische/-r, außerirdisches Wesen **II**
alive [ə'laɪv] am Leben **IV**
all [ɔ:l] alle/-s; ganz **I**
all day [ɔ:l 'deɪ] den ganzen Tag **II**
all kinds of [ɔ:l 'kaɪndz‿əv] allerhand, vielerlei; alle möglichen **V U1,** 18
all of it ['ɔ:l‿əv‿ɪt] alle/-s (davon); ganz **II**
all the time [ˌɔ:l ðə 'taɪm] die ganze Zeit **II**
pledge of **allegiance** [ˌpledʒ‿əv ə'li:dʒns] Treueeid **IV**
allergic to [ə'lɜ:dʒɪk tə] allergisch auf **I**
to **allow** [ə'laʊ] erlauben, gestatten **III**
to be allowed to (do sth) [bi‿ə'laʊd tə] dürfen **III**
almost ['ɔ:lməʊst] fast, beinahe **II**
alone [ə'ləʊn] allein **I**
Leave him alone! [ˌli:v hɪm‿ə'ləʊn] Lass ihn in Ruhe! **II**
along [ə'lɒŋ] entlang **IV**
to come along [ˌkʌm‿ə'lɒŋ] mitkommen **IV**
alphabet ['ælfəbet] Alphabet **I**
alphabetical [ˌælfə'betɪkl] alphabetisch **I**
already [ɔ:l'redi] schon, bereits **I**
also ['ɔ:lsəʊ] auch **III**
although [ɔ:l'ðəʊ] obwohl **II**
always ['ɔ:lweɪz] immer **I**
am [ˌeɪ'em] vormittags *(Uhrzeit)* **I**
amazement [ə'meɪzmənt] Erstaunen, Verwunderung ⟨**V U1,** 13⟩
amazing [ə'meɪzɪŋ] unglaublich; toll; erstaunlich **IV**
ambition [æm'bɪʃn] Ehrgeiz; Streben; Ambitionen; Ziel ⟨**V U2,** 35⟩
ambitious [æm'bɪʃəs] ehrgeizig **IV**
ambulance ['æmbjələns] Krankenwagen **III**
American [ə'merɪkən] Amerikanisch; amerikanisch, aus Amerika **III**; Amerikaner/-in **IV**
American football [əˌmerɪkən 'fʊtbɔ:l] American Football **III**
Native American [ˌneɪtɪv‿ə'merɪkən] Ureinwohner/-in Amerikas, Indianer/-in; indianisch **IV**

among [ə'mʌŋ] unter; inmitten ⟨**V U1,** 12⟩
ancestor ['ænsestə] Ahne/Ahnin; Vorfahre/Vorfahrin **V U1,** 17
ancient ['eɪnʃnt] alt; antik **V U4,** 70
and [ænd; ənd] und **I**
And you. [ənd 'ju:] Gleichfalls. **III**
angry ['æŋɡri] wütend, zornig, verärgert **II**
animal ['ænɪml] Tier **I**
animal home ['ænɪml həʊm] Tierheim **II**
announcement [ə'naʊnsmənt] Ankündigung; Durchsage **II**
annoying [ə'nɔɪɪŋ] ärgerlich; lästig **III**
anorak ['ænəræk] Anorak **II**
another [ə'nʌðə] noch ein/-e; ein/-e andere/-r/-s **I**
answer ['ɑ:nsə] Antwort **I**
to **answer** ['ɑ:nsə] (be)antworten **I**
answerphone ['ɑ:nsəfəʊn] Anrufbeantworter **III**
green **ant** [ˌɡri:n‿'ænt] grüne Ameise **V U1,** 17
antique [æn'ti:k] Antiquität **II**
any ['enɪ] irgendein/-e/-er; irgendwelche **I**
(not) any longer [nɒt ˌeni 'lɒŋɡə] (nicht) mehr, (nicht) länger **II**
(not) any more [nɒt ˌeni 'mɔ:] (nicht) mehr **III**
anybody ['eniˌbɒdi] irgendjemand; jeder (beliebige) **II**
anyone ['eniwʌn] irgendjemand; jeder (beliebige) **II**
anything ['eniθɪŋ] irgendetwas **II**
anyway ['eniweɪ] trotzdem; jedenfalls, sowieso **II**
anywhere ['eniweə] irgendwo; überall (egal, wo) **II**
apart from [ə'pɑ:t frəm] abgesehen von, außer **IV**
apartheid [ə'pɑ:taɪt] Apartheid **V ZI,** 10
apartment *(AE)* [ə'pɑ:tmənt] Apartment, Wohnung **IV**
to **apologize** [ə'pɒlədʒaɪz] sich entschuldigen **III**
to **appear** [ə'pɪə] auftauchen; erscheinen ⟨**V U1,** 12⟩; auftreten **V U3,** 60
to **applaud** [ə'plɔ:d] applaudieren **III**
apple ['æpl] Apfel **I**
applicant ['æplɪkənt] Bewerber/-in **V U2,** 37
application [ˌæplɪ'keɪʃn] Bewerbung **V U2,** 33
letter of application [ˌletər‿əv‿æplɪ'keɪʃn] Bewerbungsschreiben **V U2,** 33
to **apply (for)** [ə'plaɪ fə] sich bewerben (für) **V U2,** 33
appointment [ə'pɔɪntmənt] Termin **V U2,** 35

I'd **appreciate it if ...** [aɪd‿ə'pri:ʃieɪt‿ɪt ɪf] Könnten Sie/Könntest du ... ; Ich wäre Ihnen sehr verbunden, wenn ... **V U4,** 73
appreciation [əˌpri:ʃi'eɪʃn] Verständnis; Wertschätzung; Anerkennung ⟨**V U1,** 13⟩
appropriate [ə'prəʊpriət] angemessen **V U4,** 73
April ['eɪprl] April **I**
architect ['ɑ:kɪtekt] Architekt/-in **V U2,** 29
architecture ['ɑ:kɪtektʃə] Architektur **V U2,** 33
area ['eəriə] Areal; Fläche; Gebiet **III**
to **argue** ['ɑ:ɡju:] argumentieren **V U3,** 56
argument ['ɑ:ɡjəmənt] Auseinandersetzung, Streit **III**; Argument **IV**
arm [ɑ:m] Arm **II**
coat of arms [ˌkəʊt‿əv‿'ɑ:mz] Wappen **V U1,** 17
army ['ɑ:mi] Armee **II**
around [ə'raʊnd] herum, umher **II**
arrangement [ə'reɪndʒmənt] Abmachung, Vereinbarung; Plan **III**
arrival [ə'raɪvl] Ankunft **II**
to **arrive** [ə'raɪv] ankommen **II**
art [ɑ:t] Kunst **II**
arts and crafts (pl.) [ˌɑ:ts‿ənd 'krɑ:fts] Kunsthandwerk **II**
article ['ɑ:tɪkl] Artikel, Bericht *(in einer Zeitschrift, Zeitung)* **II**; Artikel *(gramm.)* **III**
artist ['ɑ:tɪst] Künstler/-in **IV**
as [æz] während; indem **IV**
as [æz; əz] als **II**
as ... as [əz ... əz] so ... wie **II**
as soon as [əz 'su:n‿əz] sobald **II**
as [æz] wie **IV**
as [æz; əz] da, weil **V U3,** 59
Asian ['eɪʃn] asiatisch; Asiate, Asiatin **III**
Asian-Pacific [ˌeɪʒn pə'sɪfɪk] asiatisch-pazifisch **V U1,** 17
to **ask** [ɑ:sk] fragen **I**
to ask about sb/sth [ɑ:sk ə'baʊt] sich nach jmdm./etw. erkundigen **III**
to ask for ... ['ɑ:sk fə] nach ... fragen **I**
to ask sb to do sth ['ɑ:sk tə] jmdn. bitten, etw. zu tun **III**
asleep [ə'sli:p] schlafend **I**
to fall asleep [fɔ:l‿ə'sli:p] einschlafen **I**
aspect ['æspekt] Aspekt, Gesichtspunkt, Blickwinkel **V U1,** 17
assembly [ə'sembli] Versammlung; Morgenappell **II**
assistant [ə'sɪstnt] Verkäufer/-in **I**; Assistent/-in **III**
shop assistant ['ʃɒp‿əˌsɪstnt] Verkäufer/-in **II**

to assume sth [ə'sju:m] annehmen ⟨**VU3**, 50⟩
at [æt; ət] in, auf, bei, an **I**
at any time [æt‿eni 'taɪm] jederzeit **IV**
at first [ət 'fɜ:st] zuerst; zunächst **II**
at half past (three) [ət ˌhɑ:f pɑ:st 'θri:] um halb (vier) **I**
at home [æt 'həʊm] zu Hause **I**
at last [ət 'lɑ:st] endlich, zu guter Letzt **III**
at least [ət 'li:st] mindestens, wenigstens **III**
at my house [ət 'maɪ haʊs] bei mir zu Hause **I**
at once [ət 'wʌns] auf einmal; sofort **I**
at the back (of) [ət ðə 'bæk‿əv] hinten; am Ende, im hinteren Teil **IV**
at the front [æt ðə 'frʌnt] vorn(e) **II**
at the front of [æt ðə 'frʌnt‿əv] an der Spitze (von), im vorderen Bereich **II**
at the weekend [æt ðə ˌwi:k'end] am Wochenende **I**
at times [ət 'taɪmz] ab und zu; hin und wieder; zeitweise ⟨**VU3**, 53⟩
not at all [nɒt ət‿'ɔ:l] überhaupt nicht, gar nicht **IV**
athlete ['æθli:t] (Leicht)Athlet/-in **III**
athletics [æθ'letɪks] Leichtathletik **III**
atmosphere ['ætməsfɪə] Atmosphäre; Stimmung **IV**
to attach [ə'tætʃ] anbringen, anfügen, anhängen **IV**
to attack [ə'tæk] angreifen **III**
to attend [ə'tend] teilnehmen, besuchen **III**
*to bring sb's **attention to sth** [brɪŋ ə'tenʃn tə] jmds. Aufmerksamkeit auf etw. lenken **VU4**, 75
to get sb's attention [get ə'tenʃn] jmdn. auf sich aufmerksam machen **III**
to attract [ə'trækt] anziehen **IV**
attraction [ə'trækʃn] Attraktion, Sehenswürdigkeit **IV**
attractive [ə'træktɪv] attraktiv **IV**
audience ['ɔ:diəns] Publikum **III**
audio ['ɔ:diəʊ] Audio-, Hör- **III**
to audition [ɔ:'dɪʃn] vorsingen, vorspielen; vortanzen; vorsprechen **II**
August ['ɔ:gəst] August **I**
aunt [ɑ:nt] Tante **I**
agony aunt ['ægəni ˌɑ:nt] Kummerkastentante **III**
Aussie *(coll)* ['ɒzi] Australier/-in; australisch *(ugs.)* **VZI**, 11
author ['ɔ:θə] Autor/-in **IV**
authoritarian [ˌɔ:θɒrɪ'teəriən] autoritär **VU4**, 69
to authorize ['ɔ:θəraɪz] genehmigen **IV**
autumn ['ɔ:təm] Herbst **I**
available [ə'veɪləbl] verfügbar, zur Verfügung stehen; erhältlich **VU2**, 33
on average [ɒn‿'ævrɪdʒ] durchschnittlich, im Durchschnitt **III**
award [ə'wɔ:d] Auszeichnung, Preis **IV**
away [ə'weɪ] weg **I**
right away [raɪt‿ə'weɪ] sofort **II**
awesome ['ɔ:səm] super, spitze; beeindruckend **III**
awful ['ɔ:fl] schrecklich, furchtbar **III**

B

back [bæk] Rückseite; Rücken **II**
at the back (of) [ət ðə 'bæk‿əv] hinten; am Ende, im hinteren Teil **IV**
like the back of my hand [laɪk ðə ˌbæk‿əv maɪ 'hænd] wie meine Westentasche, in- und auswendig **II**
back [bæk] zurück **I**
to get back [get 'bæk] zurückkommen **II**
background ['bækgraʊnd] Hintergrund **III**
backpacking ['bækpækɪŋ] Wandern; Rucksackreisen **IV**
bacon ['beɪkn] (Schinken)Speck **I**
bad [bæd] schlecht; böse **I**
bad guy ['bæd gaɪ] Bösewicht **IV**
bad luck [bæd 'lʌk] Pech, Unglück **III**
bag [bæg] Tasche **I**
a bag of . . . [ə 'bæg‿əv] eine Tüte . . . **I**
bagel ['beɪgl] Bagel *(weiches, ringförmiges Brötchen)* **IV**
baggage *(sing.)* ['bægɪdʒ] (Reise)Gepäck **II**
bagpipes *(pl.)* ['bægpaɪps] Dudelsack **II**
baker ['beɪkə] Bäcker/-in **II**
bald [bɔ:ld] glatzköpfig, kahl ⟨**VU2**, 39⟩
ball [bɔ:l] Ball **I**
cannon ball ['kænən bɔ:l] Kanonenkugel ⟨**VU4**, 78⟩
rubber ball [ˌrʌbə 'bɔ:l] Gummiball **I**
bamboo [bæm'bu:] Bambus **IV**
to ban [bæn] bannen; sperren; verbieten **VU4**, 78
band [bænd] Band, Musikgruppe **I**
boy band ['bɔɪ ˌbænd] Boygroup **I**
bandage ['bændɪdʒ] Verband **III**
bang [bæŋ] Knall, Schlag **I**
to bang [bæŋ] knallen, schlagen **I**
bank [bæŋk] Bank **VU2**, 29
banker ['bæŋkə] Banker, Bankier **VZI**, 8
snack bar ['snæk bɑ:] Café **II**
barber *(AE)* ['bɑ:bə] (Herren)friseur **IV**
barbie *(=barbecue) (coll)* ['bɑ:bi] Grillen; Grillparty **VU1**, 18
to bark [bɑ:k] bellen **I**
to bark at ['bɑ:k‿ət] anbellen **I**
base [beɪs] Base *(beim Baseball)* **III**
baseball ['beɪsbɔ:l] Baseball **III**
basic ['beɪsɪk] grundlegend, Grund-; einfach **III**
basis ['beɪsɪs] Basis, Grundlage **VU4**, 68
basketball ['bɑ:skɪtbɔ:l] Basketball **I**
bastard *(coll)* ['bɑ:stəd] Alter *(ugs.)* ⟨**VU1**, 21⟩
bat [bæt] Schläger *(beim Tischtennis, Baseball)* **III**
to bat [bæt] schlagen *(einen Ball)* **III**
bath [bɑ:θ] Badewanne ⟨**VU3**, 50⟩
bathroom ['bɑ:θru:m] Bad(ezimmer) **I**
battle ['bætl] Schlacht, Kampf **II**
*to **be** [bi:; bi] sein **I**
How are you? [ˌhaʊ‿ɑ: 'jə] Wie geht es dir/Ihnen? **I**
I'm afraid [aɪm ə'freɪd] leider **III**
I'm fine. [ˌaɪm 'faɪn] Mir geht es gut. **I**
I'm sorry. [aɪm 'sɒrɪ] Es tut mir leid. **I**
It's none of your business! [ɪts ˌnʌn‿əv jə 'bɪznɪs] Das geht dich nichts an! **II**
It's up to you. [ɪts‿ʌp tə 'ju:] Es ist an dir (zu entscheiden)./Wie du willst. **VU2**, 39
this is . . . ['ðɪs‿ɪz] hier ist . . . *(am Telefon)* **I**
to be able to (do sth) [bi‿'eɪbl tə] können, fähig sein (zu) **III**
to be about [bi ə'baʊt] gehen um, handeln von **III**
to be affected by [bi ə'fektɪd baɪ] von etw. beeinflusst sein **VU2**, 38
to be afraid (of) *(+ gerund)* [bi‿ə'freɪd‿əv] (sich) fürchten (vor), Angst haben (vor) **IV**
to be allowed to (do sth) [bi‿ə'laʊd tə] dürfen **III**
to be a pain [bi‿ə 'peɪn] einem auf die Nerven gehen **I**
to be born [bi 'bɔ:n] geboren werden **II**
to be certain to do sth [bi 'sɜ:tn] etw. sicher tun **VU2**, 41
to be connected [bi kə'nektɪd] zusammenhängen, in Zusammenhang stehen **III**
to be considered (to be) sth [bi kən'sɪdəd] als etw. gelten **VU4**, 69
to be dedicated to sth [bi 'dedɪkeɪtɪd‿tə] etw. verschrieben sein; (nur) für etw. leben ⟨**VU1**, 12⟩
to be devoted to sb/sth [bi dɪ'vəʊtɪd‿tə] jmdm./etw. (treu) ergeben sein; in etw. (völlig) aufgehen ⟨**VU1**, 12⟩
to be eager to do sth [bi 'i:gə‿tə] etw. unbedingt tun wollen, darauf erpicht sein, etw. zu tun; eifrig bemüht sein, etw. zu tun **VU4**, 75
to be fed up (with) [bi fed‿'ʌp wɪð] sauer sein, die Nase voll haben (von) **I**
to be fun [bi 'fʌn] Spaß machen; witzig sein **I**
to be gone [bi 'gɒn] verschwunden sein, weg sein **II**
to be good at [bi 'gʊd‿ət] gut sein in/bei **I**

to be good with [bi 'gʊd wɪð] gut umgehen können mit **I**
to be happy to do sth [bi 'hæpi tə ˌdu:] etw. gerne tun; etw. tun können **V U4,** 70
to be in [bi‿'ɪn] da sein **III**
to be in a hurry [bi ɪn‿ə 'hʌri] es eilig haben, in Eile sein **I**
to be in tears [ˌbi‿ɪn 'tɪəz] weinen ⟨**V U1,** 15⟩
to be interviewed for a job [bi‿'ɪntəvju:d] ein Vorstellungsgespräch haben **V U2,** 37
to be into sth [bi‿'ɪntə] sich für etw. interessieren; etw. mögen **III**
to be involved (in) [bi ɪn'vɒlvd‿ɪn] mit etw. zu tun haben **IV**
to be late [bi 'leɪt] zu spät kommen, spät dran sein **I**
to be likely to do sth [bi 'laɪkli] etw. wahrscheinlich tun **V U2,** 41
to be lost [bi 'lɒst] sich verirrt haben **II**
to be lucky [bi 'lʌki] Glück haben **I**
to be mad about sb/sth [bi 'mæd‿əˌbaʊt] verrückt nach jmdm./etw. sein **V U3,** 58
to be mad with sb [bi 'mæd‿wɪθ] auf jmdn. böse sein; auf jmdn. sauer sein **V U3,** 58
to be nervous about sth [bi 'nɜ:vəs əˌbaʊt] wg. etw. nervös sein **IV**
to be off [bi‿'ɒf] gehen **V U2,** 38
to be on [bi‿'ɒn] auf Sendung sein ⟨**V U3,** 53⟩
to be on edge [ˌbi ɒn‿'edʒ] nervös sein; gereizt sein ⟨**V U1,** 14⟩
to be on one's mind [bi‿ˌən wʌnz 'maɪnd] jmdn. beschäftigen, jmdn. umtreiben **V U4,** 79
to be on the move [bi ɒn‿ðə 'mu:v] unterwegs sein **III**
to be on top of the world [bi ɒn ˌtɒp‿əv ðə 'wɜ:ld] überglücklich sein **IV**
to be out of luck [ˌbi aʊt‿əv 'lʌk] kein Glück haben **III**
to be proud (of) [bi 'praʊd‿əv] stolz sein (auf) **III**
to be right [bi 'raɪt] Recht haben **I**
to be said to *(+ infinitive)* [bi 'sed‿tə] gelten als **V U1,** 21
to be scared for [bi 'skeəd fə] Angst haben um **I**
to be set (in) [bi 'set] spielen (in); seinen Schauplatz haben (in) **IV**
to be shocked [bi 'ʃɒkt] geschockt sein **II**
to be stuck [bi 'stʌk] festsitzen, feststecken; nicht weg können; hängen bleiben **IV**
to be supposed to *(+ infinitive)* [bi sə'pəʊzd‿tə] (etw. tun) sollen **V U1,** 21
to be terrified (of sth) [bi 'terəfaɪd‿əv] (große) Angst (vor etw.) haben ⟨**V U1,** 12⟩
to be thrilled [bi 'θrɪld] aus dem Häuschen sein vor Freude **IV**
to be tired of *(+ gerund)* [bi 'taɪəd‿əv] einer Sache/jmds. überdrüssig sein **IV**
to be trapped [bi 'træpt] eingeschlossen sein; in der Falle sitzen **III**
to be unable to do sth [bi ʌn'eɪbl tə] unfähig sein, etw. zu tun; nicht in der Lage sein, etw. zu tun **V U3,** 55
to be unlucky [bi ʌn'lʌki] Pech haben **III**
to be with ... [bi 'wɪð] bei ... sein **I**
to be worth (sth) [bi 'wɜ:θ] (etw.) wert sein **III**
to be wrong [bi 'rɒŋ] Unrecht haben, sich irren **I**
Who's in it? [hu:z 'ɪn‿ɪt] Wer spielt mit? **III**
beach [bi:tʃ] Strand **I**
beach holiday ['bi:tʃ ˌhɒlədeɪ] Strandurlaub **I**
on the beach [ɒn ðə 'bi:tʃ] am Strand **I**
to **beam** [bi:m] beamen **II**
bear [beə] Bär **IV**
polar bear ['pəʊlə beə] Eisbär **IV**
teddy bear ['tedi ˌbeə] Teddybär ⟨**V U1,** 19⟩
beautiful ['bju:tɪfl] schön; wunderbar **I**
beauty ['bju:ti] Schönheit **IV**
because [bɪ'kɒz] weil, da **I**
because of [bɪ'kɒz‿əv] wegen **V U3,** 59
*to **become** [bɪ'kʌm] werden **II**
bed [bed] Bett **I**
to go to bed [gəʊ tə 'bed] ins Bett gehen **I**
bedroom ['bedru:m] Schlafzimmer **I**
beer [bɪə] Bier **IV**
before [bɪ'fɔ:] bis (zu), vor **I**
the day before [ðə ˌdeɪ bɪ'fɔ:] am Tag vorher, am Tag zuvor **III**
before [bɪ'fɔ:] bevor **I**
to **beg (for)** [beg fə] betteln (um) **V U2,** 39
*to **begin** [bɪ'gɪn] beginnen, anfangen **II**
beginning [bɪ'gɪnɪŋ] Anfang; Beginn **III**
to **behave** [bɪ'heɪv] sich benehmen, sich verhalten **III**
behind [bɪ'haɪnd] hinter **I**
human **being** [ˌhju:mən 'bi:ɪŋ] Mensch ⟨**V U1,** 12⟩
to **believe** [bɪ'li:v] glauben **I**
He can't believe his eyes. [hi ˌkɑ:nt bɪˌli:v hɪz 'aɪz] Er traut seinen Augen nicht. **I**
Would you believe it! [ˌwʊd ju bɪ'li:v‿ɪt] Kaum zu glauben! **V U2,** 38
bell [bel] Glocke **IV**
bellow ['beləʊ] Gebrüll **III**
to **belong (to)** [bɪ'lɒŋ tə] gehören (zu) ⟨**V U1,** 21⟩
below [bɪ'ləʊ] unterhalb, unten **IV**
bench [benʃ] (Sitz)Bank **V U4,** 74
best [best] beste/-r/-s **I**
bet [bet] Wette **III**
better ['betə] besser **II**
between [bɪ'twi:n] zwischen **II**
big [bɪg] groß **I**
big deal [bɪg 'di:l] große Sache **IV**
to make it big [ˌmeɪk‿ɪt 'bɪg] groß (he)rauskommen ⟨**V U3,** 51⟩
bike [baɪk] Fahrrad **I**
mountain bike ['maʊntɪn baɪk] Mountainbike **II**
bilingual [baɪ'lɪŋgwl] zweisprachig **III**
bill [bɪl] Rechnung **II**
billion-dollar [ˌbɪliən 'dɒlə] milliardenschwer **IV**
bio *(= biography)* ['baɪəʊ] Biografie **V U4,** 77
biographical [baɪəʊ'græfɪkl] biographisch **V U4,** 77
biography [baɪ'ɒgrəfi] Biografie **III**
bird [bɜ:d] Vogel **I**
date of **birth** [ˌdeɪt‿əv 'bɜ:θ] Geburtsdatum **V U2,** 33
birthday ['bɜ:θdeɪ] Geburtstag **I**
birthday party ['bɜ:θdeɪ ˌpɑ:ti] Geburtstagsfeier **I**
Happy Birthday! [ˌhæpi 'bɜ:θdeɪ] Alles Gute zum Geburtstag! **I**
birthplace ['bɜ:θpleɪs] Geburtsort **III**
a **bit** [ə 'bɪt] ein wenig, ein bisschen **II**
bit of information [ˌbɪt‿əv‿ɪnfə'meɪʃn] eine Information **V U1,** 17
bitch *(vulg)* ['bɪtʃ] Miststück; Schlampe; Zicke *(derb)* ⟨**V U4,** 79⟩
*to **bite** [baɪt] beißen; stechen ⟨**V U1,** 19⟩
black (person) [blæk] Schwarze/-r **V ZI,** 10
black [blæk] schwarz **I**
blanket ['blæŋkɪt] (Bett)Decke ⟨**V U3,** 50⟩
*to **bleed** [bli:d] bluten **II**
block [blɒk] (Häuser)Block **V U4,** 74
blockbuster ['blɒkˌbʌstə] Kassenschlager; Bestseller **IV**
blog [blɒg] Blog; Internettagebuch **IV**
bloke *(coll)* [bləʊk] Typ *(ugs.)* ⟨**V U1,** 21⟩
blood [blʌd] Blut **III**
Bloody oath! *(coll)* [ˌblʌdi 'əʊθ] Ist (doch) wahr! *(ugs.)* ⟨**V U1,** 21⟩
blouse [blaʊz] Bluse ⟨**V U1,** 14⟩
*to **blow** [bləʊ] wehen, blasen ⟨**V U4,** 78⟩
blue [blu:] blau **I**
board [bɔ:d] Tafel; Brett **I**
boarding school ['bɔ:dɪŋ ˌsku:l] Internat **II**
boat [bəʊt] Boot, Schiff **I**
bobsleigh ['bɒbsleɪ] Bob **III**
body ['bɒdi] Körper **II**
body language ['bɒdi ˌlæŋgwɪdʒ] Körpersprache **V U2,** 37

dead body [ˌded 'bɒdi] Leiche **VU2,** 28
Bollywood ['bɒliwʊd] Bollywood *(indische Filmindustrie: Bombay + Hollywood)* **VZI,** 9
book [bʊk] Buch **I**
address book [ə'dres ˌbʊk] Adressbuch **I**
exercise book ['eksəsaɪz ˌbʊk] Heft **I**
to **book** [bʊk] buchen, reservieren **III**
bookworm ['bʊkwɜ:m] Bücherwurm **III**
boot [bu:t] Stiefel **II**
booth [bu:ð] Stand; Bude ⟨**VU1,** 14⟩
border ['bɔ:də] Grenze **IV**
*to get **bored** [get 'bɔ:d] sich langweilen **III**
boring ['bɔ:rɪŋ] langweilig **I**
*to be **born** [bi 'bɔ:n] geboren werden **II**
borough ['bʌrə] Bezirk, Stadtteil **IV**
to **borrow** ['bɒrəʊ] (sich) ausleihen **II**
boss [bɒs] Boss, Chef **II**
both [bəʊθ] beide **II**
to not **bother (with sth)** [nɒt 'bɒðə] sich nicht (um etw.) kümmern **IV**
bottle ['bɒtl] Flasche **I**
to **bottle up sth** [ˌbɒtl‿'ʌp] etw. unterdrücken ⟨**VU1,** 15⟩
bottom ['bɒtəm] unteres Ende, Boden **I**
on the bottom [ɒn ðə 'bɒtəm] unten **I**
boulder ['bəʊldə] Felsblock, Felsbrocken **IV**
bowl [bəʊl] Schüssel **I**
box [bɒks] Box, Kasten, Kästchen, Schachtel **I**
a box of … [ə 'bɒks‿əv] eine Schachtel …, ein Karton … **I**
boy [bɔɪ] Junge **I**
boy band ['bɔɪ ˌbænd] Boygroup **I**
boyfriend ['bɔɪfrend] Freund *(in einer Paarbeziehung)* **III**
bracket ['brækɪt] Klammer **VU3,** 58
brain(s) [breɪn, breɪnz] Gehirn; Verstand **VU3,** 55
brain power ['breɪn paʊə] Intelligenz **VU3,** 55
brake [breɪk] Bremse **III**
brand [brænd] Marke **IV**
brave [breɪv] mutig; tapfer **IV**
bread [bred] Brot **II**
break [breɪk] Pause **II**
commercial break [kəˌmɜ:ʃl 'breɪk] Werbepause **III**
*to **break** [breɪk] (zer)brechen, kaputtgehen **I**
to break up [breɪk‿'ʌp] (sich) auflösen; auseinandergehen **VZI,** 8
breakdown ['breɪkdaʊn] (Nerven)zusammenbruch **IV**
breakfast ['brekfəst] Frühstück **I**
to have breakfast [hæv 'brekfəst] frühstücken **I**

breath [breθ] Atem; Atemzug; Luft **VU1,** 15
breath [breθ] Atem; Atemzug **VU1,** 13
to hold one's breath [ˌhəʊld wʌnz 'breθ] den Atem anhalten, die Luft anhalten ⟨**VU1,** 13⟩
to take a deep breath [teɪk‿ə ˌdi:p 'breθ] tief einatmen, tief Luft holen ⟨**VU4,** 79⟩
breathtaking ['breθˌteɪkɪŋ] atemberaubend **IV**
bridge [brɪdʒ] Brücke **I**
brilliant ['brɪliənt] toll, prima; glänzend **II**
too brilliant for words [tu: 'brɪliənt fə ˌwɜ:dz] zu schön, um es in Worte zu fassen **IV**
*to **bring** [brɪŋ] (mit)bringen **I**
to bring plates *(coll)* [brɪŋ 'pleɪts] Essen mitbringen *(ugs.)* ⟨**VU1,** 21⟩
to bring sb's attention to sth [brɪŋ ə'tenʃn tə] jmds. Aufmerksamkeit auf etw. lenken **VU4,** 75
British ['brɪtɪʃ] britisch **I**
Briton ['brɪtn] Brite, Britin **III**
brochure ['brəʊʃə] Broschüre **I**
broken ['brəʊkn] gebrochen, kaputt **II**
brother ['brʌðə] Bruder **I**
brotherhood ['brʌðəhʊd] Brüderlichkeit **VU4,** 68
brown [braʊn] braun **I**
web **browser** ['web ˌbraʊzə] Webbrowser **III**
to **brush one's teeth** [brʌʃ wʌnz 'ti:θ] (seine) Zähne putzen **III**
Brussels sprout [ˌbrʌslz 'spraʊt] Rosenkohl **III**
buffalo pl. **buffalo** ['bʌfləʊ] Büffel **III**
*to **build** [bɪld] bauen **I**
builder ['bɪldə] Bauarbeiter/-in **VU2,** 38
building ['bɪldɪŋ] Gebäude **II**
bully ['bʊli] Rabauke, Rüpel, Tyrann **II**
to **bully** ['bʊli] jmdn. tyrannisieren; jmdn. drangsalieren **VU4,** 74
to **bum around** [bʌm ə'raʊnd] herumziehen ⟨**VU2,** 38⟩
to **bump into** [bʌmp‿'ɪntə] zusammenstoßen (mit) **II**
burger ['bɜ:gə] Hamburger **II**
burglar ['bɜ:glə] Einbrecher/-in **III**
*to **burn** [bɜ:n] (ver)brennen **II**
bus pl. **buses** [bʌs; bʌsɪz] Bus **I**
bus stop ['bʌs ˌstɒp] Bushaltestelle **I**
bush [bʊʃ] Busch *(Buschlandschaft)*; Wildnis ⟨**VU1,** 12⟩
business ['bɪznɪs] Geschäft; Branche **IV**
business people ['bɪznɪs,pɪpl] Geschäftsleute **IV**
It's none of your business! [ɪts ˌnʌn‿əv ‿ə 'bɪznɪs] Das geht dich nichts an! **II**
to **busk** [bʌsk] Straßenmusik machen **VU3,** 59
busker ['bʌskə] Straßenmusikant/-in **II**

busy (with) ['bɪzi ˌwɪð] beschäftigt (mit) **I**
but [bʌt; bət] außer ⟨**VU3,** 52⟩
but [bʌt] aber **I**
button ['bʌtn] Knopf ⟨**VU3,** 53⟩
*to **buy** [baɪ] kaufen **I**
buzz [bʌz] geschäftiges Treiben; Durcheinander ⟨**VU1,** 14⟩
by [baɪ] von **III**; *(spätestens)* bis **III**; um **VZI,** 8
by *(+ gerund)* [baɪ] indem **VU4,** 71
by (Underground) [baɪ] mit (der U-Bahn), per **I**
by force [baɪ 'fɔ:s] gewaltsam, mit Gewalt **VU4,** 70
bye [baɪ] tschüss **I**

C

cab *(AE)* [kæb] Taxi **IV**
cactus ['kæktəs] Kaktus **IV**
café ['kæfeɪ] Café **I**
jazz café ['dʒæz ˌkæfeɪ] Jazzcafé **I**
cafeteria [kæfə'tɪəriə] Cafeteria **I**
cake [keɪk] Kuchen, Torte **I**
Californian [ˌkælɪ'fɔ:niən] Kalifornier/-in; kalifornisch **IV**
(phone) **call** ['fəʊn ˌkɔ:l] (Telefon)Anruf **I**
to take a call [ˌteɪk‿ə 'kɔ:l] (Telefon) abheben, einen Anruf entgegennehmen **III**
to **call** [kɔ:l] rufen, schreien **I**; nennen **I**; anrufen **III**
to call about sth [kɔ:l‿ə'baʊt] wegen/bezüglich etw. anrufen **IV**
to call in [kɔ:l‿'ɪn] bei laufender Sendung/während einer Sendung anrufen **VZI,** 8
to call sb names [ˌkɔ:l ˌsʌmbɒdi 'neɪmz] jmdn. beschimpfen **VU4,** 74
caller ['kɔ:lə] Anrufer/-in **III**
calm [kɑ:m] ruhig, friedlich **I**
camera ['kæmrə] Fotoapparat, Kamera **I**
to **camp** [kæmp] campen, zelten, kampieren **IV**
campaign [kæm'peɪn] Kampagne; Aktion **VU2,** 40
campsite ['kæmpsaɪt] Campingplatz, Zeltplatz **II**
can [kæn; kən] können, dürfen **I**
Canadian [kə'neɪdiən] Kanadier/-in; kanadisch **VZI,** 10
cancer ['kænsə] Krebs **VZI,** 11
skin cancer ['skɪn ˌkænsə] Hautkrebs **VZI,** 11
candle ['kændl] Kerze **I**
candy *(AE)* ['kændi] Süßigkeiten **IV**
cannon ball ['kænən bɔ:l] Kanonenkugel ⟨**VU4,** 78⟩
canoe [kə'nu:] Kanu **II**
canyon ['kænjən] Schlucht, Canyon **IV**
capital ['kæpɪtl] Hauptstadt **II**

captain ['kæptɪn] Kapitän **I**
car [kɑ:] Auto **I**
card [kɑ:d] Karte, Spielkarte **I**; Chip, Speicherkarte *(für Digitalkameras)* **I**
e-card ['ɪ:kɑ:d] E-Card **III**
cue card ['kju: ˌkɑ:d] Stichwortkarte ⟨**VU3,** 53⟩
top-up card ['tɒp‿ʌp kɑ:d] Aufladekarte *(fürs Handy)* **II**
I don't **care!** [aɪ ˌdəʊnt 'keə] Das ist mir egal! **III**
to care (about sth) [keə] (etw.) wichtig nehmen **IV**
to care about sb ['keər‿əˌbaʊt] etw. für jmdn empfinden ⟨**VU1,** 15⟩
career [kə'rɪə] Beruf; Laufbahn **VU2,** 28
careful ['keəfl] vorsichtig; sorgfältig **II**
caretaker ['keəteɪkə] Hausmeister/-in **I**
carpet ['kɑ:pɪt] Teppich ⟨**VU3,** 50⟩; **VU4,** 75
carriage ['kærɪdʒ] Wagen, Wagon **II**
to **carry** ['kæri] tragen; befördern **II**
cartoon [kɑ:'tu:n] Cartoon **III**
to **carve out** [kɑ:v 'aʊt] gestalten **IV**
cashier [kə'ʃɪə] Kassierer/-in **IV**
casino [kə'si:nəʊ] (Spiel)kasino **IV**
cast [kɑ:st] Besetzung, Ensemble **III**
*to **cast** [kɑ:st] jmdm. eine Rolle (in einem Film) geben **III**
casting ['kɑ:stɪŋ] Casting, Rollenbesetzung **III**
castle ['kɑ:sl] Burg, Schloss **I**
sand castle ['sænd ˌkɑ:sl] Sandburg **I**
casual ['kæʒuəl] informell, zwanglos; lässig **IV**
cat [kæt] Katze **I**
cat food ['kæt ˌfu:d] Katzenfutter **I**
*to **catch** [kætʃ] nehmen *(Bus, Zug)*; (ein)fangen **I**
catch phrase ['kætʃ freɪz] Slogan **VU3,** 58
category ['kætəgri] Kategorie **IV**
Catholic ['kæθlɪk] Katholik/-in; katholisch **III**
catwalk ['kætwɔ:k] Laufsteg; Catwalk ⟨**VU1,** 14⟩
cause [kɔ:z] Sache ⟨**VU1,** 14⟩; Grund, Ursache **VU3,** 59; Sache **VU4,** 71
to **cause** [kɔ:z] verursachen **VU4,** 74
cave [keɪv] Höhle **II**
CD [ˌsi:'di:] CD **I**
to **celebrate** ['seləbreɪt] feiern **II**
celeb(rity) [sə'lebrɪti] berühmte Persönlichkeit **III**
cell [sel] Zelle ⟨**VU3,** 53⟩
cell phone *(AE)* ['selfəʊn] Handy, Mobiltelefon **IV**
cent [sent] Cent *(Währung)* **IV**
centre ['sentə] Zentrum, Center **I**
information centre [ˌɪnfə'meɪʃn 'sentə] Touristeninformation **I**
century ['sentʃri] Jahrhundert **III**

cereal *(no pl.)* ['sɪəriəl] Frühstückszerealie, Getreideprodukt *(z. B. Cornflakes oder Müsli)* **III**
*to be **certain to do sth** [bi 'sɜ:tn] etw. sicher tun **VU2,** 41
chair [tʃeə] Stuhl **I**
challenge ['tʃælɪndʒ] Herausforderung **III**
champion ['tʃæmpiən] Gewinner/-in, Sieger/-in; Champion **II**
chance [tʃɑ:ns] Chance; Gelegenheit, Möglichkeit **III**
to take the chance [ˌteɪk ðə 'tʃɑ:ns] es darauf ankommen lassen, das Risiko eingehen **III**
change [tʃeɪndʒ] Münzgeld, Wechselgeld **II**; (Ver)Änderung **VZI,** 9
to **change** [tʃeɪndʒ] umsteigen; wechseln **II**; (sich) verändern **III**
changing places [ˌtʃeɪndʒɪŋ 'pleɪsɪz] Ortswechsel **III**
changing room ['tʃeɪndʒɪŋ ru:m] Umkleidekabine **II**
channel ['tʃænl] Kanal; Programm **III**
character ['kærəktə] Charakter; Figur **II**
characterization [ˌkærəktraɪ'zeɪʃn] (Personen)Beschreibung, Charakterisierung **VU1,** 15; **VU1,** 13
charity ['tʃærɪti] Wohltätigkeitsverein **II**
flow **chart** ['fləʊ ˌtʃɑ:t] Flussdiagramm **II**
charts [tʃɑ:ts] Hitparade **II**
to **chase** [tʃeɪs] verfolgen **I**
on **chat** [ɒn 'tʃæt] im Chat, beim Chatten **III**
to **chat** [tʃæt] chatten; plaudern **III**
chatroom ['tʃætrʊm] Chatroom **III**
cheap [tʃi:p] billig, preiswert **I**
to **cheat** [tʃi:t] mogeln, betrügen **IV**
check *(AE)* [tʃek] Rechnung **IV**
to **check** [tʃek] (über)prüfen; kontrollieren **II**
to check out [tʃek 'aʊt] auschecken, abchecken **IV**
check-in ['tʃekɪn] Einchecken **I**
check-out ['tʃekaʊt] Auschecken **I**
to **cheer** [tʃɪə] (zu)jubeln, anfeuern **III**
cheerleader ['tʃɪəˌli:də] Cheerleader *(Mädchen, das in einer Gruppe eine Sportmannschaft anfeuert)* **IV**
cheese [tʃi:z] Käse **I**
chemical ['kemɪkl] Chemikalie **III**
chemistry set ['kemɪstri set] Chemiekasten **I**
chick *(coll)* [tʃɪk] Puppe *(ugs.)* ⟨**VU1,** 21⟩
chicken ['tʃɪkɪn] Huhn; Hähnchen, Hühnchen **I**
child pl. **children** ['tʃaɪld; 'tʃɪldrn] Kind **I**
child labour [ˌtʃaɪld 'leɪbə] Kinderarbeit **VU4,** 68
only child [ˌəʊnli 'tʃaɪld] Einzelkind **I**
childhood ['tʃaɪldhʊd] Kindheit **VU2,** 38
Chinese [tʃaɪ'ni:z] Chinesisch; chinesisch; aus China; Chinese/ Chinesin **IV**

chips *(pl.)* [tʃɪps] Pommes frites **II**
fish and chips [ˌfɪʃ‿n‿'tʃɪps] Fisch und Pommes frites **II**
chocka *(coll)* ['tʃɒkə] (über)voll *(ugs.)* ⟨**VU1,** 21⟩
chocolate ['tʃɒklət] Schokolade **I**
choice [tʃɔɪs] Wahl; Auswahl **IV**
to make a choice [ˌmeɪk‿ə 'tʃɔɪs] eine Wahl treffen **VU3,** 58
male voice **choir** [ˌmeɪl vɔɪs 'kwaɪə] Männerchor **III**
*to **choose** [tʃu:z] (aus)wählen **I**
Christmas ['krɪsməs] Weihnachten **II**
church [tʃɜ:tʃ] Kirche **I**
cinema ['sɪnəmə] Kino **I**
city ['sɪti] Großstadt **I**
civil rights [ˌsɪvl 'raɪts] Bürgerrechte **VZI,** 10
to **clap** [klæp] klatschen **I**
class [klɑ:s] (Schul)Klasse **I**; Unterricht(sstunde); Kurs **IV**
class trip [ˌklɑ:s 'trɪp] Klassenfahrt, Klassenausflug **I**
middle class [ˌmɪdl 'klɑ:s] Mittelschicht **VZI,** 10
classmate ['klɑ:smeɪt] Klassenkamerad/-in **II**
classroom ['klɑ:srʊm] Klassenzimmer **I**
classroom phrases *(pl.)* ['klɑ:srʊm ˌfreɪzɪz] Redewendungen für den Unterricht **I**
adverbial **clause** [əd'vɜ:biəl ˌklɔ:z] Adverbialsatz **VU2,** 42
contact clause ['kɒntækt ˌklɔ:z] *Relativsatz ohne Relativpronomen* **III**
defining relative clause [dɪ'faɪnɪŋ ˌrelətɪv klɔ:z] notwendiger Relativsatz **IV**
main clause ['meɪn klɔ:z] Hauptsatz **II**
non-defining relative clause ['nɒndɪˌfaɪnɪŋ ˌrelətɪv klɔ:z] nicht-notwendiger Relativsatz **IV**
relative clause [ˌrelətɪv 'klɔ:z] Relativsatz **III**
to **clean** [kli:n] säubern, reinigen **III**
clean [kli:n] sauber **III**
cleaning lady ['kli:nɪŋ ˌleɪdi] Putzfrau **III**
cleaning product ['kli:nɪŋ ˌprɒdʌkt] Reinigungsmittel, Putzmittel **III**
to **clear the table** [ˌklɪə ðə 'teɪbl] den Tisch abräumen **II**
clear [klɪə] klar, verständlich **I**
clever ['klevə] schlau, klug, intelligent **II**
cliché ['kli:ʃeɪ] Klischee **II**
click [klɪk] Klicken; Klick **III**
to **click on** ['klɪk‿ɒn] anklicken **I**
cliff [klɪf] Klippe; Kliff **IV**
climate ['klaɪmət] Klima **IV**
climax ['klaɪmæks] Höhepunkt **VU1,** 20
to **climb** [klaɪm] (hinauf)steigen, hinaufklettern, erklimmen **I**
rock **climbing** ['rɒk ˌklaɪmɪŋ] Klettern **II**

clock [klɒk] Uhr **I**
alarm clock [əˈlɑːm ˌklɒk] Wecker **I**
o'clock [əˈklɒk] Uhr *(Zeitangabe bei vollen Stunden)* **I**
to **close** [kləʊz] schließen, zumachen **I**
to close off [kləʊz‿ˈɔːf] (ab)sperren, abriegeln **IV**
close [kləʊs] genau; nahe **III**
closed [kləʊzd] geschlossen, zu **IV**
close-up [ˈkləʊsʌp] Nahaufnahme **VU3,** 58
clothes *(pl.)* [kləʊðz] Kleidung, Kleider **I**
clothing [ˈkləʊðɪŋ] Kleidung **VU4,** 77
cloud [klaʊd] Wolke **II**
to have one's head in the clouds [həv wʌnz ˌhed‿ɪn ðə ˈklaʊdz] über den Dingen schweben; in höheren Regionen schweben **VU2,** 34
cloudless [ˈklaʊdləs] wolkenlos, klar **IV**
cloudy [ˈklaʊdi] wolkig **II**
club [klʌb] Klub, Verein **I**
computer club [kəmˈpjuːtə ˌklʌb] Computerklub **I**
cooking club [ˈkʊkɪŋ ˌklʌb] Kochklub **I**
coach [kəʊtʃ] Reisebus **III**
coal mine [ˈkəʊl maɪn] Kohlenbergwerk, Kohlengrube **III**
coast [kəʊst] Küste **I**
coast-to-coast [kəʊst‿tə‿ˈkəʊst] von Küste zu Küste; landesweit **IV**
coat of arms [ˌkəʊt‿əv‿ˈɑːmz] Wappen **VU1,** 17
cocaine *(no pl.)* [kəˈkeɪn] Kokain **IV**
dress **code** [ˈdres kəʊd] Kleiderordnung; Bekleidungsvorschriften **IV**
coffee [ˈkɒfiː] Kaffee **IV**
cold [kəʊld] Erkältung **III**
cold [kəʊld] kalt **I**
collaborative [kəˈlæbrətɪv] zusammenarbeitend **VU2,** 40
to **collect** [kəˈlekt] (ein)sammeln **I**
college [ˈkɒlɪdʒ] Universität *(in den USA)* **IV**
colloquial [kəˈləʊkwiəl] umgangssprachlich **IV**
to **colonise** [ˈkɒlənaɪz] kolonisieren ⟨**VU1,** 15⟩
colony [ˈkɒləni] Kolonie **III**
penal colony [ˈpiːnl ˌkɒləni] Strafkolonie **VU1,** 17
colour [ˈkʌlə] Farbe **I**
*to **come** [kʌm] kommen **I**
Come on! [kʌm‿ˈɒn] Komm schon!/ Komm jetzt! **I**
to come along [ˌkʌm‿əˈlɒŋ] mitkommen **IV**
to come in [kʌm ˈɪn] hereinkommen **I**
to come over [kʌm ˈəʊvə] herüberkommen, vorbeischauen **I**
to come up to [kʌm‿ˈʌp tə] zukommen auf **II**
comedy [ˈkɒmədi] Komödie **III**
comfortable [ˈkʌmftəbl] bequem; behaglich; angenehm **VU3,** 51; **VU3,** 53
to feel comfortable [ˌfiːl ˈkʌmftəbl] sich wohl fühlen **VU3,** 51; **VU3,** 53
comfy *(= comfortable)* [ˈkʌmfi] bequem **VU3,** 59
comic [ˈkɒmɪk] Comic(heft) **III**
coming [ˈkʌmɪŋ] kommende/-r/-s **IV**
comma [ˈkɒmə] Komma **III**
command [kəˈmɑːnd] Befehl **III**
comment [ˈkɒment] Kommentar **II**
to **comment (on)** [ˈkɒment‿ɒn] kommentieren **IV**
commercial [kəˈmɜːʃl] Werbespot **III**
commercial break [kəˌmɜːʃl ˈbreɪk] Werbepause **III**
common [ˈkɒmən] üblich, gewöhnlich; (weit) verbreitet **VU4,** 79
communication skills [kəˌmjuːnɪˈkeɪʃn ˌskɪlz] Sprechfertigkeiten, Kommunikationsfertigkeiten **I**
community [kəˈmjuːnəti] Gemeinde; Gemeinschaft **IV**
company [ˈkʌmpəni] Firma, Unternehmen **IV**
comparative [kəmˈpærətɪv] Komparativ **II**
to **compare (with/to)** [kəmˈpeə] vergleichen (mit) **II**
comparison [kəmˈpærɪsn] Vergleich **II**
compass [ˈkʌmpəs] Kompass **II**
competition [ˌkɒmpəˈtɪʃn] Wettbewerb **I**; Konkurrenz **VU2,** 30
competitive [kəmˈpetɪtɪv] konkurrenzfähig, wettbewerbsfähig **VU2,** 29
to **complain** [kəmˈpleɪn] sich beschweren, sich beklagen **VU4,** 71
to **complete** [kəmˈpliːt] vervollständigen **I**; fertig stellen **III**
completely [kəmˈpliːtli] völlig **IV**
compound [ˈkɒmpaʊnd] Kompositum *(zusammengesetztes Wort)* **II**
computer [kəmˈpjuːtə] Computer **I**
computer club [kəmˈpjuːtə ˌklʌb] Computerklub **I**
computer shop [kəmˈpjuːtə ˌʃɒp] Computergeschäft **I**
to **concentrate** [ˈkɒnsntreɪt] (sich) konzentrieren **III**
concept [ˈkɒnsept] Vorstellung, Idee; Konzept **VU4,** 70
concert [ˈkɒnsət] Konzert **III**
conclusion [kənˈkluːʒn] Schluss; Schlussfolgerung **IV**
conference [ˈkɒnfrns] Konferenz, Tagung **III**
press conference [ˈpres ˌkɒnfrns] Pressekonferenz **III**
confidence [ˈkɒnfɪdns] Vertrauen; Zuversicht **IV**
confident [ˈkɒnfɪdnt] selbstsicher, selbstbewusst **VU1,** 13; **VU1,** 14
Congress [ˈkɒŋgres] Congress *(Parlament der USA)* **VU4,** 70
conjunction [kənˈdʒʌŋkʃn] Konjunktion **IV**
*to be **connected** [bi kəˈnektɪd] zusammenhängen, in Zusammenhang stehen **III**
connecting [kəˈnektɪŋ] verbindend **II**
connecting line [kəˈnektɪŋ ˌlaɪn] Verbindungslinie **III**
connection [kəˈnekʃn] Verbindung ⟨**VU3,** 51⟩
pros and **cons** *(pl.)* [ˌprəʊz‿n ˈkɒnz] Pro und Kontra **III**
*to be **considered (to be) sth** [bi kənˈsɪdəd] als etw. gelten **VU4,** 69
construction [kənˈstrʌkʃn] Konstruktion; Aufbau **IV**
construction [kənˈstrʌkʃn] Bau **VU2,** 28
consulate [ˈkɒnsjʊlət] Konsulat **VU1,** 18
contact clause [ˈkɒntækt ˌklɔːz] *Relativsatz ohne Relativpronomen* **III**
to **contact** [ˈkɒntækt] (telefonisch) erreichen, sich in Verbindung setzen **III**
contagious [kənˈteɪdʒəs] ansteckend ⟨**VU1,** 19⟩
context [ˈkɒntekst] Kontext, Zusammenhang **III**
continent [ˈkɒntɪnənt] Kontinent, Erdteil **VZI,** 11
to **continue** [kənˈtɪnjuː] weitergehen, -fahren, -reisen **III**; weiterreden; weitermachen **III**
continuing [kənˈtɪnjuɪŋ] ständig; andauernd **VU4,** 68
continuous [kənˈtɪnjuəs] ununterbrochen, dauernd; kontinuierlich ⟨**VU1,** 12⟩
contract [ˈkɒntrækt] Vertrag **III**
contradiction [ˌkɒntrəˈdɪkʃn] Widerspruch; Widersprüchlichkeit **VU4,** 77
contrast [ˈkɒntrɑːst] Kontrast, Unterschied **III**
to **control** [kənˈtrəʊl] kontrollieren; steuern **III**
controversy [ˈkɒntrəvɜːsi] Kontroverse; Auseinandersetzung ⟨**VU4,** 79⟩
conversation [ˌkɒnvəˈseɪʃn] Konversation, Gespräch, Unterhaltung **II**
convict [ˈkɒnvɪkt] Sträfling **VU1,** 17
to **convince** [kənˈvɪns] überzeugen **III**
cook [kʊk] Koch, Köchin **I**
to **cook** [kʊk] kochen **II**
cooking club [ˈkʊkɪŋ ˌklʌb] Kochklub **I**
cool [kuːl] cool, super **I**
cop *(coll)* [kɒp] *(ugs. für Polizist/-in)* **IV**
copy [ˈkɒpi] Exemplar **III**
to **copy** [ˈkɒpi] abschreiben, abmalen **I**; nachmachen **III**

corner ['kɔ:nə] Ecke **II**
to **correct** [kə'rekt] korrigieren, berichtigen **I**
correct [kə'rekt] richtig **I**
corridor ['kɒrɪdɔ:] Gang, Flur, Korridor **II**
cos *(coll)* [kʌz] weil ⟨**V U4,** 79⟩
*to **cost** [kɒst] kosten **II**
costume ['kɒstju:m] Kostüm **III**
couch potato ['kaʊtʃ pə,teɪtəʊ] Fernsehglotzer/-in, Couchpotato **III**
***could** [kʊd] konnte(n) **II**
could you [kʊd ju:] Könnten Sie/ Könntest du … ? **II**
student **council** [,stju:dnt 'kaʊnsl] Schülerrat **IV**
to **count** [kaʊnt] zählen **I**
counter ['kaʊntə] Theke; Schalter **IV**
country ['kʌntri] Land **II**
couple ['kʌpl] Paar **IV**
courage ['kʌrɪdʒ] Mut, Tapferkeit, Courage **V U4,** 74
course [kɔ:s] Kurs **II**
of course [əv 'kɔ:s] natürlich, selbstverständlich **I**
court [kɔ:t] Spielfeld **III**
cousin ['kʌzn] Cousin, Cousine **I**
to **cover** ['kʌvə] bedecken; abdecken **V U3,** 50; **V U3,** 52
covered wagon [,kʌvəd 'wægən] Planwagen **IV**
cow [kaʊ] Kuh **I**
to **crack** [kræk] (zer)brechen; (zer)springen **III**
arts and **crafts** *(pl.)* [,ɑ:ts‿ənd 'krɑ:fts] Kunsthandwerk **II**
craftspeople *(pl.)* ['krɑ:fts,pi:pl] Handwerker *(Pl.)* **II**
crash [kræʃ] Zusammenstoß **III**
to **crash** [kræʃ] aufprallen, zusammenstoßen **I**; abstürzen *(Flugzeug)* **IV**
crazy ['kreɪzi] verrückt **II**
to drive someone crazy [draɪv ,sʌmwʌn 'kreɪzi] jmdn. verrückt machen **III**
to go crazy [gəʊ 'kreɪzi] ausflippen, durchdrehen **III**
to **create** [kri'eɪt] (er)schaffen **III**
creative [kri'eɪtɪv] kreativ ⟨**V U3,** 51⟩
creative writing [kri,eɪtɪv 'raɪtɪŋ] kreatives Schreiben **IV**
creature ['kri:tʃə] Kreatur, Lebewesen; Geschöpf ⟨**V U1,** 12⟩
credit ['kredɪt] Guthaben **II**
cricket ['krɪkɪt] Kricket **III**
crime [kraɪm] Kriminalität; Verbrechen **IV**
criminal ['krɪmɪnl] Kriminelle/-r; Verbrecher/-in **V U1,** 17
criminal ['krɪmɪnl] kriminell; verbrecherisch **IV**
crisp [krɪsp] Kartoffelchip **I**
critical ['krɪtɪkl] kritisch **IV**
to **criticize** ['krɪtɪsaɪz] kritisieren **IV**
crocodile ['krɒkədaɪl] Krokodil **V U1,** 17
to **cross** [krɒs] überqueren, über … gehen **I**
crow's nest ['krəʊz ,nest] Ausguck, Krähennest **I**
crowd [kraʊd] Menschenmenge **III**; Clique **IV**
home crowd ['həʊm ,kraʊd] heimisches Publikum **II**
crowded ['kraʊdɪd] überfüllt **V ZI,** 10
crust [krʌst] Kruste, Rinde **III**
to **cry** [kraɪ] weinen; schreien, rufen **II**
crystal ['krɪstl] Kristall **I**
CU ['si: ju:] bis bald *(Abkürzung in SMS oder E-Mail)* **I**
cue card ['kju: ,kɑ:d] Stichwortkarte ⟨**V U3,** 53⟩
cult [kʌlt] Kult **III**
culture ['kʌltʃə] Kultur **III**
pop culture ['pɒp ,kʌltʃə] Popkultur **V ZI,** 8
cup [kʌp] Tasse **II**
a cup of [ə 'kʌp‿əv] eine Tasse … **I**
cupboard ['kʌbəd] Schrank **I**
to **cure** [kjʊə] heilen; kurieren **V U2,** 39
curious ['kjʊəriəs] neugierig **III**
*to go **curly** [gəʊ 'kɜ:li] sich kräuseln **III**
curry ['kʌri] Curry *(Gewürz oder Gericht)* **III**
curtain ['kɜ:tn] Vorhang **III**
customer ['kʌstəmə] Kunde/Kundin **I**
customs *(sing.)* ['kʌstəmz] Zoll **II**
*to **cut** [kʌt] (sich) schneiden **III**
CV *(= Curriculum Vitae)* [,si:'vi:] Lebenslauf **V U2,** 33

D

dachshund ['dækshənd] Dackel **II**
dad [dæd] Papa, Vati **I**
daily ['deɪli] täglich **I**
dance [dɑ:ns] Tanz(veranstaltung); Ball **IV**
to **dance** [dɑ:ns] tanzen **I**
dancer ['dɑ:nsə] Tänzer/-in **II**
dancing lessons *(pl.)* ['dɑ:nsɪŋ ,lesnz] Tanzunterricht, Tanzstunden **I**
danger ['deɪndʒə] Gefahr **III**
dangerous ['deɪndʒrəs] gefährlich **III**
dark [dɑ:k] dunkel **I**
date [deɪt] Datum **I**; Verabredung, Date **IV**
date of birth [,deɪt‿əv 'bɜ:θ] Geburtsdatum **V U2,** 33
dated ['deɪtɪd] veraltet, überholt **V U4,** 80
daughter ['dɔ:tə] Tochter **II**
day [deɪ] Tag **I**
a day [ə 'deɪ] pro Tag **II**
all day [ɔ:l 'deɪ] den ganzen Tag **II**
days of the week *(pl.)* [,deɪz‿ɒv ðə 'wi:k] Wochentage *(pl.)* **I**
G'day! *(= Good day!)* [gə'daɪ] Guten Tag./Hallo./Hi. *(Begrüßung in Australien)* **V ZI,** 11
open day [,əʊpn 'deɪ] Tag der offenen Tür **III**
the day before [ðə ,deɪ bɪ'fɔ:] am Tag vorher, am Tag zuvor **III**
these days ['ði:z deɪz] heutzutage **V U3,** 55
two days earlier [,tu: deɪz 'ɜ:liə] vor zwei Tagen, zwei Tage zuvor **III**
dead [ded] tot **I**
dead body [,ded 'bɒdi] Leiche **V U2,** 28
deadline ['dedlaɪn] (Abgabe)Termin **V U2,** 30
to meet a deadline [,mi:t‿ə 'dedlaɪn] einen (Abgabe)Termin einhalten **V U2,** 30
deaf [def] taub ⟨**V U3,** 52⟩
big **deal** [bɪg 'di:l] große Sache **IV**
*to **deal with** ['di:l wɪð] sich befassen mit, umgehen mit **III**
drug **dealer** ['drʌg ,di:lə] Drogenhändler/-in **IV**
dear [dɪə] Schatz **I**; Lieber …, Liebe … *(Anrede in Briefen)* **II**
Oh dear! [əʊ 'dɪə] Oje! **II**
death [deθ] Tod ⟨**V U1,** 12⟩; **V U4,** 78
debating [dɪ'beɪtɪŋ] Debattieren **IV**
December [dɪ'sembə] Dezember **I**
to **decide** [dɪ'saɪd] (sich) entscheiden **III**
to decide on sth [dɪ'saɪd‿ɒn] sich für etw. entscheiden **V U2,** 34
decision [dɪ'sɪʒn] Entscheidung **III**
to make a decision [,meɪk‿ə dɪ'sɪʒn] eine Entscheidung treffen **III**
*to be **dedicated to sth** [bi 'dedɪkeɪtɪd‿tə] etw. verschrieben sein; (nur) für etw. leben ⟨**V U1,** 12⟩
deep [di:p] tief **IV**
to **defeat** [dɪ'fi:t] besiegen **III**
defining relative clause [dɪ'faɪnɪŋ ,relətɪv klɔ:z] notwendiger Relativsatz **IV**
definite ['defɪnət] bestimmt **III**
definitely ['defɪnətli] bestimmt, mit Bestimmtheit; definitiv, eindeutig **IV**
definition [,defɪ'nɪʃn] Definition **III**
delay [dɪ'leɪ] Verzögerung, Verspätung **III**
deliberate [dɪ'lɪbrət] bewusst, absichtlich **II**
delicious [dɪ'lɪʃəs] köstlich **IV**
to **deliver** [dɪ'lɪvə] liefern **V U1,** 17
delivery [dɪ'lɪvri] (Aus)lieferung; Zustellung **IV**
democracy [dɪ'mɒkrəsi] Demokratie **V ZI,** 9; **V U4,** 69
democratic [,demə'krætɪk] demokratisch **V U4,** 69
department store [dɪ'pɑ:tmənt ,stɔ:] Kaufhaus **I**
police department [pə'li:s dɪ,pɑ:tmənt] Polizeidienststelle **III**

departure [dɪ'pɑ:tʃə] Abflug, Abreise **II**
to **depend (on)** [dɪ'pend‿ɒn] abhängen (von) **V U1,** 16
to **describe** [dɪ'skraɪb] beschreiben **I**
desert ['dezət] Wüste **IV**
design [dɪ'zaɪn] Design; Gestaltung **IV**
to **design** [dɪ'zaɪn] entwerfen; gestalten **V U2,** 30
desk [desk] Schreibtisch **I**; Schalter **II**
to **destroy** [dɪ'strɔɪ] zerstören **V ZI,** 11
detail ['di:teɪl] Detail, Einzelheit **III**
detention [dɪ'tenʃn] Nachsitzen **IV**
to **develop** [dɪ'veləp] (sich) entwickeln **IV**
developing world [dɪ'veləpɪŋ ˌwɜ:ld] Entwicklungsländer; Schwellenländer **V U4,** 68
development [dɪ'veləpmənt] Entwicklung **IV**
Tasmanian **devil** [tæzˌmeɪniən 'devl] Beutelteufel ⟨**V U1,** 19⟩
*to be **devoted to sb/sth** [bi dɪ'vəʊtɪd‿tə] jmdm./etw. (treu) ergeben sein; in etw. (völlig) aufgehen ⟨**V U1,** 12⟩
diabetes [ˌdaɪə'bi:ti:z] Diabetes, Zuckerkrankheit **II**
diagram ['daɪəgræm] Diagramm **IV**
dialect ['daɪəlekt] Dialekt **V ZI,** 9
dialogue ['daɪəlɒg] Dialog **I**
diary ['daɪəri] Tagebuch **I**
dictator [dik'teɪtə] Diktator/-in **V U4,** 70
dictionary ['dɪkʃnri] Wörterbuch **I**
to **die** [daɪ] sterben **I**
to die away [ˌdaɪ ə'weɪ] schwinden; nachlassen ⟨**V U1,** 12⟩
to die out [daɪ 'aʊt] aussterben ⟨**V U1,** 19⟩
difference ['dɪfrns] Unterschied **III**
to make a difference (to sth) [ˌmeɪk‿ə‿'dɪfrns] etw. verändern **V U4,** 75
different ['dɪfrnt] anders, unterschiedlich **I**
difficult ['dɪfɪklt] schwierig **III**
*to **dig** [dɪg] graben **IV**
digital ['dɪdʒɪtl] digital ⟨**V U3,** 51⟩
dignity ['dɪgnəti] Würde **V U4,** 68
diner *(AE)* ['daɪnə] *einfaches Restaurant mit Theke und Tischen* **IV**
dingo ['dɪŋgəʊ] Dingo *(austral. Wildhund)* ⟨**V U1,** 19⟩
dinner ['dɪnə] Abendessen **III**
dinosaur ['daɪnəsɔ:] Dinosaurier **II**
direct [dɪ'rekt] direkt, offen **V U1,** 13; **V U1,** 15
direct speech [ˌdɪrekt 'spi:tʃ] direkte Rede **III**
direction [dɪ'rekʃn] Richtung **V U2,** 34; Anweisung, Instruktion **V U3,** 58
directly [dɪ'rektli] direkt, ohne Umwege **V U3,** 50; **V U3,** 53
director [dɪ'rektə] Regisseur/-in **III**
dirty ['dɜ:ti] dreckig, schmutzig **I**
disabled [dɪ'seɪbld] behindert **III**
disadvantage [ˌdɪsəd'vɑ:ntɪdʒ] Nachteil **IV**
to **disagree** [ˌdɪsə'gri:] anderer Meinung sein; nicht einverstanden sein **IV**
to **disappear** [ˌdɪsə'pɪə] verschwinden **III**
disappointing [ˌdɪsə'pɔɪntɪŋ] enttäuschend **III**
disaster [dɪ'zɑ:stə] Katastrophe, Unglück; Desaster ⟨**V U1,** 13⟩
Discman ['dɪskmæn] Discman **I**
disco ['dɪskəʊ] Disco, Diskothek **III**
discount ['dɪskaʊnt] Rabatt, Preisnachlass ⟨**V U4,** 76⟩
to **discover** [dɪ'skʌvə] entdecken **III**
discrimination [dɪˌskrɪmɪ'neɪʃn] Diskriminierung ⟨**V U1,** 15⟩; ⟨**V U4,** 76⟩
to **discuss** [dɪ'skʌs] diskutieren **III**
discussing [dɪ'skʌsɪŋ] Diskutieren **III**
discussion [dɪ'skʌʃn] Diskussion **IV**
disease [dɪ'zi:z] (Infektions)Krankheit **V U2,** 39
disguised [dɪs'gaɪzd] verborgen; verkleidet, maskiert ⟨**V U3,** 52⟩
dish [dɪʃ] Gericht **V ZI,** 9
dishwasher ['dɪʃwɒʃə] Spülmaschine **II**
dislike [dɪslaɪk] Abneigung **IV**
to **dislike** [dɪs'laɪk] nicht mögen ⟨**V U1,** 12⟩
dissonant ['dɪsnənt] dissonant, nicht harmonierend **V U4,** 78
distance ['dɪstns] Distanz, Entfernung **III**
to **distract** [dɪ'strækt] ablenken **III**
divorced from [dɪ'vɔ:st frəm] geschieden von **I**
DIY *(= Do-it-yourself)* [ˌdi:aɪ'waɪ] Heimwerken **III**
DJ ['di: ˌdʒeɪ] DJ, Discjockey **I**
*to **do** [du:; də; du] machen, tun **I**
to be certain to do sth [bi 'sɜ:tn] etw. sicher tun **V U2,** 41
to be happy to do sth [bi 'hæpi tə ˌdu:] etw. gerne tun; etw. tun können **V U4,** 70
to be likely to do sth [bi 'laɪkli] etw. wahrscheinlich tun **V U2,** 41
to do a good job [du: ə gʊd 'dʒɒb] gute Arbeit leisten **IV**
to do the shopping [ˌdu: ðə 'ʃɒpɪŋ] Einkäufe machen, Besorgungen machen **II**
to do well [du: 'wel] gute Leistungen erbringen **IV**
to get sb to do sth ['get ˌsʌmbədi tə 'du: ˌsʌmθɪŋ] jmdn. dazu bewegen, etwas zu tun **III**
to happen to do sth [ˌhæpn tʊ 'du: ˌsʌmθɪŋ] zufällig etw. tun **IV**
to have sth done [ˌhæv 'dʌn] etw. machen lassen **V U1,** 17
to let sb do sth [let] jmdm. erlauben, etw. zu tun; etw. zulassen **V U1,** 17
to make sb do sth [meɪk] jmdn. veranlassen, etw. zu tun **V U1,** 17
to stop sb doing sth [stɒp] jmdn. davon abhalten, etw. zu tun ⟨**V U3,** 52⟩
dock [dɒk] Dock **III**
doctor ['dɒktə] Arzt, Ärztin **II**
dog [dɒg] Hund **I**
doghouse ['dɒghaʊs] Hundehütte **I**
dog-tired [dɒg'taɪəd] hundemüde **I**
dollar ['dɒlə] Dollar *(Währung)* **IV**
to **dominate** ['dɒmɪneɪt] dominieren; jmdn./etw. beherrschen **V ZI,** 8
door [dɔ:] Tür **I**
next door [nekst 'dɔ:] nebenan **II**
doorbell ['dɔ:bel] Türklingel **III**
double standard [ˌdʌbl 'stændəd] Doppelmoral **IV**; **V U4,** 79
dove [dʌv] Taube ⟨**V U4,** 78⟩
down [daʊn] herunter, hinunter, nach unten, hinab **I**
to **download** ['daʊnləʊd] herunterladen **II**
downstairs [daʊn'steəz] unten, im Untergeschoss **I**
downtown *(AE)* [ˌdaʊn'taʊn] im Stadtzentrum **IV**
drama ['drɑ:mə] Theater; Drama **II**
in a **draw** [ɪn‿ə 'drɔ:] unentschieden **III**
*to **draw** [drɔ:] zeichnen **I**; anlocken, anziehen ⟨**V U1,** 15⟩
drawing ['drɔ:ɪŋ] Bild; Zeichnung **V U2,** 41
dream [dri:m] Traum **I**
*to **dream** [dri:m] träumen **III**
dress [dres] Kleid **III**
dress code ['dres kəʊd] Kleiderordnung; Bekleidungsvorschriften **IV**
*to get **dressed** [get 'drest] sich anziehen **III**
drink [drɪŋk] Getränk **I**
*to **drink** [drɪŋk] trinken **I**
*to **drive** [draɪv] fahren **I**
to drive someone crazy [draɪv ˌsʌmwʌn 'kreɪzi] jmdn. verrückt machen **III**
driver ['draɪvə] Fahrer/-in **I**
driver's license *(AE)* ['draɪvəz ˌlaɪsns] Führerschein **IV**
legal **driving age** [ˌli:gl 'draɪvɪŋ eɪdʒ] *(Mindestalter für den Führerscheinerwerb)* **IV**
drop [drɒp] Tropfen ⟨**V U3,** 53⟩
to **drop** [drɒp] fallen lassen **IV**
to drop out of [drɒp 'aʊt‿əv] abbrechen **IV**
to **drown** [draʊn] ertrinken; ertränken **III**
drug [drʌg] Droge **IV**; Medikament, Arznei(mittel) **V U2,** 39
drug dealer ['drʌg ˌdi:lə] Drogenhändler/-in **IV**
drummer ['drʌmə] Schlagzeuger/-in **II**

drums *(pl.)* [drʌmz] Schlagzeug **I**
*to get **drunk** [get 'drʌŋk] sich betrinken **IV**
dry [draɪ] trocken **IV**
dude *(coll)* [du:d] Mann *(ugs.)* **IV**
dungeon ['dʌndʒn] Verlies **II**
during *(+ noun)* ['djʊərɪŋ] während *(+ Substantiv)* **III**
duty ['dju:ti] Pflicht **I**
to **dye** [daɪ] färben **II**
dynamic [daɪ'næmɪk] dynamisch **V U3,** 55

E

each [i:tʃ] jede/-r/-s **II**
each other [i:tʃ‿'ʌðə] einander, sich (gegenseitig) **III**
*to be **eager to do sth** [bi 'i:gə‿tə] etw. unbedingt tun wollen, darauf erpicht sein, etw. zu tun; eifrig bemüht sein, etw. zu tun **V U4,** 75
eagle ['i:gl] Adler **III**
ear [ɪə] Ohr **I**
early ['ɜ:li] früh **I**
to **earn** [ɜ:n] verdienen **III**
earth [ɜ:θ] Boden **II**
earthquake ['ɜ:θkweɪk] Erdbeben **II**
east [i:st] Osten **I**
east of ['i:st‿əv] östlich von **I**
easy ['i:zi] leicht, einfach **I**
Easy for you to say [ˌi:zi fə 'ju: tə 'seɪ] Du hast leicht reden. **IV**
easy-peasy [ˌi:zi'pi:zi] babyleicht **I**
*to **eat** [i:t] essen **I**
to eat up [i:t 'ʌp] aufessen **III**
eatery ['i:tri] Kantine, Restaurant **I**
e-card ['ɪ:kɑ:d] E-Card **III**
economy [ɪ'kɒnəmi] Wirtschaft **IV**
*to be on **edge** [ˌbi ɒn‿'edʒ] nervös sein; gereizt sein ⟨**V U1,** 14⟩
to **edit (out)** [ˌedɪt 'aʊt] etw. herausschneiden ⟨**V U3,** 50⟩
peer **editing** ['pɪər‿ˌedɪtɪŋ] *(Kritik/ Kontrolle durch Gleichaltrige)* **V U1,** 20
editor ['edɪtə] Herausgeber/-in; Redakteur/-in; Lektor/-in **IV**
education [edʒʊ'keɪʃn] Erziehung, Bildung **II**
higher education [ˌhaɪə edʒʊ'keɪʃn] Hochschulbildung; Hochschulwesen **V U2,** 28
effect [ɪ'fekt] Effekt; Wirkung **V U3,** 55
sound effect ['saʊnd‿ɪˌfekt] Geräuscheffekt, Toneffekt ⟨**V U3,** 51⟩
egg [eg] Ei **I**
Eh? [eɪ] Was? Nicht wahr? **I**
eight [eɪt] acht **I**
eighteen [ˌeɪ'ti:n] achtzehn **I**
the 1800s [ðə eɪˌti:n 'hʌndrədz] das 19. Jahrhundert **IV**
eighty ['eɪti] achtzig **I**

to **elect** [ɪ'lekt] wählen **IV**
election [ɪ'lekʃn] Wahl **V ZI,** 10
electronics *(pl.)* [ˌelek'trɒnɪks] Elektronik **IV**
element ['elɪmənt] Element **IV**
elephant ['elɪfənt] Elefant **III**
elevator *(AE)* ['elɪveɪtə] Aufzug, Lift **IV**
eleven [ɪ'levn] elf **I**
Elizabethan [ɪˌlɪzə'bi:θn] elisabethanisch **III**
else [els] sonst **II**
what else [ˌwɒt‿'els] was (sonst) noch **II**
e-mail ['i:meɪl] E-Mail **I**
embarrassing [ɪm'bærəsɪŋ] peinlich **II**
emergency [ɪ'mɜ:dʒnsi] Notfall, Notlage **III**
emotion [ɪ'məʊʃn] Gefühl, Emotion ⟨**V U3,** 53⟩
emotional [ɪ'məʊʃnl] emotional; gefühlsmäßig **V U4,** 78
empire ['empaɪə] Reich; Kaiserreich **III**
to **employ sb** [ɪm'plɔɪ] jmdn. beschäftigen; jmdn. einstellen, jmdn. anstellen **V U2,** 30
employer [ɪm'plɔɪə] Arbeitgeber/-in **V U2,** 37
employment [ɪm'plɔɪmənt] Beschäftigung; Anstellung **V U2,** 41
empress ['emprəs] Kaiserin **III**
empty ['emti] leer **I**
emu ['i:mju:] Emu **V U1,** 17
Encl. [ɪn'kləʊzd] Anlage **V U2,** 33
to **enclose** [ɪn'kləʊz] beifügen, beilegen **V U2,** 33
end [end] Ende, Schluss **II**
to **end** [end] enden **I**
to end in thin air [ˌend‿ɪn θɪn‿'eə] im Nichts enden **II**
ending ['endɪŋ] Schluss, Ende **II**
endless ['endləs] endlos **IV**
endlessness ['endləsnəs] Weite; Unendlichkeit **V ZI,** 11
enemy ['enəmi] Feind/-in **II**
search **engine** ['sɜ:tʃˌendʒɪn] Suchmaschine **III**
steam engine ['sti:m ˌendʒɪn] Dampfmaschine **III**
engineer [ˌendʒɪ'nɪə] Ingenieur/-in **III**
English ['ɪŋglɪʃ] Englisch **I**; englisch, aus England **I**
in English [ɪn‿'ɪŋglɪʃ] auf Englisch **I**
English-speaking ['ɪŋglɪʃˌspi:kɪŋ] englischsprachig **II**
to **enjoy** [ɪn'dʒɔɪ] genießen **I**
to enjoy oneself [ɪn'dʒɔɪ] Spaß haben; sich amüsieren **III**
enjoyable [ɪn'dʒɔɪəbl] angenehm; unterhaltsam **V U2,** 41
enough [ɪ'nʌf] genug, genügend **II**
to **enter** ['entə] einreisen; hineingehen, hereinkommen; betreten **II**
entertainment *(no pl.)* [ˌentə'teɪnmənt] Unterhaltung **III**

entrance ['entrəns] Eingang **II**
environment [ɪn'vaɪərnmənt] Umwelt; Umgebung **IV**
environmental [ɪnˌvaɪərn'mentl] die Umwelt betreffend **IV**
environmental protection [ɪnˌvaɪərnˌmentl prə'tekʃn] Umweltschutz **IV**
equal ['i:kwəl] gleich **V U4,** 69
equal opportunity [ˌi:kwəl‿ˌɒpə'tju:nəti] Chancengleichheit **V U4,** 69
racial **equality** [ˌreɪʃl‿ɪ'kwɒləti] Rassengleichheit **V U4,** 68
equipment [ɪ'kwɪpmənt] Ausstattung, Ausrüstung **II**
er [ɜ:] äh **I**
escalator ['eskəleɪtə] Rolltreppe **II**
to **escape (from)** [ɪ'skeɪp] (ent)fliehen, entkommen ⟨**V U3,** 53⟩
especially [ɪ'speʃli] besonders, vor allem **III**
espresso [es'presəʊ] Espresso **V U2,** 34
etc. *(= et cetera)* [ɪt'setrə] usw. *(= und so weiter)* **I**
euro ['jʊərəʊ] Euro *(Währung)* **II**
European [ˌjʊərə'pi:ən] europäisch, aus Europa; Europäer/-in **I**
European Union [ˌjʊərəˌpi:ən 'ju:njən] Europäische Union **III**
even ['i:vn] sogar, selbst **I**
not even [nɒt 'i:vn] (noch) nicht einmal **I**
evening ['i:vnɪŋ] Abend **I**
in the evening [ɪn ði‿'i:vnɪŋ] abends **I**
one evening [wʌn‿'i:vnɪŋ] eines Abends **I**
event [ɪ'vent] Ereignis, Veranstaltung **III**
train of events [ˌtreɪn‿əv‿ɪ'vents] Reihe von Vorfällen/Ereignissen ⟨**V U1,** 13⟩
ever ['evə] jemals **II**
every ['evri] jede/-r/-s **I**
every ten minutes [ˌevri ten 'mɪnɪts] alle zehn Minuten **I**
everybody ['evribɒdi] jeder; alle **II**
everyday ['evrideɪ] alltäglich **V U4,** 73
everyone ['evriwʌn] jeder **I**
everything ['evriθɪŋ] alles **I**
everywhere ['evriweə] überall **I**
evolution [ˌi:və'lu:ʃn] Evolution, Entwicklung **III**
exact [ɪg'zækt] genau, exakt **III**
exactly [ɪg'zæktli] genau **III**
exam [ɪg'zæm] Prüfung; Examen **V U2,** 28
to pass an exam [ˌpɑ:s ən‿ɪg'zæm] eine Prüfung bestehen **V U2,** 39
to take an exam [ˌteɪk‿ən‿ɪg'zæm] eine Prüfung schreiben; ein Examen schreiben **V U2,** 28
examination [ɪgˌzæmɪ'neɪʃn] Untersuchung; Prüfung ⟨**V U1,** 12⟩

to **examine** [ɪɡ'zæmɪn] untersuchen, kontrollieren **II**
example [ɪɡ'zɑ:mpl] Beispiel **I**
exchange [ɪks'tʃeɪndʒ] Austausch **III**
to **exchange** [ɪks'tʃeɪndʒ] austauschen **III**
excited [ɪk'saɪtɪd] aufgeregt, begeistert **I**
excitement [ɪk'saɪtmənt] Aufregung ⟨**VU3,** 59⟩
exciting [ɪk'saɪtɪŋ] spannend, aufregend **II**
exclusive [ɪks'klu:sɪv] exklusiv **IV**
Excuse me. [ɪk'skju:s mi] Entschuldigung./Entschuldigen Sie. **I**
exercise ['eksəsaɪz] Übung **I**
exercise book ['eksəsaɪz ˌbʊk] Heft **I**
exhibition [ˌeksɪ'bɪʃn] Ausstellung **III**
exile ['eksaɪl] im Exil lebende Person **IV**
to **exist** [ɪɡ'zɪst] bestehen **III**
exotic [ɪɡ'zɒtɪk] exotisch **VU1,** 17
to **expect** [ɪk'spekt] erwarten **II**
expectation [ˌekspek'teɪʃn] Erwartung **IV**
expensive [ɪk'spensɪv] teuer **I**
experience *(no pl.)* [ɪk'spɪəriəns] Erfahrung **IV**
work experience ['wɜ:k‿ɪkˌspɪəriəns] Praktikum; Berufserfahrung **VU2,** 28
to **experience** [ɪk'spɪəriəns] erfahren, erleben **IV**
to **explain** [ɪk'spleɪn] erklären **I**
explanation [ˌeksplə'neɪʃn] Erklärung; Erläuterung **IV**
explorer [ɪk'splɔ:rə] Forscher/-in; Forschungsreisende/-r **IV**
to **express** [ɪk'spres] ausdrücken **IV**
expression [ɪk'spreʃn] Ausdruck, Wendung; Äußerung ⟨**VU2,** 41⟩
extra ['ekstrə] Extra, Zusatz **III**
extra ['ekstrə] zusätzlich **III**
extra ['ekstrə] mehr **III**
extra large (XL) ['ekstrə ˌlɑ:dʒ] besonders groß **I**
extract ['ekstrækt] Auszug; Exzerpt ⟨**VU3,** 52⟩
extreme [ɪk'stri:m] extrem, radikal **IV**
extremely [ɪk'stri:mli] äußerst, sehr **IV**
eye [aɪ] Auge **I**
He can't believe his eyes. [hi ˌkɑ:nt bɪˌli:v hɪz 'aɪz] Er traut seinen Augen nicht. **I**
in the twinkling of an eye [ɪn ðə ˌtwɪŋklɪŋ‿əvn‿'aɪ] im Nu; im Handumdrehen ⟨**VU1,** 13⟩

F

face [feɪs] Gesicht **I**
face to face [ˌfeɪs tə 'feɪs] Auge in Auge; von Angesicht zu Angesicht ⟨**VU1,** 12⟩
to make a face [meɪk ə 'feɪs] ein Gesicht ziehen **II**
to throw sth back in sb's face [θrəʊ ˌbæk ɪn ˌsʌmbədiz 'feɪs] jmdm. etw. wieder auftischen ⟨**VU1,** 15⟩
facelift ['feɪslɪft] Lifting; *(hier:)* Renovierung, Verschönerung **III**
fact [fækt] Fakt, Tatsache **II**
factory ['fæktri] Fabrik; Werk **III**
factual text [ˌfæktʃʊəl 'tekst] Sachtext **III**
fair [feə] gerecht, fair **I**
fake [feɪk] künstlich **IV**
fall *(AE)* [fɔ:l] Herbst **IV**
*to **fall** [fɔ:l] (hin)fallen **I**
to fall asleep [fɔ:l‿ə'sli:p] einschlafen **I**
to fall in love [ˌfɔ:l‿ɪn 'lʌv] sich verlieben **II**
to fall off [fɔ:l 'ɒf] herunterfallen, (hinunter)fallen **III**
to fall out of [fɔ:l‿'aʊt‿əv] herausfallen aus **II**
to fall over [fɔ:l 'əʊvə] umfallen, hinfallen **I**
false [fɔ:ls] falsch **II**
fame [feɪm] Ruhm **IV**
familiar [fə'mɪliə] vertraut **IV**
family ['fæmli] Familie **I**
family fun ['fæmli ˌfʌn] Spaß für die ganze Familie **I**
family tree ['fæmli ˌtri:] Familienstammbaum **I**
host family ['həʊst ˌfæmli] Gastfamilie **II**
famous ['feɪməs] berühmt **I**
fan [fæn] Fan, Anhänger/-in **II**
fantastic [fæn'tæstɪk] fantastisch, großartig **III**
far [fɑ:] weit **III**
so far ['səʊ fɑ:] bis jetzt **II**
fare [feə] Fahrpreis **II**
farm [fɑ:m] Bauernhof **I**
farmer ['fɑ:mə] Farmer/-in, Landwirt/-in **III**
farmhand ['fɑ:mhænd] Landarbeiter/-in **I**
fashion ['fæʃn] Mode **II**
fashion model ['fæʃn ˌmɒdl] Model, Mannequin **II**
fast [fɑ:st] schnell **I**
fast-food [ˌfɑ:st'fu:d] Fastfood **IV**
father ['fɑ:ðə] Vater **I**
fave *(= favourite)* [feɪv] Lieblings- **III**
favourite ['feɪvrɪt] Lieblings- **I**
fear [fɪə] Angst, Furcht **IV**
fearless ['fɪələs] furchtlos **IV**
to **feature** ['fi:tʃə] etw. groß herausbringen; etw. zeigen *(in einem Film etc.)* **IV**
to feature (sth) ['fi:tʃə] (etw.) aufweisen **VU4,** 77
February ['februri] Februar **I**
federal ['fedrl] Bundes-; föderalistisch **IV**
*to **feed** [fi:d] füttern **I**; ernähren **III**
to be fed up (with) [bi fed‿'ʌp wɪð] sauer sein, die Nase voll haben (von) **I**
*to **feel** [fi:l] (sich) fühlen **II**
to feel comfortable [ˌfi:l 'kʌmftəbl] sich wohl fühlen **VU3,** 51; **VU3,** 53
to feel like *(+ gerund)* ['fi:l laɪk] Lust haben (auf/zu) **IV**
to feel sorry for [fi:l 'sɒri] Mitleid haben mit; bedauern **III**
to feel sth [fi:l] etw. meinen, etw. glauben **IV**
feeling ['fi:lɪŋ] Gefühl **III**
female ['fi:meɪl] weiblich ⟨**VU3,** 53⟩
ferris wheel ['ferɪs ˌwi:l] Riesenrad **I**
ferry ['feri] Fähre **II**
festival ['festɪvl] Fest, Festival **I**
kite festival ['kaɪt ˌfestɪvl] Drachenfest **I**
a **few** [ə 'fju:] ein paar, einige; wenige **I**
science **fiction** [ˌsaɪəns 'fɪkʃn] Sciencefiction **II**
to **fidget** ['fɪdʒɪt] (herum)zappeln ⟨**VU1,** 12⟩
field [fi:ld] Wiese, Weide, Acker **I**; Gebiet, Bereich **II**; (Spiel)Feld **III**
fifteen [fɪf'ti:n] fünfzehn **I**
fifty ['fɪfti] fünfzig **I**
fight [faɪt] Kampf, Streit **II**
*to **fight** [faɪt] kämpfen; sich streiten **I**
to fight over [faɪt‿'əʊvə] sich streiten um **I**
figure ['fɪɡə] Figur **IV**; Persönlichkeit; Gestalt **VZI,** 10
file [faɪl] Akte **III**; Datei ⟨**VU3,** 51⟩
to **fill** [fɪl] füllen ⟨**VU3,** 52⟩
to fill in [fɪl‿'ɪn] ausfüllen **I**
filler ['fɪlə] Füllwort **III**
film [fɪlm] Film **I**
to **film** [fɪlm] filmen, drehen **III**
to **filter sth** ['fɪltə] etw. filtern **VU3,** 55
final ['faɪnl] letzte/-r/-s **IV**
finally ['faɪnli] schließlich, endlich, zum Schluss **I**
*to **find** [faɪnd] finden **I**
to find one's way around [ˌfaɪnd wʌnz ˌweɪ ə'raʊnd] sich zurecht finden **IV**
to find out [faɪnd‿'aʊt] herausfinden **II**
fine [faɪn] in Ordnung, gut **I**
I'm fine. [ˌaɪm 'faɪn] Mir geht es gut. **I**
finger ['fɪŋɡə] Finger **II**
to **finish** ['fɪnɪʃ] (be)enden, fertig stellen **I**
fire ['faɪə] Feuer **II**
to **fire** [faɪə] *(hier:)* antreiben; anspornen ⟨**VU2,** 35⟩
to fire back [faɪə 'bæk] zurückschlagen ⟨**VU4,** 79⟩
firefighter ['faɪəˌfaɪtə] Feuerwehrmann/ Feuerwehrfrau **III**
firm [fɜ:m] Firma **III**
first [fɜ:st] zuerst, als Erstes **I**; erste/-r/-s **I**

at first [ət 'fɜ:st] zuerst; zunächst **II**
first language ['fɜ:st ˌlæŋgwɪdʒ] Muttersprache **III**
first name ['fɜ:st neɪm] Vorname **IV**
First things first. [ˌfɜ:st θɪŋz 'fɜ:st] Das Wichtigste zuerst. **III**
in the first place [ɪn ðə 'fɜ:st ˌpleɪs] überhaupt erst, von vornherein **IV**
first-time [ˌfɜ:s'taɪm] erstmalig **VU1,** 17
fish pl. **fish** [fɪʃ] Fisch **I**
fish and chips [ˌfɪʃ‿n‿'tʃɪps] Fisch und Pommes frites **II**
fishing ['fɪʃɪŋ] Fischerei; Angeln, Fischen **II**
fit [fɪt] fit, in Form **II**
to keep fit [ki:p 'fɪt] fit bleiben **II**
fitness ['fɪtnəs] Fitness **II**
five [faɪv] fünf **I**
fixed [fɪkst] fest, unbeweglich ⟨**VU2,** 35⟩
to **flap** [flæp] flattern, (mit den Flügeln) schlagen **III**
flashback ['flæʃbæk] Rückblende, Flashback ⟨**VU3,** 52⟩
flat [flæt] Wohnung **I**
flavour ['fleɪvə] Geschmack, Geschmacksrichtung, Aroma, Sorte **I**
flight [flaɪt] Flug **II**
floor [flɔ:] Fußboden **III**
flour [flaʊə] Mehl **I**
flow chart ['fləʊ ˌtʃɑ:t] Flussdiagramm **II**
to **flow** [fləʊ] fließen; strömen **VU4,** 77
flower [flaʊə] Blume **I**
flu [flu:] Grippe **II**
fluent ['flu:ənt] fließend **VU2,** 34
*to **fly** [flaɪ] fliegen **I**
flying ['flaɪɪŋ] fliegend, Flug- **III**
to **focus (on)** ['fəʊkəs‿ɒn] sich konzentrieren (auf) **VU4,** 77
fog [fɒg] Nebel **II**
foggy ['fɒgi] neblig **II**
folder ['fəʊldə] Ordner, Mappe **I**
to **follow** ['fɒləʊ] hinterhergehen; (be)folgen **II**
followed by ['fɒləʊd baɪ] gefolgt von ⟨**VU1,** 19⟩
the **following** [ðə 'fɒləʊɪŋ] folgende/-r/-s **III**
food [fu:d] Essen, Nahrung(smittel) **I**
cat food ['kæt ˌfu:d] Katzenfutter **I**
foot pl. **feet** [fʊt; fi:t] Fuß **I**; Fuß *(Längenmaß: 30,48 cm)* **IV**
on foot [ɒn 'fʊt] zu Fuß **III**
football ['fʊtbɔ:l] Fußball **I**
American football [əˌmerɪkən 'fʊtbɔ:l] American Football **III**
footy *(Australian rules football) (coll)* ['fʊti] *(ugs. für die Sportart 'Australian rules football')* ⟨**VU1,** 14⟩
for [fɔ:; fə] für **I**; seit **IV**
for ages [fə 'eɪdʒɪz] seit einer Ewigkeit ⟨**VU3,** 57⟩
for (many) hours [fə ˌmeni 'aʊəz] stundenlang **I**
for laughs [fə 'lɑ:fs] zum Spaß **III**
for sale [fɔ: 'seɪl] zu verkaufen **IV**
for (many) years [fə ˌmeni 'jɪəz] jahrelang **I**
force [fɔ:s] Kraft; Gewalt, Stärke ⟨**VU1,** 13⟩; **VU4,** 70
by force [baɪ 'fɔ:s] gewaltsam, mit Gewalt **VU4,** 70
to **force sth** [fɔ:s] etw. mit Gewalt tun **IV**
forced [fɔ:st] erzwungen **VZI,** 11
weather **forecast** ['weðə ˌfɔ:kɑ:st] Wettervorhersage **VU2,** 34
foreign ['fɒrɪn] ausländisch; fremd **VZI,** 8
foreign language [ˌfɒrɪn 'læŋgwɪdʒ] Fremdsprache **VU2,** 28
foreshadowing [fɔ:'ʃædəʊɪŋ] Vorahnung **VU1,** 20
forest ['fɒrɪst] Wald **VZI,** 10
forever [fə'revə] für immer; ewig **VU4,** 78
*to **forget** [fə'get] vergessen **I**
to forget about sb/sth [fə'get əˌbaʊt] jmdn./etw. vergessen **II**
fork [fɔ:k] Gabel **II**
form [fɔ:m] Form **I**; Art **II**; Formular **VU1,** 18
to **form** [fɔ:m] bilden, formen ⟨**VU1,** 15⟩
formal ['fɔ:ml] formell; förmlich; formal **VU1,** 21
fortress ['fɔ:trəs] Festung **III**
forty ['fɔ:ti] vierzig **I**
forum ['fɔ:rəm] Forum ⟨**VU3,** 53⟩
to **found** [faʊnd] gründen **IV**
fountain ['faʊntɪn] Springbrunnen **III**
four [fɔ:] vier **I**
four of them ['fɔ:r‿əv ðəm] vier davon *(Personen, Tiere …)* **I**
fourteen [fɔ:'ti:n] vierzehn **I**
fox [fɒks] Fuchs **I**
to **free** [fri:] befreien **VU4,** 70
free [fri:] frei **II**; kostenlos **III**
freedom *(no pl.)* ['fri:dəm] Freiheit; Unabhängigkeit **IV**
freedom of speech [ˌfri:dəm‿əv 'spi:tʃ] Redefreiheit **VU4,** 68
free time ['fri: ˌtaɪm] Freizeit **I**
French [frenʃ] Französisch; französisch **II**
the French *(pl.)* [ðə 'frenʃ] die Franzosen **IV**
fresh [freʃ] frisch **I**
Friday ['fraɪdeɪ] Freitag **I**
friend [frend] Freund **I**
to make friends [ˌmeɪk 'frendz] Freundschaft schließen **II**
friendly ['frendli] freundlich, nett **II**
in a friendly way [ɪn‿ə ˌfrendli 'weɪ] freundlich *(Adverb)* **II**
friendship ['frendʃɪp] Freundschaft **III**
frightened ['fraɪtnd] verängstigt ⟨**VU3,** 52⟩
frightening ['fraɪtnɪŋ] furchterregend **III**
Frisbee ['frɪzbi] Frisbeescheibe **II**
from [frɒm; frəm] von … entfernt **I**; aus, von **I**
from now [frəm 'naʊ] in **VU3,** 60
from … to ['frəm tə] von … bis **I**
Where are you from? [ˌweər‿ə jə 'frɒm] Woher kommst du? **I**
at the **front** [æt ðə 'frʌnt] vorn(e) **II**
at the front of [æt ðə 'frʌnt‿əv] an der Spitze (von), im vorderen Bereich **II**
in front of [ɪn 'frʌnt‿əv] vor **I**
frozen ['frəʊzn] (tief)gefroren **III**
fruit [fru:t] Obst, Frucht **II**
frustrated [frʌs'treɪtɪd] frustriert ⟨**VU3,** 53⟩
frustration [frʌs'treɪʃn] Frust; Enttäuschung; Frustration ⟨**VU1,** 15⟩
fucking *(vulg)* ['fʌkɪŋ] Scheiß- *(derb)* ⟨**VU1,** 14⟩
full [fʊl] voll **II**
fun [fʌn] Spaß **II**
to be fun [bi 'fʌn] Spaß machen; witzig sein **I**
to have fun [hæv 'fʌn] Spaß haben, sich amüsieren **I**
to make fun of [ˌmeɪk 'fʌn‿əv] sich lustig machen über **III**
funny ['fʌni] lustig, witzig **I**
furious ['fjʊəriəs] wütend **IV**
furniture ['fɜ:nɪtʃə] Möbel **I**
further ['fɜ:ðə] weiter **VU4,** 77
future ['fju:tʃə] Zukunft **II**

G

gallery ['gæləri] (Kunst)Galerie **II**
game [geɪm] Spiel **I**
game show ['geɪm ˌʃəʊ] Spielshow **II**
garage ['gærɑ:ʒ] Garage; Werkstatt; Tankstelle **I**
garbage *(AE)* ['gɑ:bɪdʒ] Müll; Abfall **IV**
garden ['gɑ:dn] Garten **I**
gardener ['gɑ:dnə] Gärtner/-in **VU2,** 38
gas station *(AE)* ['gæs ˌsteɪʃn] Tankstelle **IV**
gash [gæʃ] tiefe Schnittwunde **III**
to **gasp** [gɑ:sp] tief einatmen, tief Luft holen; keuchen **III**
gate [geɪt] Tor, Pforte **IV**
ticket gate ['tɪkɪt ˌgeɪt] Fahrkartenschranke **II**
gateway ['geɪtweɪ] (Eingangs)tor **IV**
gay [geɪ] schwul; Schwuler **VU4,** 69
general ['dʒenrl] allgemein **VU4,** 80
generation [ˌdʒenə'reɪʃn] Generation **IV**
generous as can be [ˌdʒenrəs əz kən 'bi:] so großzügig, wie man nur sein kann ⟨**VU1,** 15⟩
genitive ['dʒenɪtɪv] Genitiv **II**
gentle ['dʒentl] sanft, liebenswürdig **II**
geography [dʒi'ɒgrəfi] Geografie; Erdkunde **II**

German ['dʒɜ:mən] Deutsch; deutsch, aus Deutschland **I**
German teacher ['dʒɜ:mən ˌti:tʃə] Deutschlehrer/-in **I**
gerund ['dʒernd] Gerundium **IV**
*to **get** [get] holen, bringen; bekommen **I**; werden **II**
Don't get your hopes up too high. [dəʊnt get jɔ: ˌhəʊps ʌp tu: 'haɪ] Mach dir nicht zu viele Hoffnungen. **III**
Get lost! [get 'lɒst] Hau ab! **II**
to get back [get 'bæk] zurückkommen **II**
to get bored [get 'bɔ:d] sich langweilen **III**
to get dressed [get 'drest] sich anziehen **III**
to get drunk [get 'drʌŋk] sich betrinken **IV**
to get in the way [ˌget‿ɪn ðə 'weɪ] stören, im Weg stehen **III**
to get into [get‿'ɪntə] (ein)steigen **I**
to get into trouble [ˌget‿ɪntə 'trʌbl] in Schwierigkeiten geraten **II**
to get lost [get 'lɒst] sich verirren **I**
to get lumped in with [ˌget lʌmpt‿'ɪn wɪð] in einen Topf geworfen werden ⟨**VU1,** 15⟩
to get married [get 'mærid] heiraten **VU3,** 56
to get named *(coll)* [get 'neɪmd] beschimpft werden ⟨**VU4,** 79⟩
to get off [get‿'ɒf] aussteigen **II**
to get on [get‿'ɒn] einsteigen **II**; auskommen **III**
to get one's act together [ˌget wʌnz‿'ækt təˌgeðə] sich zusammenreißen **VU2,** 38
to get one's own back [get wʌnz‿'əʊn bæk] jmdm. eins auswischen, sich rächen **II**
to get out of the way [get ˌaʊt‿əv ðə 'weɪ] aus dem Weg gehen **IV**
to get ready [get 'redi] sich vorbereiten; sich fertig machen **III**
to get rid of [get 'rɪd‿əv] loswerden **III**
to get sb's attention [get ə'tenʃn] jmdn. auf sich aufmerksam machen **III**
to get sb to do sth ['get ˌsʌmbədi tə 'du: ˌsʌmθɪŋ] jmdn. dazu bewegen, etwas zu tun **III**
to get through sth [get 'θru:] etw. überstehen **VU4,** 74
to get tired of [get 'taɪəd‿əv] etwas satt bekommen **III**
to get to ['get tə] kommen zu, kommen nach, erreichen **I**
to get up [get 'ʌp] aufstehen **I**
to get used to (sth) [get‿'ju:zd tə] sich an (etwas) gewöhnen **II**
to get used to *(+gerund)* [get‿'ju:zd tə] sich gewöhnen (an) **IV**
You've got me there! [jʊv ˌgɒt mi 'ðeə] Da habt ihr mich kalt erwischt! **I**
ghost [gəʊst] Geist **III**
giant [dʒaɪənt] Riesen-, riesig **III**
gift [gɪft] Talent, Gabe **VU2,** 39
girl [gɜ:l] Mädchen **I**
girlfriend ['gɜ:lfrend] Freundin *(in einer Paarbeziehung)* **III**
gist [dʒɪst] das Wesentliche **III**
*to **give** [gɪv] geben; schenken **I**
giving advice [ˌgɪvɪŋ əd'vaɪs] einen Rat geben **III**
to give a (group) presentation [gɪv‿ə ˌgru:p‿ˌprezn'teɪʃn] eine (Gruppen)Präsentation machen **II**
to give one's opinion [ˌgɪv wʌnz ə'pɪnjən] seine Meinung äußern **III**
to give reasons [gɪv 'ri:znz] Gründe nennen, Gründe angeben **II**
to give sb a hand [gɪv ˌsʌmbədi‿ə‿'hænd] jmdm. helfen **IV**
to give tours [gɪv 'tʊəz] Stadtrundfahrten leiten **I**
to give up [gɪv‿'ʌp] aufgeben **II**
glad [glæd] froh **II**
glass [glɑ:s] Glas **II**
glass-bottom ['glɑ:s ˌbɒtm] Glasboden- **VU1,** 16
glasses *(pl.)* ['glɑ:sɪz] Brille **III**
glory ['glɔ:ri] Ruhm; Ehre ⟨**VU4,** 79⟩
*to **go** [gəʊ] gehen, fahren **I**; führen **I**
Go ahead. [gəʊ‿ə'hed] Mach nur! **VU3,** 51; **VU3,** 53
Go, ... go! [gəʊ ... 'gəʊ] Los, ..., los!/Lauf(t), ..., lauf(t)! **IV**
Let's go! [lets 'gəʊ] Lass(t) uns anfangen!/Lass(t) uns gehen! **I**
to be gone [bi 'gɒn] verschwunden sein, weg sein **II**
to go [tʊ 'gəʊ] zum Mitnehmen **IV**
to go back [gəʊ 'bæk] zurückgehen **I**
to go crazy [gəʊ 'kreɪzi] ausflippen, durchdrehen **III**
to go curly [gəʊ 'kɜ:li] sich kräuseln **III**
to go down [gəʊ 'daʊn] hinuntergehen; entlanggehen **I**; nach unten gehen **I**; sinken; nachlassen ⟨**VU3,** 57⟩
to go home [gəʊ 'həʊm] nach Hause gehen **I**
to go on [gəʊ‿'ɒn] weitermachen, fortfahren **I**; (an)dauern **III**
to go on holiday [gəʊ ɒn 'hɒlədeɪ] in Urlaub gehen, in Urlaub fahren **I**
to go out with [gəʊ‿'aʊt wɪð] (aus)gehen mit **III**
to go over [gəʊ 'əʊvə] hinübergehen ⟨**VU3,** 57⟩
to go shopping [gəʊ 'ʃɒpɪŋ] einkaufen gehen **I**
to go surfing [gəʊ 'sɜ:fɪŋ] surfen gehen **I**
to go to bed [gəʊ tə 'bed] ins Bett gehen **I**
to go up [gəʊ 'ʌp] nach oben gehen **I**
to go with [gəʊ 'wɪð] passen zu, gehören zu **I**
to go wrong [gəʊ 'rɒŋ] schiefgehen **IV**
What's going on? [wɒts ˌgəʊɪŋ‿'ɒn] Was ist denn hier los? **III**
goal [gəʊl] Tor **I**
Oh my **God!** [əʊ ˌmaɪ 'gɒd] Oh mein Gott! **IV**
the gods *(lit)* [ðə 'gɒdz] die Götter *(literarisch)* ⟨**VU1,** 13⟩
goggles *(pl.)* ['gɒglz] Skibrille, Schwimmbrille **III**
gold [gəʊld] Gold **III**
gold medal [gəʊld 'medl] Goldmedaille **III**
golden ['gəʊldn] golden **IV**
golf [gɒlf] Golf **II**
good [gʊd] gut **I**
a good way to ... [ə‿gʊd 'weɪ tə] eine gute Möglichkeit ... **II**
G'day! *(= Good day!)* [gə'daɪ] Guten Tag./Hallo./Hi. *(Begrüßung in Australien)* **VZI,** 11
good guy ['gʊd gaɪ] der Gute **IV**
Good luck! [ˌgʊd 'lʌk] Viel Glück! **II**
Good morning. [gʊd 'mɔ:nɪŋ] Guten Morgen. **I**
to be good at [bi 'gʊd‿ət] gut sein in/bei **I**
to be good with [bi 'gʊd wɪð] gut umgehen können mit **I**
goodbye [gʊd'baɪ] auf Wiedersehen **I**
to say goodbye (to) [seɪ gʊd'baɪ] sich verabschieden (von) **IV**
good-looking [ˌgʊd'lʊkɪŋ] gut aussehend **II**
gossip ['gɒsɪp] Klatsch; Tratsch; Gerede **VU3,** 55
*to **have (got)** [hæv 'gɒt] besitzen, haben **I**
government ['gʌvnmənt] Regierung **III**
to **grab** [græb] schnappen; greifen **IV**; (er)greifen; schnappen **VU2,** 38
grade *(AE)* [greɪd] Klasse *(AE)*; Note *(AE)* **IV**
grammar ['græmə] Grammatik **I**
grammar school ['græmə ˌsku:l] Gymnasium **II**
grandad ['grændæd] Opa **I**
grandfather ['grænˌfɑ:ðə] Großvater **I**
grandma ['grænmɑ:] Oma **I**
grandmother ['grænˌmʌðə] Großmutter **I**
grandparents [grændpeərənts] Großeltern **IV**
grass [grɑ:s] Gras **I**
great [greɪt] groß, riesig **I**; toll, großartig **I**

great-great-grandmother [ˌgreɪ-tgreɪt'grænmʌðə] Ururgroßmutter **III**
Greek [gri:k] griechisch, aus Griechenland; Griechisch **I**
green [gri:n] grün **I**
green ant [ˌgri:n‿'ænt] grüne Ameise **V U1,** 17
to **greet** [gri:t] (be)grüßen **IV**
grey [greɪ] grau **I**
grid [grɪd] Raster, Tabelle **I**
ground [graʊnd] (Erd)Boden, Erde ⟨**V U3,** 52⟩
to stand one's ground [ˌstænd wʌnz 'graʊnd] sich behaupten ⟨**V U4,** 79⟩
group [gru:p] Gruppe **I**
*to **grow** [grəʊ] wachsen **III**
to grow up [grəʊ‿'ʌp] erwachsen werden; aufwachsen **III**
witchetty **grub** [ˌwɪtʃəti 'grʌb] Witchetty-Made; Holzbohrerlarve **V U1,** 17
grumpy ['grʌmpi] mürrisch, schlecht gelaunt **III**
guarantee [ˌgærn'ti:] Garantie **IV**
to **guard** [gɑ:d] bewachen **IV**
to **guess** [ges] (er)raten; vermuten **I**
guest [gest] Gast **IV**
guide [gaɪd] Führer/-in **II**
guidebook ['gaɪdbʊk] Reiseführer **II**
guilt [gɪlt] Schuld; Schuldgefühl ⟨**V U1,** 13⟩
guitar [gɪ'tɑ:] Gitarre **I**
gun [gʌn] Schusswaffe **III**
gust of laughter [ˌgʌst‿əv 'lɑ:ftə] Lachanfall ⟨**V U1,** 13⟩
guy [gaɪ] Typ, Kerl; *(pl.)* Leute **III**
bad guy ['bæd gaɪ] Bösewicht **IV**
good guy ['gʊd gaɪ] der Gute **IV**
you guys *(coll)* [ju 'gaɪz] ihr; euch **IV**
gym(nasium) [dʒɪm; dʒɪm'neɪziəm] Turnhalle **IV**
gymnastics *(pl.)* [dʒɪm'næstɪks] Gymnastik **IV**

H

hair [heə] Haar, Haare **II**
hairdresser ['heədresə] Friseur/-in **V U2,** 32
half pl. **halves** [hɑ:f; hɑ:vz] (die) Hälfte; Halbzeit **III**
half [hɑ:f] halb **I**
half-sister ['hɑ:fˌsɪstə] Halbschwester **I**
half-time [ˌhɑ:f'taɪm] Halbzeit **III**
*to meet **halfway** [mi:t hɑ:f'weɪ] (sich auf halbem Weg) entgegenkommen **III**
hall [hɔ:l] Halle, Saal **II**; Flur, Korridor **II**
hand [hænd] Hand **I**
Hands on! [hændz‿'ɒn] Pack's an! **I**
like the back of my hand [laɪk ðə ˌbæk‿əv maɪ 'hænd] wie meine Westentasche, in- und auswendig **II**
to give sb a hand [gɪv ˌsʌmbədi‿ə‿'hænd] jmdm. helfen **IV**
to hold hands [həʊld 'hændz] Händchen halten **II**
to shake hands [ʃeɪk 'hændz] sich die Hand geben **IV**
handful ['hænfʊl] Handvoll ⟨**V U1,** 14⟩
to **handle** ['hændl] umgehen mit; handhaben; bedienen **V U4,** 79
*to **hang** [hæŋ] hängen **II**
to hang out (with) [ˌhæŋ 'aʊt wɪð] sich treffen (mit); rumhängen (mit) **III**
to **happen** ['hæpn] passieren, geschehen **I**
to happen to do sth [ˌhæpn tʊ 'du: ˌsʌmθɪŋ] zufällig etw. tun **IV**
happily ever after ['hæpɪli evə‿ɑ:ftə] glücklich und zufrieden bis an ihr Lebensende **IV**
happiness ['hæpɪnəs] Glück; Zufriedenheit; Fröhlichkeit **IV**
happy ['hæpi] glücklich, fröhlich **I**
Happy Birthday! [ˌhæpi 'bɜ:θdeɪ] Alles Gute zum Geburtstag! **I**
to be happy to do sth [bi 'hæpi tə ˌdu:] etw. gerne tun; etw. tun können **V U4,** 70
harbour ['hɑ:bə] Hafen **I**
hard [hɑ:d] stark **II**; schwierig, schwer; hart **II**
to try hard [traɪ 'hɑ:d] sich anstrengen **II**
hardly ['hɑ:dli] kaum **V U3,** 55
harmless ['hɑ:mləs] harmlos, ungefährlich ⟨**V U1,** 12⟩
harmonious [hɑ:'məʊniəs] harmonisch, wohlklingend **V U4,** 78
hat [hæt] Hut **III**
to **hate** [heɪt] hassen, nicht mögen **III**
*to **have** [hæv] haben, besitzen **II**; essen; trinken **II**
to have (got) [hæv 'gɒt] besitzen, haben **I**
to have a party [hæv ə 'pɑ:ti] eine Party feiern **I**
to have breakfast [hæv 'brekfəst] frühstücken **I**
to have fun [hæv 'fʌn] Spaß haben, sich amüsieren **I**
to have no idea [hæv ˌnəʊ‿aɪ'dɪə] keine Ahnung haben **III**
to have one's head in the clouds [həv wʌnz ˌhed‿ɪn ðə 'klaʊdz] über den Dingen schweben; in höheren Regionen schweben **V U2,** 34
to have sth done [ˌhæv 'dʌn] etw. machen lassen **V U1,** 17
to have to ['hæv tə] müssen **III**
You've got a point. [ju:v gɒt‿ə 'pɔɪnt] Da ist was dran. **III**
he [hi:] er **I**
head [hed] Kopf **II**
head of state [ˌhed‿əv 'steɪt] Staatsoberhaupt **V ZI,** 10
to have one's head in the clouds [həv wʌnz ˌhed‿ɪn ðə 'klaʊdz] über den Dingen schweben; in höheren Regionen schweben **V U2,** 34
headache ['hedeɪk] Kopfschmerzen, Kopfweh **II**
heading ['hedɪŋ] Überschrift, Titel **I**
headline ['hedlaɪn] Schlagzeile **III**
health [helθ] Gesundheit **II**
healthy ['helθi] gesund **II**
*to **hear** [hɪə] hören **I**
heart [hɑ:t] Herz **I**
to learn by heart [ˌlɜ:n baɪ 'hɑ:t] auswendig lernen **I**
heartless ['hɑ:tləs] herzlos, unbarmherzig **IV**
the heavens *(lit)* [ðə 'hevnz] das Firmament *(literarisch)*, der Himmel *(literarisch)* ⟨**V U1,** 13⟩
heavy ['hevi] schwer, stark **II**
heavy industry [ˌhevi 'ɪndəstri] Schwerindustrie **III**
heir [eə] Erbe/Erbin **III**
helicopter ['helɪkɒptə] Helikopter, Hubschrauber **II**
hell [hel] Hölle **V U4,** 75
Hello. [hel'əʊ] Hallo. **I**
to say hello [seɪ hel'əʊ] jmdn. begrüßen **I**
to say hello to [seɪ hel'əʊ tə] grüßen, Grüße ausrichten **I**
helmet ['helmət] Helm **III**
help [help] Hilfe **I**
to **help** [help] helfen **I**
to help oneself (to) [help wʌn'self tə] sich bedienen **III**
helpful ['helpfl] hilfsbereit; hilfreich, nützlich **II**
helpless ['helpləs] hilflos **IV**
her [hɜ:] ihr/-e **I**
here [hɪə] hier **I**; hierher, hierhin **I**
Here it is. [ˌhɪər‿ɪt‿'ɪz] Hier ist es. **I**
Here you are. [ˌhɪə ju‿'ɑ:] Bitte schön. **I**
in here [ɪn 'hi:ə] hier drin **I**
over here [ˌəʊvə 'hɪə] hierher **IV**
hero pl. **heroes** ['hɪərəʊ, 'hɪərəʊz] Held, Helden **II**
herself [hɜ:'self] selber **III**
to **hesitate** ['hezɪteɪt] zögern ⟨**V U1,** 14⟩
Hey! [heɪ] Hey! **I**
Hi. [haɪ] Hi./Hallo. **I**
*to **hide** [haɪd] (sich) verstecken **II**
high [haɪ] hoch; groß **II**; high *(auf Drogen sein)* **IV**
higher education [ˌhaɪə edʒʊ'keɪʃn] Hochschulbildung; Hochschulwesen **V U2,** 28
high school ['haɪ ˌsku:l] High School *(weiterführende Schule in den USA, Oberstufe)* **IV**
highlight ['haɪlaɪt] Highlight **IV**
high-tech ['haɪtek] hoch technisiert **II**

highway *(AE)* ['haɪweɪ] Bundesstraße, Highway **IV**
hike [haɪk] Wanderung **II**
to hike [haɪk] wandern **IV**
hiker ['haɪkə] Wanderer/-in **II**
hill [hɪl] Berg; Hügel **II**
himself [hɪm'self] selber **III**
Hindi ['hɪndi:] Hindi **VZI,** 9
hint [hɪnt] Hinweis, Tipp; Andeutung **VU1,** 20
hippy ['hɪpəʊ] Hippie ⟨**VU2,** 38⟩
to hire [haɪə] einstellen **IV**
his [hɪz] sein/-e **I**
Hispanic [hɪ'spænɪk] Lateinamerikaner/-in; hispanisch, lateinamerikanisch **IV**
historical [hɪ'stɒrɪkl] historisch, geschichtlich **VU4,** 77
history ['hɪstri] Geschichte **II**
***to hit** [hɪt] schlagen; treffen **II**
to hit the slopes [ˌhɪt ðə 'sləʊps] auf die (Ski)piste gehen **IV**
hm [m] hm **I**
hobby pl. **hobbies** ['hɒbi; 'hɒbiz] Hobby **I**
ice **hockey** ['aɪs ˌhɒki] Eishockey **III**
***to hold** [həʊld] halten, festhalten **I**
to hold back [həʊld 'bæk] (zurück)halten ⟨**VU1,** 15⟩
to hold hands [həʊld 'hændz] Händchen halten **II**
to hold one's breath [ˌhəʊld wʌnz 'breθ] den Atem anhalten, die Luft anhalten ⟨**VU1,** 13⟩
to hold sb back [ˌhəʊld 'bæk] jmdn. zurückhalten ⟨**VU2,** 35⟩
to hold sb down [ˌhəʊld 'daʊn] jmdn. niedrig halten; jmdn. unterdrücken ⟨**VU4,** 79⟩
to hold up [həʊld 'ʌp] hochhalten **I**
hole [həʊl] Loch **I**
holiday(s) ['hɒlədeɪ; 'hɒlədeɪz] Ferien, Urlaub **I**
beach holiday ['bi:tʃ ˌhɒlədeɪ] Strandurlaub **I**
planning your holidays [ˌplænɪŋ jə 'hɒlədeɪz] den Urlaub planen **I**
to go on holiday [gəʊ ɒn 'hɒlədeɪ] in Urlaub gehen, in Urlaub fahren **I**
holiday-maker ['hɒlədeɪˌmeɪkə] Urlauber-/in **I**
home [həʊm] Zuhause **I**
animal home ['ænɪml həʊm] Tierheim **II**
at home [æt 'həʊm] zu Hause **I**
Home alone. [həʊm ə'ləʊn] Allein zu Hause. **III**
home crowd ['həʊm ˌkraʊd] heimisches Publikum **II**
home page ['həʊm ˌpeɪdʒ] Homepage **I**
home sweet home ['həʊm ˌswi:t 'həʊm] trautes Heim *(Sprichwort)* **I**
old people's home [əʊld 'pi:plz həʊm] Altersheim **III**
on the way home [ˌɒn ðe weɪ 'həʊm] auf dem Weg nach Hause **I**
to go home [gəʊ 'həʊm] nach Hause gehen **I**
homeless ['həʊmləs] obdachlos **VU4,** 77
homeowner ['həʊmˌəʊnə] Hauseigentümer/-in **IV**
homework ['həʊmwɜ:k] Hausaufgabe/-n **I**
Hooray! [hʊ'reɪ] Hurra! **I**
to **hop** [hɒp] hüpfen **II**
hope [həʊp] Hoffnung **II**
Don't get your hopes up too high. [dəʊnt get jɔ: ˌhəʊps ʌp tu: 'haɪ] Mach dir nicht zu viele Hoffnungen. **III**
to **hope** [həʊp] hoffen **II**
hopefully ['həʊpfli] hoffentlich **IV**
hopeless ['həʊpləs] hoffnungslos **IV**
horizon [hə'raɪzn] Horizont ⟨**VU3,** 52⟩
horrible ['hɒrəbl] schrecklich, furchtbar **II**
horror ['hɒrə] Horror, Schrecken, Entsetzen **II**
horse [hɔ:s] Pferd **I**
hospital ['hɒspɪtl] Krankenhaus, Hospital **II**
host [həʊst] Gastgeber/-in **II**
host family ['həʊst ˌfæmli] Gastfamilie **II**
youth **hostel** ['ju:θ ˌhɒstl] Jugendherberge **II**
hot [hɒt] heiß; gefragt **III**; *(hier:)* groß **VU2,** 34
hotel [həʊ'tel] Hotel **II**
hot-headed [hɒt'hedɪd] hitzköpfig **II**
hotline ['hɒtlaɪn] Hotline **III**
hotly ['hɒtli] hitzig, erregt ⟨**VU1,** 14⟩
hottie *(coll.)* ['hɒti] gutaussehende Person, attraktive Person ⟨**VU1,** 21⟩
hour [aʊə] Stunde **I**
for (many) hours [fə ˌmeni 'aʊəz] stundenlang **I**
house [haʊs] Haus **I**
at my house [ət 'maɪ haʊs] bei mir zu Hause **I**
to move (house) [mu:v 'haʊs] umziehen **III**
houseboat ['haʊsbəʊt] Hausboot **III**
housewife pl. **housewives** ['haʊswaɪf, 'haʊswaɪvz] Hausfrau **III**
how [haʊ] wie **I**
How about ... ? [haʊ ə'baʊt] Wie wäre es mit ...? **I**
How are you? [ˌhaʊ‿ɑ: 'jə] Wie geht es dir/Ihnen? **I**
How many ... ? [haʊ 'meni] Wie viele ... ? **I**
How much ... ? [haʊ 'mʌtʃ] Wie viel ... ? **I**
How much is ... ? ['haʊ mʌtʃ‿ɪz] Wie viel kostet ... ? **I**
How old are you? [haʊ‿'əʊld‿ɑ: 'ju:] Wie alt bist du? **I**
How to ... ['haʊ tə] Wie man ... **I**
however [haʊ'evə] jedoch **IV**
Howzit! ['haʊzɪt] Hallo. *(Begrüßung in Südafrika)* **VZI,** 10
huge [hju:dʒ] riesig, riesengroß; gewaltig **IV**
huh [hʌ; hə] (nicht) wahr **VU1,** 17
human ['hju:mən] menschlich ⟨**VU3,** 53⟩; **VU4,** 68
human being [ˌhju:mən 'bi:ɪŋ] Mensch ⟨**VU1,** 12⟩
human rights [ˌhju:mən 'raɪts] Menschenrechte **VU4,** 68
a/one **hundred** [ə 'hʌndrəd; wʌn 'hʌndrəd] einhundert **I**
hungry ['hʌŋgri] hungrig **II**
hurry ['hʌri] Eile, Hast **I**
to be in a hurry [bi ɪn‿ə 'hʌri] es eilig haben, in Eile sein **I**
to **hurry** ['hʌri] sich beeilen ⟨**VU1,** 14⟩
to hurry up [ˌhʌri 'ʌp] sich beeilen **I**
*to **hurt** [hɜ:t] verletzen; weh tun **II**
hypocritical [ˌhɪpə'krɪtɪkl] heuchlerisch, scheinheilig ⟨**VU1,** 15⟩

I

I [aɪ] ich **I**
I didn't mean to ... [aɪ ˌdɪdnt 'mi:n tə] Ich wollte nicht ... **III**
I'd like to ... *(= I would like to)* [aɪd 'laɪk tə] ich möchte .../ich würde gerne ... **I**
I don't care! [aɪ ˌdəʊnt 'keə] Das ist mir egal! **III**
I'd rather [aɪd 'rɑ:ðə] ich würde lieber **III**
I see. [aɪ 'si:] Ich verstehe./Aha! **III**
ice [aɪs] Eis **III**
ice hockey ['aɪs ˌhɒki] Eishockey **III**
ice skating ['aɪs ˌskeɪtɪŋ] Schlittschuhlaufen **II**
ice-cream [ˌaɪs'kri:m] Eis(creme) **I**
idea [aɪ'dɪə] Idee **I**
to have no idea [hæv ˌnəʊ‿aɪ'dɪə] keine Ahnung haben **III**
idealistic [aɪˌdɪə'lɪstɪk] idealistisch **VU4,** 78
identification [aɪdentɪfɪ'keɪʃn] Identifizierung, Identifikation **II**
to **identify** [aɪ'dentɪfaɪ] aufzeigen; identifizieren **VU4,** 70
idiot ['ɪdiət] Idiot/-in **II**
if [ɪf] wenn, falls; ob **I**
if-clause ['ɪfklɔ:z] if-Satz **II**
to **ignore** [ɪg'nɔ:] ignorieren, außer Acht lassen **IV**
ill [ɪl] krank; schlecht **II**
illegal [ɪ'li:gl] illegal; rechtswidrig; unrechtmäßig **IV**

illusion [ɪ'lu:ʒn] Trugbild, Illusion; Täuschung ⟨**V U3,** 52⟩
image ['ɪmɪdʒ] Image, Ruf **V U2,** 32
imaginative [ɪ'mædʒɪnətɪv] einfallsreich, fantasievoll **V U2,** 41
to **imagine** [ɪ'mædʒɪn] sich (etwas) vorstellen **II**
immigrant ['ɪmɪgrənt] Immigrant/-in, Einwanderer/Einwanderin **IV**
immigration [ˌɪmɪ'greɪʃn] Immigration, Einwanderung **IV**
impolite [ˌɪmp'laɪt] unhöflich **IV**
importance [ɪm'pɔ:tns] Bedeutung, Wichtigkeit **V U3,** 55
of no importance [əv ˌnəʊ ɪm'pɔ:tns] ohne Bedeutung **V U3,** 55
important [ɪm'pɔ:tnt] wichtig **I**
impression [ɪm'preʃn] Eindruck **IV**
to make a good/bad impression (on sb) [ˌmeɪk‿ə gʊd ɪm'preʃn‿ɒn] einen guten/schlechten Eindruck (auf jmdn.) machen **V U2,** 37
to **improve** [ɪm'pru:v] (sich) verbessern **II**
impulse ['ɪmpʌls] Impuls ⟨**V U1,** 12⟩
in [ɪn] aktuell, in, trendy **II**
in [ɪn] in **I**; aus, von, jede/-r/-s (zweite/dritte …) **III**
in a draw [ɪn‿ə 'drɔ:] unentschieden **III**
in a friendly way [ɪn‿ə ˌfrendli 'weɪ] freundlich *(Adverb)* **II**
in English [ɪn‿'ɪŋglɪʃ] auf Englisch **I**
in front of [ɪn 'frʌnt‿əv] vor **I**
in here [ɪn 'hi:ə] hier drin **I**
in place of [ɪn 'pleɪs‿əv] (an)statt, an Stelle von **V U2,** 30
in reply to [ɪn rɪ'plaɪ tə] als Antwort auf, als Reaktion auf **V U3,** 55
in spite of [ɪn 'spaɪt‿əv] trotz **V U4,** 71
in the evening [ɪn ði‿'i:vnɪŋ] abends **I**
in the first place [ɪn ðə 'fɜ:st ˌpleɪs] überhaupt erst, von vornherein **IV**
in the middle of [ɪn ðə 'mɪdl‿əv] mitten in **V U2,** 39
in the street [ɪn ðə 'stri:t] auf der Straße **I**
incredulously [ɪn'kredjələsli] ungläubig; fassungslos ⟨**V U1,** 14⟩
indefinite [ɪn'defɪnət] unbestimmt **III**
independence [ˌɪndɪ'pendəns] Unabhängigkeit **V ZI,** 10
independent [ˌɪndɪ'pendənt] unabhängig **III**
index ['ɪndeks] Index **V U4,** 69
Indian ['ɪndiən] Indianer/-in; indianisch **IV**; Inder/-in; indisch **V ZI,** 9
indigenous [ɪn'dɪdʒɪnəs] einheimisch **V ZI,** 11
indirect speech [ˌɪndɪrekt 'spi:tʃ] indirekte Rede **III**
individual [ˌɪndɪ'vɪdʒuəl] Einzelperson; Einzelne/-r; Individuum **V U4,** 70
industrial [ɪn'dʌstriəl] Industrie- **IV**
Industrial Revolution [ɪnˌdʌstriəl revˈlu:ʃn] Industrielle Revolution **III**
industry ['ɪndəstri] Industrie, Industrieanlage **III**
heavy industry [ˌhevi 'ɪndəstri] Schwerindustrie **III**
oil industry ['ɔɪl‿ˌɪndəstri] Ölindustrie **II**
infectious [ɪn'fekʃəs] ansteckend ⟨**V U1,** 13⟩
infinitive [ɪn'fɪnətɪv] Infinitiv **II**
influence ['ɪnfluəns] Einfluss **V ZI,** 8
info *(= information)* ['ɪnfəʊ] Infos (= Informationen) **V U3,** 59
to **inform** [ɪn'fɔ:m] informieren **II**
information *(no pl.)* [ˌɪnfə'meɪʃn] Information, Informationen **I**
bit of information [ˌbɪt‿əv‿ɪnfə'meɪʃn] eine Information **V U1,** 17
information centre [ˌɪnfə'meɪʃn 'sentə] Touristeninformation **I**
ingredient [ɪn'gri:diənt] Zutat **V U4,** 73
in-line skating [ˌɪnlaɪn 'skeɪtɪŋ] Inlineskates fahren **II**
inquisitive [ɪn'kwɪzətɪv] neugierig; wissbegierig; fragend ⟨**V U1,** 12⟩
inside [ɪn'saɪd] innen, im Innern; hinein, nach drinnen; in **II**
instant ['ɪnstənt] sofortige/-r/-s ⟨**V U1,** 13⟩
instead [ɪn'sted] stattdessen ⟨**V U1,** 14⟩
instead of [ɪn'sted‿əv] (an)statt, anstelle von **V U3,** 58
instructor [ɪn'strʌktə] Lehrer/-in **IV**
musical **instrument** [ˌmju:zɪkl‿'ɪnstrəmənt] Musikinstrument **II**
to **integrate** ['ɪntɪgreɪt] (sich) integrieren; (sich) einfügen; *(hier:) (Schulen für Schwarze zugänglich machen)* **V U4,** 74
integration [ˌɪntɪ'greɪʃn] Integration, Integrierung; Eingliederung **V U4,** 74
to **intensify** [ɪn'tensɪfaɪ] intensivieren; verstärken ⟨**V U1,** 12⟩
interactive [ˌɪntər'æktɪv] interaktiv **III**
to **interest** ['ɪntrəst] interessieren **V U1,** 16
interested in ['ɪntrəstɪd] interessiert an **I**
interesting ['ɪntrəstɪŋ] interessant **I**
Internet ['ɪntənet] Internet **I**
to surf on the Internet [ˌsɜ:f‿ɒn ði‿'ɪntənet] im Internet surfen **I**
to **interrupt** [ˌɪntə'rʌpt] unterbrechen **IV**
interview ['ɪntəvju:] Interview; Befragung **II**; Vorstellungsgespräch ⟨**V U2,** 36⟩
to **interview** ['ɪntəvju:] interviewen **III**
to be interviewed for a job [bi‿'ɪntəvju:d] ein Vorstellungsgespräch haben **V U2,** 37
interviewer ['ɪntəvju:ə] Leiter/-in eines Vorstellungsgesprächs; Interviewer/-in **V U2,** 37
into ['ɪntə] in (hinein) **I**
to **intrigue sb** [ɪn'tri:g] jmdn. faszinieren ⟨**V U1,** 12⟩
to **introduce** [ˌɪntrə'dju:s] einführen, einleiten **III**
introduction [ˌɪntrə'dʌkʃn] Einführung **IV**
invention [ɪn'venʃn] Erfindung **III**
inversion [ɪn'vɜ:ʃn] Inversion **V U3,** 56
invitation [ˌɪnvɪ'teɪʃn] Einladung **I**
to **invite** [ɪn'vaɪt] einladen **I**
to invite … out [ɪnˌvaɪt 'aʊt] … (zu etwas) einladen **I**
*to be **involved (in)** [bi ɪn'vɒlvd‿ɪn] mit etw. zu tun haben **IV**
irregular [ɪ'regjələ] unregelmäßig **II**
island ['aɪlənd] Insel **I**
issue ['ɪʃu:, 'ɪsju:] Angelegenheit, Thema, Problem **V U3,** 55
it [ɪt] es **I**
it says … [ɪt 'sez] hier steht … **V U2,** 30
It's a pity. [ˌɪts‿ə 'pɪti] Das ist schade./Es ist schade … **III**
It's two pounds. [ɪts ˌtu: 'paʊndz] Es kostet zwei Pfund. **I**
It's up to you. [ɪts‿ˌʌp tə 'ju:] Es ist an dir (zu entscheiden)./Wie du willst. **V U2,** 39
IT *(= Information Technology)* [ˌaɪ'ti:] Informatik; Informationstechnik **V ZI,** 8
Italian [ɪ'tæliən] italienisch, aus Italien; Italienisch **I**
italics [ɪ'tælɪks] Kursivschrift **V U3,** 58
its [ɪts] sein **I**
itself [ɪt'self] selbst **III**

J

life-**jacket** ['laɪfˌdʒækɪt] Schwimmweste, Rettungsweste **II**
jail [dʒeɪl] Gefängnis **IV**
January ['dʒænjuri] Januar **I**
jealous (of) ['dʒeləs‿əv] neidisch; eifersüchtig **III**
jeans *(pl.)* [dʒi:nz] Jeans **I**
jewellery ['dʒu:əlri] Schmuck **III**
job [dʒɒb] Arbeit, Aufgabe, Tätigkeit **I**
to do a good job [du: ə gʊd 'dʒɒb] gute Arbeit leisten **IV**
to **jog** [dʒɒg] joggen **II**
to **join** [dʒɔɪn] beitreten **II**
joint *(coll)* [dʒɔɪnt] Laden *(ugs.)* **IV**
joke [dʒəʊk] Witz **I**
to **joke** [dʒəʊk] scherzen **III**
journalist ['dʒɜ:nlɪst] Journalist/-in **IV**
journey ['dʒɜ:ni] Reise **III**
joy [dʒɔɪ] Freude **IV**
joyless ['dʒɔɪləs] freudlos **IV**

judge [dʒʌdʒ] Richter/-in **II**; Juror/-in ⟨**V U3,** 57⟩
to judge sb/sth by sth ['dʒʌdʒ baɪ] jmdn./etw. beurteilen; jmdn./etw. einschätzen **V U4,** 75
judo ['dʒu:dəʊ] Judo **II**
July [dʒʊ'laɪ] Juli **I**
jumbled ['dʒʌmbld] durcheinander geraten, vermischt **I**
jump [dʒʌmp] Sprung **III**
ski jump ['ski: dʒʌmp] Skispringen **III**
to jump [dʒʌmp] springen **I**
to jump out of one's skin [ˌdʒʌmp‿aʊt‿əv wʌnz 'skɪn] sich zu Tode erschrecken **III**
ski jumper ['ski: ˌdʒʌmpə] Skispringer/-in **III**
June [dʒu:n] Juni **I**
junk [dʒʌŋk] Gerümpel; Ramsch **III**
junkie ['dʒʌŋki] Junkie **III**
just [dʒʌst] gerade (eben), soeben **I**; nur **I**; einfach **I**
just about [dʒʌst‿ə'baʊt] gerade noch (so) ⟨**V U2,** 38⟩
just now [ˌdʒʌst 'naʊ] gerade, im Augenblick **I**
Just you wait! [dʒʌst ju‿'weɪt] Wirst schon sehen! **V U2,** 34

K

kangaroo [ˌkæŋgr'u:] Känguru **V ZI,** 11
karaoke machine [ˌkæri'əʊki mə'ʃi:n] Karaokegerät **I**
***to keep** [ki:p] behalten, aufbewahren **I**; belassen **IV**
to keep *(+ gerund)* [ki:p] etwas weiter/immer wieder tun **IV**
to keep + *adj.* [ki:p] … bleiben **II**
to keep fit [ki:p 'fɪt] fit bleiben **II**
to keep out [ki:p‿'aʊt] draußen halten; draußen bleiben **III**
keyword ['ki:wɜ:d] Stichwort; Schlüsselbegriff **III**
kick [kɪk] Tritt, Stoß **III**
to kick [kɪk] schießen; treten **I**
kid [kɪd] Kind, Jugendlicher, Jugendliche **I**
to kill [kɪl] töten, umbringen **II**
killer *(coll)* ['kɪlə] Killer-, Wahnsinns- ⟨**V U3,** 51⟩
kind [kaɪnd] Art, Sorte **II**
all kinds of [ɔ:l 'kaɪndz‿əv] allerhand, vielerlei; alle möglichen **V U1,** 18
kind [kaɪnd] freundlich, nett **II**
king [kɪŋ] König **II**
kiss [kɪs] Kuss **IV**
to kiss [kɪs] küssen **II**
kitchen ['kɪtʃɪn] Küche **I**
kite [kaɪt] Drachen **I**
kite festival ['kaɪt ˌfestɪvl] Drachenfest **I**

knee [ni:] Knie **II**
knife pl. **knives** [naɪf; naɪvz] Messer **II**
knight [naɪt] Ritter **III**
***to know** [nəʊ] kennen; wissen **I**
I don't know! [ˌaɪ dəʊnt 'nəʊ] Ich weiß (es) nicht! **I**
knowledge ['nɒlɪdʒ] Kenntnisse; Wissen **V U2,** 33
koala [kəʊ'ɑ:lə] Koala **V ZI,** 11
laughing kookaburra [ˌlɑ:fɪŋ 'kʊkəˌbʌrə] Kookaburra, Lachender Hans ⟨**V U1,** 19⟩

L

label ['leɪbl] (Schallplatten)label ⟨**V U3,** 51⟩
labour ['leɪbə] Arbeit **V U4,** 68
child labour [ˌtʃaɪld 'leɪbə] Kinderarbeit **V U4,** 68
lack (of) [læk] Mangel (an); Fehlen (von) ⟨**V U1,** 12⟩
lady ['leɪdi] Dame; Frau **III**
cleaning lady ['kli:nɪŋ ˌleɪdi] Putzfrau **III**
lake [leɪk] See **II**
LAN *(= Local Area Network)* [læn; ˌləʊkl ˌeəriə 'netwɜ:k] LAN **III**
land [lænd] Land **I**
on land [ɒn 'lænd] an Land **III**
to land [lænd] landen **II**
landowner ['lændˌəʊnə] Grundbesitzer/-in **V U4,** 70
landscape ['lændskeɪp] Landschaft **III**
language ['læŋgwɪdʒ] Sprache **I**
body language ['bɒdi ˌlæŋgwɪdʒ] Körpersprache **V U2,** 37
first language ['fɜ:st ˌlæŋgwɪdʒ] Muttersprache **III**
foreign language [ˌfɒrɪn 'læŋgwɪdʒ] Fremdsprache **V U2,** 28
second language ['seknd ˌlæŋgwɪdʒ] Zweitsprache **III**
laptop ['læptɒp] Laptop **I**
large (L) [lɑ:dʒ] groß **I**
extra large (XL) ['ekstrə ˌlɑ:dʒ] besonders groß **I**
last [lɑ:st] letzte/-r/-s **I**
at last [ət 'lɑ:st] endlich, zu guter Letzt **III**
last name ['lɑ:st neɪm] Familienname, Nachname **IV**
late [leɪt] (zu) spät **I**
2L8 (= too late) [tu: 'leɪt] zu spät *(Abkürzung in SMS oder E-Mail)* **III**
Sorry I'm late. [ˌsɒri‿aɪm 'leɪt] Tut mir leid, dass ich zu spät komme. **I**
to be late [bi 'leɪt] zu spät kommen, spät dran sein **I**
to be late for school [bi ˌleɪt fə 'sku:l] zu spät zur Schule kommen **I**
later ['leɪtə] später **I**
See you later. [si: jə 'leɪtə] Bis später. **II**

the latest ['leɪtɪst] der/die/das neueste ⟨**V U3,** 57⟩
Latin ['lætɪn] Latein **II**
for laughs [fə 'lɑ:fs] zum Spaß **III**
to laugh [lɑ:f] lachen **I**
to laugh at ['lɑ:f‿ət] auslachen **II**
laughing kookaburra [ˌlɑ:fɪŋ 'kʊkəˌbʌrə] Kookaburra, Lachender Hans ⟨**V U1,** 19⟩
laughter ['lɑ:ftə] Gelächter, Lachen ⟨**V U1,** 13⟩
gust of laughter [ˌgʌst‿əv 'lɑ:ftə] Lachanfall ⟨**V U1,** 13⟩
law [lɔ:] Gesetz **IV**
lawyer ['lɔɪə] Anwalt/Anwältin, Jurist/-in **V U2,** 29
***to lay** [leɪ] legen ⟨**V U1,** 19⟩
to lay the table [ˌleɪ ðə 'teɪbl] den Tisch decken **II**
ozone layer ['əʊzəʊn ˌleɪə] Ozonschicht **V ZI,** 11
lazy ['leɪzi] faul **IV**
***to lead** [li:d] führen **V ZI,** 8
leader ['li:də] Führer/-in, Anführer/-in **V ZI,** 10
leaflet ['li:flət] Broschüre; Informationsblatt; Prospekt **V U2,** 30
leap [li:p] Sprung, Satz **III**
***to learn** [lɜ:n] lernen **I**
to learn by heart [ˌlɜ:n baɪ 'hɑ:t] auswendig lernen **I**
learner ['lɜ:nə] Lernende/-r **II**
least [li:st] am wenigsten **V U4,** 69
at least [ət 'li:st] mindestens, wenigstens **III**
***to leave** [li:v] (ver)lassen; abfahren **II**; hinterlassen **III**
Leave him alone! [ˌli:v hɪm‿ə'ləʊn] Lass ihn in Ruhe! **II**
left [left] linke/-r/-s; links **I**
on the left [ɒn ðə 'left] auf der linken Seite, links **I**
on your left/right [ɒn jə 'left, 'raɪt] links/rechts, auf der linken/rechten Seite **I**
leg [leg] Bein **I**
legal ['li:gl] legal; rechtlich; Rechts- **IV**
legal driving age [ˌli:gl 'draɪvɪŋ eɪdʒ] *(Mindestalter für den Führerscheinerwerb)* **IV**
leisure ['leʒə] Freizeit, Freizeit- **III**
***to lend (to)** [lend] leihen; verleihen **II**
length [leŋθ] Länge ⟨**V U1,** 12⟩
lesbian ['lezbiən] lesbisch; Lesbe **V U4,** 69
less [les] weniger **III**
lesson ['lesn] Unterrichtsstunde **I**
dancing lessons *(pl.)* ['dɑ:nsɪŋ ˌlesnz] Tanzunterricht, Tanzstunden **I**
***to let** [let] lassen **I**
let's (= let us) [lets; let‿'ʌs] lass(t) uns **I**
Let's go! [lets 'gəʊ] Lass(t) uns anfangen!/Lass(t) uns gehen! **I**

let's listen [lets 'lɪsn] lass(t) uns zuhören **I**
to let go of [let 'gəʊ‿əv] loslassen **IV**
to let sb do sth [let] jmdm. erlauben, etw. zu tun; etw. zulassen **VU1,** 17
to let sb down [let ˌsʌmbədi 'daʊn] jmdn. im Stich lassen; jmdn. enttäuschen **IV**
to let up [let‿'ʌp] nachlassen; aufhören **IV**
letter ['letə] Buchstabe **I**
letter of application [ˌletər‿əv‿æplɪ'keɪʃn] Bewerbungsschreiben **VU2,** 33
level ['levl] Niveau, Level; Höhe **II**
sea level ['si: ˌlevl] Meeresspiegel **IV**
library ['laɪbri] Bibliothek **II**
driver's license *(AE)* ['draɪvəz ˌlaɪsns] Führerschein **IV**
to **lick** [lɪk] (ab)lecken **I**
lie [laɪ] Lüge **III**
to tell a lie [ˌtel‿ə 'laɪ] lügen **III**
*to **lie** [laɪ] liegen **II**
life pl. **lives** [laɪf; laɪvz] Leben **I**
life-jacket ['laɪfˌdʒækɪt] Schwimmweste, Rettungsweste **II**
lifestyle ['laɪfstaɪl] Lebensart, Lifestyle **IV**
to **lift** [lɪft] (hoch)heben, anheben **IV**
light [laɪt] Licht; Lampe **II**
lighthouse ['laɪthaʊs] Leuchtturm **I**
soft **lighting** [sɒft 'laɪtɪŋ] Dämmerlicht **VU3,** 58
lights *(pl.)* [laɪts] Beleuchtung **III**
like [laɪk] Vorliebe **IV**
to **like** [laɪk] mögen **I**
I'd like to ... *(= I would like to)* [aɪd 'laɪk tə] ich möchte .../ich würde gerne ... **I**
I don't like them. [aɪ dəʊnt 'laɪk ˌðəm] Sie gefallen mir nicht. **I**
like [laɪk] wie **I**
like the back of my hand [laɪk ðə ˌbæk‿əv maɪ 'hænd] wie meine Westentasche, in- und auswendig **II**
like this [laɪk 'ðɪs] so, auf diese Weise **I**
What is ... like? [ˌwɒt‿ɪz 'laɪk] Wie ist ... ? **II**
what it looks like [ˌwɒt‿ɪt 'lʊks laɪk] wie es aussieht **I**
likely ['laɪkli] wahrscheinlich ⟨**VU3,** 50⟩
to be likely to do sth [bi 'laɪkli] etw. wahrscheinlich tun **VU2,** 41
limit ['lɪmɪt] Limit; Grenze; Beschränkung ⟨**VU2,** 35⟩
line [laɪn] Linie; Zeile **I**; (Telefon)Leitung **III**; Schlange **IV**
connecting line [kə'nektɪŋ ˌlaɪn] Verbindungslinie **III**
time line ['taɪm laɪn] Zeitstrahl **II**
to **link** [lɪŋk] verbinden **I**
linking sounds [ˌlɪŋkɪŋ 'saʊndz] das Verbinden von Lauten **I**

lion [laɪən] Löwe ⟨**VU1,** 12⟩
lip [lɪp] Lippe ⟨**VU3,** 52⟩
list [lɪst] Liste **I**
shopping list ['ʃɒpɪŋ ˌlɪst] Einkaufszettel **II**
to **listen** ['lɪsn] zuhören **I**
let's listen [lets 'lɪsn] lass(t) uns zuhören **I**
to listen for ['lɪsn fə] heraushören **I**
to listen to ['lɪsn tə] jmdm. zuhören **I**; hören auf **III**
Listening ['lɪsnɪŋ] *(hier:)* Hörverstehensübung **I**
little ['lɪtl] klein **I**; wenig **I**
a little [ə 'lɪtl] ein wenig, etwas **I**
to **live** [lɪv] wohnen, leben **I**
live [laɪv] live ⟨**VU3,** 53⟩; **VU3,** 56
living room ['lɪvɪŋ ru:m] Wohnzimmer **I**
standard of living [ˌstændəd‿əv 'lɪvɪŋ] Lebensstandard **IV**
local ['ləʊkl] hiesig, örtlich, lokal **VU3,** 59
loch [lɒx] See *(in Schottland)* **II**
locker ['lɒkə] Schließfach **II**
lodge [lɒdʒ] *Hotel oder Pension in nordamerikanischen Berggebieten* **IV**
Londoner ['lʌndənə] Londoner/-in **II**
lonely ['ləʊnli] einsam **III**
long [lɒŋ] lang **I**
(not) any longer [nɒt ˌeni 'lɒŋgə] (nicht) mehr, (nicht) länger **II**
look [lʊk] Aussehen **III**
to **look** [lʊk] schauen, sehen, gucken **I**; nachschauen, suchen **I**; aussehen **I**
to look after [lʊk‿'ɑ:ftə] sich kümmern um; aufpassen auf **I**
to look around sth [lʊk‿ə'raʊnd] sich etw. ansehen **IV**
to look at ['lʊk‿æt] anschauen, ansehen **I**
to look for ['lʊk fə] suchen (nach) **I**
to look forward to [ˌlʊk 'fɔ:wəd tə] sich freuen auf **IV**
to look the part [ˌlʊk ðə 'pɑ:t] danach aussehen ⟨**VU1,** 14⟩
to look up [lʊk‿'ʌp] nachschlagen, nachschauen **I**
what it looks like [ˌwɒt‿ɪt 'lʊks laɪk] wie es aussieht **I**
looks *(pl.)* [lʊks] Aussehen **IV**
lord [lɔ:d] Lord, Herr **III**
lorry ['lɒri] Lastwagen **II**
*to **lose** [lu:z] verlieren **II**
Get lost! [get 'lɒst] Hau ab! **II**
to be lost [bi 'lɒst] sich verirrt haben **II**
to get lost [get 'lɒst] sich verirren **I**
loss [lɒs] Verlust **VU4,** 70
a **lot of** [ə 'lɒt‿əv] viel/-e, eine Menge **I**
lots of ['lɒts‿əv] viel/-e, jede Menge **I**
loud [laʊd] laut **I**
love [lʌv] Liebe Grüße, Herzliche Grüße *(am Briefende)* **II**; null *(Tennis)* **III**; Liebe **III**

love at first sight [ˌlʌv‿ət fɜ:st 'saɪt] Liebe auf den ersten Blick **IV**
to fall in love [ˌfɔ:l‿ɪn 'lʌv] sich verlieben **II**
to **love** [lʌv] lieben **I**
I'd love to ... *(= I would love to)* [aɪd 'lʌv tə] Ich würde sehr gern ... **IV**
low [ləʊ] niedrig **IV**
luck [lʌk] Glück **III**
bad luck [bæd 'lʌk] Pech, Unglück **III**
Good luck! [ˌgʊd 'lʌk] Viel Glück! **II**
to be out of luck [ˌbi aʊt‿əv 'lʌk] kein Glück haben **III**
What a stroke of luck! [wɒt‿ə ˌstrəʊk‿əv 'lʌk] Was für ein Glückstreffer! **III**
luckily ['lʌkɪli] glücklicherweise **IV**
lucky ... ['lʌki] ... Glückliche/-r **II**
That was lucky! [ˌðæt wəz 'lʌki] Glück gehabt! **III**
to be lucky [bi 'lʌki] Glück haben **I**
You were lucky there! [jʊ wə ˌlʌki 'ðeə] Da hast du aber Glück gehabt! **III**
ludicrous ['lu:dɪkrəs] lächerlich; absurd, grotesk ⟨**VU1,** 13⟩
lunch [lʌnʃ] Mittagessen **I**
lunchtime ['lʌnʃtaɪm] Mittagszeit, Mittagspause **I**
the **lungs** *(pl.)* [lʌŋz] die Lunge **III**
luxurious [lʌg'ʒʊriəs] luxuriös, Luxus- **VU2,** 41
luxury ['lʌkʃri] Luxus **IV**
lyrics *(pl.)* ['lɪrɪks] Liedtext ⟨**VU3,** 50⟩; **VU4,** 80

M

machine [mə'ʃi:n] Maschine, Apparat, Gerät; Automat **I**
karaoke machine [ˌkæri'əʊki mə'ʃi:n] Karaokegerät **I**
washing machine ['wɒʃɪŋ məˌʃi:n] Waschmaschine ⟨**VU3,** 50⟩
*to be **mad about sb/sth** [bi 'mæd‿əˌbaʊt] verrückt nach jmdm./etw. sein **VU3,** 58
to be mad with sb [bi 'mæd‿wɪθ] auf jmdn. böse sein; auf jmdn. sauer sein **VU3,** 58
magazine [ˌmægə'zi:n] Zeitschrift **I**
magic ['mædʒɪk] Magie, Zauberei **III**
magnet ['mægnət] Magnet **IV**
voice **mail** ['vɔɪs meɪl] Voicemail; Mailbox **III**
main [meɪn] Haupt- **III**
main clause ['meɪn klɔ:z] Hauptsatz **II**
mainly ['meɪnli] hauptsächlich, in erster Linie; vorwiegend **VU2,** 30
*to **make** [meɪk] machen, bilden **I**
Make up your mind! [ˌmeɪk‿'ʌp jə 'maɪnd] Entscheide dich! **I**

to make a choice [ˌmeɪk‿ə 'tʃɔɪs] eine Wahl treffen **VU3,** 58
to make a decision [ˌmeɪk‿ə dɪ'sɪʒn] eine Entscheidung treffen **III**
to make a difference (to sth) [ˌmeɪk‿ə'dɪfrns] etw. verändern **VU4,** 75
to make a face [meɪk ə 'feɪs] ein Gesicht ziehen **II**
to make a good/bad impression (on sb) [ˌmeɪk‿ə gʊd ɪm'preʃn‿ɒn] einen guten/schlechten Eindruck (auf jmdn.) machen **VU2,** 37
to make a point [ˌmeɪk‿ə 'pɔɪnt] etw. anmerken **IV**
to make friends [ˌmeɪk 'frendz] Freundschaft schließen **II**
to make fun of [ˌmeɪk 'fʌn‿əv] sich lustig machen über **III**
to make it ['meɪk‿ɪt] es schaffen **III**
to make it big [ˌmeɪk‿ɪt 'bɪg] groß (he)rauskommen ⟨**VU3,** 51⟩
to make money [ˌmeɪk 'mʌni] Geld verdienen **II**
to make sb do sth [meɪk] jmdn. veranlassen, etw. zu tun **VU1,** 17
to make sth up [ˌmeɪk‿'ʌp] etw. erfinden; sich etw. ausdenken **VU2,** 39
to make sure [meɪk 'ʃɔ:] sich versichern **III**
make-up ['meɪkʌp] Make-up **III**
male [meɪl] männlich ⟨**VU3,** 53⟩; Mann **VU4,** 68
male voice choir [ˌmeɪl vɔɪs 'kwaɪə] Männerchor **III**
shopping **mall** ['ʃɒpɪŋ ˌmɔ:l] Einkaufszentrum **IV**
man pl. **men** [mæn; men] Mann **I**
to **manage (to do sth)** ['mænɪdʒ] (es) schaffen (etw. zu tun) **III**
management ['mænɪdʒmənt] Management, Geschäftsführung, Unternehmensleitung **VU2,** 29
manager ['mænɪdʒə] Geschäftsführer/-in **I**
personnel manager [pɜ:sn'el ˌmænədʒə] Personalchef/-in **VU2,** 29
maniac ['meɪniæk] Verrückte/-r, Wahnsinnige/-r **III**
mankind [mæn'kaɪnd] Menschheit **III**
many ['meni] viele **I**
How many ... ? [haʊ 'meni] Wie viele ... ? **I**
map [mæp] Stadtplan, Landkarte **I**
treasure map ['treʒə ˌmæp] Schatzkarte **I**
marathon ['mærəθn] Marathon **III**
March [mɑ:tʃ] März **I**
the third of March [ðə ˌθɜ:d‿əv 'mɑ:tʃ] der dritte März **I**
mark [mɑ:k] Note **VU4,** 71
to **mark** [mɑ:k] markieren; kennzeichnen ⟨**VU1,** 21⟩
market ['mɑ:kɪt] Markt **I**
marketing ['mɑ:kɪtɪŋ] Marketing; Vermarktung; Vertrieb **VZI,** 8
married to ['mærid tə] verheiratet mit **I**
to get married [get 'mærid] heiraten **VU3,** 56
to **marry** ['mæri] heiraten **III**
marsupial [mɑ:'su:piəl] Beuteltier ⟨**VU1,** 19⟩
mask [mɑ:sk] Maske **III**
to **master** ['mɑ:stə] mastern ⟨**VU3,** 51⟩
match [mætʃ] Wettkampf; Spiel; Match **II**
to **match** [mætʃ] zuordnen **I**
mate [meɪt] (Schiffs)Offizier; Freund, Freundin **I**
material [mə'tɪəriəl] Material **IV**
raw material [ˌrɔ: mə'tɪəriəl] Rohstoff **III**
material [mə'tɪəriəl] materiell **VU4,** 77
Maths [mæθs] Mathematik **II**
may [meɪ] (vielleicht) können; dürfen **I**
May I? [meɪ‿aɪ] Darf ich? **II**
May [meɪ] Mai **I**
maybe ['meɪbi] vielleicht **I**
me [mi:] mich; mir **I**
Me? [mi:; mi] Ich? **I**
meal [mi:l] Mahlzeit, Essen **I**
*to **mean** [mi:n] bedeuten; meinen **I**
I didn't mean to ... [aɪ ˌdɪdnt 'mi:n tə] Ich wollte nicht ... **III**
mean [mi:n] knauserig, geizig **II**; gemein ⟨**VU4,** 74⟩
meaning ['mi:nɪŋ] Bedeutung **I**
meat [mi:t] Fleisch **II**
gold **medal** [gəʊld 'medl] Goldmedaille **III**
media-mad ['mi:diəmæd] medienverrückt **VU3,** 50
medicine ['medsn] Medizin, Medikamente **VU2,** 39
medium pl. **media** ['mi:diəm, 'mi:diə] Medium, Medien **III**
medium (M) ['mi:diəm] mittel(groß) **I**
medium shot ['mi:diəm ʃɒt] Halbnahe *(Kameraeinstellung)* **VU3,** 58
*to **meet** [mi:t] (sich) treffen **I**; kennenlernen **III**
Nice to meet you. [ˌnaɪs tə 'mi:t ju:] Nett, dich/Sie/euch kennenzulernen. **IV**
Pleased to meet you. [ˌpli:zd tə 'mi:t‿ju] Sehr erfreut./Freut mich, Sie/dich kennenzulernen. **II**
to meet a deadline [ˌmi:t‿ə 'dedlaɪn] einen (Abgabe)Termin einhalten **VU2,** 30
to meet halfway [mi:t hɑ:f'weɪ] (sich auf halbem Weg) entgegenkommen **III**
meeting people ['mi:tɪŋ ˌpi:pl] Leute kennenlernen, Leute treffen **I**
meeting point ['mi:tɪŋ pɔɪnt] Treffpunkt **IV**
melodious [mə'ləʊdiəs] melodiös, wohlklingend ⟨**VU1,** 13⟩
melody ['melədi] Melodie ⟨**VU3,** 50⟩
member ['membə] Mitglied **IV**
to **mend** [mend] heilen; reparieren **I**
to **mention** ['menʃn] erwähnen **III**
menu ['menju:] Speisekarte **II**
mess [mes] Unordnung, Durcheinander **I**
What a mess! [wɒt‿ə 'mes] Was für eine Unordnung! **I**
message ['mesɪdʒ] Nachricht **II**; Botschaft; Message **VU4,** 80
metal ['metl] Metall **III**
meteorologist [ˌmi:tir'ɒlədʒɪst] Meteorologe/-in **VU2,** 34
meteorology [ˌmi:tir'ɒlədʒi] Meteorologie **VU2,** 34
metre ['mi:tə] Meter **II**
Mexican ['meksɪkən] Mexikaner/-in; mexikanisch, aus Mexiko **IV**
microphone (mike) ['maɪkrəfəʊn, maɪk] Mikrofon ⟨**VU3,** 51⟩
microwave ['maɪkrəʊweɪv] Mikrowelle **III**
mid- [mɪd] Mitte **IV**
in the **middle of** [ɪn ðə 'mɪdl‿əv] mitten in **VU2,** 39
middle class [ˌmɪdl 'klɑ:s] Mittelschicht **VZI,** 10
middle name ['mɪdl ˌneɪm] zweiter Vorname **III**
Middle Ages ['mɪdl‿eɪdʒɪz] Mittelalter **VU4,** 70
***might** [maɪt] könnte/-n **III**
mile [maɪl] Meile **I**
milestone ['maɪlstəʊn] Meilenstein **IV**
milk [mɪlk] Milch **I**
to **milk** [mɪlk] melken **I**
million ['mɪljən] Million **II**
millions of ['mɪljənz‿əv] Millionen von **II**
mind [maɪnd] Gedanken; Geist, Verstand **VU4,** 77
Make up your mind! [ˌmeɪk‿'ʌp jə 'maɪnd] Entscheide dich! **I**
to be on one's mind [bi‿ən wʌnz 'maɪnd] jmdn. beschäftigen, jmdn. umtreiben **VU4,** 79
to **mind** [maɪnd] etwas dagegen haben; einem etwas ausmachen **III**
Never mind! [ˌnevə 'maɪnd] Schon gut. **III**
coal **mine** ['kəʊl maɪn] Kohlenbergwerk, Kohlengrube **III**
minority [maɪ'nɒrəti] Minderheit **VZI,** 10
minute ['mɪnɪt] Minute **I**
mirror ['mɪrə] Spiegel **VU4,** 72
to **miss** [mɪs] vermissen **II**; verpassen; nicht teilnehmen **IV**
to miss a point [ˌmɪs‿ə‿'pɔɪnt] nicht verstehen, worum es geht ⟨**VU4,** 76⟩
to miss sth [mɪs] etw. verpassen; etw. versäumen ⟨**VU1,** 21⟩

missing ['mɪsɪŋ] fehlend, verschwunden **I**
missionary ['mɪʃnri] Missionar/-in **III**
to **mist up** [mɪst‿'ʌp] (sich) beschlagen **III**
mistake [mɪ'steɪk] Fehler **II**
to **misuse** [mɪs'ju:s] missbrauchen **IV**
to **mix** [mɪks] (ver)mischen; mixen **IV**
mixed [mɪkst] gemischt **I**
mmm [m] mmm, lecker **I**
mob [mɒb] Mob, (Menschen)Menge; Pöbel **V U4,** 74
mobile ['məʊbaɪl] Handy, Mobiltelefon **I**
mobility [məʊ'bɪləti] Mobilität **IV**
model ['mɒdl] Modell ⟨**V U3,** 57⟩
fashion model ['fæʃn ˌmɒdl] Model, Mannequin **II**
role model ['rəʊl ˌmɒdl] Vorbild **V U4,** 74
modern ['mɒdn] modern **III**
mom *(AE)* [mɒm] Mama **IV**
moment ['məʊmənt] Moment, Augenblick **I**
monarch ['mɒnək] Monarch/-in **V ZI,** 10
Monday ['mʌndeɪ] Montag **I**
money ['mʌni] Geld **I**
pocket money ['pɒkɪt ˌmʌni] Taschengeld **II**
to make money [ˌmeɪk 'mʌni] Geld verdienen **II**
to raise money [reɪz 'mʌni] Geld sammeln, Geld aufbringen **III**
monkey ['mʌŋki] Affe **I**
monster ['mɒnstə] Monster **II**
month [mʌnθ] Monat **I**
mood [mu:d] Stimmung; Laune **IV**
moon [mu:n] Mond **III**
more [mɔ:] mehr; weitere **I**
(not) any more [nɒt ˌeni 'mɔ:] (nicht) mehr **III**
morning ['mɔ:nɪŋ] Morgen, Vormittag **I**
Good morning. [gʊd 'mɔ:nɪŋ] Guten Morgen. **I**
this morning [ðɪs 'mɔ:nɪŋ] heute Morgen **I**
mosaic [mə'zeɪɪk] Mosaik **IV**
most [məʊst] das meiste; die meisten **II**
mother ['mʌðə] Mutter **I**
mother tongue ['mʌðə tʌŋ] Muttersprache **II**
motionless ['məʊʃnləs] reg(ungs)los, bewegungslos ⟨**V U1,** 12⟩
motorway ['məʊtəweɪ] Autobahn **III**
mountain ['maʊntɪn] Berg **I**
mountain bike ['maʊntɪn baɪk] Mountainbike **II**
mouse pl. **mice** [maʊs; maɪs] Maus **I**
mouth [maʊθ] Mund **II**
*to be on the **move** [bi ɒn‿ðə 'mu:v] unterwegs sein **III**
to **move** [mu:v] (sich) bewegen **II**
to move (house) [mu:v 'haʊs] umziehen **III**
to move in [mu:v 'ɪn] *(hier:)* Kontrolle übernehmen ⟨**V U1,** 15⟩
movement ['mu:vmənt] Bewegung ⟨**V U1,** 12⟩; **V U4,** 74
movie *(AE)* ['mu:vi] Film **IV**
moving ['mu:vɪŋ] Umziehen **IV**
MP3 player [ˌempi:'θri: ˌpleɪə] MP3-Player **III**
Mr ['mɪstə] Herr *(Anrede)* **I**
Mrs ['mɪsɪz] Frau *(Anrede)* **I**
Ms [mɪz] Frau *(Anrede)* **IV**
much [mʌtʃ] viel **I**
How much ... ? [haʊ 'mʌtʃ] Wie viel ... ? **I**
How much is ... ? ['haʊ mʌtʃ‿ɪz] Wie viel kostet ... ? **I**
to **muck out** [mʌk‿'aʊt] ausmisten **I**
mug [mʌg] Becher **I**
multimedia [ˌmʌlti'mi:diə] Multimedia; multimedial **V U2,** 30
to **multi-task** ['mʌltiˌtɑ:sk] mehrere Dinge gleichzeitig tun **V U3,** 55
multi-track ['mʌltitræk] mehrspurig ⟨**V U3,** 51⟩
mum [mʌm] Mama **I**
mural ['mjuərl] Wandgemälde **IV**
to **murder sb** ['mɜ:də] jmdn. ermorden, jmdn. umbringen **V U4,** 75
museum [mju:'zi:əm] Museum **I**
music ['mju:zɪk] Musik **I**
musical instrument [ˌmju:zɪkl‿'ɪnstrəmənt] Musikinstrument **II**
musician [mju:'zɪʃn] Musiker/-in **V U2,** 29
must [mʌst] müssen **I**
mustn't ['mʌsnt] nicht dürfen **I**
a **must-see** [ə ˌmʌst 'si:] ... muss man gesehen haben **III**
my [maɪ] mein/-e **I**
My name is .... [maɪ 'neɪm‿ɪz] Ich heiße ... **I**
myself [maɪ'self] selbst **III**
mythical [mɪθɪkl] sagenhaft, sagenumwoben **IV**

N

nakedness ['neɪkɪdnəs] Nacktheit ⟨**V U1,** 12⟩
Namáste! [nʌ'mʌsteɪ] Guten Tag. *(Begrüßung in Indien)* **V ZI,** 9
name [neɪm] Name **I**
first name ['fɜ:st neɪm] Vorname **IV**
last name ['lɑ:st neɪm] Familienname, Nachname **IV**
middle name ['mɪdl ˌneɪm] zweiter Vorname **III**
My name is .... [maɪ 'neɪm‿ɪz] Ich heiße ... **I**
to call sb names [ˌkɔ:l ˌsʌmbɒdi 'neɪmz] jmdn. beschimpfen **V U4,** 74
to get named *(coll)* [get 'neɪmd] beschimpft werden ⟨**V U4,** 79⟩
What's your name? [wɒts jɔ: 'neɪm] Wie heißt du? **I**
narrow ['nærəʊ] eng, schmal **IV**
nasty ['nɑ:sti] böse, gemein **I**; gefährlich; schlimm **IV**
national park [ˌnæʃnl 'pɑ:k] Nationalpark, Naturpark **IV**
nationality [ˌnæʃn'æləti] Nationalität **I**
Native American [ˌneɪtɪv‿ə'merɪkən] Ureinwohner/-in Amerikas, Indianer/-in; indianisch **IV**
natural ['nætʃrl] natürlich, Natur- **IV**
nature ['neɪtʃə] Natur **IV**
near [nɪə] nahe, in der Nähe von **I**
nearby [ˌnɪə'baɪ] in der Nähe ⟨**V U1,** 14⟩; **V U1,** 17
necessary ['nesəsri] nötig, notwendig, erforderlich ⟨**V U1,** 19⟩; **V U4,** 70
neck [nek] Hals, Nacken, Genick **II**
need [ni:d] Notwendigkeit; Bedarf **V U4,** 70
to **need** [ni:d] brauchen **I**
negative ['negətɪv] Verneinungsform **III**
negative ['negətɪv] negativ, verneint **II**
negligence ['neglɪdʒəns] Nachlässigkeit; Fahrlässigkeit ⟨**V U1,** 14⟩
neighbour ['neɪbə] Nachbar/-in **I**
neighbourhood ['neɪbəhʊd] Nachbarschaft **IV**
nervous ['nɜ:vəs] nervös, aufgeregt **I**
to be nervous about sth [bi 'nɜ:vəs əˌbaʊt] wg. etw. nervös sein **IV**
social **networking site** [ˌsəʊʃl 'netwɜ:kɪŋ ˌsaɪt] Online-Netzwerk ⟨**V U3,** 51⟩; **V U3,** 54
never ['nevə] nie, niemals **I**
Never mind! [ˌnevə 'maɪnd] Schon gut. **III**
new [nju:] neu **I**
news *(sing.)* [nju:z] Nachricht(en), Neuigkeit(en) **II**
newsagent ['nju:zˌeɪdʒnt] Zeitschriftengeschäft **I**
newsletter ['nju:sˌletə] Newsletter; Rundschreiben **IV**
newspaper ['nju:sˌpeɪpə] Zeitung **III**
popular newspaper [ˌpɒpjələ 'nju:sˌpeɪpə] Boulevardzeitung **III**
New Yorker [ˌnju: 'jɔ:kə] New Yorker/-in **IV**
next [nekst] nächste/-r/-s **I**
next door [nekst 'dɔ:] nebenan **II**
next to ['nekst tə] neben **I**
nice [naɪs] nett, sympathisch **I**; schön, gut **I**
Nice to meet you. [ˌnaɪs tə 'mi:t ju:] Nett, dich/Sie/euch kennenzulernen. **IV**
nickname ['nɪkneɪm] Spitzname **III**
night [naɪt] Nacht; Abend **I**
nightclub ['naɪtklʌb] Nachtklub **IV**
nil [nɪl] null *(beim Sport)* **III**

nine [naɪn] neun **I**
nineteen [ˌnaɪnˈtiːn] neunzehn **I**
ninety [ˈnaɪnti] neunzig **I**
no [nəʊ] kein/-e **I**
no sign of [nəʊ ˈsaɪn‿əv] keine Spur von; kein Anzeichen von ⟨**VU1,** 14⟩
no way [nəʊ ˈweɪ] keine Möglichkeit; kein Weg ⟨**VU3,** 53⟩; auf keinen Fall; keineswegs **VU3,** 56
No way! [ˌnəʊ ˈweɪ] Was?!/Echt?!/Nie im Leben! **III**
no [nəʊ] nein **I**
nobody [ˈnəʊbədi] niemand **II**
to nod [nɒd] nicken **III**
noise [nɔɪz] Lärm, Krach; Geräusch **III**
none [nʌn] keine/-r/-s **IV**
It's none of your business! [ɪts ˌnʌn‿əv jə ˈbɪznɪs] Das geht dich nichts an! **II**
non-stop [ˌnɒnˈstɒp] nonstop, ununterbrochen **VU3,** 55
noodle [ˈnuːdl] Nudel **III**
normal [ˈnɔːml] normal **II**
normal type [ˈnɔːml taɪp] Normalschrift **VU3,** 58
Norman [ˈnɔːmən] Normanne, Normannin; normannisch **III**
north [nɔːθ] Norden **I**
North Sea [ˌnɔːθ ˈsiː] Nordsee **I**
up North [ʌp ˈnɔːθ] im Norden **III**
nose [nəʊz] Nase **II**
not [nɒt] nicht **I**
not at all [nɒt ət‿ˈɔːl] überhaupt nicht, gar nicht **IV**
not even [nɒt ˈiːvn] (noch) nicht einmal **I**
not until [nɒt ʌnˈtɪl] erst (dann), wenn **III**
note [nəʊt] Notiz, Nachricht **I**
to take notes [teɪk ˈnəʊts] sich Notizen machen **I**
nothing [ˈnʌθɪŋ] nichts **II**
to notice [ˈnəʊtɪs] bemerken; wahrnehmen **IV**
noun [naʊn] Nomen, Hauptwort **I**
novel [ˈnɒvl] Roman **IV**
November [nəˈvembə] November **I**
now [naʊ] jetzt, nun, gerade **I**
right now [raɪt ˈnaʊ] jetzt, sofort, gerade **I**
nowhere [ˈnəʊweə] nirgendwo; nirgendwohin **III**
number [ˈnʌmbə] Nummer, Hausnummer; Zahl **I**
nurse [nɜːs] Krankenschwester, Krankenpfleger **VU2,** 29

O

o'clock [əˈklɒk] Uhr *(Zeitangabe bei vollen Stunden)* **I**
Bloody oath! *(coll)* [ˌblʌdi ˈəʊθ] Ist (doch) wahr! *(ugs.)* ⟨**VU1,** 21⟩
object [ˈɒbdʒɪkt] Objekt, Satzergänzung **I**
obnoxious [əbˈnɒkʃəs] unausstehlich; unmöglich; widerwärtig **VU4,** 78
observation platform [ˌɒbzəˈveɪʃn ˌplætfɔːm] Aussichtsplattform **IV**
observer [əbˈzɜːvə] Beobachter/-in; Zuschauer/-in **VU4,** 74
obvious [ˈɒbviəs] offensichtlich **IV**
ocean [ˈəʊʃn] Ozean **I**
October [ɒkˈtəʊbə] Oktober **I**
odd [ɒd] seltsam, komisch **III**
oddity [ˈɒdɪti] Eigenartigkeit, Kuriosität **III**
of [ɒv; əv] von **I**
four of them [ˈfɔːr‿əv ðəm] vier davon *(Personen, Tiere …)* **I**
of course [əv ˈkɔːs] natürlich, selbstverständlich **I**
of no importance [əv ˌnəʊ ɪmˈpɔːtns] ohne Bedeutung **VU3,** 55
off [ɒf] reduziert ⟨**VU4,** 76⟩
to be off [bi‿ˈɒf] gehen **VU2,** 38
to offend [əˈfend] beleidigen; verletzen **VU4,** 79
to offer [ˈɒfə] (an)bieten **III**
office [ˈɒfɪs] Büro **II**
post office [ˈpəʊst‿ˌɒfɪs] Postamt **II**
official [əˈfɪʃl] offiziell **III**
offside [ˌɒfˈsaɪd] abseits **III**
often [ˈɒfn] oft, häufig **I**
oh [əʊ] null *(bei Telefonnummern)* **I**
Oh! [əʊ] Oh! **I**
Oh dear! [əʊ ˈdɪə] Oje! **II**
Oh my God! [əʊ ˌmaɪ ˈgɒd] Oh mein Gott! **IV**
oil [ɔɪl] Öl **II**
oil industry [ˈɔɪl‿ˌɪndəstri] Ölindustrie **II**
oil platform [ˈɔɪl ˌplætfɔːm] Bohrinsel **II**
OK [əʊˈkeɪ] okay **I**
ol' *(= old)* [əʊl] alt ⟨**VU2,** 38⟩
old [əʊld] alt **I**
year-old [jɪər‿ˈəʊld] -jährig/-e/-r **II**
How old are you? [haʊ‿ˈəʊld‿ɑː ˈjuː] Wie alt bist du? **I**
old people's home [əʊld ˈpiːplz həʊm] Altersheim **III**
old-fashioned [əʊldˈfæʃnd] altmodisch **III**
oldies *(coll)* [ˈəʊldiz] die Alten *(ugs.)*; Eltern ⟨**VU1,** 21⟩
Olympic [əˈlɪmpɪk] Olympia-, olympisch **II**
on [ɒn] an(geschaltet) **II**
on [ɒn] auf; an **I**
on chat [ɒn ˈtʃæt] im Chat, beim Chatten **III**
on a train [ɒn‿ə ˈtreɪn] im Zug **I**
on average [ɒn‿ˈævrɪdʒ] durchschnittlich, im Durchschnitt **III**
on foot [ɒn ˈfʊt] zu Fuß **III**
on one's own [ɒn wʌnz‿ˈəʊn] (ganz) allein(e) **III**
on one's own terms [ɒn wʌnz ˌəʊn ˈtɜːmz] unter den eigenen Bedingungen ⟨**VU1,** 15⟩
on stage [ɒn ˈsteɪdʒ] auf der Bühne **II**
on the beach [ɒn ðə ˈbiːtʃ] am Strand **I**
on the bottom [ɒn ðə ˈbɒtəm] unten **I**
on the left [ɒn ðə ˈleft] auf der linken Seite, links **I**
on the right [ɒn ðə ˈraɪt] auf der rechten Seite, rechts **I**
on the top [ɒn ðə ˈtɒp] oben **I**
on time [ɒn ˈtaɪm] pünktlich **III**
on top of [ɒn ˈtɒp‿əv] auf … hinauf, oben (auf) **I**
on Tuesdays [ɒn ˈtjuːzdeɪz] dienstags **I**
on TV [ɒn ˌtiːˈviː] im Fernsehen **I**
on your right/left [ɒn jə ˈraɪt, ˈleft] rechts/links, auf der rechten/linken Seite **I**
once [wʌns] einmal **III**
at once [ət ˈwʌns] auf einmal; sofort **I**
Once upon a time … [ˈwʌns‿əˌpɒn‿ə ˈtaɪm] Es war einmal … **III**
one [wʌn] eins **I**
one by one [ˌwʌn baɪ ˈwʌn] eine/-r/-s nach dem/der anderen **III**
one evening [wʌn‿ˈiːvnɪŋ] eines Abends **I**
one Saturday afternoon [wʌn ˈsætədeɪ ˌɑːftəˈnuːn] an einem Samstag Nachmittag **I**
one-dimensional [wʌndaɪˈmenʃnl] eindimensional **VU4,** 77
online [ˌɒnˈlaɪn] online **I**
only [ˈəʊnli] einzige/-r/-s **II**
only child [ˌəʊnli ˈtʃaɪld] Einzelkind **I**
only [ˈəʊnli] erst, bloß; nur **II**
onto [ˈɒntə] auf … hinauf **II**
Oops! [uːps] Hoppla! **I**
to open [ˈəʊpn] öffnen, aufmachen **I**; eröffnen **III**
open [ˈəʊpn] geöffnet, offen; aufgeschlagen **I**
open day [ˌəʊpn ˈdeɪ] Tag der offenen Tür **III**
open-air [ˌəʊpnˈeə] Openair-, Freilicht-, im Freien **III**
opening [ˈəʊpnɪŋ] Öffnung; Öffnen **IV**
opinion [əˈpɪnjən] Meinung **III**
in sb's opinion [ɪn ˌsʌmbədiz əˈpɪnjən] jmds. Meinung nach **IV**
to give one's opinion [ˌgɪv wʌnz əˈpɪnjən] seine Meinung äußern **III**
opportunity [ˌɒpəˈtjuːnəti] Gelegenheit; Chance **VU2,** 29
equal opportunity [ˌiːkwəl‿ˌɒpəˈtjuːnəti] Chancengleichheit **VU4,** 69
opposite [ˈɒpəzɪt] Gegenteil **II**

opposite ['ɒpəzɪt] gegenüber **I**
or [ɔ:] oder **I**; sonst **III**
orange ['ɒrɪndʒ] orange **I**
orchestra ['ɔ:kɪstrə] Orchester **I**
order ['ɔ:də] Reihenfolge **I**; Bestellung **VZI,** 8
to **order** ['ɔ:də] bestellen **II**
ordinary ['ɔ:dnri] gewöhnlich, normal **VU4,** 74
organisation [ˌɔ:gnaɪ'zeɪʃn] Organisation **VU2,** 41
to **organise** ['ɔ:gənaɪz] organisieren **III**
orienteering [ˌɔ:riən'tɪərɪŋ] Orientierungslauf **II**
other ['ʌðə] andere/-r/-s, weitere/-r/-s **I**
each other [i:tʃ‿'ʌðə] einander, sich (gegenseitig) **III**
the others [ði‿'ʌðəz] die anderen **I**
Ouch! [aʊtʃ] Aua! **III**
*ought to ['ɔ:t‿tə] sollte **III**
our [aʊə; ɑ:] unser/-e **I**
ourselves [aʊə'selvz] selber **III**
out [aʊt] heraus, hinaus, nach draußen **I**
out of ['aʊt‿əv] aus … heraus **II**
out of this world [ˌaʊt‿əv ðɪs 'wɜ:ld] spitze; abgefahren **IV**
out West [aʊt 'west] draußen im Westen **IV**
outback ['aʊtbæk] Outback *(australisches Hinterland)* **VZI,** 11
outdoor [ˌaʊt'dɔ:] Freiluft-; Outdoor- **IV**
outline ['aʊtlaɪn] Umriss, Silhouette **III**
outside [ˌaʊt'saɪd] außen, draußen, im Freien; außerhalb **I**
oval ['əʊvl] oval, eiförmig **III**
over ['əʊvə] vorüber **IV**
over ['əʊvə] über **I**
over here [ˌəʊvə 'hɪə] hierher **IV**
over there [ˌəʊvə 'ðeə] (nach) dort drüben **I**
overalls *(pl.)* ['əʊvrɔ:lz] Overall ⟨**VU1,** 14⟩
overprotective [ˌəʊvəprə'tektɪv] überfürsorglich ⟨**VU1,** 13⟩
to **overreact** [ˌəʊvri'ækt] überreagieren ⟨**VU1,** 12⟩
overweight [ˌəʊvə'weɪt] übergewichtig **II**
to **own** [əʊn] besitzen **II**
own [əʊn] eigene/-r/-s **I**
her own room [hər‿ˌəʊn 'ru:m] ihr eigenes Zimmer **I**
on one's own [ɒn wʌnz‿'əʊn] (ganz) allein(e) **III**
on one's own terms [ɒn wʌnz ˌəʊn 'tɜ:mz] unter den eigenen Bedingungen ⟨**VU1,** 15⟩
to get one's own back [get wʌnz‿'əʊn bæk] jmdm. eins auswischen, sich rächen **II**
owner ['əʊnə] Besitzer/-in **I**
ozone layer ['əʊzəʊn ˌleɪə] Ozonschicht **VZI,** 11

P

to **pack** [pæk] (ein)packen **I**
page [peɪdʒ] Seite **I**
home page ['həʊm ˌpeɪdʒ] Homepage **I**
pain [peɪn] Schmerz **II**
to be a pain [bi‿ə 'peɪn] einem auf die Nerven gehen **I**
painful ['peɪnfl] schmerzhaft; schmerzlich **IV**
paint [peɪnt] Farbe **II**
to **paint** [peɪnt] (an)malen, streichen **II**
painting ['peɪntɪŋ] Gemälde **IV**
pair [peə] Paar **I**
a pair of [ə 'peər‿əv] ein Paar **III**
palace ['pælɪs] Palast **II**
pants *(AE)* [pænts] Hose **IV**
paper ['peɪpə] Papier **II**
paper *(= newspaper)* ['peɪpə] Zeitung **VU2,** 40; **VU3,** 59
papers *(pl.)* ['peɪpəz] Unterlagen, Papiere **IV**
paragraph ['pærəgrɑ:f] Paragraph, Absatz **III**
paramedic [ˌpærə'medɪk] Sanitäter/-in **III**
parents *(pl.)* ['peərnts] Eltern **I**
park [pɑ:k] Park **I**
theme park ['θi:m pɑ:k] Themenpark **II**
national park [ˌnæʃnl 'pɑ:k] Nationalpark, Naturpark **IV**
to **park** [pɑ:k] parken **I**
parliament ['pɑ:ləmənt] Parlament **VU4,** 69
part [pɑ:t] Teil **I**
to look the part [ˌlʊk ðə 'pɑ:t] danach aussehen ⟨**VU1,** 14⟩
to take part (in) [teɪk 'pɑ:t] teilnehmen (an) **IV**
to **part** [pɑ:t] sich teilen; auseinandergehen ⟨**VU1,** 15⟩
part-Aboriginal [ˌpɑ:t æbə'rɪdʒnl] teils Aborigine ⟨**VU1,** 14⟩
participle ['pɑ:tɪsɪpl] Partizip **IV**
partner ['pɑ:tnə] Partner/-in **I**
part-time [ˌpɑ:t'taɪm] Teilzeit-, Halbtags- **VU2,** 38
party ['pɑ:ti] Party, Feier **I**
birthday party ['bɜ:θdeɪ ˌpɑ:ti] Geburtstagsfeier **I**
to have a party [hæv ə 'pɑ:ti] eine Party feiern **I**
to **pass** [pɑ:s] *(ein Gesetz)* verabschieden **VU4,** 70; vorbeigehen; vorübergehen; vorbeikommen **VU4,** 74
to pass an exam [ˌpɑ:s ən‿ɪg'zæm] eine Prüfung bestehen **VU2,** 39
passenger ['pæsndʒə] Passagier/-in, Beifahrer/-in, Fahrgast **II**
passive ['pæsɪv] Passiv **III**
passive progressive [ˌpæsɪv prə'gresɪv] Verlaufsform des Passivs **IV**

passport ['pɑ:spɔ:t] (Reise)Pass **II**
past [pɑ:st] Vergangenheit **II**
past perfect [ˌpɑ:st 'pɜ:fɪkt] Plusquamperfekt **III**
past perfect progressive [ˌpɑ:st ˌpɜ:fɪkt prə'gresɪv] Verlaufsform des Plusquamperfekts **IV**
past [pɑ:st] nach *(bei Uhrzeitangaben)* **I** ; über … hinaus **IV**
path [pɑ:θ] Pfad, Weg **II**
pathway ['pɑ:θweɪ] Pfad, Weg **IV**
patient ['peɪʃnt] Patient/-in **III**
patient ['peɪʃnt] geduldig **II**
patriot ['peɪtriət] Patriot/-in **VU4,** 70
pause [pɔ:z] Pause **II**
to **pause** [pɔ:z] (eine kurze) Pause machen; innehalten ⟨**VU1,** 15⟩
pay [peɪ] Lohn; Gehalt **VU2,** 31
*to **pay** [peɪ] bezahlen **II**
P.E. *(= Physical Education)* [pi:'j‿i:; ˌfɪzɪkl‿edʒʊ'keɪʃn] Sportunterricht **II**
peace [pi:s] Frieden **IV**
peaceful ['pi:sfl] friedlich **VU4,** 77
peer editing ['pɪər‿edɪtɪŋ] *(Kritik/ Kontrolle durch Gleichaltrige)* **VU1,** 20
pen [pen] Füller **I**
penal colony ['pi:nl ˌkɒləni] Strafkolonie **VU1,** 17
penalty ['penlti] Elfmeter; Strafe **III**
pencil ['pensl] Bleistift **I**
pencil-case ['pensl keɪs] Federmäppchen **I**
penny pl. **pence** [peni; pens] Penny, Pence *(brit. Währungseinheit)* **I**
people *(pl.)* ['pi:pl] Leute *(pl.)*, Menschen *(pl.)* **I**
old people's home [əʊld 'pi:plz həʊm] Altersheim **III**
per [pɜ:; pə] pro **I**
per cent [pə'sent] Prozent **III**
verb of **perception** [ˌvɜ:b‿əv pə'sepʃn] Verb der Wahrnehmung **VU2,** 35
perfect ['pɜ:fɪkt] perfekt, vollkommen **II**
to **perform** [pə'fɔ:m] aufführen, auftreten **II**
performer [pə'fɔ:mə] Darsteller/-in; Künstler/-in ⟨**VU3,** 53⟩
perfume ['pɜ:fju:m] Parfüm **II**
perhaps [pə'hæps] vielleicht **III**
period ['pɪəriəd] (Unterrichts)stunde **IV**
person pl. **people** ['pɜ:sn; pi:pl] Person, Mensch **I**
personal ['pɜ:snəl] persönlich **II**
Personally, … ['pɜ:snli] Ich persönlich … **IV**
personnel manager [pɜ:sn'el ˌmænədʒə] Personalchef/-in **VU2,** 29
perspective [pə'spektɪv] Perspektive, Blickwinkel **VU1,** 20
pet [pet] Haustier **I**
phone [fəʊn] Telefon **I**
cell phone *(AE)* ['selfəʊn] Handy, Mobiltelefon **IV**

phone call ['fəʊn ˌkɔ:l] (Telefon)Anruf **I**
phone number ['fəʊn ˌnʌmbə] Telefonnummer **I**
to **phone** [fəʊn] anrufen **I**
photo ['fəʊtəʊ] Foto **I**
to **photograph** ['fəʊtəgrɑ:f] fotografieren **III**
photographer [fə'tɒgrəfə] Fotograf/-in **IV**
phrasal verb [ˌfreɪzl 'vɜ:b] *phrasal verb (Verb + Präposition oder Partikel)* **IV**
phrase [freɪz] Satz, Redewendung **I**
catch phrase ['kætʃ freɪz] Slogan **V U3,** 58
classroom phrases *(pl.)* ['klɑ:srʊm ˌfreɪzɪz] Redewendungen für den Unterricht **I**
physical ['fɪzɪkl] körperlich **II**
to **pick up** [pɪk‿'ʌp] abholen, mitnehmen **I**; aufheben **II**; aufschnappen ⟨**V U3,** 50⟩
pick-pocketing ['pɪkˌpɒkɪtɪŋ] Taschendiebstahl **V U4,** 70
pick-up ['pɪkʌp] Pick-up, Kleintransporter **I**
picnic ['pɪknɪk] Picknick **I**
picture ['pɪktʃə] Bild **I**
piece [pi:s] Stück **II**
pier [pɪə] Pier, Hafendamm **I**
pig [pɪg] Schwein **I**
pigeon ['pɪdʒən] Taube **II**
pile [paɪl] Stapel, Haufen **III**
pink [pɪŋk] rosa, pink **I**
pip [pɪp] Kern **III**
pipe [paɪp] Rohr **III**
pirate ['paɪrət] Pirat, Seeräuber **I**
pitch [pɪtʃ] Spielfeld, Platz **III**
to **pitter-patter** ['pɪtəˌpætə] prasseln, klopfen, trappeln **I**
It's a **pity.** [ˌɪts‿ə 'pɪti] Das ist schade./Es ist schade … **III**
pizza ['pi:tsə] Pizza **I**
pizza place ['pi:tsə ˌpleɪs] Pizzeria **I**
place [pleɪs] Ort **I**; Platz **III**
changing places [ˌtʃeɪndʒɪŋ 'pleɪsɪz] Ortswechsel **III**
in place of [ɪn 'pleɪs‿əv] (an)statt, an Stelle von **V U2,** 30
in the first place [ɪn ðə 'fɜ:st ˌpleɪs] überhaupt erst, von vornherein **IV**
placement ['pleɪsmənt] Praktikum **V U2,** 33
plan [plæn] Plan **II**
to **plan** [plæn] planen **I**
plane [pleɪn] Flugzeug **II**
planet ['plænɪt] Planet **II**
plank [plæŋk] Brett, Planke **I**
planner ['plænə] Kalender, Planer **II**
planning your holidays [ˌplænɪŋ jə 'hɒlədeɪz] den Urlaub planen **I**
plant [plɑ:nt] Pflanze **III**
plate [pleɪt] Teller **II**
to bring plates *(coll)* [brɪŋ 'pleɪts] Essen mitbringen *(ugs.)* ⟨**V U1,** 21⟩
platform ['plætfɔ:m] Bahnsteig; Plattform **II**
observation platform [ˌɒbzə'veɪʃn ˌplætfɔ:m] Aussichtsplattform **IV**
oil platform ['ɔɪl ˌplætfɔ:m] Bohrinsel **II**
platypus pl. **platypi** ['plætɪpəs, 'plætɪpaɪ] Schnabeltier **V ZI,** 11
play [pleɪ] Spiel, Theaterstück **II**
role play ['rəʊl pleɪ] Rollenspiel **I**
to **play** [pleɪ] spielen **I**; (ab)spielen *(CD, Radio etc.)* **I**
to play a trick on [ˌpleɪ‿ə 'trɪk‿ɒn] einen Streich spielen **II**
player ['pleɪə] (Mit)Spieler/-in **II**
MP3 player [ˌempi:'θri: ˌpleɪə] MP3-Player **III**
playground ['pleɪgraʊnd] Schulhof; Spielplatz **I**
please [pli:z] bitte **I**
Pleased to meet you. [ˌpli:zd tə 'mi:t‿ju] Sehr erfreut./Freut mich, Sie/dich kennenzulernen. **II**
pledge of allegiance [ˌpledʒ‿əv ə'li:dʒns] Treueeid **IV**
plot [plɒt] Handlung **IV**
plural ['plʊərl] Plural, Mehrzahl **I**
plus (+) [plʌs] aufwärts **V U2,** 30
pm [ˌpi:'em] nachmittags *(Uhrzeit)* **I**
poacher ['pəʊtʃə] Wilderer **IV**
pocket ['pɒkɪt] Tasche, Hosentasche **II**
pocket money ['pɒkɪt ˌmʌni] Taschengeld **II**
pod [pɒd] Gondel **II**
poem ['pəʊɪm] Gedicht **I**
poet ['pəʊɪt] Dichter/-in **III**
poetic [pəʊ'etɪk] poetisch, dichterisch **V U4,** 78
point [pɔɪnt] Punkt **IV**
to miss a point [ˌmɪs‿ə‿'pɔɪnt] nicht verstehen, worum es geht ⟨**V U4,** 76⟩
meeting point ['mi:tɪŋ pɔɪnt] Treffpunkt **IV**
point of view [ˌpɔɪnt‿əv‿'vju:] Ansicht, Einstellung; Standpunkt ⟨**V U1,** 14⟩; **V U1,** 16
to make a point [ˌmeɪk‿ə 'pɔɪnt] etw. anmerken **IV**
turning point ['tɜ:nɪŋ ˌpɔɪnt] Wendepunkt **V U1,** 20
You've got a point. [ju:v gɒt‿ə 'pɔɪnt] Da ist was dran. **III**
to **point** [pɔɪnt] zeigen **I**; **IV**
polar bear ['pəʊlə beə] Eisbär **IV**
police [pə'li:s] Polizei **I**
police department [pə'li:s dɪˌpɑ:tmənt] Polizeidienststelle **III**
police officer [pəˌli:s 'ɒfɪsə] Polizeibeamte/-r **III**
police state [pə'li:s ˌsteɪt] Polizeistaat **V ZI,** 10
police station [pə'li:s ˌsteɪʃn] Polizeirevier, Polizeiwache **I**
secret police [ˌsi:krət pə'li:s] Geheimpolizei **V U4,** 70
Polish ['pəʊlɪʃ] polnisch, aus Polen; Polnisch **I**
polite [pə'laɪt] höflich **I**
politeness [pə'laɪtnəs] Höflichkeit **II**
politically active [pəˌlɪtɪkli 'æktɪv] politisch engagiert ⟨**V U1,** 14⟩
politician [ˌpɒlɪ'tɪʃn] Politiker/-in **V U2,** 39
politics pl. **politics** ['pɒlətɪks] Politik **IV**
Pooh! [pu:] Igitt! **I**
pool [pu:l] Pool **III**
the **poor** [ðə 'pɔ:] die Armen **III**
poor [pɔ:; pʊə] arm **II**
poorly ['pɔ:li] schlecht **IV**
pop culture ['pɒp ˌkʌltʃə] Popkultur **V ZI,** 8
pop star ['pɒp stɑ:] Popstar **I**
popular ['pɒpjələ] beliebt, populär **II**
popular newspaper [ˌpɒpjələ 'nju:sˌpeɪpə] Boulevardzeitung **III**
popularity [ˌpɒpjə'lærəti] Popularität; Beliebtheit **V U4,** 79
population [ˌpɒpjə'leɪʃn] Einwohner(zahl); Bevölkerung **IV**
portrait ['pɔ:trɪt] Portrait; Konterfei **V ZI,** 10
to **portray** [pɔ:'treɪ] darstellen **IV**
position [pə'zɪʃn] Position **V U4,** 68
position of power [pəˌzɪʃn‿əv 'paʊə] Machtposition **V U4,** 68
positive ['pɒzətɪv] positiv **II**
possibility [ˌpɒsə'bɪləti] Möglichkeit **V ZI,** 9
possible ['pɒsəbl] möglich **IV**
post office ['pəʊst‿ɒfɪs] Postamt **II**
to **post** [pəʊst] online stellen; posten **V U1,** 17
postbox ['pəʊstbɒks] Briefkasten *(öffentlich)* **II**
postcard ['pəʊskɑ:d] Postkarte **I**
poster ['pəʊstə] Poster **I**
couch **potato** ['kaʊtʃ pəˌteɪtəʊ] Fernsehglotzer/-in, Couchpotato **III**
pouch [paʊtʃ] Beutel ⟨**V U1,** 19⟩
pound [paʊnd] Pfund *(Währung)* **I**
It's two pounds. [ɪts ˌtu: 'paʊndz] Es kostet zwei Pfund. **I**
poverty ['pɒvəti] Armut **V ZI,** 9
pow [paʊ] peng **IV**
power ['paʊə] Strom, Elektrizität, Energie **III**; Macht **V U3,** 50
brain power ['breɪn paʊə] Intelligenz **V U3,** 55
position of power [pəˌzɪʃn‿əv 'paʊə] Machtposition **V U4,** 68
practical ['præktɪkl] praktisch **V U2,** 29
practice ['præktɪs] Training **IV**
to **practise** ['præktɪs] üben **II**
prairie ['preəri] Prärie **III**

preconception [ˌpriːkənˈsepʃn] vorgefasste Meinung ⟨**VU1,** 13⟩
preconception [ˌpriːkənˈsepʃən] vorgefasste Meinung **VU1,** 17
to **predict** [prɪˈdɪkt] vorhersagen, voraussagen **VU2,** 34
predictable [prɪˈdɪktəbl] vorhersehbar, voraussagbar; berechenbar **IV**
prediction [prɪˈdɪkʃn] Vorhersage, Voraussage ⟨**VU2,** 36⟩
pre-digested [ˌpriːdaɪˈdʒestɪd] vorverdaut ⟨**VU1,** 12⟩
to **prefer** [prɪˈfɜː] vorziehen **IV**
Premiership [ˈpremiərʃɪp] *erste Division, vgl. Deutsche Bundesliga* **II**
to **prepare** [prɪˈpeə] vorbereiten; zubereiten **III**
preposition [ˌprepəˈzɪʃn] Präposition **II**
pre-reading [priːˈriːdɪŋ] vor dem Lesen **III**
prescription [prɪˈskrɪpʃn] Rezept *(für Arzneimittel)* **II**
present [ˈpreznt] Geschenk **I**
present [ˈpreznt] Gegenwart; Präsens **I**
present perfect [ˌpreznt ˈpɜːfɪkt] das Perfekt **II**
present perfect progressive [ˌpreznt ˌpɜːfɪkt prəˈgresɪv] Verlaufsform des Perfekts **IV**
present progressive [ˌpreznt prəˈgresɪv] Verlaufsform des Präsens/der Gegenwart **I**
simple present [ˌsɪmpl ˈpreznt] Gegenwart, Präsens **I**
to **present** [prɪˈzent] präsentieren **IV**
presentation [ˌpreznˈteɪʃn] Präsentation, Vortrag **II**
to give a (group) presentation [gɪv‿ə ˌgruːp‿ˌpreznˈteɪʃn] eine (Gruppen)Präsentation machen **II**
president [ˈprezɪdnt] Präsident/-in **VZI,** 10
press conference [ˈpres ˌkɒnfrns] Pressekonferenz **III**
to **press** [pres] drücken ⟨**VU3,** 53⟩
pressure [ˈpreʃə] Druck **IV**
to **pretend (sth)** [prɪˈtend] (etw.) vortäuschen, (etw.) vorgeben ⟨**VU3,** 52⟩; **VU4,** 78
pretty [ˈprɪti] hübsch **IV**
pretty [ˈprɪti] ziemlich **IV**
pretty much [ˌprɪti ˈmʌtʃ] fast, nahezu **IV**
price [praɪs] Preis **II**
priest [priːst] Priester **II**
primary school [ˈpraɪmri ˌskuːl] Grundschule **I**
princess [prɪnˈses] Prinzessin **III**
princess-like [prɪnˈsesˌlaɪk] prinzessinenhaft **VU1,** 20
principal *(AE)* [ˈprɪnsɪpl] Schulleiter/-in **IV**
to **print** [prɪnt] (etw. in Druckschrift) schreiben; drucken **VU2,** 33
prison [ˈprɪzn] Gefängnis **III**
prisoner [ˈprɪznə] Gefangene/-r **II**
privacy [ˈprɪvəsi] Privatsphäre, Intimsphäre; Privatleben **IV**
private [ˈpraɪvɪt] privat **IV**
prize [praɪz] Preis, Gewinn **I**
probably [ˈprɒbəbli] möglicherweise, wahrscheinlich **III**
problem [ˈprɒbləm] Problem **I**
product [ˈprɒdʌkt] Produkt, Erzeugnis **III**
cleaning product [ˈkliːnɪŋ ˌprɒdʌkt] Reinigungsmittel, Putzmittel **III**
profile [ˈprəʊfaɪl] Profil; Porträt **IV**
programme [ˈprəʊgræm] Programm; Sendung **III**; Programmheft **III**
project [ˈprɒdʒekt] Projekt **I**
to **promise** [ˈprɒmɪs] versprechen **II**
to **promote sth** [prəˈməʊt] für etw. werben ⟨**VU3,** 50⟩
pronoun [ˈprəʊnaʊn] Pronomen, Fürwort **I**
self-pronoun [ˈself ˌprəʊnaʊn] Reflexivpronomen **III**
relative pronoun [ˌrelətɪv ˈprəʊnaʊn] Relativpronomen **III**
to **pronounce** [prəˈnaʊns] aussprechen **IV**
pronunciation [prəˌnʌnsiˈeɪʃn] Aussprache **IV**
properly [ˈprɒpli] richtig; anständig **VU4,** 75
proportion [prəˈpɔːʃn] Anteil **VU4,** 69
props *(pl.)* [prɒps] Requisiten **III**
pros and cons *(pl.)* [ˌprəʊz‿n ˈkɒnz] Pro und Kontra **III**
protection [prəˈtekʃn] Schutz ⟨**VU1,** 19⟩
environmental protection [ɪnˌvaɪərnˌmentl prəˈtekʃn] Umweltschutz **IV**
protective [prəˈtektɪv] fürsorglich ⟨**VU1,** 13⟩
protest [ˈprəʊtest] Protest **VU4,** 69
to **protest** [prəʊˈtest] protestieren ⟨**VU3,** 52⟩; **VU4,** 68
Protestant [ˈprɒtɪstnt] Protestant/-in; protestantisch **III**
*to **be proud (of)** [bi ˈpraʊd‿əv] stolz sein (auf) **III**
to **prove** [pruːv] beweisen **VU3,** 51; **VU3,** 53
to prove sb wrong [ˌpruːv ˈrɒŋ] beweisen, dass jmd. Unrecht hat **VU3,** 53
to **provide sb/sth with** [prəʊˈvaɪd wɪð] jmdn./etw. mit etw. versorgen; jmdm./etw. etw. bieten ⟨**VU1,** 12⟩
P.S.E. *(= Personal and Social Education)* [ˌpiːjesˈiː; ˌpɜːsnəl‿ənd ˌsəʊʃl‿edʒʊˈkeɪʃn] Sozialkunde **II**
the **public** [ðə ˈpʌblɪk] die Öffentlichkeit **III**
public [ˈpʌblɪk] öffentlich **I**
public transportation *(no pl.)* [ˌpʌblɪk ˌtrænspɔːˈteɪʃn] öffentliche Verkehrsmittel **IV**
to **pull** [pʊl] ziehen **IV**
pullover [ˈpʊləʊvə] Pullover **II**
Punjabi [pʌnˈdʒɑːbiː] Pandschabi; pandschabisch **III**
pupil [ˈpjuːpl] Schüler-/in **I**
purple [ˈpɜːpl] violett, lila **I**
purpose [ˈpɜːpəs] Ziel; Absicht; Zweck ⟨**VU1,** 12⟩
purr [pɜː] *(Schnurren einer Katze)* **I**
purse [pɜːs] Geldbeutel **III**
to **push** [pʊʃ] stoßen, schieben, drücken, schubsen **II**; drängeln **IV**
push-button [ˈpʊʃˌbʌtn] Druckknopf- ⟨**VU1,** 12⟩
*to **put** [pʊt] stellen, setzen, legen **I**
to put in [pʊt ˈɪn] einsetzen **I**
to put on (a play) [ˌpʊt‿ɒn‿ə ˈpleɪ] (ein Theaterstück) aufführen **III**
to put sb off [pʊt‿ˈɒf] jmdn. von etw. abbringen; jmdm. etw. verleiden **VU2,** 30
to put sth into words [pʊt ˌɪntə ˈwɜːdz] etw. in Worte fassen **IV**
pyramid [ˈpɪrəmɪd] Pyramide **VU4,** 71

Q

qualification [ˌkwɒlɪfɪˈkeɪʃn] Qualifikation; Befähigung **IV**
to **qualify** [ˈkwɒlɪfaɪ] die (nötigen) Voraussetzungen/Bedingungen erfüllen **VU4,** 69
quality [ˈkwɒləti] Qualität; Qualitäts- **III**; Eigenschaft, Merkmal **VU2,** 32
quarter [ˈkwɔːtə] Viertel **I**
queen [kwiːn] Königin **II**
question [ˈkwestʃən] Frage **I**
question tag [ˈkwestʃən ˌtæg] Frageanhängsel, Bestätigungsfrage **II**
question word [ˈkwestʃən ˌwɜːd] Fragewort **I**
questionnaire [ˌkwestʃəˈneə] Fragebogen **VU2,** 29
queue [kjuː] Schlange **II**
to **queue** [kjuː] anstehen, sich anstellen **III**
quick [kwɪk] schnell **II**
quiet [kwaɪət] leise, ruhig, still **I**
*to **quit** [kwɪt] aufgeben **IV**; aufhören; aufgeben **IV**
quite [kwaɪt] ziemlich; ganz, völlig **III**
quiz [kwɪz] Quiz, Ratespiel **I**

R

race [reɪs] Wettlauf, Rennen **III**; Rasse ⟨**VU4,** 76⟩
racial equality [ˌreɪʃl‿ɪˈkwɒləti] Rassengleichheit **VU4,** 68

racism ['reɪsɪzm] Rassismus **V U4,** 74
racist ['reɪsɪst] rassistisch; Rassist/-in **V ZI,** 10
racket ['rækɪt] Schläger *(Tennis-)* **III**
radio ['reɪdiəʊ] Radio **I**
radio station ['reɪdiəʊ ˌsteɪʃn] Radiosender **I**
rage [reɪdʒ] Wut, Zorn ⟨**V U1,** 14⟩
rags-to-riches [ˌrægz tə‿'rɪtʃɪz] vom Tellerwäscher zum Millionär **IV**
railroad *(AE)* ['reɪlrəʊd] Eisenbahn **IV**
railway ['reɪlweɪ] Eisenbahn **III**
railway system ['reɪlweɪ ˌsɪstəm] Eisenbahnnetz **V U2,** 28
rain [reɪn] Regen **I**
to **rain** [reɪn] regnen **I**
rainforest ['reɪnˌfɒrɪst] Regenwald **V ZI,** 11
rainy ['reɪni] regnerisch **II**
to **raise** [reɪz] *(hier:)* strecken ⟨**V U1,** 13⟩
to raise money [reɪz 'mʌni] Geld sammeln, Geld aufbringen **III**
rally ['ræli] (Massen)Versammlung ⟨**V U1,** 14⟩
ramp [ræmp] Rampe **III**
ranger *(AE)* [reɪndʒə] Ranger **IV**
rap [ræp] Rap **I**
I'd **rather** [aɪd 'rɑːðə] ich würde lieber **III**
rating ['reɪtɪŋ] Einstufung **IV**
raw [rɔː] roh; unbehandelt ⟨**V U3,** 51⟩
raw material [ˌrɔː mə'tɪəriəl] Rohstoff **III**
R.E. *(= Religious Education)* [ɑː'r‿iː; rɪˌlɪdʒəs‿edʒʊ'keɪʃn] Religion *(Schulfach)* **II**
to **reach** [riːtʃ] erreichen **V U2,** 28
to **react** [ri'ækt] reagieren **IV**
reaction [ri'ækʃn] Reaktion **IV**
*to **read** [riːd] lesen **I**
to read to [riːd 'tə] jmdm. vorlesen **I**
reader ['riːdə] Leser/-in **II**
ready ['redi] fertig, bereit **I**
to get ready [get 'redi] sich vorbereiten; sich fertig machen **III**
real [rɪəl] echt, richtig, wirklich **II**
realistic [ˌrɪə'lɪstɪk] realistisch **III**
reality [ri'æləti] Realität; Wirklichkeit **IV**
to **realize** ['rɪəlaɪz] erkennen, realisieren **IV**
really ['rɪəli] wirklich **II**
reason ['riːzn] Grund **II**
to give reasons [gɪv 'riːznz] Gründe nennen, Gründe angeben **II**
to **receive** [rɪ'siːv] erhalten, bekommen **V U4,** 70
recent ['riːsnt] kürzlich; neueste/-r/-s; letzte/-r/-s **V U4,** 69
recently ['riːsntli] kürzlich, vor kurzem, neulich; in letzter Zeit **III**
recipe ['resɪpi] Rezept **I**
reckless ['rekləs] leichtsinnig, unbesonnen; rücksichtslos **IV**

to **recognize** ['rekəgnaɪz] erkennen **IV**
to **recommend** [ˌrekə'mend] empfehlen **III**
record ['rekɔːd] Schallplatte **II**; Rekord **III**; Bericht; Dokumentation ⟨**V U3,** 53⟩
to **record** [rɪ'kɔːd] aufnehmen; aufzeichnen **V ZI,** 8
recorder [rɪ'kɔːdə] Aufnahmegerät ⟨**V U3,** 51⟩
recording [rɪ'kɔːdɪŋ] Aufnahme; Aufzeichnung ⟨**V U3,** 50⟩
to **recruit** [rɪ'kruːt] rekrutieren **V U4,** 70
red [red] rot **I**
red-back (spider) [ˌredbæk 'spaɪdə] Rotrückenspinne ⟨**V U1,** 19⟩
red-herring [ˌred'herɪŋ] Ablenkungsmanöver **V U1,** 20
to **reduce** [rɪ'djuːs] reduzieren; verringern ⟨**V U3,** 57⟩
ref *(= referee)* [ref] Schiri *(= Schiedsrichter)* **V U3,** 59
referee [ˌrefə'riː] Schiedsrichter/-in **III**
reference ['refrns] Referenz(schreiben) **V U2,** 33; Anspielung; Erwähnung, Bezugnahme **V U4,** 77
reflexive [rɪ'fleksɪv] reflexiv **III**
refrain [rɪ'freɪn] Refrain **V U4,** 80
regime [reɪ'ʒiːm] Regime **V U4,** 69
region ['riːdʒn] Region; Gegend **III**
regional ['riːdʒnl] regional **III**
register ['redʒɪstə] Klassenbuch; Namensliste **II**; Sprachebene, Register **IV**
to take the register [ˌteɪk ðə 'redʒɪstə] Anwesenheitskontrolle durchführen **II**
to **regret sth** [rɪ'gret] etw. bedauern ⟨**V U1,** 14⟩
regular ['regjələ] regelmäßig; gleichmäßig **II**; normal; üblich **IV**
regulation [ˌregjə'leɪʃn] Regelung; Regulierung; Vorschrift **V ZI,** 8
rehearsal [rɪ'hɜːsl] Probe **III**
to **rehearse** [rɪ'hɜːs] proben **III**
reign [reɪn] Herrschaft **III**
to **relate to (sb/sth)** [rɪ'leɪt‿tə] eine Beziehung/Zugang zu jmdm./etw. finden **V U4,** 80
relations *(pl.)* [rɪ'leɪʃnz] Verhältnis; Beziehungen **V ZI,** 11
relationship [rɪ'leɪʃnʃɪp] Beziehung **V U4,** 69
relative ['relətɪv] Verwandte/-r **III**
relative ['relətɪv] relativ **V U4,** 70
non-defining relative clause ['nɒndɪˌfaɪnɪŋ ˌrelətɪv klɔːz] nicht-notwendiger Relativsatz **IV**
relative clause [ˌrelətɪv 'klɔːz] Relativsatz **III**
relative pronoun [ˌrelətɪv 'prəʊnaʊn] Relativpronomen **III**
relatively ['relətɪvli] relativ ⟨**V U3,** 50⟩
to **relax** [rɪ'læks] (sich) entspannen, (sich) ausruhen; sich beruhigen **III**

relaxed [rɪ'lækst] entspannt; locker, gelassen **IV**
to **release** [rɪ'liːs] veröffentlichen; herausbringen ⟨**V U3,** 51⟩
reliable [rɪ'laɪəbl] verlässlich, zuverlässig; vertrauenswürdig **V U2,** 29
religion [rɪ'lɪdʒn] Religion **V U4,** 68
religious [rɪ'lɪdʒəs] religiös, gläubig **II**
relocation [ˌriːlə'kəɪʃn] Umsiedlung **V ZI,** 11
to **remember** [rɪ'membə] sich erinnern (an); denken an **I**
to **remind sb (about)** [rɪ'maɪnd] jmdn. erinnern (an) **II**
reminder [rɪ'maɪndə] Erinnerung; Mahnung **V ZI,** 10
to **reopen** [ˌriː'əʊpn] wiedereröffnen **IV**
to **repeat** [rɪ'piːt] wiederholen **I**
to **replace sb/sth (by sb/sth)** [rɪ'pleɪs] jmdn./etw. (durch jmdn./etw.) ersetzen ⟨**V U3,** 53⟩
reply [rɪ'plaɪ] Antwort **III**
in reply to [ɪn rɪ'plaɪ tə] als Antwort auf, als Reaktion auf **V U3,** 55
to **reply** [rɪ'plaɪ] antworten, erwidern, entgegnen **III**
report [rɪ'pɔːt] Bericht **II**
to **report** [rɪ'pɔːt] berichten, wiedergeben **III**
reporting what someone said [rɪˌpɔːtɪŋ wɒt sʌmwʌn 'sed] wiedergeben, was jemand gesagt hat **III**
reporter [rɪ'pɔːtə] Reporter/-in **II**
to **represent** [ˌreprɪ'zent] repräsentieren; darstellen **V U4,** 68
*to **reread** [riː'riːd] noch einmal lesen **III**
to **rescue** ['reskjuː] retten **III**
research [riː'sɜːtʃ] Recherche; Forschung; Untersuchung **III**
to **research** [rɪ'sɜːtʃ] recherchieren; erforschen; untersuchen **IV**
reservation [ˌrezə'veɪʃn] Reservierung **III**; Reservat **IV**
respect [rɪ'spekt] Respekt **IV**
to **respect** [rɪ'spekt] respektieren **IV**
respectful [rɪ'spektfl] respektvoll **V U4,** 73
the **rest** [ðə 'rest] der Rest **II**
restaurant ['restrɑːŋ] Restaurant, Gaststätte **I**
restroom *(AE)* ['restrʊm] Toilette **IV**
result [rɪ'zʌlt] Ergebnis, Resultat **IV**
*to **retell** [riː'tel] nacherzählen; nochmals erzählen **I**
return [rɪ'tɜːn] Hin- und Rückfahrkarte **III**
to **return** [rɪ'tɜːn] zurückkehren, zurückkommen **V U1,** 20
review [rɪ'vjuː] Kritik **IV**
revision [rɪ'vɪʒn] Wiederholung **I**
Industrial **Revolution** [ɪnˌdʌstriəl revə'luːʃn] Industrielle Revolution **III**

*to **rewrite** [ri:'raɪt] umschreiben; neu schreiben **III**
rhyme [raɪm] Reim **I**
rhythm ['rɪðm] Rhythmus **IV**
rich [rɪtʃ] reich **I**
*to get **rid of** [get 'rɪd‿əv] loswerden **III**
*to **ride** [raɪd] reiten, fahren **I**
right [raɪt] Recht **VU4,** 68
civil rights [ˌsɪvl 'raɪts] Bürgerrechte **VZI,** 10
human rights [ˌhju:mən 'raɪts] Menschenrechte **VU4,** 68
right [raɪt] rechte/-r/-s; rechts **I**; richtig **I**
Right? [raɪt] Stimmt's?/Nicht wahr? **III**
on the right [ɒn ðə 'raɪt] auf der rechten Seite, rechts **I**
on your right/left [ɒn jə 'raɪt, 'left] rechts/links, auf der rechten/linken Seite **I**
to be right [bi 'raɪt] Recht haben **I**
to turn right [ˌtɜ:n 'raɪt] (nach) rechts abbiegen **I**
right away [raɪt‿ə'weɪ] sofort **II**
right now [raɪt 'naʊ] jetzt, sofort, gerade **I**
*to **ring** [rɪŋ] klingeln, läuten **I**
ripper *(coll)* ['rɪpə] geil *(ugs.)* ⟨**VU1,** 21⟩
*to **rise** [raɪz] (an)steigen **VU2,** 30
risk [rɪsk] Risiko **II**
to take a risk [ˌteɪk‿ə 'rɪsk] ein Risiko eingehen **II**
to **risk (sth)** [rɪsk] (etw.) riskieren **II**
river ['rɪvə] Fluss **I**
road [rəʊd] Straße **I**
road trip ['rəʊd trɪp] Tour, Trip **VU1,** 20
to **roar** [rɔ:] (auf)heulen, dröhnen; brüllen **VU3,** 51; **VU3,** 52
robe [rəʊb] Gewand **VU4,** 77
rock [rɒk] Fels, Riff, Stein **I**
rock and roll [ˌrɒk‿n 'rəʊl] Rock 'n' Roll **II**
rock climbing ['rɒk ˌklaɪmɪŋ] Klettern **II**
rock wallaby [ˌrɒk 'wɒləbi] Wallaby *(austral. Beuteltier)* ⟨**VU1,** 12⟩
rocky ['rɒki] felsig, steinig **I**
rodeo ['rəʊdiəʊ] Rodeo **IV**
role [rəʊl] Rolle **II**
role model ['rəʊl ˌmɒdl] Vorbild **VU4,** 74
role play ['rəʊl pleɪ] Rollenspiel **I**
Roman ['rəʊmən] Römer/-in; römisch **II**
Romanian [rʊ'meɪniən] Rumäne/Rumänin; rumänisch, aus Rumänien; Rumänisch **VU4,** 70
romantic [rə'mæntɪk] romantisch **VU3,** 58
roo *(coll)* [ru:] Känguru *(ugs.)* **VZI,** 11
roof [ru:f] Dach **III**
rooftop terrace [ˌru:ftɒp 'terɪs] Dachterrasse **VU1,** 18
rookie ['rʊki] Neuling **IV**
room [ru:m] Zimmer, Raum **I**
changing room ['tʃeɪndʒɪŋ ru:m] Umkleidekabine **II**
living room ['lɪvɪŋ ru:m] Wohnzimmer **I**
waiting room ['weɪtɪŋ ˌrʊm] Wartezimmer **VU2,** 35
rope [rəʊp] Seil **IV**
round [raʊnd] rund **VU2,** 39
from all **round the world** [frəm‿'ɔ:l ˌraʊnd ðə 'wɜ:ld] aus aller Welt **I**
round the garden [raʊnd ðə 'gɑ:dn] durch den ganzen Garten **I**
route [ru:t] *(Bezeichnung einer amerikanischen Bundesstraße)*; Strecke, Route **IV**
routine [ru:'ti:n] Routine **I**
to **row** [rəʊ] rudern **I**
rowing ['rəʊɪŋ] Rudern **III**
royal ['rɔɪəl] königlich **II**
to **rub out** [rʌb‿'aʊt] wegreiben, ausradieren **II**
rubber ['rʌbə] Radiergummi **I**
rubber ball [ˌrʌbə 'bɔ:l] Gummiball **I**
rubbish ['rʌbɪʃ] Unsinn, Quatsch; Müll; Gerümpel **III**
Don't rubbish me! *(coll)* [ˌdəʊnt rʌbɪʃ 'mi:] Mach mich nicht fertig!; Kritisiere mich nicht! *(ugs.)* ⟨**VU1,** 21⟩
rude [ru:d] unhöflich; unverschämt **III**
rugby ['rʌgbi] Rugby **III**
to **ruin** ['ru:ɪn] zerstören, ruinieren **I**
rule [ru:l] Regel **I**
ruler ['ru:lə] Lineal **I**
rumor ['ru:mə] Gerücht **VU4,** 79
*to **run** [rʌn] laufen, rennen **I**
to run after [rʌn‿'ɑ:ftə] hinterherrennen **I**
to run away [rʌn‿ə'weɪ] weglaufen **I**
running time ['rʌnɪŋ‿taɪm] Laufzeit **IV**
Russian ['rʌʃn] russisch, aus Russland; Russisch **I**

S

sad [sæd] traurig **I**
safe [seɪf] sicher, ungefährlich **I**
safety ['seɪfti] Sicherheit **II**
to **sail** [seɪl] segeln **I**
salad ['sæləd] Salat **II**
for **sale** [fɔ: 'seɪl] zu verkaufen **IV**
the **same** [ðə 'seɪm] der-/die-/dasselbe, der/die/das Gleiche **I**
same-sex [seɪm'seks] gleichgeschlechtlich **VU4,** 69
sand [sænd] Sand **I**
sand castle ['sænd ˌkɑ:sl] Sandburg **I**
sandwich ['sænwɪdʒ] Sandwich **I**
sandy ['sændi] sandig **I**
satisfactory [ˌsætɪs'fæktri] zufriedenstellend **VU4,** 69
Saturday ['sætədeɪ] Samstag **I**
to **save** [seɪv] sparen **II**; retten **III**; speichern ⟨**VU3,** 51⟩
Saxon ['sæksn] Sachse, Sächsin; sächsisch **III**
to **say** [seɪ] sagen **I**
Easy for you to say [ˌi:zi fə 'ju: tə 'seɪ] Du hast leicht reden. **IV**
it says ... [ɪt 'sez] hier steht ... **VU2,** 30
saying what you've got ['seɪɪŋ ˌwɒt jʊv 'gɒt] sagen, was jemand hat **I**
to be said to *(+ infinitive)* [bi 'sed‿tə] gelten als **VU1,** 21
to say goodbye (to) [seɪ gʊd'baɪ] sich verabschieden (von) **IV**
to say hello [seɪ hel'əʊ] jmdn. begrüßen **I**
to say hello to [seɪ hel'əʊ tə] grüßen, Grüße ausrichten **I**
to **scan** [skæn] durchsuchen, abtasten **III**
scanning ['skænɪŋ] Durchsuchen nach Details; Abtasten **III**
scared [skeəd] verängstigt **I**
to be scared for [bi 'skeəd fə] Angst haben um **I**
scarf pl. **scarves** [skɑ:f; skɑ:vz] Schal, Tuch **I**
scary ['skeəri] beängstigend, unheimlich **I**
scene [si:n] Szene **III**
school [sku:l] Schule **I**
boarding school ['bɔ:dɪŋ ˌsku:l] Internat **II**
grammar school ['græmə ˌsku:l] Gymnasium **II**
high school ['haɪ ˌsku:l] High School *(weiterführende Schule in den USA, Oberstufe)* **IV**
primary school ['praɪmri ˌsku:l] Grundschule **I**
school day ['sku:l deɪ] Schultag **I**
schools officer ['sku:lz ˌɒfɪsə] *(hier:)* Beauftragter/Beauftragte für Schulklassen **I**
to be late for school [bi ˌleɪt fə 'sku:l] zu spät zur Schule kommen **I**
schoolbag ['sku:lbæg] Schultasche **I**
science ['saɪəns] (Natur)Wissenschaft **II**
science fiction [ˌsaɪəns 'fɪkʃn] Sciencefiction **II**
scientist ['saɪəntɪst] Wissenschaftler/-in **III**
score *(for movie etc.)* [skɔ:] (Titel)musik **IV**
to **score** [skɔ:] punkten; ein Tor schießen **II**
to score *(coll)* [skɔ:] jmdn. ins Bett kriegen *(ugs.)* ⟨**VU4,** 79⟩
Scot [skɒt] Schotte/Schottin **II**
Scottish ['skɒtɪʃ] schottisch **II**
scream [skri:m] Schrei **III**

to scream [skri:m] schreien, kreischen **III**
screen [skri:n] Bildschirm **IV**
screenplay ['skri:npleɪ] Drehbuch **IV**
script [skrɪpt] Drehbuch, Skript **III**
sea [si:] Meer, die See **I**
North Sea [ˌnɔ:θ 'si:] Nordsee **I**
sea level ['si: ˌlevl] Meeresspiegel **IV**
search engine ['sɜ:tʃ ˌendʒɪn] Suchmaschine **III**
seaside ['si:saɪd] (Meeres)Küste **I**
seaside town [ˌsi:saɪd 'taʊn] Küstenstadt **I**
season ['si:zn] Jahreszeit; Saison **I**
seat [si:t] Sitz, Sitzplatz **III**
second ['seknd] Sekunde **I**
second language ['seknd ˌlæŋgwɪdʒ] Zweitsprache **III**
secret ['si:krət] Geheimnis **II**
secret ['si:krət] geheim **III**
secret police [ˌsi:krət pə'li:s] Geheimpolizei **V U4,** 70
*to **see** [si:] sehen **I**
to see sb [si:] mit jmdm. zusammen sein **V U3,** 56
a must-see [ə ˌmʌst 'si:] … muss man gesehen haben **III**
I see. [aɪ 'si:] Ich verstehe./Aha! **III**
See you later. [si: jə 'leɪtə] Bis später. **II**
See you there. [si: jə 'ðeə] Wir sehen uns dort. **I**
to **seem** [si:m] scheinen **III**
segregation [ˌsegrɪ'geɪʃn] (Rassen)Trennung **V U4,** 74
self-catering [ˌself'keɪtrɪŋ] Selbstversorger- **III**
selfish ['selfɪʃ] selbstsüchtig **III**
self-pronoun ['self ˌprəʊnaʊn] Reflexivpronomen **III**
*to **sell** [sel] verkaufen **I**
semester [sɪ'mestə] (Schul)halbjahr, Semester **IV**
semicircle ['semɪˌsɜ:kl] Halbkreis ⟨**V U1,** 15⟩
*to **send** [send] schicken **II**
sensation [sen'seɪʃn] Sensation **IV**
sixth sense [ˌsɪksθ 'sens] sechster Sinn **III**
sensitive ['sensɪtɪv] empfindlich **V U4,** 73
sentence ['sentəns] Satz **I**
separated ['sepreɪtɪd] getrennt **V ZI,** 11
separateness ['seprətnəs] Getrenntheit; Isolation **V ZI,** 10
September [sep'tembə] September **I**
serious ['sɪəriəs] ernst **IV**
Seriously! ['sɪəriəsli] Im Ernst! ⟨**V U3,** 50⟩
servant ['sɜ:vnt] Bedienstete/-r; Diener/-in **III**
to **serve** [sɜ:v] servieren **IV**; (be)dienen; servieren **V U2,** 34
service ['sɜ:vɪs] Service, Dienst; Verbindung *(Zug, Bus)* **III**
support service [sə'pɔ:t ˌsɜ:vɪs] *(hier:)* Beratungsstelle **V U2,** 30
*to be **set (in)** [bi 'set] spielen (in); seinen Schauplatz haben (in) **IV**
to set one's sights [ˌset wʌnz 'saɪts] sich Ziele stecken ⟨**V U2,** 35⟩
to set (sb) up [set 'ʌp] jmdn. übers Ohr hauen **IV**
setting ['setɪŋ] Schauplatz; Rahmen **IV**
settlement ['setlmənt] Siedlung **V ZI,** 11
settler ['setlə] Siedler/-in **IV**
seven ['sevn] sieben **I**
seventeen [ˌsevn'ti:n] siebzehn **I**
seventy ['sevnti] siebzig **I**
sex [seks] Geschlecht **V U4,** 68
s-genitive [es'dʒenɪtɪv] s-Genitiv **I**
*to **shake** [ʃeɪk] zittern, beben **II**; schütteln **II**
to shake hands [ʃeɪk 'hændz] sich die Hand geben **IV**
Shall I … ? [ʃæl‿aɪ] Soll ich … ? **II**
shame [ʃeɪm] Scham; Schande, Schmach ⟨**V U1,** 12⟩
shampoo [ʃæm'pu:] Shampoo **V U3,** 56
to **share** [ʃeə] teilen **II**
shark [ʃɑ:k] Hai **II**
she [ʃi:] sie **I**
shed [ʃed] Stall **I**; Schuppen, Gartenhäuschen **I**
sheep pl. **sheep** [ʃi:p] Schaf **I**
sheila *(coll)* ['ʃi:lə] Puppe *(ugs. für Frau)* ⟨**V U1,** 21⟩
shelf pl. **shelves** [ʃelf; ʃelvz] Regal(brett) **I**
*to **shine** [ʃaɪn] scheinen; glänzen **III**
ship [ʃɪp] Schiff **I**
shipload ['ʃɪpləʊd] Schiffsladung **V U1,** 17
shock [ʃɒk] Schock, Schreck **I**
*to be **shocked** [bi 'ʃɒkt] geschockt sein **II**
shocking [ʃɒkɪŋ] schockierend **IV**
shoe [ʃu:] Schuh **I**
*to **shoot** [ʃu:t] schießen **III**
to shoot sb up [ʃu:t‿'ʌp] jmdn. schnell hinauf befördern **IV**
shop [ʃɒp] Geschäft, Laden **I**
computer shop [kəm'pju:tə ˌʃɒp] Computergeschäft **I**
shop assistant ['ʃɒp‿əˌsɪstnt] Verkäufer/-in **II**
sports shop ['spɔ:ts ˌʃɒp] Sportgeschäft **I**
shopper ['ʃɒpə] (Ein)Käufer/-in ⟨**V U1,** 14⟩
shopping ['ʃɒpɪŋ] Einkaufen **I**
shopping list ['ʃɒpɪŋ ˌlɪst] Einkaufszettel **II**
shopping mall ['ʃɒpɪŋ ˌmɔ:l] Einkaufszentrum **IV**
to do the shopping [ˌdu: ðə 'ʃɒpɪŋ] Einkäufe machen, Besorgungen machen **II**
to go shopping [gəʊ 'ʃɒpɪŋ] einkaufen gehen **I**
short [ʃɔ:t] kurz **I**; klein **II**
shorthand ['ʃɔ:thænd] Kurzschrift, Stenografie **V U1,** 16
shorts *(pl.)* [ʃɔ:ts] Shorts, kurze Hose ⟨**V U1,** 14⟩
shot [ʃɒt] Schuss, Schlag **II**; (Kamera)Einstellung **V U3,** 58
medium shot ['mi:diəm ʃɒt] Halbnahe *(Kameraeinstellung)* **V U3,** 58
wide shot ['waɪd ʃɒt] Totale *(Kameraeinstellung)* **V U3,** 58
should [ʃʊd] sollte **I**
shoulder ['ʃəʊldə] Schulter **II**
shout [ʃaʊt] Schrei, Ruf **III**
to **shout** [ʃaʊt] rufen, schreien **I**
show [ʃəʊ] Show, Schau, Aufführung **III**
game show ['geɪm ˌʃəʊ] Spielshow **II**
talk show ['tɔ:k ˌʃəʊ] Talkshow **IV**
*to **show** [ʃəʊ] zeigen **I**
to show up [ˌʃəʊ‿'ʌp] auftauchen **IV**
show-business ['ʃəʊˌbɪznɪs] Showbusiness **IV**
to **shrug** [ʃrʌg] mit den Achseln/Schultern zucken **V U3,** 58
to **shuffle** ['ʃʌfl] mischen **I**; schlurfen **V U4,** 74
Shut up! [ʃʌt‿'ʌp] Halt die Klappe! **III**
shuttle ['ʃʌtl] Pendelzug **II**
shy [ʃaɪ] schüchtern **II**
sick [sɪk] schlecht, übel; krank **II**
side [saɪd] Seite **III**
sides [saɪdz] Skript beim Casting **III**
sight [saɪt] Sicht, Anblick **IV**
to set one's sights [ˌset wʌnz 'saɪts] sich Ziele stecken ⟨**V U2,** 35⟩
sights *(pl.)* [saɪts] Sehenswürdigkeiten **I**
sightseeing ['saɪtsi:ɪŋ] Besichtigungstour **II**
sign [saɪn] Schild, Zeichen **II**
no sign of [nəʊ 'saɪn‿əv] keine Spur von; kein Anzeichen von ⟨**V U1,** 14⟩
to **sign** [saɪn] unterschreiben **III**
signal ['sɪgnl] Zeichen, Signal **I**
signature ['sɪgnətʃə] Unterschrift **V U2,** 33
silence ['saɪləns] Stille; Schweigen; Ruhe ⟨**V U1,** 13⟩
silent ['saɪlənt] still; ruhig; schweigsam **V U4,** 74
silently ['saɪləntli] leise; schweigend; lautlos **IV**
silly ['sɪli] Dummkopf **I**
silly ['sɪli] albern, dumm **I**
simple ['sɪmpl] einfach, simpel **II**
simple present [ˌsɪmpl 'preznt] Gegenwart, Präsens **I**
since [sɪns] seit **IV**; da **V U3,** 59
Yours **sincerely** [jɔ:z sɪn'sɪəli] Mit freundlichen Grüßen **V U2,** 33
*to **sing** [sɪŋ] singen **I**

singer ['sɪŋə] Sänger/-in **II**
singing lessons ['sɪŋɪŋ ˌlesnz] Gesangsunterricht, Gesangsstunden **II**
single ['sɪŋgl] Single *(CD)* **II**; einfache Fahrkarte **III**
third person **singular** [θɜːd ˌpɜːsn 'sɪŋgjələ] dritte Person Singular (Einzahl) **I**
*to **sink** [sɪŋk] untergehen, sinken **I**
Sioux pl. **Sioux** [suː, suːz] Sioux-Indianer **III**
Sir [sɜː] Sir *(Anrede für einen Ritter)* **II**
sister ['sɪstə] Schwester **I**
*to **sit** [sɪt] sitzen **I**
to sit down [sɪt 'daʊn] sich hinsetzen **I**
social networking **site** [ˌsəʊʃl 'netwɜːkɪŋ ˌsaɪt] Online-Netzwerk ⟨**VU3,** 51⟩; **VU3,** 54
situation [ˌsɪtju'eɪʃn] Situation **III**
six [sɪks] sechs **I**
sixteen [ˌsɪk'stiːn] sechzehn **I**
sixth sense [ˌsɪksθ 'sens] sechster Sinn **III**
sixty ['sɪksti] sechzig **I**
size [saɪz] Größe **I**
skateboard ['skeɪtbɔːd] Skateboard **I**
skateboarding ['skeɪtbɔːdɪŋ] Skateboardfahren **III**
skater ['skeɪtə] Skater/-in **III**
in-line **skating** [ˌɪnlaɪn 'skeɪtɪŋ] Inlineskates fahren **II**
ski [skiː] Ski **III**
ski jump ['skiː dʒʌmp] Skispringen **III**
ski jumper ['skiː ˌdʒʌmpə] Skispringer/-in **III**
to **ski** [skiː] Ski fahren **IV**
skier ['skiːə] Skifahrer/-in **IV**
skill [skɪl] Fertigkeit **I**
communication skills [kəˌmjuːnɪ'keɪʃn ˌskɪlz] Sprechfertigkeiten, Kommunikationsfertigkeiten **I**
to **skim** [skɪm] überfliegen **III**
skimming ['skɪmɪŋ] Überfliegen **III**
skin [skɪn] Haut; Fell **III**
skin cancer ['skɪn ˌkænsə] Hautkrebs **VZI,** 11
to jump out of one's skin [ˌdʒʌmp‿aʊt‿əv wʌnz 'skɪn] sich zu Tode erschrecken **III**
skirt [skɜːt] Rock **II**
sky [skaɪ] Himmel **II**
skydiving ['skaɪˌdaɪvɪŋ] Fallschirmspringen **IV**
skyscraper ['skaɪskreɪpə] Wolkenkratzer **IV**
to **slam shut** [slæm 'ʃʌt] zuschlagen, zuknallen ⟨**VU3,** 52⟩
to **slander (sb/sth)** ['slɑːndə] (jmdn./etw.) verleumden ⟨**VU4,** 79⟩
slave [sleɪv] Sklave/Sklavin **VU4,** 70
slavery ['sleɪvri] Sklaverei **VU4,** 70
sleep [sliːp] Schlaf **III**
*to **sleep** [sliːp] schlafen **I**
*to **slide** [slaɪd] gleiten; rutschen **III**
*to **slink away** [ˌslɪŋk ə'weɪ] davonschleichen ⟨**VU1,** 12⟩
to **slip** [slɪp] (aus)rutschen **IV**
slob *(coll)* [slɒb] Assi *(ugs.)* ⟨**VU1,** 14⟩
slope [sləʊp] (Ski)piste; (Ab)hang **IV**
to hit the slopes [ˌhɪt ðə 'sləʊps] auf die (Ski)piste gehen **IV**
slot [slɒt] Schlitz **IV**
to **slouch off** [slaʊtʃ 'ɒf] davonzockeln ⟨**VU1,** 14⟩
to **slow down** [sləʊ 'daʊn] langsamer werden **III**
slow [sləʊ] langsam **I**
slum [slʌm] Slum, Elendsviertel **III**
small [smɔːl] klein **I**
small talk ['smɔːl ˌtɔːk] Smalltalk **III**
smell [smel] Geruch, Duft, Gestank **I**
*to **smell** [smel] riechen; duften **III**
smile [smaɪl] Lächeln **IV**
to **smile** [smaɪl] lächeln **I**
to smile at ['smaɪl‿ət] anlächeln **II**
smoke [sməʊk] Rauch **I**
to **smoke** [sməʊk] rauchen **II**
smooth [smuːθ] glatt **III**
to **smuggle** ['smʌgl] schmuggeln **VU4,** 70
snack bar ['snæk bɑː] Café **II**
sneeze [sniːz] Nieser ⟨**VU1,** 13⟩
to **sneeze** [sniːz] niesen ⟨**VU1,** 13⟩
snow [snəʊ] Schnee **III**
to **snow** [snəʊ] schneien **III**
so [səʊ] so **I**
so far ['səʊ fɑː] bis jetzt **II**
so [səʊ] also, folglich, deshalb **I**
soap *(no pl.)* [səʊp] Seife **III**
soap (opera) ['səʊp ˌɒprə] Seifenoper, Soap **III**
soccer ['sɒkə] Fußball **III**
social ['səʊʃl] sozial, Gesellschaft- **II**
social networking site [ˌsəʊʃl 'netwɜːkɪŋ ˌsaɪt] Online-Netzwerk ⟨**VU3,** 51⟩; **VU3,** 54
social work ['səʊʃl ˌwɜːk] Sozialarbeit **VU2,** 29
society [sə'saɪəti] Gesellschaft **VZI,** 10
sofa ['səʊfə] Sofa, Couch **I**
soft lighting [sɒft 'laɪtɪŋ] Dämmerlicht **VU3,** 58
software ['sɒftweə] Software ⟨**VU3,** 51⟩
soldier ['səʊldʒə] Soldat/-in **II**
solution [sə'luːʃn] Lösung **VU4,** 80
to **solve** [sɒlv] lösen **IV**
some [sʌm] einige, ein paar; etwas **I**
somebody ['sʌmbədi] jemand **II**
someone ['sʌmwʌn] jemand **II**
something ['sʌmθɪŋ] etwas **II**
sometimes ['sʌmtaɪmz] manchmal **I**
somewhere ['sʌmweə] irgendwo **II**
son [sʌn] Sohn **II**
song [sɒŋ] Lied, Song **I**
soon [suːn] bald **I**
as soon as [əz 'suːn‿əz] sobald **II**
I'm **sorry.** [aɪm 'sɒrɪ] Es tut mir leid. **I**
Sorry I'm late. [ˌsɒri‿aɪm 'leɪt] Tut mir leid, dass ich zu spät komme. **I**
to feel sorry for [fiːl 'sɒri] Mitleid haben mit; bedauern **III**
to **sort** [sɔːt] sortieren **I**
to sort out [sɔːt 'aʊt] klären, regeln **I**
soul [səʊl] Seele ⟨**VU2,** 35⟩; **VU4,** 77
sound [saʊnd] Geräusch **I**; Laut **I**
sound effect ['saʊnd‿ɪˌfekt] Geräuscheffekt, Toneffekt ⟨**VU3,** 51⟩
to **sound** [saʊnd] klingen **III**
source [sɔːs] Quelle **VU3,** 54
south [saʊθ] Süden **I**
southbound ['saʊθbaʊnd] in Richtung Süden **II**
southern ['sʌðən] südlich **IV**
souvenir [ˌsuːvn'ɪə] Andenken, Souvenir **I**
space [speɪs] Raum; Fläche **IV**
spaghetti [spə'geti] Spaghetti **I**
Spanish ['spænɪʃ] spanisch, aus Spanien; Spanisch **I**
*to **speak (to)** [spiːk tə] sprechen (mit) **I**
to speak out (about sth) [ˌspiːk‿'aʊt] seine Meinung deutlich vertreten; sich zu etw. äußern **VU4,** 75
speaker ['spiːkə] Sprecher/-in **II**
special ['speʃl] besondere/-r/-s **I**
specific [spə'sɪfɪk] genau **VU4,** 80
direct **speech** [ˌdɪrekt 'spiːtʃ] direkte Rede **III**
freedom of speech [ˌfriːdəm‿əv 'spiːtʃ] Redefreiheit **VU4,** 68
indirect speech [ˌɪndɪrekt 'spiːtʃ] indirekte Rede **III**
*to **speed** [spiːd] beschleunigen; sausen, flitzen **IV**
spell [spel] Zauber, Bann; Zauberspruch ⟨**VU1,** 13⟩
*to **spell** [spel] buchstabieren **I**
to spell sth [spel] *(hier:)* etw. bedeuten ⟨**VU1,** 14⟩
speller ['spelə] jemand, der gut/schlecht in Rechtschreibung ist **II**
spelling ['spelɪŋ] Rechtschreibung **II**
*to **spend** [spend] verbringen *(Urlaub, Zeit etc.)* **I**
to spend (on) [spend] ausgeben (für) **II**
spider ['spaɪdə] Spinne **II**
red-back (spider) [ˌredbæk 'spaɪdə] Rotrückenspinne ⟨**VU1,** 19⟩
spinach *(no pl.)* ['spɪnɪtʃ] Spinat **III**
spirit ['spɪrɪt] Geist **VU4,** 68
in **spite of** [ɪn 'spaɪt‿əv] trotz **VU4,** 71
*to **split up** [splɪt‿'ʌp] sich trennen **III**
spoken ['spəʊkn] gesprochen **VU3,** 56
spokesperson ['spəʊksˌpɜːsn] (PR-)Sprecher/-in **IV**
spoon [spuːn] Löffel **II**
sport [spɔːt] Sport, Sportart **I**

sports shop ['spɔ:ts ˌʃɒp] Sportgeschäft **I**
*to **spread** [spred] (sich) verbreiten **V U4,** 70
spring [sprɪŋ] Frühling **I**
Brussels **sprout** [ˌbrʌslz 'spraʊt] Rosenkohl **III**
sq. *(=square)* [skweə] Quadrat *(Flächeneinheit)* **V ZI,** 9
Sssh! [ʃ] Psst! **I**
stage [steɪdʒ] Bühne **III**
on stage [ɒn 'steɪdʒ] auf der Bühne **II**
stamp [stæmp] Briefmarke **II**
stance [stɑ:ns] Haltung ⟨**V U1,** 14⟩
*to **stand** [stænd] ertragen, ausstehen **III**
to stand (up) [stænd 'ʌp] (auf)stehen **I**
to stand one's ground [ˌstænd wʌnz 'graʊnd] sich behaupten ⟨**V U4,** 79⟩
double **standard** [ˌdʌbl 'stændəd] Doppelmoral **IV**; **V U4,** 79
standard of living [ˌstændəd‿əv 'lɪvɪŋ] Lebensstandard **IV**
star [stɑ:] Star **I**
pop star ['pɒp stɑ:] Popstar **I**
to **star** [stɑ:] die Hauptrolle spielen *(Film, Theater)* **IV**
stare [steə] Starren, starrer Blick ⟨**V U1,** 12⟩
to **stare** [steə] (an)starren **IV**
to stare sb/sth down [steə 'daʊn] jmdn./etw. zum Wegsehen zwingen ⟨**V U1,** 12⟩
to **start** [stɑ:t] anfangen, beginnen **I**
state [steɪt] Zustand **IV**; (Bundes)staat; Land **IV**
head of state [ˌhed‿əv 'steɪt] Staatsoberhaupt **V ZI,** 10
police state [pə'li:s ˌsteɪt] Polizeistaat **V ZI,** 10
to **state** [steɪt] erklären; aussagen; nennen **V U4,** 68
statement ['steɪtmənt] Äußerung, Erklärung **IV**
station ['steɪʃn] Station, Bahnhof **I**
gas station *(AE)* ['gæs ˌsteɪʃn] Tankstelle **IV**
radio station ['reɪdiəʊ ˌsteɪʃn] Radiosender **I**
statistics *(pl.)* [stə'tɪstɪks] Statistik ⟨**V U2,** 28⟩
stative ['steɪtɪv] **V U3,** 55
statue ['stætʃu:] Statue, Standbild **IV**
status ['steɪtəs] Status **V ZI,** 8
status symbol ['steɪtəs ˌsɪmbl] Statussymbol **V U4,** 77
to **stay** [steɪ] bleiben **II**
to stay out [steɪ 'aʊt] wegbleiben **IV**
*to **steal** [sti:l] stehlen **II**
steam engine ['sti:m ˌendʒɪn] Dampfmaschine **III**

steel [sti:l] Stahl **III**
step [step] Schritt, Stufe **III**
to **step (on)** [step] treten (auf); steigen (auf) **IV**
*to **step out of line** [ˌstep aʊt‿əv 'laɪn] aus der Reihe tanzen ⟨**V U1,** 15⟩
step-father ['stepˌfɑ:ðə] Stiefvater **I**
stereotype ['steriəʊtaɪp] Klischee, Stereotyp **V U2,** 28
stewardess ['stju:ədɪs] Stewardess **III**
stick [stɪk] Stock, Schläger **III**; Stock; Zweig; *(hier:) sehr dünne Arme und Beine, wie Stöckchen* **V U2,** 39
*to **stick out** [stɪk] (her)vorstehen, herausstehen **IV**
to be stuck [bi 'stʌk] festsitzen, feststecken; nicht weg können; hängen bleiben **IV**
still [stɪl] noch, immer noch **I**
*to **stink** [stɪŋk] stinken **I**
stomach ['stʌmək] Magen, Bauch **II**
stop [stɒp] Haltestelle **II**
to **stop** [stɒp] aufhören, beenden **I**
to stop sb doing sth [stɒp] jmdn. davon abhalten, etw. zu tun ⟨**V U3,** 52⟩
store *(AE)* [stɔ:] Laden, Geschäft **IV**
department store [dɪ'pɑ:tmənt ˌstɔ:] Kaufhaus **I**
storey ['stɔ:ri] Stock(werk) **IV**
storm [stɔ:m] Sturm, Unwetter, Gewitter **I**
to **storm away** [ˌstɔ:m‿ə'weɪ] davonstürmen ⟨**V U1,** 15⟩
stormy ['stɔ:mi] stürmisch **I**
story ['stɔ:ri] Geschichte, Erzählung **I**
storyline ['stɔ:rilaɪn] Handlung **IV**
straight [streɪt] gerade(aus); direkt **I**
straight on [streɪt‿'ɒn] geradeaus **I**
strange [streɪndʒ] merkwürdig, seltsam; fremd **III**
stranger ['streɪndʒə] Fremde/-r ⟨**V U1,** 12⟩
strategy ['strætədʒi] Strategie ⟨**V U1,** 12⟩
street [stri:t] Straße **I**
in the street [ɪn ðə 'stri:t] auf der Straße **I**
stress [stres] Betonung **III**
to **stress** [stres] betonen, hervorheben **III**
stretch [stretʃ] Abschnitt; Strecke; Stück **IV**
strict [strɪkt] streng **II**
strong [strɒŋ] stark, kräftig **I**
structure ['strʌktʃə] Struktur; Aufbau **IV**
to **strut** [strʌt] herumstolzieren ⟨**V U1,** 14⟩
student ['stju:dnt] Schüler/-in, Student/-in **II**
student council [ˌstju:dnt 'kaʊnsl] Schülerrat **IV**
studio ['stju:diəʊ] Studio **III**
to **study** ['stʌdi] studieren; lernen **V U2,** 28
stuff *(no pl.)* [stʌf] Zeug **IV**

stupid ['stju:pɪd] Blödmann, Dummkopf **V U2,** 34
stupid ['stju:pɪd] dumm, blöd **IV**
style [staɪl] Stil **II**
subject ['sʌbdʒɪkt] Subjekt, Satzgegenstand **I**; Schulfach; Thema **II**
substitute ['sʌbstɪtju:t] Ersatz ⟨**V U4,** 76⟩
suburb ['sʌbɜ:b] Vorort **IV**
subway *(AE)* ['sʌbweɪ] U-Bahn **IV**
success [sək'ses] Erfolg **II**
successful [sək'sesfl] erfolgreich **V U2,** 41
such [sʌtʃ] solche/-r/-s **III**
to **suck** [sʌk] lutschen **V U3,** 58
suddenly ['sʌdnli] plötzlich, auf einmal **I**
to **suffer** ['sʌfə] leiden **V U2,** 39
suffix ['sʌfɪks] Suffix, Nachsilbe **V U2,** 41
sugar ['ʃʊgə] Zucker **I**
to **suggest** [sə'dʒest] vorschlagen **III**
suggestion [sə'dʒestʃn] Vorschlag **III**
suit [su:t] Anzug; Kostüm **II**
to **suit sb** [su:t] passen zu **V U2,** 29
suitable ['su:təbl] geeignet; passend **V U2,** 37
to **summarize sth** ['sʌməraɪz] etw. (kurz) zusammenfassen **V U3,** 55
summer ['sʌmə] Sommer **I**
sun [sʌn] Sonne **I**
Sunday ['sʌndeɪ] Sonntag **I**
sunglasses *(pl.)* ['sʌnˌglɑ:sɪz] Sonnenbrille **I**
sunny ['sʌni] sonnig **II**
sunset ['sʌnset] Sonnenuntergang **IV**
super ['su:pə] super **III**
superlative [su:'pɜ:lətɪv] Superlativ **II**
supermarket ['su:pəˌmɑ:kɪt] Supermarkt **II**
superpower ['su:pəˌpaʊə] Supermacht **V ZI,** 8
support service [sə'pɔ:t ˌsɜ:vɪs] *(hier:)* Beratungsstelle **V U2,** 30
to **support** [sə'pɔ:t] unterstützen **IV**
*to **be supposed to** *(+ infinitive)* [bi sə'pəʊzd‿tə] (etw. tun) sollen **V U1,** 21
sure [ʃɔ:; ʃʊə] sicher **I**
to make sure [meɪk 'ʃɔ:] sich versichern **III**
to **surf** [sɜ:f] (wind)surfen **I**
to go surfing [gəʊ 'sɜ:fɪŋ] surfen gehen **I**
to surf on the Internet [ˌsɜ:f‿ɒn ði‿'ɪntənet] im Internet surfen **I**
surfer ['sɜ:fə] Surfer/-in **IV**
surfie *(coll)* ['sɜ:fi] Surfer/-in ⟨**V U1,** 21⟩
surprise [sə'praɪz] Überraschung **I**
to **surprise** [sə'praɪz] überraschen **III**
surprising [sə'praɪzɪŋ] überraschend **IV**
surroundings *(pl.)* [sə'raʊndɪŋz] Umgebung **IV**
survey ['sɜ:veɪ] Umfrage; Studie **V ZI,** 9
to **survive** [sə'vaɪv] überleben **I**
survivor [sə'vaɪvə] Überlebende/-r ⟨**V U1,** 12⟩

to swallow ['swɒləʊ] (hinunter)schlucken ⟨**V U4,** 79⟩
*__to swear__ [sweə] fluchen **IV**
sweat [swet] Schweiß **III**
sweatshirt ['swetʃɜ:t] Sweatshirt **I**
sweatshop ['swetʃɒp] Ausbeuterbetrieb **V U4,** 75
sweet [swi:t] süß **I**
sweets *(pl.)* [swi:ts] Süßigkeiten **I**
sweet shop ['swi:t ˌʃɒp] Süßwarenladen **I**
swept-back [swept 'bæk] zurückgekämmt ⟨**V U1,** 14⟩
*__to swim__ [swɪm] schwimmen **I**
swimmer ['swɪmə] Schwimmer/-in **II**
swimming ['swɪmɪŋ] Schwimmen **III**
swimming pool ['swɪmɪŋ ˌpu:l] Schwimmbad, Schwimmbecken **I**
to go swimming [gəʊ 'swɪmɪŋ] schwimmen gehen **I**
swimsuit ['swɪmsu:t] Badeanzug **I**
symbol ['sɪmbl] Symbol ⟨**V U1,** 19⟩
status symbol ['steɪtəs ˌsɪmbl] Statussymbol **V U4,** 77
sympathy ['sɪmpəθi] Mitleid, Mitgefühl; Verständnis **IV**
system ['sɪstəm] System **V ZI,** 10
railway system ['reɪlweɪ ˌsɪstəm] Eisenbahnnetz **V U2,** 28
systematic [ˌsɪstə'mætɪk] systematisch; gezielt **V ZI,** 11

T

table ['teɪbl] Tisch **I**
to clear the table [ˌklɪə ðə 'teɪbl] den Tisch abräumen **II**
to lay the table [ˌleɪ ðə 'teɪbl] den Tisch decken **II**
tablet ['tæblət] Tablette **II**
tactful ['tæktfl] taktvoll **V U2,** 29
question **tag** ['kwestʃən ˌtæg] Frageanhängsel, Bestätigungsfrage **II**
*__to take__ [teɪk] (weg)nehmen **I**; (mit)nehmen; bringen **I**; dauern, (Zeit) brauchen **III**
Take your time. [ˌteɪk jɔ: 'taɪm] Lass dir Zeit. **III**
to take a call [ˌteɪk‿ə 'kɔ:l] (Telefon) abheben, einen Anruf entgegennehmen **III**
to take a deep breath [teɪk‿ə ˌdi:p 'breθ] tief einatmen, tief Luft holen ⟨**V U4,** 79⟩
to take an exam [ˌteɪk‿ən‿ɪg'zæm] eine Prüfung schreiben; ein Examen schreiben **V U2,** 28
to take a photo [ˌteɪk‿ə 'fəʊtəʊ] ein Foto machen **I**
to take a risk [ˌteɪk‿ə 'rɪsk] ein Risiko eingehen **II**
to take a tour [ˌteɪk‿ə 'tʊə] sich auf eine Rundreise begeben **V ZI,** 9
to take away [teɪk‿ə'weɪ] wegnehmen ⟨**V U2,** 35⟩
to take notes [teɪk 'nəʊts] sich Notizen machen **I**
to take off [teɪk‿'ɒf] abnehmen, ausziehen, herunternehmen **I**; abheben **II**
to take out [teɪk‿'aʊt] ausführen **I**
to take part (in) [teɪk 'pɑ:t] teilnehmen (an) **IV**
to take sb's word for it [teɪk ˌsʌmbədiz 'wɜ:d fɔ:r‿ɪt] jmdm. glauben **IV**
to take the chance [ˌteɪk ðə 'tʃɑ:ns] es darauf ankommen lassen, das Risiko eingehen **III**
to take the register [ˌteɪk ðə 'redʒɪstə] Anwesenheitskontrolle durchführen **II**
to take turns [teɪk 'tɜ:nz] sich abwechseln **I**
talk [tɔ:k] Gespräch, Unterhaltung; Unterredung **III**
small talk ['smɔ:l ˌtɔ:k] Smalltalk **III**
talk show ['tɔ:k ˌʃəʊ] Talkshow **IV**
to **talk** [tɔ:k] sprechen, reden **I**
to talk about [tɔ:k ə'baʊt] sprechen über **I**
to talk to [tɔ:k tə] sprechen mit, reden mit **I**
talkwise ['tɔ:kwaɪz] „redegewandt" **III**
tall [tɔ:l] groß; hoch **II**
target ['tɑ:gɪt] Ziel(scheibe) **V U4,** 79
Tasmanian devil [tæzˌmeɪniən 'devl] Beutelteufel ⟨**V U1,** 19⟩
taste [teɪst] Geschmack **III**
to **taste** [teɪst] schmecken **III**
tasty ['teɪsti] lecker **I**
taxi ['tæksi] Taxi **I**
tea [ti:] Tee **I**; (frühes) Abendessen **III**
*__to teach__ [ti:tʃ] unterrichten, lehren, beibringen **I**
teacher ['ti:tʃə] Lehrer/-in **I**
German teacher ['dʒɜ:mən ˌti:tʃə] Deutschlehrer/-in **I**
team [ti:m] Team, Gruppe **I**
*__to be in tears__ [ˌbi‿ɪn 'tɪəz] weinen ⟨**V U1,** 15⟩
*__to tear apart__ [teər‿ə'pɑ:t] auseinanderreißen; zerreißen **V ZI,** 11
technical ['teknɪkl] technisch **V U2,** 29
technology [tek'nɒlədʒi] Technologie; Computerunterricht **II**
teddy bear ['tedi ˌbeə] Teddybär ⟨**V U1,** 19⟩
teen [ti:n] Teenager; Jugendliche/-r **IV**
teenager ['ti:neɪdʒə] Teenager; Jugendliche/-r **II**
telegram ['telɪgræm] Telegramm **III**
telephone ['telɪfəʊn] Telefon **III**
teletext ['telɪˌtekst] Videotext **V U3,** 56
television ['telɪvɪʒn] Fernsehapparat, Fernseher; Fernsehen **V U3,** 50; **V U3,** 52
*__to tell__ [tel] erzählen, sagen **I**
to tell a lie [ˌtel‿ə 'laɪ] lügen **III**
to tell the time [ˌtel ðə 'taɪm] die Uhr lesen **I**
telly *(= television)* ['teli] Fernseher, Glotze **V U3,** 59
temperature ['temprətʃə] Fieber; Temperatur **II**
ten [ten] zehn **I**
tennis ['tenɪs] Tennis **III**
tense [tens] Zeit, Zeitform *(grammatisch)* **II**
tense shift ['tens ʃɪft] Zeitenverschiebung *(gramm.)* ⟨**V U4,** 76⟩
tent [tent] Zelt **V U2,** 38
term [tɜ:m] Begriff **IV**
on one's own terms [ɒn wʌnz ˌəʊn 'tɜ:mz] unter den eigenen Bedingungen ⟨**V U1,** 15⟩
terminal ['tɜ:mɪnl] Terminal **II**
rooftop **terrace** [ˌru:ftɒp 'terɪs] Dachterrasse **V U1,** 18
terrible ['terəbl] schrecklich, schlimm, furchtbar **I**
terrified ['terəfaɪd] erschrocken; verängstigt **V U4,** 74
to be terrified (of sth) [bi 'terəfaɪd‿əv] (große) Angst (vor etw.) haben ⟨**V U1,** 12⟩
territory ['terɪtri] Gebiet, Revier, Territorium **I**
terrorist ['terərɪst] Terrorist/-in **IV**
test [test] Test, Prüfung **I**
to **test** [test] testen, prüfen **II**
text [tekst] Text **I**; SMS **II**
factual text [ˌfæktʃʊəl 'tekst] Sachtext **III**
to **text** [tekst] eine SMS schicken **I**
than [ðæn; ðən] als **II**
to **thank** [θæŋk] danken **IV**
thank you ['θæŋk ju] danke **I**
thanks [θæŋks] danke **I**
thanks a lot [ˌθæŋks‿ə 'lɒt] vielen Dank **I**
thanks to ['θæŋks tə] dank (dir/Ihnen), wegen **I**
that [ðæt] so *(Betonung)* **II**
that [ðæt; ðət] dass **I**
that [ðæt] das; jenes **I**
that day [ðæt 'deɪ] an jenem Tag **I**
That was lucky! [ˌðæt wəz 'lʌki] Glück gehabt! **III**
that [ðæt; ðət] der, dem, den, die, das *(Relativpronomen)* **III**
the [ðə; ði] der, die *(auch pl.)*, das **I**
the French *(pl.)* [ðə 'frenʃ] die Franzosen **IV**
the six/... of us [ðə 'sɪks‿əv‿əs] uns sechs **II**
the ... the ... [ðə ... ðə] je ... desto ... **II**
theatre ['θɪətə] Theater **II**

their [ðeə] ihr, ihre *(Plural)* **I**

them [ðem; ðəm] sie *(Plural)* **I**

theme [θi:m] Thema; Motto **II**

theme park ['θi:m pɑ:k] Themenpark **II**

themselves [ðəm'selvz] selber **III**

then [ðen] dann, danach **I**

there [ðeə] da, dort **I**; dorthin, dahin **I**

over there [ˌəʊvə 'ðeə] (nach) dort drüben **I**

There she is. ['ðeə ʃi‿ɪz] Da ist sie ja. **I**

You've got me there! [jʊv ˌgɒt mi 'ðeə] Da habt ihr mich kalt erwischt! **I**

therefore ['ðeəfɔ:] deshalb, deswegen, daher **VU3,** 59

these [ði:z] diese (hier) **I**

these days ['ði:z deɪz] heutzutage **VU3,** 55

they [ðeɪ] sie **I**

thick [θɪk] dick **VU4,** 73

thief pl. **thieves** [θi:f; θi:vz] Dieb, Diebin **I**

thin [θɪn] dünn **II**

to end in thin air [ˌend‿ɪn θɪn‿'eə] im Nichts enden **II**

thing [θɪŋ] Ding, Sache **I**

First things first. [ˌfɜ:st θɪŋz 'fɜ:st] Das Wichtigste zuerst. **III**

thingummy *(coll)* ['θɪŋəmi] der/die/das Dings(da) *(ugs.)* ⟨**VU2,** 41⟩

*to **think** [θɪŋk] (nach)denken, finden, glauben **I**

to think about [θɪŋk‿ə'baʊt] halten von, denken über **I**

to think of ['θɪŋk‿əv] halten von, denken über **I**; (sich) ausdenken, sich etwas einfallen lassen **I**

third [θɜ:d] dritte/-r/-s **I**

the third of March [ðə ˌθɜ:d‿əv 'mɑ:tʃ] der dritte März **I**

thirteen [θɜ:'ti:n] dreizehn **I**

thirty ['θɜ:ti] dreißig **I**

this [ðɪs] diese/-r/-s **I**

like this [laɪk 'ðɪs] so, auf diese Weise **I**

this is ... ['ðɪs‿ɪz] hier ist ... *(am Telefon)* **I**

this morning [ðɪs 'mɔ:nɪŋ] heute Morgen **I**

thongs *(pl.)* [θɒŋz] Flip-Flops *(AE; Aus)* ⟨**VU1,** 14⟩

those [ðəʊz] diese (dort), jene **I**

though [ðəʊ] (je)doch **VU4,** 77

thought [θɔ:t] Gedanke **VU4,** 77

a, one **thousand** [ə 'θaʊznd; wʌn 'θaʊznd] eintausend **I**

threatening ['θretnɪŋ] bedrohlich ⟨**VU1,** 12⟩

three [θri:] drei **I**

*to be **thrilled** [bi 'θrɪld] aus dem Häuschen sein vor Freude **IV**

thriller ['θrɪlə] Thriller; spannender Krimi; Schauergeschichte **III**

throne [θrəʊn] Thron **III**

through [θru:] durch **II**

*to **throw** [θrəʊ] werfen **I**

to throw around [ˌθrəʊ‿ə'raʊnd] hin und her werfen; herumwerfen **VU2,** 38

to throw sth back in sb's face [θrəʊ ˌbæk ɪn ˌsʌmbədiz 'feɪs] jmdm. etw. wieder auftischen ⟨**VU1,** 15⟩

thunderstorm ['θʌndəstɔ:m] Gewitter **II**

Thursday ['θɜ:zdeɪ] Donnerstag **I**

ticket ['tɪkɪt] Ticket, Fahrschein; Eintrittskarte **II**

ticket gate ['tɪkɪt ˌgeɪt] Fahrkartenschranke **II**

to **tidy (up)** [taɪdi 'ʌp] aufräumen, in Ordnung bringen **III**

to **tie** [taɪ] binden, zubinden **III**

to tie up [taɪ‿'ʌp] fesseln **VU3,** 59

tiger ['taɪgə] Tiger **I**

tight [taɪt] fest, eng **III**

till [tɪl] bis ⟨**VU4,** 78⟩

time [taɪm] Zeit **I**; Mal **II**

all the time [ˌɔ:l ðə 'taɪm] die ganze Zeit **II**

at any time [æt‿eni 'taɪm] jederzeit **IV**

at the same time [ət ðə ˌseɪm 'taɪm] zur selben Zeit, gleichzeitig **I**

at times [ət 'taɪmz] ab und zu; hin und wieder; zeitweise ⟨**VU3,** 53⟩

from time to time [frəm ˌtaɪm tə 'taɪm] von Zeit zu Zeit **I**

It's time to go home. [ɪts ˌtaɪm tə gəʊ 'həʊm] Es ist Zeit, nach Hause zu gehen. **I**

Once upon a time ... ['wʌns‿əˌpɒn‿ə 'taɪm] Es war einmal ... **III**

on time [ɒn 'taɪm] pünktlich **III**

running time ['rʌnɪŋ‿taɪm] Laufzeit **IV**

Take your time. [ˌteɪk jɔ: 'taɪm] Lass dir Zeit. **III**

time line ['taɪm laɪn] Zeitstrahl **II**

to tell the time [ˌtel ðə 'taɪm] die Uhr lesen **I**

What time is it, please? [wɒt 'taɪm‿ɪz‿ɪt ˌpli:z] Wie spät ist es, bitte? **I**

timebox ['taɪmbɒks] Zeitmaschine **II**

timeless ['taɪmləs] zeitlos **VU4,** 80

timetable ['taɪmteɪbl] Stundenplan; Fahrplan **II**

tin [tɪn] Dose, Büchse **I**

tiny ['taɪni] klein, winzig **I**

tip [tɪp] Tipp, Ratschlag **I**

tired ['taɪəd] müde **I**

dog-tired [dɒg'taɪəd] hundemüde **I**

to be tired of *(+ gerund)* [bi 'taɪəd‿əv] einer Sache/jmds. überdrüssig sein **IV**

to get tired of [get 'taɪəd‿əv] etwas satt bekommen **III**

title ['taɪtl] Titel **I**

to [tu:; tʊ; tə] nach, zu, in **I**; an **I**; vor *(bei Uhrzeitangaben)* **I**

To us! [tə‿'ʌs] Auf uns! **IV**

toast [təʊst] Toast **II**

today [tə'deɪ] heute **I**

toe [təʊ] Zeh **II**

together [tə'geðə] zusammen; gemeinsam **I**

toilet ['tɔɪlət] Toilette **I**

tolerance ['tɒlrns] Toleranz **VU4,** 68

tolerant ['tɒlrnt] tolerant **VU4,** 73

to **tolerate sth** ['tɒlreɪt] etw. tolerieren; etw. dulden **VU4,** 69

tomorrow [tə'mɒrəʊ] morgen **II**

tone [təʊn] (Signal)Ton **III**

tongue [tʌŋ] Zunge **II**

mother tongue ['mʌðə tʌŋ] Muttersprache **II**

too [tu:] auch **I**; zu **I**

too brilliant for words [tu: 'brɪliənt fə ˌwɜ:dz] zu schön, um es in Worte zu fassen **IV**

too much [tu: 'mʌtʃ] zu viel **I**

tooth pl. **teeth** [tu:θ; ti:θ] Zahn **I**

to brush one's teeth [brʌʃ wʌnz 'ti:θ] (seine) Zähne putzen **III**

top [tɒp] oberes Ende, Spitze **I**; Top **II**

on the top [ɒn ðə 'tɒp] oben **I**

on top of [ɒn 'tɒp‿əv] auf ... hinauf, oben (auf) **I**

to be on top of the world [bi ɒn ˌtɒp‿əv ðə 'wɜ:ld] überglücklich sein **IV**

top 10 [ˌtɒp 'ten] Top 10, die besten Zehn **I**

topic ['tɒpɪk] Thema **III**

top-up card ['tɒp‿ʌp kɑ:d] Aufladekarte *(fürs Handy)* **II**

tornado [tɔ:'neɪdəʊ] Tornado ⟨**VU2,** 38⟩

total ['təʊtl] gesamt ⟨**VU3,** 53⟩

tour [tʊə] Reise, Tour, Rundgang **I**

to give tours [gɪv 'tʊəz] Stadtrundfahrten leiten **I**

to take a tour [ˌteɪk‿ə 'tʊə] sich auf eine Rundreise begeben **VZI,** 9

tourist ['tʊərɪst] Tourist/-in **I**

towards [tə'wɔ:dz] in Richtung; auf ... zu, darauf zu **IV**

towel ['taʊəl] Handtuch **IV**

tower ['taʊə] Turm **III**

town [taʊn] Stadt **I**

seaside town [ˌsi:saɪd 'taʊn] Küstenstadt **I**

township ['taʊnʃɪp] Township *(von Schwarzen und Farbigen bewohnte, abseits der Städte gelegene Siedlungen in Südafrika)* **VZI,** 10

toy [tɔɪ] Spielzeug **II**

track [træk] Gleis; Spur **III**; Bahn, Laufbahn; Weg **III**; (Ton)Spur **VU3,** 51

tradition [trə'dɪʃn] Tradition **III**

traffic ['træfɪk] Verkehr **II**

tragedy ['trædʒədi] Tragödie ⟨**VU3,** 59⟩

trail [treɪl] Weg, Pfad **IV**

trailer ['treɪlə] Wohnwagen **VU2,** 38

train [treɪn] Zug **I**

on a train [ɒn͜ ə 'treɪn] im Zug **I**
train of events [ˌtreɪn͜ əv͜ ɪ'vents] Reihe von Vorfällen/Ereignissen ⟨**V U1,** 13⟩
to **train** [treɪn] trainieren **II**
to train sb (in sth) ['treɪn͜ ɪn] jmdn. (in etw.) ausbilden **V U2,** 30
trainer ['treɪnə] Trainer/-in **II**
trainers ['treɪnəz] Turnschuhe **II**
training ['treɪnɪŋ] Training, Ausbildung **II**
transcontinental [ˌtrænsˌkɒntɪ'nentl] transkontinental **IV**
to **translate** [trænz'leɪt] übersetzen **III**
transport *(no pl.)* ['trænspɔ:t] Verkehrsmittel, Beförderung **I**
public **transportation** *(no pl.)* [ˌpʌblɪk ˌtrænspɔ:'teɪʃn] öffentliche Verkehrsmittel **IV**
*to be **trapped** [bi 'træpt] eingeschlossen sein; in der Falle sitzen **III**
trash *(AE)* [træʃ] Abfall, Müll **IV**
travel agency ['trævl ˌeɪdʒnsi] Reisebüro **III**
Tube travel ['tju:b ˌtrævl] U-Bahn-Fahren **II**
to **travel** ['trævl] reisen, fahren **II**
travelcard ['trævlkɑ:d] Netzkarte **II**
traveller ['trævlə] Reisende/-r **III**
travelling ['trævlɪŋ] (das) Reisen **II**
treasure ['treʒə] Schatz **I**
treasure map ['treʒə ˌmæp] Schatzkarte **I**
to **treat** [tri:t] behandeln **IV**
tree [tri:] Baum **I**
trend [trend] Trend; Entwicklung; Richtung **IV**
trendy ['trendi] trendy **III**
tribe [traɪb] (Volks)stamm **IV**
trick [trɪk] Trick, Kunststück **I**
card trick ['kɑ:d ˌtrɪk] Kartenkunststück **I**
to play a trick on [ˌpleɪ͜ ə 'trɪk͜ ɒn] einen Streich spielen **II**
trip [trɪp] Reise, Fahrt, Ausflug **I**
class trip [ˌklɑ:s 'trɪp] Klassenfahrt, Klassenausflug **I**
road trip ['rəʊd trɪp] Tour, Trip **V U1,** 20
trouble ['trʌbl] Ärger, Schwierigkeiten **I**; Sorge; Problem **IV**
to get into trouble [ˌget͜ ɪntə 'trʌbl] in Schwierigkeiten geraten **II**
trousers *(pl.)* ['traʊzəz] Hose **II**
true [tru:] wahr **II**
truly ['tru:li] wirklich, wahrhaftig ⟨**V U2,** 35⟩
truth [tru:θ] Wahrheit **IV**
to **try** [traɪ] versuchen, probieren **II**
to try hard [traɪ 'hɑ:d] sich anstrengen **II**
to try on [traɪ͜ 'ɒn] anprobieren **I**
to try out [traɪ͜ 'aʊt] ausprobieren **III**
T-shirt ['ti:ʃɜ:t] T-Shirt **I**
tube [tju:b] Tube **III**
Tube [tju:b] U-Bahn **II**
Tube travel ['tju:b ˌtrævl] U-Bahn-Fahren **II**
Tuesday ['tju:zdeɪ] Dienstag **I**
tundra ['tʌndrə] Tundra **V ZI,** 10
tunnel ['tʌnl] Tunnel **I**
Turkish ['tɜ:kɪʃ] türkisch, aus der Türkei; Türkisch **I**
*to take **turns** [teɪk 'tɜ:nz] sich abwechseln **I**
Your turn. ['jɔ: tɜ:n] Du bist dran. **I**
to **turn** [tɜ:n] einbiegen, abbiegen **I**; (sich) drehen ⟨**V U1,** 21⟩; (herum)drehen **V U2,** 38
to turn away from sb/sth [ˌtɜ:n͜ ə'weɪ frəm] sich von jmdm./etw. abwenden **V U3,** 58
to turn into [tɜ:n͜ 'ɪntə] (sich) verwandeln in; werden **III**
to turn off [tɜ:n͜ 'ɒf] abschalten, ausschalten **III**
to turn on sb/sth ['tɜ:n͜ ɒn] sich gegen jmdn./etw. wenden ⟨**V U1,** 15⟩
to turn out to be [tɜ:n͜ 'aʊt tə ˌbi:] sich herausstellen als **IV**
to turn right [ˌtɜ:n 'raɪt] (nach) rechts abbiegen **I**
to turn to sb ['tɜ:n͜ tə] sich an jmdn. wenden; sich jmdm./etw. zuwenden ⟨**V U1,** 14⟩
turning point ['tɜ:nɪŋ ˌpɔɪnt] Wendepunkt **V U1,** 20
tutor ['tju:tə] Klassenlehrer/-in **I**
tutor group ['tju:tə gru:p] Klasse *(in einer englischen Schule)* **I**
tutorial [tju:'tɔ:riəl] Tutorium **II**
tutorial [tju:'tɒ:riəl] Anleitung ⟨**V U3,** 51⟩
TV [ˌti:'vi:] Fernseher **I**
on TV [ɒn ˌti:'vi:] im Fernsehen **I**
twelve [twelv] zwölf **I**
twenty ['twenti] zwanzig **I**
twenty-one [ˌtwenti'wʌn] einundzwanzig **I**
twin [twɪn] Zwilling, Zwillings- **III**
in the **twinkling of an eye** [ɪn ðə ˌtwɪŋklɪŋ͜ əvn͜ 'aɪ] im Nu; im Handumdrehen ⟨**V U1,** 13⟩
two [tu:] zwei **I**
type [taɪp] Typ, Art, Sorte **III**
normal type ['nɔ:ml taɪp] Normalschrift **V U3,** 58
typically ['tɪpɪkli] typisch **IV**
tyrant ['taɪrənt] Tyrann/-in **V U4,** 77

U

ugh [ʊh] i, igitt **I**
ugly ['ʌgli] hässlich **IV**
uh [ə] äh **I**
um [əm] ähm **III**
umpire ['ʌmpaɪə] Schiedsrichter/-in **III**
*to be **unable to do sth** [bi ʌn'eɪbl tə] unfähig sein, etw. zu tun; nicht in der Lage sein, etw. zu tun **V U3,** 55
unable [ʌn'eɪbl] unfähig, außerstande **V U3,** 55
unchanging [ʌn'tʃəɪndʒɪŋ] unveränderlich, gleich bleibend ⟨**V U1,** 12⟩
uncle ['ʌŋkl] Onkel **I**
uncontrolled [ˌʌnkən'trəʊld] unkontrolliert ⟨**V U1,** 13⟩
under ['ʌndə] unter **I**
Underground ['ʌndəgraʊnd] U-Bahn **I**
to **underline** [ˌʌndə'laɪn] unterstreichen **I**
*to **understand** [ˌʌndə'stænd] verstehen **II**
uneducated [ʌn'edʒʊkeɪtɪd] ungebildet **V U4,** 77
unforgettable [ˌʌnfə'getəbl] unvergesslich **IV**
unfortunately [ʌn'fɔ:tʃnətli] leider; unglücklicherweise **IV**
ungrateful [ʌn'greɪtfl] undankbar ⟨**V U1,** 15⟩
uni(versity) ['ju:nɪ, ˌju:nɪ'vɜ:səti] Uni(versität) ⟨**V U1,** 14⟩
uniform ['ju:nɪfɔ:m] Uniform **II**
European **Union** [ˌjʊərəˌpi:ən 'ju:njən] Europäische Union **III**
unique [ju:'ni:k] einzigartig **V ZI,** 11
unit ['ju:nɪt] Lektion, Kapitel, Einheit **I**
universal [ju:nɪ'vɜ:sl] allgemein, universell **II**
universe ['ju:nɪvɜ:s] Universum **II**
university [ˌju:nɪ'vɜ:səti] Universität **V U2,** 31
*to be **unlucky** [bi ʌn'lʌki] Pech haben **III**
until [ʌn'tɪl] bis **II**
not until [nɒt ʌn'tɪl] erst (dann), wenn **III**
unusual [ʌn'ju:ʒl] ungewöhnlich **III**
It's **up to you.** [ɪts͜ ʌp tə 'ju:] Es ist an dir (zu entscheiden)./Wie du willst. **V U2,** 39
What's up? [wɒts͜ 'ʌp] Was ist los? **I**
*to come **up to** [kʌm͜ 'ʌp tə] zukommen auf **II**
up North [ʌp 'nɔ:θ] im Norden **III**
upside-down [ˌʌpsaɪd 'daʊn] auf den Kopf gestellt **V U2,** 38
upstairs [ʌp'steəz] oben, im Obergeschoss **I**
UR *(= you are)* [ju: 'ɑ:] du bist *(Abkürzung in SMS oder E-Mail)* **III**
us [ʌs; əs] uns **I**
to **use** [ju:z] benutzen, verwenden, gebrauchen **I**
to get used to (sth) [get͜ 'ju:zd tə] sich an (etwas) gewöhnen **II**

to get used to *(+gerund)* [get͜ ˈjuːzd tə] sich gewöhnen (an) **IV**
used to (+ infinitive) [ˈjuːs͜ tə] früher; pflegte(n) zu **V U1,** 17
useful [ˈjuːsfl] nützlich, hilfreich **I**
usually [ˈjuːʒli] gewöhnlich, normalerweise **I**

V

vacation *(AE)* [vəˈkeɪʃn] Ferien, Urlaub **IV**
values *(pl.)* [ˈvæljuːz] Werte, Wertvorstellungen **IV**
van [væn] Lieferwagen, Transporter **III**
vegetable [ˈvedʒtəbl] Gemüse **II**
vegetarian [ˌvedʒɪˈteəriən] Vegetarier/-in **III**
verb [vɜːb] Verb, Zeitwort **I**
phrasal verb [ˌfreɪzl ˈvɜːb] *phrasal verb (Verb + Präposition oder Partikel)* **IV**
verb of perception [ˌvɜːb͜ əv pəˈsepʃn] Verb der Wahrnehmung **V U2,** 35
version [ˈvɜːʃn] Version **V U1,** 17
very [ˈveri] sehr **I**
vet [vet] Tierarzt, Tierärztin **I**
Victorian [vɪkˈtɔːriən] viktorianisch; Viktorianer/-in **III**
video [ˈvɪdiəʊ] Video **I**
view [vjuː] (Aus)Sicht, (Aus)Blick **II**; Ansicht, Einstellung; Standpunkt **V U3,** 56
in sb's view [ɪn ˈsʌmbədiz vjuː] jmds. Meinung nach **IV**
point of view [ˌpɔɪnt͜ əv͜ ˈvjuː] Ansicht, Einstellung; Standpunkt ⟨**V U1,** 14⟩; **V U1,** 16
viewer [ˈvjuːə] (Fernseh)Zuschauer/-in ⟨**V U3,** 53⟩; **V U3,** 60
village [ˈvɪlɪdʒ] Dorf **I**
violence *(no pl.)* [ˈvaɪəlns] Gewalt **III**
violent [ˈvaɪəlnt] gewalttätig **III**
vision [ˈvɪʒn] Vision **III**
to **visit** [ˈvɪzɪt] besuchen **I**
visitor [ˈvɪzɪtə] Besucher/-in **I**
vocabulary [vəˈkæbjəlri] Vokabular, Wortschatz **I**
vocals [ˈvəʊklz] Gesang ⟨**V U3,** 51⟩
voice [vɔɪs] Stimme **II**
male voice choir [ˌmeɪl vɔɪs ˈkwaɪə] Männerchor **III**
voice mail [ˈvɔɪs meɪl] Voicemail; Mailbox **III**
voice-over [ˈvɔɪsəʊvə] Offkommentar; Hintergrundkommentar **V U3,** 58
volleyball [ˈvɒlibɔːl] Volleyball **I**
volunteer [ˌvɒlənˈtɪə] Freiwillige/-r; ehrenamtliche/-r Helfer/-in **V U2,** 33
to **vote** [vəʊt] wählen; (für/gegen jmdn.) stimmen **V U4,** 70
to **vote for** [ˈvəʊt fɔː] wählen; stimmen für **II**

W

waggle [ˈwægl] wackeln; fuchteln ⟨**V U1,** 13⟩
covered **wagon** [ˌkʌvəd ˈwægən] Planwagen **IV**
to **wait** [weɪt] warten **I**
Just you wait! [dʒʌst ju͜ ˈweɪt] Wirst schon sehen! **V U2,** 34
to wait for [ˈweɪt fə] warten auf **I**
waiter [ˈweɪtə] Kellner, Bedienung **II**
waiting room [ˈweɪtɪŋ ˌrʊm] Wartezimmer **V U2,** 35
waitress [ˈweɪtrɪs] Kellnerin, Bedienung **II**
*to **wake up** [weɪk͜ ˈʌp] aufwecken; aufwachen **I**
to **walk** [wɔːk] gehen *(zu Fuß)* **I**
to walk past [wɔːk ˈpɑːst] vorbeigehen, vorbeilaufen **III**
to walk the dog [wɔːk ðə ˈdɒg] den Hund ausführen **I**
walkabout [ˈwɔːkəbaʊt] *(eine rituelle, sechsmonatige Wanderung durch das Outback, auf die die Aborigines ihre dreizehnjährigen Jungen schicken)* ⟨**V U1,** 12⟩
wall [wɔːl] Wand, Mauer **I**
rock **wallaby** [ˌrɒk ˈwɒləbi] Wallaby *(austral. Beuteltier)* ⟨**V U1,** 12⟩
wallet [ˈwɒlɪt] Brieftasche; Geldbörse **V U2,** 40
to **want** [wɒnt] wollen, mögen **I**
I want to ... [aɪ ˈwɒnt tə] ich möchte .../ich will ... **I**
to want to know [ˌwɒnt tə ˈnəʊ] wissen wollen **I**
war [wɔː] Krieg **IV**
World War II [ˌwɜːld ˌwɔː ˈtuː] der Zweite Weltkrieg **III**
wardrobe [ˈwɔːdrəʊb] Kleiderschrank **I**
warm [wɔːm] warm **I**
to **warn sb** [wɔːn] jmdn. warnen; jmdn. ermahnen **III**
warning [ˈwɔːnɪŋ] Warnung **II**
to **wash** [wɒʃ] waschen **I**; wegschwemmen, wegspülen ⟨**V U4,** 78⟩
to wash up [wɒʃ͜ ˈʌp] abwaschen, abspülen **II**
washing machine [ˈwɒʃɪŋ məˌʃiːn] Waschmaschine ⟨**V U3,** 50⟩
to **waste** [weɪst] verschwenden **IV**
watch [wɒtʃ] Armbanduhr **II**
to **watch** [wɒtʃ] ansehen; beobachten **I**
to watch out [wɒtʃ ˈaʊt] aufpassen **I**
water [ˈwɔːtə] Wasser **I**
to **water** [ˈwɔːtə] gießen, bewässern **IV**
waterfront [ˈwɔːtəfrʌnt] Hafenviertel; Ufer **III**
wave [weɪv] Welle, Woge **I**; Wink **III**
to **wave** [weɪv] winken **III**
wax [wæks] Wachs **III**
waxed [wækst] gewachst **II**
way [weɪ] Weg **I**; Art und Weise **II**
a good way to ... [ə͜ ˌgʊd ˈweɪ tə] eine gute Möglichkeit ... **II**
no way [nəʊ ˈweɪ] keine Möglichkeit; kein Weg ⟨**V U3,** 53⟩; auf keinen Fall; keineswegs **V U3,** 56
No way! [ˌnəʊ ˈweɪ] Was?!/Echt?!/Nie im Leben! **III**
on his way [ˌɒn hɪz ˈweɪ] auf dem Weg, unterwegs **I**
to find one's way around [ˌfaɪnd wʌnz ˌweɪ əˈraʊnd] sich zurecht finden **IV**
to get in the way [ˌget͜ ɪn ðə ˈweɪ] stören, im Weg stehen **III**
to get out of the way [get ˌaʊt͜ əv ðə ˈweɪ] aus dem Weg gehen **IV**
way out [weɪ ˈaʊt] Ausweg **IV**
we [wiː; wi] wir **I**
weak [wiːk] schwach **II**
weakness [ˈwiːknəs] Schwäche ⟨**V U1,** 12⟩; **V U2,** 41
wealth [welθ] Wohlstand; Reichtum **V ZI,** 10
weapon [ˈwepən] Waffe ⟨**V U1,** 12⟩
*to **wear** [weə] anhaben, tragen **II**
to wear off [weər͜ ˈɒf] nachlassen **IV**
weather [ˈweðə] Wetter **II**
weather forecast [ˈweðə ˌfɔːkɑːst] Wettervorhersage **V U2,** 34
web [web] Netz **II**
web browser [ˈweb ˌbraʊzə] Webbrowser **III**
website [ˈwebsaɪt] Website **II**
Wednesday [ˈwenzdeɪ] Mittwoch **I**
weed [wiːd] Unkraut **IV**
week [wiːk] Woche **I**
days of the week *(pl.)* [ˌdeɪz͜ ɒv ðə ˈwiːk] Wochentage *(pl.)* **I**
weekend [ˌwiːkˈend] Wochenende **I**
at the weekend [æt ðə ˌwiːkˈend] am Wochenende **I**
to **weigh** [weɪ] wiegen **II**
weight [weɪt] Gewicht **IV**
weird [wɪəd] merkwürdig, seltsam **III**
welcome [ˈwelkəm] Empfang **III**
You're **welcome.** [jɔː ˈwelkəm] Bitte schön./Nichts zu danken./Gern geschehen. **I**
welcome [ˈwelkəm] Willkommen **II**
well [wel] gut **II**
to do well [duː ˈwel] gute Leistungen erbringen **IV**
well [wel] tja, nun **I**
welly pl. **wellies** [ˈweli; weliz] Gummistiefel **I**
Welsh [welʃ] walisisch; Walisisch **III**
west [west] Westen **I**
out West [aʊt ˈwest] draußen im Westen **IV**
western [ˈwestən] westlich **V U4,** 70
wet [wet] nass **II**
what [wɒt] was **I**

What about … ? [wɒt‿ə'baʊt] Was ist mit … ? **I**
What a stroke of luck! [wɒt‿ə ˌstrəʊk‿əv 'lʌk] Was für ein Glückstreffer! **III**
what else [ˌwɒt‿'els] was (sonst) noch **II**
What is … like? [ˌwɒt‿ɪz 'laɪk] Wie ist … ? **II**
what it looks like [ˌwɒt‿ɪt 'lʊks laɪk] wie es aussieht **I**
what's (= what is) [wɒts; ˌwɒt 'ɪz] was ist **I**
What's going on? [wɒts ˌgəʊɪŋ‿'ɒn] Was ist denn hier los? **III**
What's up? [wɒts‿'ʌp] Was ist los? **I**
What's your name? [wɒts jɔ: 'neɪm] Wie heißt du? **I**
What time is it, please? [wɒt 'taɪm‿ɪz‿ɪt ˌpli:z] Wie spät ist es, bitte? **I**
whatsit *(coll)* ['wɒtsɪt] Dingsda, Dings *(ugs.)* **V U2**, 34
wheel [wi:l] Steuerrad, Steuer, Rad **I**
wheelchair ['wi:ltʃeə] Rollstuhl **III**
when [wen] wenn, als **I**; wann **I**
where [weə] wo, wohin, woher **I**
Where are you from? [ˌweər‿ə jə 'frɒm] Woher kommst du? **I**
wherever [weə'revə] wo(hin) auch immer, egal wo(hin) **III**
whether ['weðə] ob **III**
which [wɪtʃ] welche/-r/-s **I**
which [wɪtʃ] der, dem, den, die, das *(Relativpronomen)* **III**
while [waɪl] während **II**
to whirl around [ˌwɜ:l‿ə'raʊnd] sich abrupt umdrehen, herumfahren ⟨**V U1**, 13⟩
whistle ['wɪsl] Pfiff, Pfeifen **III**
white [waɪt] weiß **I**
whiz-kid ['wɪzkɪd] kluger Kopf **V U2**, 30
who [hu:] wer **I**
Who's in it? [hu:z 'ɪn‿ɪt] Wer spielt mit? **III**
who [hu:] die *(Relativpronomen)* **III**
whoever [hu:'evə] wer auch immer **III**
whole [həʊl] ganz **I**
whore *(vulg)* [hɔ:] Nutte; Flittchen *(derb)* ⟨**V U4**, 79⟩
whose [hu:z] dessen, deren *(Relativpronomen)* **III**
why [waɪ] warum **I**
wicked *(coll)* ['wɪkɪd] super, cool **II**
wide shot ['waɪd ʃɒt] Totale *(Kameraeinstellung)* **V U3**, 58
wife pl. **wives** [waɪf, waɪvz] Ehefrau **II**
wild [waɪld] wild **I**
will [wɪl] Wille **I**
***to win** [wɪn] gewinnen **I**
wind [wɪnd] Wind **I**
window ['wɪndəʊ] Fenster **I**
windy ['wɪndi] windig **I**
wing [wɪŋ] Flügel **III**
winner ['wɪnə] Gewinner/-in **I**
winter ['wɪntə] Winter **I**
wise [waɪz] weise **III**
wish [wɪʃ] Wunsch **IV**
to wish [wɪʃ] (sich) wünschen **III**
witch [wɪtʃ] Hexe **III**
witchetty grub [ˌwɪtʃəti 'grʌb] Witchetty-Made; Holzbohrerlarve **V U1**, 17
with [wɪð] mit **I**
to be with … [bi 'wɪð] bei … sein **I**
without [wɪ'ðaʊt] ohne **II**
woman pl. **women** ['wʊmən; 'wɪmɪn] Frau **I**
wonder ['wʌndə] Wunder **I**
to wonder ['wʌndə] sich fragen **III**
wonderful ['wʌndəfl] wunderbar **IV**
wood [wʊd] Holz **III**
Woof! [wʊf] Wau! **I**
Woosh! [wʊʃ] Zisch! **I**
word [wɜ:d] Wort **I**
question word ['kwestʃən ˌwɜ:d] Fragewort **I**
signal word ['sɪgnl ˌwɜ:d] Signalwort **I**
too brilliant for words [tu: 'brɪliənt fə ˌwɜ:dz] zu schön, um es in Worte zu fassen **IV**
to put sth into words [pʊt ˌɪntə 'wɜ:dz] etw. in Worte fassen **IV**
to take sb's word for it [teɪk ˌsʌmbədiz 'wɜ:d fɔ:r‿ɪt] jmdm. glauben **IV**
word bank ['wɜ:d ˌbæŋk] Wortsammlung **I**
word order ['wɜ:d‿ˌɔ:də] Wortstellung, Satzstellung **I**
word web ['wɜ:d web] Wortnetz **I**
wordwise ['wɜ:dwaɪz] „wortschlau", „wortgewandt" **I**
work [wɜ:k] Arbeit **II**
social work ['səʊʃl ˌwɜ:k] Sozialarbeit **V U2**, 29
work experience ['wɜ:k‿ɪkˌspɪəriəns] Praktikum; Berufserfahrung **V U2**, 28
to work [wɜ:k] funktionieren **I**; arbeiten **I**
to work one's way up [ˌwɜ:k wʌnz weɪ 'ʌp] sich hocharbeiten **V U2**, 30
to work out [ˌwɜ:k‿'aʊt] funktionieren, klappen **V U2**, 34
worker ['wɜ:kə] Arbeiter/-in **II**
to work out sth [ˌwɜ:k‿'aʊt] etw. verstehen, hinter etw. kommen ⟨**V U3**, 53⟩
workplace ['wɜ:kpleɪs] Arbeitsplatz; Arbeitsstätte **V U2**, 42
workshop ['wɜ:kʃɒp] Werkstatt; Workshop **III**
workstation ['wɜ:kˌsteɪʃn] Arbeitsplatzrechner; Workstation ⟨**V U3**, 51⟩
world [wɜ:ld] Welt **I**
developing world [dɪ'veləpɪŋ ˌwɜ:ld] Entwicklungsländer; Schwellenländer **V U4**, 68
in the world [ɪn ðə 'wɜ:ld] auf der Welt **I**
out of this world [ˌaʊt‿əv ðɪs 'wɜ:ld] spitze; abgefahren **IV**
to be on top of the world [bi ɒn ˌtɒp‿əv ðə 'wɜ:ld] überglücklich sein **IV**
World Heritage Site [wɜ:ld 'herɪtɪdʒ saɪt] Welterbestätte; *(von der UNESCO anerkanntes Weltkulturerbe)* **V U1**, 16
World War II [ˌwɜ:ld ˌwɔ: 'tu:] der Zweite Weltkrieg **III**
worried ['wʌrɪd] beunruhigt, besorgt **I**
to worry ['wʌri] sich Sorgen machen **I**
Don't worry. [dəʊnt 'wʌri] Mach dir keine Sorgen. **I**
worry-wart ['wʌriwɔ:t] *(jmd., der sich ständig Sorgen macht)*; Grübler/-in **V U1**, 20
worth [wɜ:θ] Wert ⟨**V U4**, 79⟩
***to be worth (sth)** [bi 'wɜ:θ] (etw.) wert sein **III**
I'd appreciate it if … [aɪd‿ə'pri:ʃieɪt‿ɪt ɪf] Könnten Sie/Könntest du … ; Ich wäre Ihnen sehr verbunden, wenn … **V U4**, 73
I'd like to … *(= I would like to)* [aɪd 'laɪk tə] ich möchte …/ich würde gerne … **I**
I'd love to … *(= I would love to)* [aɪd 'lʌv tə] Ich würde sehr gern … **IV**
Would you believe it! [ˌwʊd ju bɪ'li:v‿ɪt] Kaum zu glauben! **V U2**, 38
Wow! [waʊ] Wow!/Toll! **I**
***to write** [raɪt] schreiben **I**
to write down [raɪt 'daʊn] aufschreiben **I**
creative writing [kriˌeɪtɪv 'raɪtɪŋ] kreatives Schreiben **IV**
written ['rɪtn] schriftlich **V U3**, 56
wrong [rɒŋ] falsch **I**
to be wrong [bi 'rɒŋ] Unrecht haben, sich irren **I**
to go wrong [gəʊ 'rɒŋ] schiefgehen **IV**
to prove sb wrong [ˌpru:v 'rɒŋ] beweisen, dass jmd. Unrecht hat **V U3**, 53

Y

yard [jɑ:d] (Hinter)hof; Garten **IV**
yeah *(coll)* [jeə] ja **IV**
year [jɪə] Jahr; Jahrgangsstufe, Klasse, Schuljahr **I**
for (many) years [fə ˌmeni 'jɪəz] jahrelang **I**
year-old [ˌjɪər‿'əʊld] -jährig/-e/-r **II**
yellow ['jeləʊ] gelb **I**
yes [jes] ja **I**

yesterday ['jestədeɪ] gestern **II**
yet [jet] schon; noch **II**
you [ju:] du **I**
And you. [ənd 'ju:] Gleichfalls. **III**
you guys *(coll)* [ju 'gaiz] ihr; euch **IV**
young [jʌŋ] jung **I**
your [jɔ:] dein, deine **I**; euer, eure; Ihr(e) **I**
Yours sincerely [ˌjɔ:z sɪn'sɪəli] Mit freundlichen Grüßen **VU2,** 33
yourself [jɔ:'self] dich selbst **I**; selber **III**
yourselves [jɔ:'selvz] selber **III**
youth [ju:θ] Jugend **III**
youth hostel ['ju:θ ˌhɒstl] Jugendherberge **II**
yuk [jʌk] i, igitt **I**
yummy *(coll)* ['jʌmi] lecker **VU1,** 17

Z

zero ['zɪərəʊ, əʊ] null **I**
zoo [zu:] Zoo **I**
to **zoom in** [zu:m'ɪn] heranzoomen, heranfahren **VU3,** 58
zoom-in [zu:m'ɪn] Heranzoomen, Heranfahren **I**
Zzz ... [z] Schnarch! **I**

Male names

Adam ['ædəm] **II**
Alan ['ælən] **VU3,** 55
Alex ['ælɪks] **III**
Angelo ['ænðʒləʊ] **VU1,** 20
Angus ['æŋgəs] **II**
Ben [ben] **I**
Bill [bɪl] **II**
Blake [bleɪk] **VU1,** 17
Bob [bɒb] **II**
Brian [braɪən] **IV**
Brooklyn ['brʊklɪn] **IV**
Bruce [bru:s] **II**
Carlos ['kɑ:lɒs] **IV**
Charlie ['tʃɑ:li] **II**
Christof ['krɪstɒf] ⟨**VU3,** 52⟩
Clarence ['klærns] **III**
Cody ['kəʊdi] **IV**
Danny ['dæni] **III**
Dave [deɪv] **VU3,** 60
David ['deɪvɪd] **I**
Dean [di:n] **IV**
Derrick ['derɪk] **VU1,** 16
Diego [di'eɪgəʊ] **IV**
Don [dɒn] **II**
Donovan ['dɒnəvən] **VU1,** 20
Dustin ['dʌstɪn] **IV**
Ed [ed] **IV**
Eddie ['edi] Eddie **III**
Edward ['edwəd] **II**
Emilio [ɪ'mɪliəʊ] **IV**
Frank [fræŋk] **II**
Gavin ['gævɪn] **III**
Harold ['hærəld] **III**
Iqbal ['ɪkbæl] **VU4,** 75
Jake [dʒeɪk] **III**
James [dʒeɪmz] **I**
Jay [dʒeɪ] **IV**; **VU3,** 55
Jesse ['dʒesi] **VU2,** 40
Jim [dʒɪm] **IV**
Jimmy ['dʒɪmi] **VU2,** 38
Joey ['dʒəʊi] **II**
Jon [dʒɒn] **II**
Jonathan ['dʒɒnəθn] **I**
Joseph ['dʒəʊzɪf] **II**
Josh [dʒɒʃ] **VU4,** 74
Justin ['dʒʌstɪn] **II**
Kevin ['kevɪn] **II**
Kyle [kaɪl] **IV**
Lance [lɑ:ns] **IV**
Leo ['li:əʊ] ⟨**VU4,** 76⟩
Luke [lu:k] **III**
Marco ['mɑ:kəʊ] **VU2,** 28
Marcus ['mɑ:kəs] **II**
Mario ['mæriəʊ] **IV**
Mark [mɑ:k] **III**
Martin ['mɑ:tɪn] **I**
Matt [mæt] **III**
Max [mæks] **III**
Michael ['maɪkl] **III**
Micky ['mɪki] **II**
Mike [maɪk] **VU3,** 56
Nelson ['nelsn] **I**
Nick [nɪk] **III**
Oscar ['ɒskə] **IV**
Perry ['peri] **IV**
Pete [pi:t] **II**
Peter ['pi:tə] ⟨**VU1,** 12⟩
Phil [fɪl] **I**
Philip ['fɪlɪp] **III**
Reginald ['redʒɪnld] **III**
Rhodri ['rɒdri] **III**
Richard ['rɪtʃəd] **I**
Ritchie ['rɪtʃi] **IV**
Rob [rɒb] **I**
Robert ['rɒbət] **II**
Romeo ['rəʊmiəʊ] **III**
Ryan [raɪən] **III**
Sam [sæm] **I**
Samuel ['sæmjʊəl] **I**
Scott [skɒt] **I**
Sean [ʃɔ:n] **IV**
Shane [ʃɑ:n] **IV**
Tariq ['tærɪk] **III**
Ted [ted] **I**
Terry ['teri] **I**
Tim [tɪm] **I**
Timothy ['tɪməθi] **III**
Todd [tɒd] **IV**
Tom [tɒm] **I**
Truman ['tru:mən] ⟨**VU3,** 52⟩
Walter ['wɒltə] **II**
Wayne [weɪn] **II**
Wilfred ['wɪlfrɪd] **IV**
William ['wɪljəm] **III**

Female names

Alena [ə'li:nə] ⟨**VU1,** 21⟩
Alexia [ə'leksiə] ⟨**VU1,** 21⟩
Amanda [ə'mændə] **I**
Amy ['eɪmi] **III**
Andi ['ændi] **VU3,** 54
Angela ['ændʒlə] ⟨**VU1,** 14⟩
Ann [æn] **VU3,** 56
Anne [æn] **II**
Aouda [ə'u:də] **III**
Beverly ['bevli] **IV**
Briana [bri'ænə] **VU3,** 54
Caitlin ['keɪtlɪn] **IV**
Cathia ['kæθɪə] **IV**
Cheryl ['tʃerl] ⟨**VU1,** 15⟩
Chloe ['kləʊi] **III**
Colleen ['kɒli:n] **II**
Conchita [kɒn'ʃi:tə] **IV**
Dani ['dæni] **VU1,** 20
Debbie ['debi] **I**
Denise [də'ni:z] **I**
Diana [daɪ'ænə] **II**
Diane [daɪ'æn] **IV**
Donna ['dɒnə] **IV**
Elena ['elənə] **I**
Elsie ['elsi] **I**
Emma ['emə] **I**
Eva ['i:və] **IV**
Farah ['fɑ:rə] **I**
Fiona [fi'əʊnə] **I**
Gayathriy ['gaɪətri] **II**
Grace [greɪs] **I**
Gracey ['greɪsi] ⟨**VU1,** 14⟩
Gwendolyn ['gwendəlɪn] **III**
Henrietta [ˌhenri'etə] **III**
Ivy ['aɪvi] **IV**
Jade [dʒeɪd] **I**
Jane [dʒeɪn] **II**
Janelle [dʒə'nel] **IV**
Janice ['dʒænɪs] **II**
Jessie ['dʒesi] **IV**
Jill [dʒɪl] **II**
Julie ['dʒu:li] **II**
Juliet ['dʒu:liət] **III**
Katie ['keɪti] **II**
Kelly ['keli] **III**; **IV**
Kelsey ['kelsi] **III**
Kim [kɪm] **I**
Laura ['lɔ:rə] **VU3,** 55
Leanne [li'æn] **III**
Linda ['lɪndə] **III**
Lisa ['li:sə] **I**
Lucy ['lu:si] ⟨**VU2,** 36⟩; **VU3,** 60
Maria [mə'ri:ə] **II**
Mariah [mə'raɪə] **III**
Marsha ['mɑ:ʃə] **III**
Mary ['meəri] **II**
Maudeline ['mɔ:dlɪn] **IV**

Megan ['megən] **III**
Mel [mel] **III**
Miriam ['mɪriəm] **III**
Molly ['mɒli] **II**
Mya ['maɪə] **IV**
Naomi ['neɪəmi] **VU2,** 28
Nasreen [nəs'ri:n] **I**
Nicola ['nɪklə] **I**
Nicole [nɪ'kəʊl] **II**
Nisha ['nɪʃə] **II**
Olivia [ɒl'ɪviə] **IV**
Penny ['peni] **VU3,** 60
Polly ['pɒli] **II**
Rachel ['reɪtʃl] **I**
Rhona ['rəʊnə] **III**
Ruby ['ru:bi] **VU1,** 20
Rukhshana [ruk'ʃanə] **II**
Sarah ['seərə] **I**
Serena [sə'ri:nə] **III**
Sheri ['ʃeri] **IV**
Shirin ['ʃɪrɪn] **III**
Shirley ['ʃɜ:li] ⟨**VU1,** 14⟩
Shirlyn ['ʃɜ:lɪn] **IV**
Stacy ['steɪsi] ⟨**VU4,** 81⟩
Stella ['stelə] **VU3,** 54
Sue [su:] **I**
Susan ['su:zn] **I**
Susie ['su:zi] **VU3,** 59
Sylvia ['sɪlviə] **IV**
Tanya ['tɑ:njə] ⟨**VU4,** 81⟩
Tess [tes] **I**
Tina ['ti:nə] **II**
Tori ['tɔ:ri] **IV**
Tracy ['treɪsi] **I**
Venus ['vi:nəs] **III**
Vicky ['vɪki] **III**
Wendy ['wendi] ⟨**VU1,** 14⟩
Yoko ['jəʊkəʊ] **I**
Zeba ['zi:bə] **III**
Zoe ['zəʊi] **VU4,** 70

Surnames

Barker ['bɑ:kə] **I**
Barnes [bɑ:nz] **IV**
Bennett ['benet] **VU3,** 55
Berners-Lee [ˌbɜ:nəz'li:] **III**
Broker ['brəʊkə] **VU2,** 38
Brook [brʊk] **I**
Brown [braʊn] **I**
Burbank ['bɜ:bæŋk] ⟨**VU3,** 52⟩
Carlton ['kɑ:ltn] **II**
Carter ['kɑ:tə] **I**
Church [tʃɜ:tʃ] **II**
Clooney ['klu:ni] **II**
Collins ['kɒlɪnz] **III**
Cumberland ['kʌmbələnd] **III**
Darling ['dɑ:lɪŋ] **I**
Devine [dɪ'vaɪn] **II**
Doro ['dɒrəʊ] **IV**
Dougherty ['dɒxəti] **VU3,** 54
Douglas ['dʌgləs] **II**
Duffy ['dʌfi] **VU3,** 54
Flood [flʌd] **VU2,** 40
Freeman ['fri:mən] **VU3,** 60
García [gɑ:'siə] **IV**
Gomez ['gəʊmez] **IV**
Gonzaga [gɒn'zɑ:gə] **IV**
Goodman ['gʊdmæn] **IV**
Green [gri:n] **I**
Jackson ['dʒæksn] **I**
Khan [kɑ:n] **III**
Kumar [ku:'mɑ:] **II**
Lacy ['leɪsi] **III**
Levinson ['levɪnsn] **IV**
Lotric ['lɒtrɪtʃ] **III**
MacGregor [mə'gregə] **II**
MacMouse [mək'maʊs] **II**
Masih [mʌ'si] **VU4,** 75
McGeoch [mə'gɪəx] **II**
McHughes [mək'hju:z] **VU4,** 74
Moise [mɔɪs] **IV**
Negrete [nɪ'gri:teɪ] **IV**
Nelson ['nelsn] **I**
Newman ['nju:mən] **I**
O'Shea [ə'ʃeɪ] **IV**
Patterson ['pætəsn] **III**
Peterson ['pi:təsn] **I**
Pilch [pɪltʃ] **I**
Pinner ['pɪnə] **II**
Redfern ['redfɜ:n] **II**
Reese [ri:s] **VU1,** 16
Riverdale ['rɪvədeɪl] **IV**
Robinson ['rɒbɪnsn] **III**
Serafino [ˌserə'fi:nəʊ] **VU1,** 17
Simpson ['sɪmsən] **II**
Sims [sɪmz] **VU3,** 54
Slade [sleɪd] ⟨**VU3,** 51⟩
Smith [smɪθ] **I**
Spencer ['spensə] **I**
Stavros ['stævrəs] **I**
Steward ['stju:əd] **II**
Stirling ['stɜ:lɪŋ] **III**
Taylor ['teɪlə] **I**
Tiny ['taɪni] **I**
Tohomas [tə'həʊməs] **II**
Warner ['wɔ:nə] **IV**
Webb-Miller [web'mɪlə] **VU2,** 33
Wendover ['wendəʊvə] **I**
Whitecloud ['waɪtklaʊd] **IV**
Williams ['wɪljəmz] **II**

Place names

Aberdeen [ˌæbə'di:n] **II**
Abertawe ['æbətɔ:] **III**
Albert Dock [ˌælbət 'dɒk] **III**
Amsterdam Avenue ['æmstəˌdæm 'ævenju:] **IV**
Bamburgh ['bæmbrə] **I**
Bannockburn ['bænəkbɜ:n] **II**
Berlin [bɜ:'lɪn] **I**
Birmingham ['bɜ:mɪŋəm] **III**; **III**
Blackheath Park [ˌblækhi:θ 'pɑ:k] **I**
Bond Street ['bɒnd ˌstri:t] **II**
Boston ['bɒstn] **IV**
Boulogne [bʊ'lɔɪn] **II**
Brighton ['braɪtn] **I**
Brisbane ['brɪzbən] ⟨**VU1,** 14⟩
Bristol ['brɪstl] **I**
the **Bronx** [ðə 'brɒŋks] **IV**
Calais ['kæleɪ] **II**
Calgary ['kælgri] **III**
Canary Wharf [kə'neəri ˌwɔ:f] **I**
Cardiff ['kɑ:dɪf] **I**
Central Park [ˌsentrl 'pɑ:k] **IV**
Charlotte ['ʃɑ:lət] ⟨**VU3,** 53⟩
Charlton ['tʃɑ:ltn] **I**
Chicago [ʃɪ'kɑ:gəʊ] **IV**
Chinatown ['tʃaɪnətaʊn] **IV**
Church Street ['tʃɜ:tʃ ˌstri:t] **I**
Covent Garden [ˌkɒvnt 'gɑ:dn] **II**
Dover ['dəʊvə] **II**
Edgecombe ['edʒkəm] **IV**
Edinburgh ['edɪnbrə] **II**
Ellis Island [ˌelɪs 'aɪlənd] **IV**
Fifth Avenue [fɪfθ 'ævənju:] **IV**
Fort William [ˌfɔ:t 'wɪljəm] **II**
Fresno ['freznəʊ] **IV**
Gatwick ['gætwɪk] **II**
Golden Mile [ˌgəʊldn 'maɪl] **I**
Goodge Street ['gu:dʒ ˌstri:t] **II**
Greenwich ['grenɪdʒ] **I**
Greenwich Park [ˌgrenɪdʒ 'pɑ:k] **I**
Greenwich Village [ˌgrenɪdʒ 'vɪlɪdʒ] **IV**
Guadalajara [ˌgwɑ:dlə'hɑ:rə] **IV**
Hamburg ['hæmbɜ:g] **II**
Harlech ['hɑ:lek] **I**
Harlem ['hɑ:ləm] **IV**
Heathrow [hi:θ'rəʊ] **II**
High Road ['haɪ ˌrəʊd] **I**
High Street ['haɪ stri:t] **VU2,** 42
Hither Farm Road ['hɪðə fɑ:m ˌrəʊd] **I**
Holburne Road ['hɒlbɜ:n ˌrəʊd] **I**
Hollywood ['hɒliwʊd] **III**
Hyde Park [ˌhaɪd 'pɑ:k] **II**
Inverness [ˌɪnvə'nes] **II**
Istanbul [ˌɪstæn'bʊl] **I**
Jackson ['dʒæksn] **IV**
Kidbrooke Park Road [ˌkɪdbrʊk 'pɑ:k ˌrəʊd] **I**
Kirkton ['kɜ:ktn] **II**
Knightsbridge ['naɪtsbrɪdʒ] **II**
Leicester ['lestə] **I**
Leicester Square ['lestə ˌskweə] **II**
Leytonstone ['leɪtnstəʊn] **II**
Liberty Island [ˌlɪbəti 'aɪlənd] **IV**
Little Rock [ˌlɪtl 'rɒk] **VU4,** 74
Liverpool ['lɪvəpu:l] **III**
London ['lʌndən] **I**
Long Island [ˌlɒŋ 'aɪlənd] **IV**
Los Angeles [lɒs 'ænʒɪli:z] **VU4,** 73
Madrid [mə'drɪd] **I**
Malaga ['mæləgə] **III**
Malibu ['mælɪbu:] **IV**
Manchester ['mæntʃɪstə] **II**
Manhattan [mæn'hætn] **IV**

Medicine Bow ['medsn ˌbəʊ] **III**
Mesquite [mes'ki:t] **IV**
Munich ['mju:nɪk] **IV**
Nairobi [naɪ'rəʊbi] **I**
New Town ['nju: taʊn] **II**
Newtown ['nju:taʊn] **VU2,** 42
New York [nju: ˌjɔ:k 'sɪti] **IV**
North Street ['nɔθ stri:t] **VU3,** 59
Observatory Station [əbˌzɜ:vətri 'steɪʃn] **I**
Old Town ['əʊld taʊn] **II**
Orlando [ɔ:'lændəʊ] **IV**
Oxford Circus Station ['ɒksfəd ˌsɜ:kəs ˌsteɪʃn] **II**
Oxford Street ['ɒksfəd ˌstri:t] **II**
Paris ['pærɪs] **I**
P'borough *(= Peterborough)* ['pi:brə] ⟨**VU2,** 36⟩
Penzance [pen'zæns] **I**
Peterborough ['pi:təbrə] **VU2,** 30
Piccadilly Circus [ˌpɪkədɪli 'sɜ:kəs] **II**
Pond Road ['pɒnd ˌrəʊd] **I**
Queens [kwi:nz] **II**
Queensway ['kwi:nzweɪ] **II**
Quincy Street Garden [ˌkwɪnsi stri:t 'gɑ:dn] **IV**
Reading ['redɪŋ] **III**
Redwood National Park ['redwʊd ˌnæʃnl 'pɑ:k] **IV**
Rhossili ['rɒsli] **III**
Richmond ['rɪtʃmənd] **II**
Rome [rəʊm] **VU4,** 70
Royal Mile [ˌrɔɪəl 'maɪl] **II**
Rutland Way [ˌrʌtlənd 'weɪ] **VU2,** 33
San Diego [ˌsæn di'eɪgəʊ] **IV**
San Francisco [ˌsæn frən'sɪskəʊ] **III**
Santa Monica [ˌsæntə 'mɒnɪkə] **IV**
Seattle [si'ætl] **IV**
Shanghai [ʃæŋ'haɪ] **I**
Silicon Valley [ˌsɪlɪkən 'væli] **III**
Southampton [saʊ'θæmtən] **III**
Southend-on-Sea [ˌsaʊθ'end‿ɒn 'si:] **I**
St. Anne's Square [snt'ænz skweə] **III**
Staten Island [ˌstætn 'aɪlənd] **IV**
Stirling ['stɜ:lɪŋ] **II**
Stockwell Street ['stɒkwel ˌstri:t] **I**
Sunrise Pass [ˌsʌnraɪz 'pɑ:s] **IV**
Swansea ['swɒnzi] **III**
Sydney ['sɪdni] **III**
Tennessee [ˌtenə'si:] **II**
Tokyo ['təʊkiəʊ] **I**
Toulouse [tu:'lu:z] **II**
Trafalgar Square [trə'fælgə skweə] **II**
Tulsa ['tʌlsə] **IV**
Tunbridge Wells [ˌtʌnbrɪdʒ 'welz] **VU3,** 55
Ulan Bator [u:ˌlɑ:n 'bɑ:tɔ:] **VU2,** 38
Venice Beach [ˌvenɪs 'bi:tʃ] **IV**
Victoria Station [vɪk'tɔ:riə ˌsteɪʃn] **II**
Waterloo Station [ˌwɔ:tə'lu: ˌsteɪʃn] **II**
Wendover Road ['wendəʊvə ˌrəʊd] **I**
Wimbledon ['wɪmbldn] **II**
Windsor ['wɪndzə] **III**
Winnipeg ['wɪnɪpeg] **VU2,** 38
Yellowstone National Park [ˌjeləʊstəʊn ˌnæʃnl 'pɑ:k] **IV**

Geographical names

Africa ['æfrɪkə] **VZI,** 8
Alaska [ə'læskə] **IV**
America [ə'merɪkə] **VZI,** 8
the **American West** [əˌmerɪkən 'west] **IV**
Arizona [ˌærɪ'zəʊnə] **IV**
Arkansas ['ɑ:kənsɔ:] **VU4,** 74
Asia ['eɪʒə] Asien **III**
Atlantic [ət'læntɪk] **III**
Australia ['ɒstreɪliə] Australien **III**
Bali ['bɑ:li] **VU1,** 17
Ben Nevis [ˌben 'nevɪs] **II**
Big Harcar Rock [bɪg ˌhɑ:kə 'rɒk] **I**
Bondi Beach [ˌbɒndaɪ 'bi:tʃ] **III**
Britain ['brɪtn] Großbritannien **I**
British Columbia [ˌbrɪtɪʃ kə'lʌmbiə] **VZI,** 10
CA *(= California)* [ˌkælɪ'fɔ:niə] **IV**
Canada ['kænədə] Kanada **II**
Channel ['tʃænl] Ärmelkanal *(Teil der Nordsee zwischen Großbritannien und Frankreich)* **II**
China ['tʃaɪnə] **III**
Colorado [ˌkɒlr'ɑ:dəʊ] **IV**
Colorado River [ˌkɒlrɑ:dəʊ 'rɪvə] **IV**
Congo ['kɒŋgəʊ] **VU2,** 39
Cornwall ['kɔ:nwɔ:l] **I**
Death Valley [ˌdeθ 'væli] **IV**
Dorchester ['dɔ:tʃɪstə] **III**
Ecuador ['ekwədɔ:] **IV**
Egypt ['i:dʒɪpt] Ägypten **III**
England ['ɪŋglənd] **I**
Essex ['esɪks] **II**
Europe ['jʊərəp] Europa **II**
Farne Islands [fɑ:n 'aɪləndz] **I**
Finland ['fɪnlənd] Finland **III**
FL *(= Florida)* ['flɒrɪdə] **IV**
France [frɑ:nts] Frankreich **II**
Germany ['dʒɜ:məni] Deutschland **I**
Gower Coast ['gaʊə kəʊst] **III**
Grand Canyon [ˌgrænd 'kænjən] **IV**
Great Barrier Reef [ˌgreɪt ˌbæriə 'ri:f] **VU1,** 16
Great Britain [ˌgreɪt 'brɪtn] Großbritannien **III**
Great Wall of China [ˌgreɪt ˌwɔ:l‿əv 'tʃaɪnə] **III**
Greece [gri:s] Griechenland **I**
Haiti ['heɪti] **IV**
Highlands ['haɪləndz] **II**
India ['ɪndiə] Indien **III**
Iowa ['aɪəʊə] **IV**
Isle of Dogs [ˌaɪl əv 'dɒgz] **I**
Italy ['ɪtli] Italien **I**
Jamaica [dʒə'meɪkə] **III**
Japan [dʒə'pæn] **III**
Lancashire ['læŋkəʃə] **II**
Latvia ['lætviə] ⟨**VU1,** 21⟩
Lithuania [ˌlɪθju'eɪniə] ⟨**VU1,** 21⟩
Loch Fyne [ˌlɒx 'faɪn] **II**
Loch Lochy [ˌlɒx 'lɒxi] **II**
Loch Lomond [ˌlɒx 'ləʊmənd] **II**
Loch Ness [ˌlɒx 'nes] **II**
Loch Rannoch [ˌlɒx 'rænəx] **II**
Loch Tay [ˌlɒx 'teɪ] **II**
Majorca [mə'jɔ:kə] **III**
Mersey ['mɜ:zi] **III**
Mexico ['meksɪkəʊ] **III**
Midwest [mɪd'west] **VU2,** 39
Mississippi [ˌmɪsɪ'sɪpi] **IV**
Montana [mɒn'tænə] **IV**
Mount Snowdon [ˌmaʊnt 'snəʊdn] **I**
Mt. McKinley [ˌmaʊnt mə'kɪnli] **IV**
Nevada [nə'vɑ:də] **III**
New Jersey [ˌnju: 'dʒɜ:zi] **IV**
New Mexico [nju: 'meksɪkəʊ] **VU2,** 38
Normandy ['nɔ:məndi] die Normandie **III**
North America [ˌnɔ:θ ə'merɪkə] Nordamerika **III**
North Carolina [ˌnɔ:θ kær'laɪnə] ⟨**VU3,** 53⟩
North Korea [ˌnɔ:θ kə'ri:ə] **VU4,** 69
OK *(= Oklahoma)* [ˌəʊklə'həʊmə] **IV**
Orange County [ˌɒrɪndʒ 'kaʊnti] **IV**
Outer Mongolia [ˌaʊtə mɒŋ'gəʊliə] **VU2,** 39
the **Pacific Northwest** [pəˌsɪfɪk nɔ:θ'west] **IV**
Pacific Ocean [pəˌsɪfɪk 'əʊʃn] **IV**
Pakistan [ˌpɑ:kɪ'stɑ:n] **III**
Panama [ˌpænə'mɑ:] **III**
Poland ['pəʊlənd] Polen **I**
Québec [kwɪ'bek, keb'ek] **VZI,** 10
River Mersey [ˌrɪvə 'mɜ:zi] **III**
River Thames [ˌrɪvə 'temz] **I**
the **Rockies** *(= the Rocky Mountains)* ['rɒkiz] **IV**
Rocky Mountains [ˌrɒki 'maʊntɪnz] **III**
Russia ['rʌʃə] Russland **I**
San Andreas Fault [ˌsæn 'ændriəs fɔ:lt] **IV**
Scotland ['skɒtlənd] Schottland **II**
Sennen Beach [ˌsenən 'bi:tʃ] **I**
The **Shetlands** [ðə 'ʃetləndz] die Shetlandinseln **II**
Singapore [ˌsɪŋə'pɔ:] **VU1,** 17
South Africa [ˌsaʊθ‿'æfrɪkə] Südafrika **III**
the **Southwest** [ˌsaʊθ'west] **IV**
Spain [speɪn] **I**
St Michael's Mount [snˌmaɪklz 'maʊnt] **I**
Sweden ['swi:dn] **VU4,** 69
Tasmania [tæz'meɪniə] ⟨**VU1,** 19⟩
Texas ['teksəs] **IV**
Tibet [tɪ'bet] **VU4,** 69
Turkey ['tɜ:ki] Türkei **I**
TX *(= Texas)* ['teksəs] **IV**
UK [ˌju:'keɪ] Vereinigtes Königreich von Großbritannien und Nordirland **II**

United States [juːˌnaɪtɪd ˈsteɪts] Vereinigte Staaten **IV**
Utah [ˈjuːtɑː] **III**
Wales [weɪlz] **I**
Washington State [ˌwɒʃɪŋtən ˈsteɪt] **IV**
Wyoming [waɪˈəʊmɪŋ] **III**
Yugoslavia [ˌjuːgəʊˈslɑːviə] Jugoslawien **III**

Other names

Abercrombie & Fitch *(A&F)* [ˌæbəkrɒmbiˌn ˈfɪtʃ] ⟨**VU4,** 76⟩
Aberdeen Hiking Club [ˌæbədiːn ˈhaɪkɪŋ klʌb] **II**
Academy Award [əˌkædəmi əˈwɔːd] **IV**
AIDS [eɪdz] **VU2,** 40
Airbus [ˈeəbʌs] **III**
A-levels [ˈeɪlevlz] *britische Abiturprüfung* **VU2,** 28
Anfield Road [ˌænfiːld ˈrəʊd] **III**
Angelo's [ˈændʒləʊz] **I**
Armada [ɑːˈmɑːdə] **III**
Bagdad Café [ˌbægdæd ˈkæfeɪ] **IV**
Barker [ˈbɑːkə] **I**
Battle of Hastings [ˌbætlˌəv ˈheɪstɪŋz] **III**
BBC *(= British Broadcasting Corporation)* [ˌbiːbiːˈsiː (ˌbrɪtɪʃ ˈbrɔːdkɑːstɪŋ kɔːprˌeɪʃn)] **II**
Beagle [ˈbiːgl] **III**
Bears [beəz] **IV**
Beatlemania [ˌbiːtlˈmeɪniə] **III**
Bebo [ˈbiːbəʊ] **VU3,** 54
the **Beeb** [ðə ˈbiːb] **III**
Berry Middle School [ˌberi ˈmɪdl skuːl] **IV**
Beryl Alpha [ˌberl ˈælfə] **II**
Bonza [ˈbɒnzə] **I**
Brent Charlie [ˌbrent ˈtʃɑːli] **II**
Britannia [brɪˈtæniə] Britannien **III**
British Airways [ˌbrɪtɪʃ ˈeəweɪz] **II**
British Empire [ˌbrɪtɪʃ ˈempaɪə] **III**
Bu [buː] **II**
Buckingham Palace [ˌbʌkɪŋəm ˈpælɪs] **II**
Busted [ˈbʌstɪd] **II**
Caddris [kædrɪs] **II**
California Aqueduct [ˌkælɪfɔːniə ˈækwɪdʌkt] **IV**
California State Water Project (CSWP) [ˌkælɪfɔːniə ˌsteɪt ˈwɔːtə ˌprɒdʒekt] **IV**
CCTV [ˌsiːsiːtiːˈviː] Videoüberwachung **II**
Cèilidh Mòr [ˌkeɪli ˈmɔː] **II**
Central Line [ˈsentrl ˌlaɪn] **II**
chicken tikka masala [ˌtʃɪkɪn ˌtɪkə məˈsɑːlə] **VZI,** 9
Chihuahua [tʃɪˈwɑːwə] **II**
Chocolate Islands [ˈtʃɒklət ˌaɪləndz] **I**
CIA [ˌsiːaɪˈeɪ] **VU4,** 70
Coaster's Café [ˌkəʊstəz ˈkæfeɪ] **II**
Commonwealth [ˈkɒmənwelθ] **III**
Connexions [kəˈnekʃnz] **VU2,** 30
Cool Cat [ˌkuːl ˈkæt] **I**
Cool Runnings [ˌkuːl ˈrʌnɪŋz] **III**
Coronation Street [kɒrəˌneɪʃn ˈstriːt] **III**
Covent Garden Market [ˌkɒvnt ˈgɑːdn ˌmɑːkɪt] **II**
CSI: Miami [siːesˈaɪ maɪˌæmi] **III**
Cumberland Hall [ˌkʌmbələnd ˈhɔːl] **III**
Cutty Sark [ˌkʌti ˈsɑːk] **I**
Danny Way [ˌdæni ˈweɪ] **III**
DAZZ [dæz] **III**
Decathlon [dɪˈkæθlɒn] **II**
Disneyland [ˈdɪznilænd] **IV**
Docklands Light Railway [ˌdɒklændz laɪt ˈreɪlweɪ] **I**
down under [ˌdaʊnˌˈʌndə] *Spitzname für Australien* **VZI,** 11
Dr Jones [ˌdɒktə ˈdʒəʊnz] **II**
EastEnders [iːstˈendəz] **III**
Eiffel Tower [ˌaɪfl ˈtaʊə] **IV**
Eisteddfod [aɪˈsteðvɒd] **III**
El Dorado [ˌel dəˈrɑːdəʊ] **IV**
Emmerdale [ˈemədeɪl] **III**
Empire State Building [ˌempaɪə ˈsteɪt ˌbɪldɪŋ] **IV**
Epic Skatepark [ˌepɪk ˈskeɪtpɑːk] **III**
ER *(= Emergency Room)* [iːˈɑːr; ɪˈmɜːdʒnsi ruːm] **III**
E.T. *(= The Extra-Terrestrial)* [ði ˌekstrətəˈrestriəl] **IV**
Facebook [ˈfeɪsbʊk] **VU3,** 54
FBI [ˌefbiːˈaɪ] **VU4,** 70
Fightstar [ˈfaɪtstɑː] **II**
Flushing Meadow Park [ˌflʌʃɪŋ ˌmedəʊ ˈpɑːk] ⟨**VU3,** 52⟩
Folgers Coffee [ˌfəʊldʒəz ˈkɒfi] ⟨**VU3,** 53⟩
Foyles [fɔɪlz] **II**
Friendster [ˈfrendstə] **VU3,** 54
GCSE *(= General Certificate of Secondary Education)* [ˌdʒiː siː es ˈiː; ˌdʒenrl seˈtɪfɪkətˌəv ˌsekəndri edʒʊˈkeɪʃn] *allg. Abschluss der weiterführenden Schulen in GB* **VU2,** 28
Gizzette Hair Gel [ˌgɪzet heə ˈgel] **III**
the **Globe Theatre** [ˈgləʊb ˌθɪətə] das Globe-Theater **III**
Gold Rush [ˈgəʊld ˌrʌʃ] **IV**
Google [ˈguːgl] **II**
Graceland [ˈgreɪslənd] **II**
Grand Canyon Skywalk Resort [grænd ˌkænjən ˌskaɪwɔːk rɪˈzɔːt] **IV**
Great expectations [ˌgreɪt ˌekspekˈteɪʃnz] ⟨**VU2,** 41⟩
Greenpeace [ˈgriːnpiːs] **VU1,** 16
Greensleeves [ˈgriːnsliːvz] **III**
Greenwich Foot Tunnel [ˌgrenɪdʒ ˈfʊt tʌnl] **I**
Greenwich Market [ˌgrenɪdʒ ˈmɑːkɪt] **I**
Guinness World of Records [ˌgɪnɪs wɜːldˌəv ˈrekɔːdz] **II**
Hadrian's Wall [ˌheɪdriənz ˈwɔːl] **III**
Hamleys [ˈhæmliz] **II**
Harrods [ˈhærədz] **II**
Historia [hɪˈstɔːriə] **III**
Hobbyland [ˈhɒbilænd] Hobbyland **I**
Hogwarts [ˈhɒgwɔːts] **II**
HTML [eɪtʃtiːemˈel] **III**
Hualapai [ˌhʊələˈpeɪ] **IV**
Hyperion [haɪˈpɪəriən] **IV**
iTunes [ˈaɪtjuːnz] ⟨**VU3,** 51⟩
Jesus [ˈdʒiːzəs] **VU2,** 38
Jubilee Line [ˈdʒuːbɪliː laɪn] **II**
Junior Mastermind [ˌdʒuːniə ˈmɑːstəmaɪnd] **VU3,** 60
Koolkats [ˈkuːlkæts] **II**
Liverpool FC [ˌlɪvəpuːl efˈsiː] **III**
Liverpool Football Club [ˌlɪvəpuːl ˈfʊtbɔːl klʌb] **III**
Londinium [lʌnˈdɪnɪəm] **II**
London Dungeon [ˌlʌndən ˈdʌndʒn] **II**
London Eye [ˌlʌndənˌˈaɪ] **II**
London Marathon [ˌlʌndən ˈmærəθn] **III**
London Zoo [ˌlʌndən ˈzuː] **III**
Lycos [ˈlaɪkəz] **III**
M4 [emˈfɔː] **III**
Madame Tussaud's [ˌmædəm tʊˈsɔːdz] **III**
Manchester United [ˌmæntʃɪstə juːˈnaɪtɪd] **II**
ManU *(= Manchester United)* [ˌmænˈjuː] **III**
Mario's Bagels [ˌmæriəʊz ˈbeɪglz] **IV**
Maritime Museum [ˈmærɪtaɪm mjuːˈziːəm] **II**
Melters [ˈmeltəz] **VU3,** 58
Mercedes [məˈseɪdiːz] **IV**
merengue [məˈreŋgə] *lateinamerikanischer Tanz- und Musikstil* **IV**
Millennium Dome [mɪˈleniəm ˌdəʊm] **I**
Mimic [ˈmɪmɪk] **VU4,** 81
Moonlight [ˈmuːnlaɪt] **III**
Mousehole Harbour [ˌmaʊzl ˈhɑːbə] **I**
Mudchute Farm [ˌmʌdʃuːt ˈfɑːm] **I**
Muriel's Wedding [ˌmjʊəriəlz ˈwedɪŋ] **VU1,** 21
Murray's [ˈmʌriz] **II**
My Space [ˈmaɪ speɪs] ⟨**VU3,** 51⟩
Napster [ˈnæpstə] ⟨**VU3,** 51⟩
National Waterfront Museum [ˌnæʃnl ˌwɔːtəfrʌnt mjuːˈziːəm] **III**
Natural History Museum [ˌnætʃrl ˈhɪstri mjuːˌziːəm] **II**
Neighbours [ˈneɪbəz] **III**
Newsflash [ˈnjuːzflæʃ] ⟨**VU3,** 59⟩
New World [ˌnjuː ˈwɜːld] **III**
New York Yankees [ˌnjuː jɔːk ˈjæŋkiz] **IV**
Olympic Games [əʊˌlɪmpɪk ˈgeɪmz] Olympiade, Olympische Spiele **III**
Out of Rosenheim [ˌaʊtˌəv ˈrəʊznhaɪm] **IV**
Oz *(coll)* [ɒz] Oz *(Spitzname für Australien)* **VU1,** 17
Palomar Community College [ˈpæləmɑː kəˈmjuːnəti ˌkɒlɪdʒ] **IV**
Passepartout [ˌpæspəˈtuː] **III**
Patriot Act [ˈpeɪtriət ækt] **VU4,** 70
People [ˈpiːpl] **IV**
Phileas Fogg [fɪˌliə ˈfɒg] **III**

Philip Randolph High School [ˌfɪlɪp ˌrændɒlf 'haɪ sku:l] IV
Piazza [pi'ætsə] II
Playstation ['pleɪˌsteɪʃn] III
Quinally [kwɪn'æli] IV
RCA [ɑ:rsi:'eɪ] III
Real Madrid [rɪˌɑ:l mə'drɪd] II
Regent's Park [ˌri:dʒnts 'pɑ:k] III
Rivermead Leisure Complex [ˌrɪvəmi:d ˌleʒə 'kɒmpleks] III
Romeo and Juliet [ˌrəʊmiəʊ‿ənd 'dʒu:liət] IV
Route 66 [ru:t] IV
Royal Observatory [ˌrɔɪəl əb'zɜ:vətri] I
Rusty ['rʌsti] I
Sayonara [sai'əʊnɑ:lɑ:] III
Seahaven ['si:heɪvn] ⟨VU3, 52⟩
Shout [ʃaʊt] III
Sidewalk ['saɪdwɔ:k] III
Skywalk ['skaɪwɔ:k] IV
Smash hits ['smæʃ hɪt] III
Spin [spɪn] III
Squeak [skwi:k] II
Starry ['stɑ:ri] III
Starstruck ['stɑ:strʌk] II
Statue of Liberty [ˌstætʃu:‿əv 'lɪbəti] IV
Strawberry Fields [ˌstrɔ:bri 'fi:ldz] IV
Superbowl ['su:pəbəʊl] III
Superteen ['su:pəti:n] II
Tallis Newsletter [ˌtælɪs 'nju:zletə] II
Tate Modern [ˌteɪt 'mɒdn] II
Teen Buzz ['ti:n bʌz] II
Thames Barrier [ˌtemz 'bæriə] I
The Lord of the Rings [ðə ˌlɔ:d‿əv ðə 'rɪŋz] III
The Oregon Trail [ði ˌɒrɪgən 'treɪl] IV
The Quarrymen [ðə 'kwɒrimən] III
The Seattle Chronicle [ðə siˌætl 'krɒnɪkl] IV
The Seattle Times [ðə siˌætl 'taɪmz] IV
The Truman Show [ðə 'tru:mən ˌʃəʊ] ⟨VU3, 52⟩
Thomas Tallis [ˌtɒməs 'tælɪs] I
Thomas Tallis School [ˌtɒməs 'tælɪs ˌsku:l] I
Tiger ['taɪgə] I
Tokyo Tigers [ˌtəʊkiəʊ 'taɪgəz] I
Tom-Toms ['tɒm tɒmz] II
Top Fit [ˌtɒp 'fɪt] II
the Tower of London [ðə ˌtaʊər‿əv 'lʌndən] III
4U [fə 'ju] I

UNESCO [ju:'neskəʊ] VU1, 16
United Nations Universal Declaration of Human Rights [ju:ˌnaɪtɪd 'neɪʃnz ju:nɪ'vɜ:sl ˌdeklə'reɪʃn‿əv ˌhju:mən 'raɪts] Allgemeine Erklärung der Menschenrechte der Vereinten Nationen VU4, 68
US Congress [ju:ˌes 'kɒŋgres] VU4, 70
US Supreme Court [ˌju:es su:'pri:m ˌkɔ:t] VU4, 74
Walk of Fame [ˌwɔ:k‿əv 'feɪm] IV
Water Park ['wɔ:tə ˌpɑ:k] I
Williamson Tunnels ['wɪljəmsn ˌtʌnlz] III
World Cup [wɜ:ld 'kʌp] Fußballweltmeisterschaft II
World Stage [ˌwɜ:ld 'steɪdʒ] III
World Trade Center [wɜ:ld 'treɪd ˌsentə] IV
World Wide Web [ˌwɜ:ld waɪd 'web] III
Yahoo ['jɑ:hu:] VU3, 54
YouTube ['ju:tju:b] ⟨VU3, 51⟩
Zerfee [zɜ:rfi:] II
Zest [zest] II

Famous names

Albert Bierstadt [ˌælbət 'bɪəstʌt] IV
Arctic Monkeys [ˌɑ:ktɪk 'mʌŋkiz] III
Aretha Franklin [əˌri:θə 'fræŋklɪn] ⟨VU4, 80⟩
The Beatles [ðə 'bi:tlz] III
Bob Dylan [bɒb 'dɪlən] VU4, 78
Captain Cook [ˌkæptɪn 'kʊk] III
50 Cent [ˌfɪfti 'sent] III
Charles Darwin [ˌtʃɑ:lz 'dɑ:wɪn] III
Charles Dickens [ˌtʃɑ:lz 'dɪkɪnz] ⟨VU2, 41⟩
Charlton Heston [ˌtʃɑ:ltn 'hestn] IV
Christina Aguilera [krɪˌsti:nə ægɪ'lerə] VU4, 79
Craig Kielburger [kreɪg 'ki:lˌbɜ:gə] VU4, 75
David Beckham [ˌdeɪvɪd 'bekəm] II
Dirk Benedict [dɜ:k 'benɪdɪkt] IV
Drew Barrymore [dru: 'bærɪmɔ:] IV
Elizabeth Eckford [ɪˌlɪzəbəθ 'ekfəd] VU4, 74
Elizabeth I [ɪˌlɪzəbəθ ðə 'fɜ:st] III
Ellen MacArthur [ˌelən mə'kɑ:θə] III
Elvis Presley [ˌelvɪs 'presli] II
Francis Drake [ˌfrɑ:nsɪs 'dreɪk] III

Gandhi ['gændi] VU4, 77
Gladys Aylward [ˌglædɪs 'eɪlwəd] III
Harry Potter [ˌhæri 'pɒtə] II
James Moloney [ˌdʒeɪmz mə'ləʊni] ⟨VU1, 15⟩
James Vance Marshall [ˌdʒeɪmz ˌvæns 'mɑ:ʃl] ⟨VU1, 13⟩
James Watt [ˌdʒeɪmz 'wɒt] III
Jeff Wall [dʒef 'wɔ:l] VU4, 81
J K Rowling [ˌdʒeɪ keɪ 'rəʊlɪŋ] VU2, 31
John Lennon [dʒɒn 'lenən] IV
John Lennon [ˌdʒɒn 'lenən] VU2, 39
Kelly Holmes [ˌkeli 'həʊmz] II
Lance Armstrong [ˌlænts 'ɑ:mstrɒŋ] III
Levi Strauss [ˌli:vaɪ 'straʊs] IV
Lily Allen [ˌlɪli 'ælən] ⟨VU3, 51⟩
Lorenzo DiLario [ləˌrenzəʊ dɪ'læriəʊ] IV
Mahatma Gandhi [məˌhɑ:tmə 'gændi] VU4, 77
Malachy Doyle [ˌmæləki 'dɔɪl] VU2, 40
Marco Polo [ˌmɑ:kəʊ 'pəʊləʊ] III
Matthew Pinsent [ˌmæθju: 'pɪnsnt] III
Matti Nykanen [ˌmati 'nɪkanən] III
Michael Phelps [ˌmaɪkl 'felps] III
Mickey Mouse ['mɪki maʊs] I
Midnight Oil [ˌmɪdnaɪt‿'ɔɪl] ⟨VU1, 21⟩
Mohandas Gandhi [məʊˌhændəz 'gændi] VU4, 77
Neil Armstrong [ni:l 'ɑ:mstrɒŋ] III
Nelson Mandela [ˌnelsn mæn'delə] VZI, 10
Orlando Bloom [ɔ:ˌlændəʊ 'blu:m] II
Paul Cookson [pɔ:l 'kʊksn] ⟨VU2, 35⟩
Philip Pirrip [ˌfɪlɪp 'pɪrɪp] ⟨VU2, 41⟩
Pink [pɪŋk] ⟨VU4, 80⟩
Queen Victoria [ˌkwi:n vɪk'tɔ:riə] III
Robbie Williams [ˌrɒbi 'wɪljəmz] III
Roger Federer [ˌrɒdʒə 'fedərə] III
Runrig ['rʌnrɪg] II
The Spice Girls ['spaɪs ˌgɜ:lz] II
Stephen Hoskins [ˌsti:vn 'hɒskɪnz] III
Tanny Grey-Thompson ['tæni ˌgreɪ'tɒmpsn] III
Thora Birch [ˌθɔ:rə 'bɜ:tʃ] IV
Tiger Woods [ˌtaɪgə 'wʊdz] III
Victoria Adams [vɪkˌtɔ:rɪə 'ædəmz] II
Vincent Kartheiser [ˌvɪnsnt kɑ:'θi:zə] IV
William Shakespeare [ˌwɪljəm 'ʃeɪkspɪə] III
William the Conqueror [ˌwɪljəm ðə 'kɒŋkrə] III
Yoko Ono [ˌjəʊkəʊ 'əʊnəʊ] IV

List of irregular verbs

infinitive	simple past	past participle	German
to **be** [bi:]	**was / were** [wɒz, wɜ:]	**been** [bi:n]	sein
to **become** [bɪ'kʌm]	**became** [bɪ'keɪm]	**become** [bɪ'kʌm]	werden
to **bleed** [bli:d]	**bled** [bled]	**bled** [bled]	bluten
to **break** [breɪk]	**broke** [brəʊk]	**broken** ['brəʊkn]	(zer)brechen; kaputtmachen
to **bring** [brɪŋ]	**brought** [brɔ:t]	**brought** [brɔ:t]	(mit)bringen
to **build** [bɪld]	**built** [bɪlt]	**built** [bɪlt]	bauen
to **burn** [bɜ:n]	**burnt / burned** [bɜ:nt, bɜ:nd]	**burnt / burned** [bɜ:nt, bɜ:nd]	(ver)brennen
to **buy** [baɪ]	**bought** [bɔ:t]	**bought** [bɔ:t]	kaufen
to **catch** [kætʃ]	**caught** [kɔ:t]	**caught** [kɔ:t]	fangen
to **choose** [tʃu:z]	**chose** [tʃəʊz]	**chosen** ['tʃəʊzn]	(aus)wählen
to **come** [kʌm]	**came** [keɪm]	**come** [kʌm]	kommen
to **cost** [kɒst]	**cost** [kɒst]	**cost** [kɒst]	kosten
to **deal (with)** [di:l]	**dealt** [delt]	**dealt** [delt]	(be)handeln
to **do** [du:]	**did** [dɪd]	**done** [dʌn]	machen, tun
to **draw** [drɔ:]	**drew** [dru:]	**drawn** [drɔ:n]	zeichnen
to **drink** [drɪŋk]	**drank** [dræŋk]	**drunk** [drʌŋk]	trinken
to **drive** [draɪv]	**drove** [drəʊv]	**driven** ['drɪvn]	fahren
to **eat** [i:t]	**ate** [et, eɪt]	**eaten** ['i:tn]	essen
to **fall** [fɔ:l]	**fell** [fel]	**fallen** ['fɔ:lən]	(herunter)fallen, hinfallen
to **feed** [fi:d]	**fed** [fed]	**fed** [fed]	füttern
to **feel** [fi:l]	**felt** [felt]	**felt** [felt]	(sich) fühlen
to **fight** [faɪt]	**fought** [fɔ:t]	**fought** [fɔ:t]	kämpfen, (sich) streiten
to **find** [faɪnd]	**found** [faʊnd]	**found** [faʊnd]	finden
to **fly** [flaɪ]	**flew** [flu:]	**flown** [fləʊn]	fliegen
to **forget** [fə'get]	**forgot** [fə'gɒt]	**forgotten** [fə'gɒtn]	vergessen
to **get** [get]	**got** [gɒt]	**got** [gɒt]	holen, bringen; (be)kommen; werden
to **give** [gɪv]	**gave** [geɪv]	**given** ['gɪvn]	geben
to **go** [gəʊ]	**went** [went]	**gone** [gɒn]	gehen
to **grow** [grəʊ]	**grew** [gru:]	**grown** [grəʊn]	wachsen
to **hang** [hæŋ]	**hung** [hʌŋ]	**hung** [hʌŋ]	hängen
to **have** [hæv]	**had** [hæd]	**had** [hæd]	haben
to **hear** [hɪə]	**heard** [hɜ:d]	**heard** [hɜ:d]	hören
to **hide** [haɪd]	**hid** [hɪd]	**hidden** ['hɪdn]	(sich) verstecken
to **hit** [hɪt]	**hit** [hɪt]	**hit** [hɪt]	schlagen; treffen
to **hold** [həʊld]	**held** [held]	**held** [held]	halten
to **hurt** [hɜ:t]	**hurt** [hɜ:t]	**hurt** [hɜ:t]	verletzen, weh tun
to **keep** [ki:p]	**kept** [kept]	**kept** [kept]	behalten
to **know** [nəʊ]	**knew** [nju:]	**known** [nəʊn]	wissen; kennen
to **lay** [leɪ]	**laid** [leɪd]	**laid** [leɪd]	legen
to **learn** [lɜ:n]	**learnt/learned** [lɜ:nt, lɜ:nd]	**learnt/learned** [lɜ:nt, lɜ:nd]	lernen

infinitive	simple past	past participle	German
to **leave** [li:v]	**left** [left]	**left** [left]	(ver)lassen, abfahren
to **lend** [lend]	**lent** [lent]	**lent** [lent]	leihen
to **let** [let]	**let** [let]	**let** [let]	lassen
to **lose** [lu:z]	**lost** [lɒst]	**lost** [lɒst]	verlieren
to **make** [meɪk]	**made** [meɪd]	**made** [meɪd]	machen, tun
to **mean** [mi:n]	**meant** [ment]	**meant** [ment]	bedeuten; meinen
to **meet** [mi:t]	**met** [met]	**met** [met]	(sich) treffen
to **pay** [peɪ]	**paid** [peɪd]	**paid** [peɪd]	(be)zahlen
to **put** [pʊt]	**put** [pʊt]	**put** [pʊt]	setzen, stellen, legen
to **read** [ri:d]	**read** [red]	**read** [red]	lesen
to **ride** [raɪd]	**rode** [rəʊd]	**ridden** ['rɪdn]	fahren, reiten
to **ring** [rɪŋ]	**rang** [ræŋ]	**rung** [rʌŋ]	klingeln, läuten
to **run** [rʌn]	**ran** [ræn]	**run** [rʌn]	rennen, laufen
to **say** [seɪ]	**said** [sed]	**said** [sed]	sagen
to **see** [si:]	**saw** [sɔ:]	**seen** [si:n]	sehen
to **sell** [sel]	**sold** [səʊld]	**sold** [səʊld]	verkaufen
to **send** [send]	**sent** [sent]	**sent** [sent]	schicken
to **shake** [ʃeɪk]	**shook** [ʃʊk]	**shaken** ['ʃeɪkn]	schütteln
to **shine** [ʃaɪn]	**shone** [ʃɒn]	**shone** [ʃɒn]	scheinen; glänzen
to **shoot** [ʃu:t]	**shot** [ʃɒt]	**shot** [ʃɒt]	schießen
to **show** [ʃəʊ]	**showed** [ʃəʊd]	**shown** [ʃəʊn]	zeigen
to **sing** [sɪŋ]	**sang** [sæŋ]	**sung** [sʌŋ]	singen
to **sink** [sɪŋk]	**sank** [sæŋk]	**sunk** [sʌŋk]	sinken
to **sit** [sɪt]	**sat** [sæt]	**sat** [sæt]	sitzen
to **sleep** [sli:p]	**slept** [slept]	**slept** [slept]	schlafen
to **slide** [slaɪd]	**slid** [slɪd]	**slid** [slɪd]	rutschen; gleiten
to **smell** [smel]	**smelt / smelled** [smelt, smeld]	**smelt / smelled** [smelt, smeld]	riechen
to **speak** [spi:k]	**spoke** [spəʊk]	**spoken** ['spəʊkn]	sprechen
to **spend** [spend]	**spent** [spent]	**spent** [spent]	ausgeben; verbringen
to **stand** [stænd]	**stood** [stʊd]	**stood** [stʊd]	stehen
to **steal** [sti:l]	**stole** [stəʊl]	**stolen** ['stəʊln]	stehlen
to **swim** [swɪm]	**swam** [swæm]	**swum** [swʌm]	schwimmen
to **take** [teɪk]	**took** [tʊk]	**taken** ['teɪkn]	(mit)nehmen, bringen
to **teach** [ti:tʃ]	**taught** [tɔ:t]	**taught** [tɔ:t]	lehren
to **tell** [tel]	**told** [təʊld]	**told** [təʊld]	erzählen, sagen
to **think** [θɪŋk]	**thought** [θɔ:t]	**thought** [θɔ:t]	denken, glauben
to **throw** [θrəʊ]	**threw** [θru:]	**thrown** [θrəʊn]	werfen
to **understand** [ˌʌndə'stænd]	**understood** [ˌʌndə'stʊd]	**understood** [ˌʌndə'stʊd]	verstehen
to **wake** [weɪk]	**woke** [wəʊk]	**woken** ['wəʊkn]	(auf)wecken; (auf)wachen
to **wear** [weə]	**wore** [wɔ:]	**worn** [wɔ:n]	anhaben, tragen
to **win** [wɪn]	**won** [wʌn]	**won** [wʌn]	gewinnen, siegen
to **write** [raɪt]	**wrote** [rəʊt]	**written** ['rɪtn]	schreiben

⟨In the classroom⟩

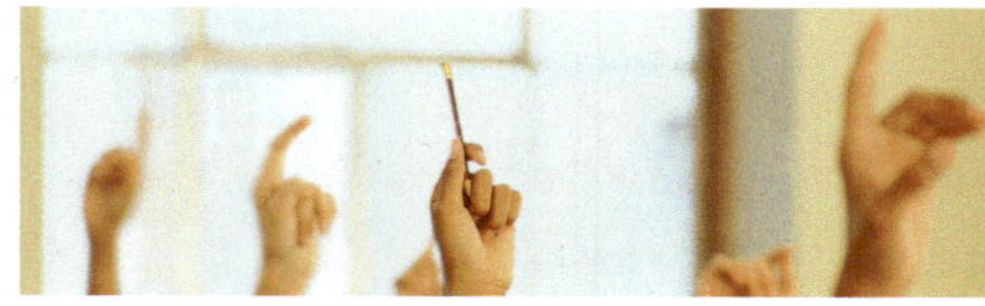

What you can say to your teacher

Could you explain that, please?	Könnten Sie das bitte erklären?
Can I say: …? Or is that wrong?	Könnte man … sagen? Oder ist das falsch?
I'd like to comment on that, please.	Das würde ich gerne kommentieren, bitte.
I don't think I understand what the author is trying to say.	Ich bin mir nicht sicher, ob ich verstehe, was uns der Autor / die Autorin sagen will.
What's … in English / German?	Was ist … auf Englisch / Deutsch?
How do you pronounce that word exactly?	Wie spricht man das Wort genau aus?
Have I written this sentence correctly?	Habe ich diesen Satz richtig geschrieben?

What your teacher can say to you

Could you give us your opinion on …?	Könntest du deine Meinung zu … äußern?
How would you interpret line 22?	Wie würdest du Zeile 22 interpretieren?
Sorry, it's not your turn yet.	Du bist leider noch nicht an der Reihe.
Just listen for gist the first time. Then listen for detail.	Hört erst mal nur das Wesentliche heraus. Dann hört die Details heraus.
Take notes while you listen.	Schreibt (Notizen) mit, während ihr zuhört.
What is the author trying to say with the words …?	Was versucht der Autor/die Autorin mit den Worten … zu sagen?
I'd like you to do peer editing.	Ich möchte, dass ihr Partnerbewertung macht.
Be fair and respectful during peer editing.	Seid fair und geht achtungsvoll miteinander um bei der Partnerbewertung.
For the next group activity, divide up into groups of three / four.	Teilt euch für die nächste Gruppenaktivität auf in Dreier- / Vierergruppen.
Keep your English folders up-to-date.	Haltet eure *English folders* auf dem Laufenden.

Presentation phrases

The topic of my presentation is …	Das Thema meines Vortrags ist …
The purpose / aim of this presentation is …	Der Zweck / Das Ziel dieser Präsentation ist …
Before I start, here's a handout with key words / phrases.	Bevor ich beginne, habe ich für euch ein Handout mit wichtigen Wörtern / Ausdrücken.
To begin with, …	Als Erstes …
My next topic / point has to do with …	Mein nächstes Thema / nächster Punkt behandelt …
Are there any questions at this point?	Gibt es zu diesem Zeitpunkt Fragen?
Let's move on to …	Machen wir jetzt weiter bei …
And now I'd like to summarize the main points.	Und nun möchte ich die Hauptpunkte zusammenfassen.

Talking about charts and numbers

As you can see in this chart …	Wie man in diesem Diagramm sehen kann, …
The results show that …	Die Ergebnisse zeigen, dass …
More / less than half / 20 per cent …	Mehr / weniger als die Hälfte / 20 Prozent …
We were surprised that …	Wir waren überrascht, dass …

Talking about stories, songs and poems

This text / extract / song deals with …	Dieser Text / Auszug / dieses Lied handelt von …
I think it's exciting / interesting / sad / well-written.	Ich finde es spannend / interessant / traurig / gut geschrieben.
I think the plot / turning point / climax is exciting / predictable / brilliant.	Ich finde die Handlung / den Wendepunkt / Höhepunkt spannend / vorhersehbar / toll.
The narrator is …	Der Erzähler / Die Erzählerin ist …
The plot is realistic / confusing.	Die Handlung ist realistisch / verwirrend.
The story has a change of perspective.	Die Geschichte hat einen Perspektivenwechsel.
The foreshadowing is well done / makes things too predictable.	Die Andeutungen sind geschickt gemacht / machen die Dinge zu vorhersehbar.
I think Alex … is an interesting / hypocritical / confident character.	Ich finde, dass Alex ein interessanter / heuchlerischer / selbstbewusster Charakater ist.
The characters are very similar to each other / totally different.	Die Charaktere ähneln einander sehr / sind total unterschiedlich.
There are contradictions in his / her character.	Es gibt Widersprüche in seinem / ihrem Charakter.
Line 12 in the song tells us that …	Zeile 12 in dem Lied sagt uns, dass …
The language of the text / song / poem is angry / emotional.	Die Sprache des Textes / Liedes / Gedichts ist aggressiv / emotional.
The song's lyrics are timeless / dated.	Die Liedtexte sind zeitlos / zeitverhaftet.
The poem is divided up into three stanzas.	Das Gedicht ist in drei Strophen unterteilt.
The rhyme scheme is ABAB / …	Das Reimschema ist ABAB / …

Discussion phrases

What do you think? / What's your opinion?	Was meinst du?
Do you have any comments on …?	Hast du irgendwelche Kommentare zu …?
In my opinion …	Meiner Meinung nach …
As far as I know …	Soweit ich weiß, …
Is that a fact or an opinion?	Ist das eine Tatsache oder eine Meinung?
I used to think that …	Früher dachte ich, dass …
Please show more respect for someone else's opinion.	Zeige bitte mehr Achtung vor der Meinung eines anderen.
I don't think it's appropriate to …	Ich glaube nicht, dass es angebracht ist, …
Are you / we in a position to judge …?	Bist du / Sind wir in einer Lage, … beurteilen zu können?

Lösungen zu den Check-out-Seiten

Unit 1 page 22

Exercise 1

Musterlösung: 1. The Aboriginals used to live all alone in Australia. Now they share the continent with Australians who came from other parts of the world and with tourists, too.
2. Many people used to come to Australia as convicts. Now they arrive as tourists on holiday.
3. The Tasmanian devil didn't use to have protection from hunters. Now there are protection areas for the 'devil'.
4. Australian cities used to be very British and very white. Now the cities have got mixed styles of architecture, and there are people from all over the world there.

Exercise 2

1. I hate my hair right now. It looks worse than ever! – Stop worrying and have it cut!
2. My kids never clean up around the house, they're so lazy. – Then make them do it – you're their father, remember?
3. Oh no, look. It's snowing, and I lost my hat last week, ugh! – Oh, I'll let you borrow mine, no problem.
4. We're never going to have the food ready before the guests arrive! – Don't worry. It's not too late to have something delivered.
5. Carol, that outfit is *so* ugly! – Dad, make him shut up, now! He's a stupid little twelve-year-old who knows *nothing* about fashion!
6. What are *you* so happy about? – Mum and Dad are letting me fly to Bali next summer!

Exercise 3

Musterlösung:

I'd like to share a weird and true story with you. I was in Sydney last summer, and one night my family and I went to one of those restaurants where you can try all the weird things like witchetty grubs, green ants, and stuff like that. We ordered a big combination plate for four, with 12 or 14 different dishes that we could all share.

Things tasted better than we had thought, actually. The green ants were really sweet and we all liked them. Then, while I was trying a strange kind of seafood, I saw something on the plate I hadn't seen before. It looked really awful, not like anything from the sea. More like something you'd find in a garden: It was as long as my little finger, with legs and wings. But I thought, "Oh well, you only live once. Tonight's the night to try everything!" So I put the thing in my mouth and felt the "crunch" as I bit down on the wings and legs. But then I thought, "Wow, this is quite tasty. Mmm!" It tasted like a crisp on the outside, and like soft cheese on the inside.

I was sad that I could only find one of these things on the plate. But then I found another one. Before I ate it, I asked the waiter if he could tell me what it was. We had ordered so many things that I couldn't remember all the names. But his face went white; I had given him a real shock with my question. He said he'd tell me what it was if I promised not to tell anybody else. I said yes, and he whispered in my ear: "Er, the thing you ate is actually not on the menu. We've, er, been having problems with cockroaches (neu: Kakerlaken) over the past few weeks, and, well, it looks like two of them found their way from the kitchen onto your plate. I'm very sorry …"

Unit 2 page 42/43

Exercise 1

In Germany you can ask the „Bundesagentur für Arbeit" to help you and inform you. Schools, pupils and parents can ask the "Berufsinformationszentren" (BIZ) there for help. They know all about jobs and careers for young people and can inform you really well. You can use the Internet to find the BIZ. Click on "Bundesagentur für Arbeit" and then "Partner vor Ort" and you'll find out where the nearest BIZ at the"Bundesagentur für Arbeit" in your area is. Then go for an interview there and tell them what you're interested in. They'll help you to make a good career choice.

Exercise 2

1. Year 10 and 11 students studying for GCSEs are under a lot of pressure.
2. People expecting a lot of us, like parents and teachers, are a problem.
3. The good grades needed to go on to A levels are not easy to get.
4. The exams taken at the end of Year 11 are really important.
5. All the kids waiting for their results in August feel very nervous.
6. Big plans made for the future can be ruined in a minute.

Exercise 3

1. After seeing/having seen an advert, Lucy phoned about the job in the shoe shop.
2. Wanting to look good, she asked to borrow her sister's (Naomi's) new skirt.
3. Hoping to get cheap shoes, Naomi said yes.
4. Having made the best impression of all the applicants, Lucy was offered the job.

5. Having read her contract, she discovered she could not get cheap shoes right away.
6. Having worked there for six months, she was finally able to make Naomi happy!

Exercise 4
Musterlösung:
a)
Application for job as assistant at tourist information centre

Dear Mrs Smith
I am writing to apply for the job as a tourist information centre assistant advertised in your advert. I have just passed my German A levels (Abitur). I am looking forward to starting a workplace and college training programme in the UK.
I have spent some time in the UK before (two exchange programmes of six weeks each) and enjoyed my time there so much that I would like to start career training in Britain. I enjoy working with people and I'm very reliable. Because I come from a foreign country, I feel that your tourist information centre would be an excellent place for me to get work experience. At the same time, I hope that having a German-speaking assistant could be very useful to you.
I hope very much that you are able to offer me the job, and I would be happy to fly to Britain for an interview. Thank you for reading this application. I look forward to hearing from you.
Yours sincerely

Musterlösung:
b)
Things you should always put in your CV:
name; address; e-mail address; telephone number; nationality; date of birth; education information; work experience information; personal profile information. You should also mention that references are available if needed.

Exercise 5
Musterlösung:
1. Maybe one day I'll be on TV, talking to the rich and famous in interviews every day.
2. It would be fun to drive around in a police car, chasing criminals all over town!
3. I might enjoy working in a zoo, taking good care of all the animals.
4. Of course I'd love to be in the England football team, playing for the European or World Cup!
5. I don't think I'd like to spend my days in school, working as a teacher because I've already spent enough time in classrooms.

Exercise 6
Musterlösung:
1. He always arrives really late for work. This morning I saw him arrive at 9.35!
2. He clearly prefers magazines to company reports. Today I noticed him reading a car magazine, with his feet up on his desk!
3. A lot of his phone calls from the office are personal ones. Yesterday I heard him talking on the phone and saying, "I love you, too, baby!"
4. He takes other people's equipment without asking. Yesterday I saw him take a pen from somebody's desk.
5. Our boss isn't too happy with him, of course. This afternoon I saw her give him an official warning.

Exercise 7
Musterlösung:
1. Good morning, nice to meet you.
2. I enjoy working with people; I like to travel myself and know what travellers need at tourist information centres; I like to work and would be a reliable assistant and team member.
3. I think that coming from Germany would be very useful to you as so many German tourists come to Britain each year; I am a reliable worker and would be a good member of your team.
4. Could you tell me what my job would be like? Could you describe an assistant's typical day? How many people work at your centre? Could you tell me more about the pay for the job of assistant? How many days of holiday could I expect the first year? May I ask how long it might be before I find out who(m) you have chosen for the job?
5. Thank you very much for your time; Thank you very much for (inviting me to) this interview; I'm looking forward to hearing from you soon.

Exercise 8
Musterlösung:
1. Having a happy family life.
2. Marrying a wonderful man/woman.
3. Getting an interesting job.
4. Having lots of good friends.
5. Always staying healthy.
6. Earning well.

Unit 3 page 60

Exercise 1
Musterlösung:
– I get up in the morning and the first thing I hear is the <u>radio</u>, so I start my day with the media.
– And because I always turn my <u>mobile</u> off during the night, I have to check it in the morning.
– I usually check my <u>e-mails</u> three or four times a day, and the first time is always while I'm having breakfast.

– I'm a music fan, so I always listen to my mp3 player on the way to school and on the way home from school.
– I often read good books and I visit lots of different websites, too, to get information on the things I'm interested in – history and music. I also surf the Internet for half an hour in the evening to see what's happening at MySpace.

Exercise 2
1. are 2. 'm talking 3. seems 4. has 5. 'm waiting 6. think 7. see 8. is 9. get 10. 're filming 11. starts 12. is going 13. 'm trying 14. 're shaking 15. hope 16. 'm getting 17. happens 18. disappears 19. 're speaking 20. sounds 21. expect 22. 're looking 23. 're sitting 24. is calling

Exercise 3
1. "YouTube is OK, but it's Facebook that I use the most."
2. "Wow, look at your shelves! You do have an amazing number of DVDs."
3. "Look at the price! No way would I pay that much for a mobile."
4. "It's a fantastic book. I'd love to be able to write stories like that myself."
5. "Well, he isn't good-looking, but he does know how to sing and dance."

Exercise 4
Musterlösung:
Dave: I predict that twenty years from now there won't be any books. How do you see it?
Penny: Oh, I see it totally differently. I don't think people are ever going to stop reading.
Dave: Well, I didn't actually say people would stop reading. I just think all words will be on screen, not paper.
Penny: I can't imagine that at all. I'm sure that for many people there'll still be a place for books.
Dave: The way I see it, the only place for books will be in museums.
Penny: Do you really think that? What about reading in bed? You can't use a computer for that.

Unit 4 page 82/83

Exercise 1
1. to agree on 2. wearing 3. doing 4. to point out 5. considering 6. looking 7. to be able 8. expressing 9. to be 10. to shout

Exercise 2
1. to make 2. hearing 3. to do 4. to become 5. to think 6. telling 7. to travel 8. being 9. finding

Exercise 3
1. to do 2. vote 3. to work 4. take 5. attend 6. to quit 7. to understand 8. to drink 9. show 10. to turn 11. to show

Exercise 4
Musterlösung:
Picture 1: Excuse me, but would you mind not making fun of the waitress? I can hear everything you're saying and I don't think it's very nice. Look at her; you can see it's hurting her feelings.
Picture 2: Excuse me, but I'd really appreciate it if you could try to keep your cigarette smoke from blowing in my direction. Would that be possible?
Picture 3: Excuse me, but if you want to continue showing each other your feelings, would you mind doing it somewhere else, where you'd have more privacy? I'm trying to enjoy my lunch break. Thanks.

Exercise 5
(Eigene Auswahl)

Exercise 6
Beispiel einer Quizfrage aus jeder Lektion:
Zoom-in: What is the name of the French-speaking part of Canada?
Unit 1: What are witchetty grubs?
Unit 2: True or false: In Britain, you send a photo along with your CV when applying for a job.
Unit 3: True or false: A stative verb expresses an action.
Unit 4: How many black students tried to attend Little Rock's Central High School in 1957?

Bildquellen:

Cov1; Cov4 Getty Images (Digital Vision), München; **3.1** shutterstock (Kitch Bain), New York; **8.1** Imago Stock & People (Jürgen Schwarz), Berlin; **8.2** shutterstock (Mehmet Dilsiz), New York; **8.3** laif (The New York Times/Redux), Köln; **9.1** shutterstock (vera bogaerts), New York; **9.2** Corbis (RF), Düsseldorf; **9.3** shutterstock (Kharidehal Abhirama Ashwin), New York; **9.4** Comstock (RF), Luxemburg; **9.5** Picture-Alliance (Brix), Frankfurt; **9.6** shutterstock (Joe Gough), New York; **9.7** Getty Images (Dream Pictures), München; **10.1** iStockphoto (laughing mango), Calgary, Alberta; **10.2** iStockphoto (Theresa Martinez), Calgary, Alberta; **10.3** Comstock, Luxemburg; **10.4** Alamy Images RM (James Nesterwitz), Abingdon, Oxon; **10.5** Corbis (Louise Gubb), Düsseldorf; **10.6** Comstock, Luxemburg; **10.7** Corbis (Gallo Images), Düsseldorf; **11.1** Mauritius (Westlight), Mittenwald; **11.2** Comstock, Luxemburg; **11.3** Avenue Images GmbH (Corbis RF), Hamburg; **11.4** Corbis (Free Agents Limited), Düsseldorf; **11.5** Alamy Images RM (Travel-Shots), Abingdon, Oxon; **11.6** Corbis (zefa/Reinhard), Düsseldorf; **12.1** Corbis (Bob Krist), Düsseldorf; **12.2** laif (Emmler), Köln; **13.1** Walkabout by James Vance Marshal; **14.1** Corbis (Michael A. Keller/zefa), Düsseldorf; **14.2** Klett-Archiv, Stuttgart; **16.1** MEV, Augsburg; **17.1** Avenue Images GmbH (Banana Stock), Hamburg; **17.2** Corbis (Ludo Kuipers), Düsseldorf; **17.3** Logo, Stuttgart; **18.1** Getty Images (Stuart Hughs), München; **19.1** Fotosearch RF (Digital Vision), Waukesha; **19.2** Klett-Archiv (Nature + Science AG), Stuttgart; **19.3** shutterstock (Patsy A. Jacks), New York; **19.4** iStockphoto (Michael Willis), Calgary, Alberta; **21.1** Getty Images (ANDREZ LIGUZ/AFP), München; **23.1** Alamy Images RM (Jack Sullivan), Abingdon, Oxon; **24.1** Corbis (Sean Davey); **24.2** Corbis (Theo Allofs/zefa), Düsseldorf; **25.1** shutterstock (Ian Scott), New York; **25.2** Wikimedia Foundation Inc. (PD), St. Petersburg FL; **25.3** iStockphoto (RF/ Michael Pettigrew), Calgary, Alberta; **26.1** Jupiter Images photos.com, Tucson, AZ; **26.2** Interfoto (Erika Groth-Schmachtenberger), München; **26.2; 26.4** Corbis (Andy Warhol), Düsseldorf; **26.3** Corbis (Andy Warhol Foundation), Düsseldorf; **26.6** aus: Tales of the Dreamtime 2006 © Bartel Publications, Mascot; **27.1; 27.2** Linden-Museum Stuttgart; **28.1** iStockphoto (Lise Gagne); **28.2** iStockphoto (Trigger Photo), Calgary, Alberta; **28.3** Corbis (Peter Dazeley/zefa), Düsseldorf; **29.1** Avenue Images GmbH (StockDisc), Hamburg; **29.2** Fotolia LLC (RF/Nicholas Sutcli), New York; **29.3** Picture-Alliance, Frankfurt; **29.4** Fotosearch RF; **29.5** Fotosearch RF (PhotoDisc), Waukesha; **31.1** Getty Images (Image Bank/Alan Thor), München; **32.1** Bananastock RF, Watlington/Oxon; **32.2** iStockphoto (RF/Lise Gagne), Calgary, Alberta; **34.1** Getty Images (Photographer's Choice/Richard Elliott), München; **35.1** Fotosearch RF, Waukesha; **37.1** ullstein bild (Himsel/Intro), Berlin; **37.2** iStockphoto (Martin Purmensky), Calgary, Alberta; **39.1** Corbis (Liz Gilbert), Düsseldorf; **39.2** laif (Hahn), Köln; **39.3** Corbis (Peter Turnley), Düsseldorf; **40.1** ullstein bild (Ton Koene), Berlin; **40.2** Picture-Alliance, Frankfurt; **40.3** Corbis (Robert Grossman), Düsseldorf; **41.1** shutterstock (Konstantin Sutyagin), New York; **41.2** Getty Images (Blend Images/Shalom Ormsby), München; **41.3** Getty Images, München; **41.4** iStockphoto (Skip ODonnell), Calgary, Alberta; **41.5** Getty Images (The Image Bank/Matthew Antrobus), München; **40.1** ullstein bild (Ton Koene), Berlin; **41.6** Charles Dickens, Klett Easy Reader B; **45.1** iStockphoto (John Carnemolla), Calgary, Alberta; **45.2** shutterstock (Raymond Yong), New York; **45.3** iStockphoto (juuce), Calgary, Alberta; **46.1** Avenue Images GmbH, Hamburg; **46.2** shutterstock (Alexander Gitlits), New York; **48.1** Picture-Alliance, Frankfurt; **48.2** www.cartoonstock.com (Geoff Thompson), Bath; **50.1** Avenue Images GmbH (Banana Stock), Hamburg; **51.1** iStockphoto (Anna Pustovaya), Calgary, Alberta; **51.2** Fotosearch RF (Brand X Pictures), Waukesha; **51.3** Getty Images (Dave Hogan), München; **51.4** Fotosearch RF (Digital Vision), Waukesha; **52.1** Interfoto, München; **54.1** Image Source (RF), Köln; **55.1** Ericsson GmbH, Düsseldorf; **58.1** Imageshop RF (Imageshop), Düsseldorf; **58.2** MEV, Augsburg; **58.3** shutterstock (Tomo Jesenicnik), New York; **58.4** iStockphoto (Anthony Ladd), Calgary, Alberta; **58.5** Schwarz, Gesa, Hamburg; **58.6** iStockphoto (Lars Nilsson), Calgary, Alberta; **59.1** N. Brown, Klett Easy Reader, Stuttgart; **63.1** iStockphoto (Quavondo Nguyen), Calgary, Alberta; **63.2** iStockphoto (Arthur Kwiatkowski), Calgary, Alberta; **63.3** iStockphoto (Damir Spanic), Calgary, Alberta; **63.4** iStockphoto (aldra), Calgary, Alberta; **63.5** iStockphoto (Jelani Memory), Calgary, Alberta; **64.1** Sulake Deutschland GmbH, Frankfurt a.M.; **66.1** Getty Images RF (Photodisc), München; **66.2** Getty Images RF, München; **68.1** Picture-Alliance (EPA/Andre Kosters), Frankfurt; **68.2** Picture-Alliance (Syed Jan Sabawoon), Frankfurt; **68.3** Fotosearch Stock Photography, Waukesha; **69.1** Picture-Alliance (Jan Woitas), Frankfurt; **69.2** shutterstock (Zdorov Kirill Vladimirovich), New York; **69.3** Imago Stock & People (GranAngular), Berlin; **70.1** laif (Shannon Stapleton/Gamma/Eyedea Presse), Köln; **74.1** Corbis (Bettmann), Düsseldorf; **75.2** (Tom Hanson); **77.1** Corbis (Bettmann), Düsseldorf; **77.2** laif (Keystone France), Köln; **78.1** Corbis (Jerry Schatzberg), Düsseldorf; **78.2** Corbis (Thierry Orban), Düsseldorf; **79.1** Picture-Alliance, Frankfurt; **79.2** Picture-Alliance (EPA/Larry W. Smith), Frankfurt; **79.3** Picture-Alliance (Rebecca Reid), Frankfurt; **80.1** Getty Images (Aretha Franklin), München; **80.2** Ullstein Bild GmbH (AKG), Berlin; **80.3** Getty Images (Andrew H. Walker), München; **81.1** Jeff Wall, Mimic (1982), Vancouver,; **84.1** Alamy Images RM (Judie Long), Abingdon, Oxon; **84.2** Corbis, Düsseldorf; **85.1** Picture-Alliance (Philadelphia Inquirer/MCT), Frankfurt; **85.2** Getty Images (America 24-7), München; **85.3** Keystone (Jose Giribas), Hamburg; **85.4** Corbis (Les Stone/ Sygma), Düsseldorf; **85.5** Logo, Stuttgart; **86.1** Alamy Images RM (vario images GmbH & Co. KG), Abingdon, Oxon; **85.6** Republican National Committee, Washington, D. C.; **87.1** shutterstock, New York; **87.2** Corbis (Paul A. Souders), Düsseldorf; **87.3** shutterstock (Luc Sesselle), New York; **87.4** Getty Images (Lutz Bongarts), München; **88.1** Alamy Images RF (Image Source Black), Abingdon, Oxon; **89.1** iStockphoto (pkruger), Calgary, Alberta; **90.1** Avenue Images GmbH (Stock Disc), Hamburg; **91.2** Action Press GmbH (Gaul), Hamburg; **91.3** Ullstein Bild GmbH (Brill), Berlin; **92.1** Ullstein Bild GmbH (Brill), Berlin; **93.1** iStockphoto (Jan Rihak), Calgary, Alberta; **93.2** Picture-Alliance (Karl Switak), Frankfurt; **93.3** iStockphoto (Anne Clark), Calgary, Alberta; **95.1** iStockphoto (Nuno Silva), Calgary, Alberta; **95.2** laif (REA), Köln; **95.3** iStockphoto (Nuno Silva), Calgary, Alberta; **96.1** Getty Images (Michael Ochs Archives), München; **97.1** Ullstein Bild GmbH (Müller-Schneck), Berlin; **97.2** Picture-Alliance (dpa-Report), Frankfurt; **98.1** Sony BMG Music Entertainment (Germany), München; **98.2** Corbis (Michael Ochs Archives), Düsseldorf; **98.2** WARNER MUSIC Group Germany, Hamburg; **98.3** Corbis (Bettmann), Düsseldorf; **98.3** Corbis (Rune Hellestad), Düsseldorf; **99.1** VISUM Foto GmbH (Georg Schoenharting), Hamburg; **101.1** Alamy Images RM (Janine Wiedel Photol), Abingdon, Oxon; **101.2** Fotosearch RF (Image Source RF), Waukesha; **101.3** Corbis (Lowell Georgia), Düsseldorf; **102.1** ; **102.2**; **102.3** Ernst Klett Verlag GmbH, Stuttgart; **102.4** Penguin Group (UK) (24 girls in 7 days by Alex Bradley), London WC2R ORL; **103.1** Carissa Pelleteri, Brooklyn, NY 11222; **103.2;103.3** Ernst Klet Verlag GmbH, Stuttgart; **216.1** DigitalVision (Digital Vision), Maintal-Dörnigheim; **222.1** Mauritius (Rene Truffy), Mittenwald; **222.2** Interfoto (Mary Evans Picture Library), München; **222.3** Wikimedia Foundation Inc. (PD), St. Petersburg FL; **222.4** JupiterImages photos.com, Tucson, AZ; **223.1** ullstein bild (Keith), Berlin; **223.2** shutterstock (RF/Kaspars Grinvalds), New York; **224.1** Kessler-Medien, Saarbrücken; **225.1; 225.2** MEV Verlag GmbH, Augsburg; **225.3** Getty Images RF (Photodisc), München

Nicht in allen Fällen war es uns möglich, den Rechteinhaber der Abbildungen ausfindig zu machen. Berechtigte Ansprüche werden selbstverständlich im Rahmen der üblichen Vereinbarungen abgegolten.

Song- und Textquellen:

S.12 Walkabout by James Vance Marshall (first published as THE CHILDREN by Michael Joseph, 1959) © James Vance Marshall, 1969; **S.14** © James Moloney, 1998. First publishes by University of Queensland Press 1998.; **S.21** © Sprint-Music, Sony/ATV Music Publishing (Germany GmbH), Berlin; **S.23** © from Down Under by Bill Bryson, published by Black Swan. Reprinted by permission of The Random House Group Ltd.; **S.35** © by Paul Cookson, The Works 3, A poet a week, Macmillan Children's Books, 2004; **S.38** © Who is Jesse Flood by Malachy Doyle, Bloomsbury Publishing; **S.50** © from How to Make Music in Your Bedroom by Nicola Slade, published by Virgin Books. Reprinted by permission of the Random House Group Ltd.; **S.52** © Newmarket Press, New York und © THE TRUMAN SHOW © Paramount Pictures. All Rights Reserved; **S.54** by Jonathan Duvvy, © BBC News Magazine, 07/03/2006; **S.61** © Reprinted with the permission of Simon Pulse, an imprint of Simon & Schuster Children's Publishing Division from UGLIES by Scott Westerfeld. Text © 2005 Scott Westerfeld.; **S.74** © America.gov; **S.78** © Special Rider Music, Für D/A/CH: Sony/ ATV Music Publishing (Germany GmbH), Berlin; **S.79** Buchu Music/Careers BMG Music Publishing/ Copyright Contol Shares/Hallelujah Productions Inc./Ole Media Management LP I/TVT Music Inc./ Xtina Music, BUG Music Musikverlagsgesellschaft, München, Musik Edition Discoton GmbH, Berlin, EMI Music Publishing Germany GmbH & Co. KG, Hamburg, Kobalt Music Publishing Ltd., London; **S.88** © Woodlands Junior School, Kent; **S. 91** © 1993 by Edition Brausebeat, Music Edition Discoton GmbH, Berlin; **S.92** "Going Home" by JB, Wulagi NT, first published by ABC Online, 13 June, 2005, is reproduced by permission of the Australian Broadcasting, Corporation and ABC Online. © 2005 ABC. All rights reserved.; **S.94** © Robert Swindells, 1993; **S.100** © by Larry Fondation 1991, Asylum Arts

More than 40,000 years ago

The first people came to Australia from south-east Asia and spread across the red continent. These people adapted perfectly to the dry climate. The Aboriginals learned how to find food and water where no one else could. They developed a rich culture of art and great spirituality. The famous Ubirr rock paintings in Kakadu National Park in the north are some of the oldest artworks in the world.

1770

For centuries people had heard of a mythical southern continent (*australis* means 'south' in Latin). The English Lieutenant (later: Captain) James Cook believed the continent existed. He discovered Australia for Britain and claimed it by order of King George III of England. Cook named eastern Australia *New South Wales*.

1788

The First Fleet, under the command of British Navy captain Arthur Phillip, arrived at *Botany Bay*, carrying about 800 convicts. Phillip founded the first British colony in Australia, a penal colony, and became its first governor.

The First Fleet 1788

The First Fleet consisted of 11 ships. The ships' journey took nearly eight months and many passengers died because of the terrible conditions aboard ship.

Starting in 1793

The first free settlers came to Australia.

1860

In the mid-19th century the Australian outback was mostly unexplored. In 1860 Robert Burke and William Wills led an expedition, crossing Australia from south to north. The journey north took nearly five months and most men died of starvation and exhaustion on their way back, including Burke and Wills.

1870

The surveyor John Forrest went on an expedition from Perth to Adelaide. It was the first west-to-east crossing of Western Australia.

John Forrest

Robert Burke

1901

Australia first consisted of six British colonies. In 1901 the colonies were united, forming the *Commonwealth of Australia* with Canberra as its capital and the British monarch as head of state.

1901–1939

Governmental *Protection Acts* deprived the Aboriginal people of their legal and civil rights. Half-Aboriginal children (children with a white Australian father and an Aboriginal mother) were separated from their families and brought to missions or reserves in order to be "civilised". They were supposed to be "assimilated" into white Australian society. These half-Aboriginal children were later called the *Stolen Generations*.
The Australian government's assimilation policy concerning Aboriginal blood lasted into the 1970s!

1945–2000

The Australian *Gold Rush* of the 1850s brought more than 600,000 people to the country, especially from Britain, but also from America, Germany and, above all, China. The peak of Asian immigration, however, was in the early 1990s when more than half of the immigrants arriving in Australia were from an Asian country. Almost 5.9 million immigrants settled in Australia, Britain and Ireland being the largest source of post-war immigrants.

1963

Indigenous peoples received full civil rights as Australian citizens.

The Aboriginal flag was first introduced on National Aborigines' Day in 1971. It represents Aboriginal identity: yellow symbolises the sun, red stands for the earth and black represents the Aboriginal people.

1986

With the *Australia Act* of 1986 the country, which was already self-governing, became fully independent of British parliament.

2001

Despite public pressure, Prime Minister John Howard refused to apologise to the *Stolen Generations* for the government's wrongdoings during its assimilation policy.

2007

Australia's cultural importance goes well beyond the country's borders: the *Sydney Opera House*, built in 1973, became world cultural heritage in 2007. Two of the most well-known Australian landmarks can also be found on the UNESCO list: *Uluru* ('Ayers Rock') in the Uluru Kata Tjuta National Park and the *Great Barrier Reef* in the Coastal Sea off the coast of Queensland (listed in 1981 and 1987 respectively).

February 2008

Kevin Rudd, Prime Minister since December 2007, officially apologised to the Aboriginals and the Stolen Generations.

Parliament today

House of Commons

One elected Member of Parliament (MP) for each of about 650 constituencies.
Each MP has to be elected directly by the voters of a constituency. The candidate with the most votes in each constituency becomes its MP.

House of Lords

About 740 non-elected members. There is now a strong movement in the House of Commons to allow only elected Lords (except the Law Lords).

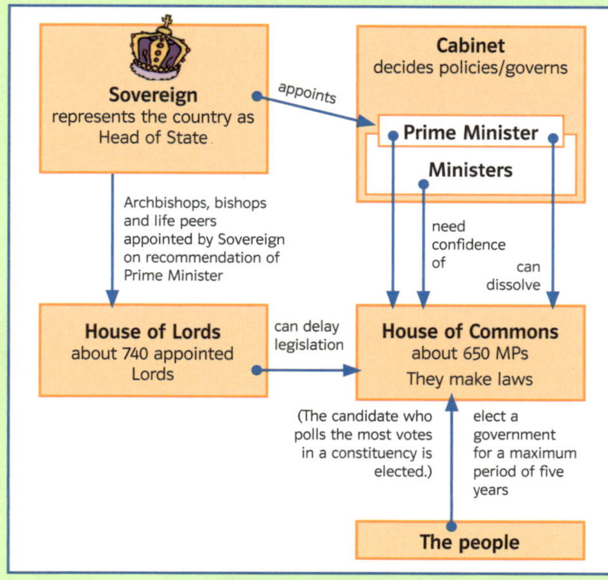

A history of Parliament

1 John, who became King of England in 1199, was unsuccessful in war. England had lots of land in France then. King John lost most of his land in France. He asked his barons to give him more money so that he could win it back, but they refused. When he tried to make them pay heavy taxes, they rebelled.
In 1215 they formed an army, captured London and forced John to sign a treaty. It was called **Magna Carta** and is one of the most important documents in English history. Here on the right are four of the 61 articles John had to agree to.

- The English Church shall be free to choose its own bishops.
- No special taxes can be created unless the barons meet and agree to them.
- Freemen should only be imprisoned if they have had a proper trial.
- The barons shall choose 25 representatives to check that the king does not break these rules.

The Lords	The King	The Commons
• The barons • Bishops • Abbots	• Parliament only met when the king wanted it to. • Parliament could not tell the king what to do, but it could stop taxes if it disagreed with them.	Representatives of the • towns/boroughs • knights

2 Most people at that time were not rich barons and churchmen, but poor peasants working on the barons' land. Magna Carta did not mention them. But it did limit the king's power, and it formed the basis for the first Parliament, which was called by Edward I in 1295. This became known as the **Model Parliament** because it had so many of the features of later Parliaments.

3 King James II became King in 1685. He tried to rule alone, so Parliament invited James's daughter Mary and her Dutch husband William of Orange to come to England as King and Queen. In 1688 William landed with a small army. Nobody wanted to fight for James, so it was a **Glorious** (and Bloodless) **Revolution**. But before they were given the crown, William and Mary had to sign a document called the **Bill of Rights** (1689), which finally made sure that Parliament was more important than the monarch.

Bill of Rights

- Parliament, not the monarch, passes laws and decides on taxes.
- Parliament keeps a check on the army.
- MPs have absolute freedom of speech.

The American government today

The United States of America has three branches of government. Each controls the other two.

Congress

Senate (100 Senators: 2 from each state)

House of Representatives (435 Congressmen/ women)

- can impeach and remove the President.
- may ignore the President's veto.
- The Senate approves the appointment of members of Supreme Court.
- The Senate approves treaties made by the President.

The President

- controls foreign policy and makes treaties.
- may veto laws made by Congress.
- can recommend laws.
- appoints members of the Supreme Court.

The Supreme Court

- watches over the Constitution and interprets the laws.
- can call laws made by Congress unconstitutional.
- can call the President's decisions unconstitutional.

The people

- elect a President for four years.
- elect Senators for six years.
- elect one third of Representatives every two years.

The American Constitution and the Bill of Rights

The War of Independence from Britain ended in 1783 with an American victory. On September 17, 1787, 39 delegates from the original 13 colonies signed the new **Constitution of the United States**.

In 1791 the **Bill of Rights** was added. This guaranteed:

Freedom of assembly

Freedom to hold public meetings.
Meetings must be peaceful and obey local laws.

Freedom of religion

Freedom of worship.
Freedom to belong to any religion, or to none.
No official state religion is allowed.

Freedom of the press

Freedom to print books, newspapers, and magazines. No one may print lies that harm other citizens ("libel").

Freedom of speech

Freedom to express ideas and opinions.
No one may use this freedom to tell lies in order to harm or to injure other citizens ("slander").

The Constitution represents two basic beliefs:

- The individual is important and must be free.
- The people have the right to choose the officials of the government (government by consent of the governed).

Freedom of petition

Freedom to encourage the government to pass laws.
Freedom to ask the government to take certain actions.

Freedom and security of citizens

No unlawful search may be made of homes. Under certain circumstances citizens may carry guns.

Rights to equal justice

All persons accused of a crime must be treated fairly and equally in a court of law.